The Metamodern Slasher Film

 21st Century Horror

Series Editors: Alice Haylett Bryan, Craig Ian Mann and Thomas Joseph Watson

Editorial Board

Stacey Abbott, Northumbria University
Simon Brown, Kingston University
Laura Loguercio Cánepa, Anhembi Morumbi University
Chris Cooke, Mayhem Film Festival
Mithuraaj Dhusiya, University of Delhi
Pembe Gözde Erdoğan, Independent Scholar
Stella Marie Gaynor, Liverpool John Moores University
Steve Halfyard, Royal Conservatoire of Scotland
Lindsay Hallam, University of East London
Erin Harrington, University of Canterbury

Rhys Jones, University of Amsterdam
Steve Jones, Northumbria University
Lynn Kozak, McGill University
Murray Leeder, University of Manitoba
Jason Middleton, University of Rochester
Patricia Pisters, University of Amsterdam
Kali Simmons, Portland State University
Ashley R. Smith, Northwestern University
Iain Robert Smith, King's College London
Lauren Stephenson, York St John University

21st Century Horror is a series of monographs and edited collections dedicated to the study of contemporary horror media, exploring the genre's continued social, cultural, political, industrial and aesthetic significance. Building on the work of the Fear 2000 conference series, it provides a publication venue for world-leading research on the genre's immediate past, present and future.

Available titles

The Metamodern Slasher Film
Steve Jones

Forthcoming titles:

The US-Mexico Borderlands in Contemporary Horror: Crossing the Boundary
Anna Marta Marini

www.edinburghuniversitypress.com/series-21st-century-horror

The Metamodern Slasher Film

Steve Jones

EDINBURGH
University Press

Edinburgh University Press is one of the leading university presses in the UK. We publish academic books and journals in our selected subject areas across the humanities and social sciences, combining cutting-edge scholarship with high editorial and production values to produce academic works of lasting importance. For more information visit our website: edinburghuniversitypress.com

© Steve Jones 2024, 2025

Grateful acknowledgement is made to the sources listed in the List of Illustrations for permission to reproduce material previously published elsewhere. Every effort has been made to trace the copyright holders, but if any have been inadvertently overlooked, the publisher will be pleased to make the necessary arrangements at the first opportunity.

Published with the support of the University of Edinburgh Scholarly Publishing Initiatives Fund.

Edinburgh University Press Ltd
13 Infirmary Street
Edinburgh, EH1 1LT

First published in hardback by Edinburgh University Press 2024

Typeset in Monotype Ehrhardt by
IDSUK (DataConnection) Ltd

A CIP record for this book is available from the British Library

ISBN 978 1 3995 2095 9 (hardback)
ISBN 978 1 399 52096 6 (paperback)
ISBN 978 1 3995 2097 3 (webready PDF)
ISBN 978 1 3995 2098 0 (epub)

The right of Steve Jones to be identified as the author of this work has been asserted in accordance with the Copyright, Designs and Patents Act 1988, and the Copyright and Related Rights Regulations 2003 (SI No. 2498).

Contents

List of Figures   vii
Acknowledgements   viii

Introduction   1
   The Slasher Subgenre: Definitions and Tropes   3
   The Structure of the Book   7
   Aims and Caveats   14

1. From Postmodern to Metamodern Slasher   20
   Metamodernism (and its Alternatives)   21
   From Postmodern Slasher Films . . .   25
   . . . to Metamodern Slasher Films   29
   A New Beginning   35

2. Investment (Epistemology)   38
   Are You Experienced?: Unreliable Perspectives and Ambiguity in *Shrooms*   42
   Three Sides to Every Story: Repetition, Reflection and Responsibility in *Triangle*   50
   Centralising Subjective Experiences   55

3. Coherence (Ontology)   60
   Pulp Friction: Metafictional Devices and Ontological Uncertainty   63
   Death Becomes Her: Structure as Catalyst for Growth in *Happy Death Day*   72
   Coherence and Meaning   79

4. Conventionality   82
   Murder Will Out: Exposing Conventions in *Behind the Mask*   86
   Bad Advice: Unorthodox Perspectives and Positional Slippage in *You Might Be the Killer*   94
   Conventional Wisdom   101

5. Subtraction 105
    Leveraging Subgenre Knowledge: From Postmodern
        Exclusion and Unoriginality to Metamodern
        Engagement and Innovation 108
    No Killer, No Cry?: Subtracting the Slasher in *I Didn't Come
        Here to Die* 113
    Structural Compression in *Murder Loves Killers Too* 119
    'Every-Victim', Every Slasher: *KillerKiller* 125
    Loss Aversion, Forward Momentum 128

6. Hypercoding 132
    Amped-Up '80s: Pleasurable Absurdism in *Dude Bro Party
        Massacre III* 135
    Any Time Now: *Detention*'s Heterochronic 'Stylish Style' 142
    Wreaking Havoc: Substance in Stylistic Excess 151

7. Nostalgia 154
    No Time Like the Present: Slasher Throwbacks and Replication 162
    Ahead of its Time: *Getting Schooled* and Revision 170
    Time and Time Again: Looking Back, Moving Forward 177

8. Remake, Sequel, Reboot, Requel 182
    Time After Time: Retconning, Retrocausality and Revis[it]ing
        the Past 188
    Dead Ringer: *Scream* (and *Scream* Again) 195
    Return to Form: Laurie's Search for Meaning in *Halloween* (2018) 201
    The Point of No Return: *Freddy's Dead* as Proto-Metamodern
        Requel 209
    Come Again?: The Metamodern Requel 217

9. The New Icons 221
    Death By Design: Creating New Icons 225
    Old School, New Context: *Hatchet* 230
    Old Dog, New Tricks: *Axe Murdering with Hackley* 241
    Subgeneric Upcycling 247

Conclusion 250

Bibliography 263
Filmography 284
Index 291

Figures

2.1 Tara is captured in an irised 'stalker' point-of-view shot in *Shrooms* (2007)   47
2.2 'You're not me' – one Jess confronts another in *Triangle* (2009)   54
3.1 Rebecca Gayheart's character breaks the fourth wall in *Urban Legends: Final Cut* (2000)   65
3.2 The protagonists witness Sully's murder onscreen in *Midnight Movie* (2008)   71
3.3 Tree's anxiety is emulated formally in *Happy Death Day* (2017)   73
4.1 Parallel interactions between Taylor and Leslie in *Behind the Mask: The Rise of Leslie Vernon* (2006)   93
4.2 An eavesdropping customer berates Chuck for advising Sam in *You Might Be the Killer* (2018)   98
5.1 Julie pays a high price for her lack of foresight in *I Didn't Come Here to Die* (2010)   118
5.2 Aggie spies on Stevie through a keyhole in *Murder Loves Killers Too* (2009)   123
6.1 Shot and reverse shot indicating that the caption 'life sucks' is present within the diegetic world of *Detention* (2011)   143
7.1 The 1980s is encapsulated by various cultural markers such as a Rubik's cube, boombox and fashion items in *Die Die Delta Pi* (2013)   165
7.2 Rusty mourns for Hillary in *Getting Schooled* (2017)   173
8.1 Parallel shots of Michael in *Halloween* (1978) and Laurie in *Halloween* (2018)   204
8.2 Freddy guns to camera *a la* Bugs Bunny in *Freddy's Dead: The Final Nightmare* (1991)   214
9.1 A design based in incongruities – Art the Clown grimaces in a pizzeria in *Terrifier* (2016)   228
9.2 Corporate 'head-hunter' – teens use 'the rules' against the slasher in *Axe Murdering with Hackley* (2016)   243
9.3 Michael Harbor presents 'Hackley 2.0' aka LaMarc in *Axe Murdering with Hackley* (2016)   245

Acknowledgements

This book has been in gestation for five(!) years, and I've had countless conversations with people about slashers and metamodernism during that time. Consequently, I'll limit this list of acknowledgements to those who have most immediately facilitated the project and its development.

Most directly, my thanks to Craig Ian Mann, Alice Haylett Bryan and Thomas Joseph Watson for inviting me to publish this book as part of the 21st Century Horror series. Extra thanks to Craig for offering such detailed comments on the manuscript, and for recommending *Clown in a Cornfield* and the *Third Saturday in October* films. Thanks too to Gillian Leslie and the team at Edinburgh University Press, and to the peer reviewers who were extremely encouraging about the initial book proposal.

During the course of the project, I have been invited to speak about it at various events. Those opportunities allowed me to distil many of this book's central ideas. If I recall correctly, the first time I mentioned the metamodern slasher was in a presentation at Abertoir Film Festival in 2018, so thanks to Gaz Bailey, Nia Edwards-Behi, Rhys Fowler and the rest of the Abertoir team: that invitation started this ball rolling. Thank you to Maša Peče and the team at Kurja Polt Film Festival for inviting me to talk about the slasher film three times (in 2019, 2021 and 2023), to Russ Hunter for organising those events and to my co-panellists at those events – Alexia Kannas, Laura Mee, Shellie McMurdo, Alison Peirse, Jamie Sexton and Johnny Walker – for the discussions that followed. Thank you to Wickham Clayton and Daniel Sheppard for inviting me to present a keynote talk on the metamodern slasher for the 2021 Slasher Studies Summer Camp: An International Conference on Slasher Theory, History and Practice (on Friday the 13th, no less!), as well as inviting me to participate in a roundtable discussion about the slasher with co-panellists Joan Hawkins and Murray Leeder. Thanks once more to Craig Ian Mann, this time alongside Chris Cooke and Oli Hicks, for inviting me to present a keynote talk on the metamodern slasher for the Fear 2000 conference in 2022, and to Stella Gaynor for chairing that session. Thanks again to Laura Mee and Shellie McMurdo, this time along with Kate Egan, for inviting me to speak about slashers at the BAFTSS Horror Studies Special Interest Group event 'Nightmares Before Christmas: Seasonal Horror on Screen' in 2022. Thanks yet again to Craig Ian Mann for chairing the session, and to my co-panellists Derek Johnston, Cat Lester and Diane Rodgers for the interesting discussion about festive horror. Additionally, thank you to anyone who asked me questions or recommended a film to me during any of these sessions.

Thanks too to Maja Krajnc and the team at *Kino!* journal for inviting me to write on the slasher for the journal in 2020 and 2022, and also for the considerable work of translating my writing into Slovenian.

Thank you to everyone I've cited, and anyone involved in making the films mentioned in this book: your work has inspired this project in innumerable ways. In particular, thanks to Garrett Hargrove, Pat Higgins and Chuck Norfolk for their interest in and kindness about my interpretations of their films.

I have already thanked Johnny, Jamie, Kate and Russ above, but thanks too to my other immediate colleagues at Northumbria, especially my office-mate Clarissa Smith (I'm sure I bored you with talk about this book numerous times), Sarah Bowman (who has a shared interest in metamodernism, but definitely not in slasher films), James Leggott, Matthew Potter and Solomon Lennox, who supported the research leave that made writing and editing this book possible. Although I didn't get the chance to talk to him about this project, my thanks too to Peter Hutchings: without him, there wouldn't be a research culture around horror at Northumbria. Thank you too to the many horror-based PhD researchers I have conversed with about slashers, especially Krista Amira Calvo, Meg Lonergan and Ami Nisa.

As ever, thank you to my friends – including many of the people I've already mentioned – for the numerous horror-themed conversations over coffee (or something stronger). Given that I've pulled multiple all-nighters watching slasher films with Martin Russell, he has probably heard more of my ideas and opinions about the subgenre than anyone else (especially in their nascent forms).

Thank you to my family for their love and support. Special thanks to my wonderful Mum for renting horror films for me when I was a kid: I'm still putting it to good use. Most of all, thank you to my partner Lydia, not only for sitting through endless hours of horror with me, but also for encouraging me at every stage of this project (and every other). I love you so much Najly.

Finally, this book is dedicated to our daughter Betty, who completed our little family just as I began drafting this manuscript. Optimism emerged as a central theme of this book (and my life) because of you. One day, I hope you'll watch *Jason Lives* with me. I'll try not to be too crushed if you think it's rubbish, but if that happens, please brace yourself for a protracted explanation about why it is one of cinema's greatest achievements :) ~

Introduction

The slasher film is considered a staple horror subgenre, but that status was hard-won. Despite being popular with audiences, the first peak of slasher film production between the late-1970s and the early-1980s was openly disparaged by critics, parent associations and feminist activists (see Dika 1990, 9; Hutchings 2004, 192; Wood 2003, 185). The slasher quickly became associated with sadism and misogyny (see Nowell 2012, 75; Platts 2020, 17). Thus, although 'the slasher film ... dominated the horror genre between 1980 and 1984' (Conrich 2010, 173), even popular horror publication *Fangoria* mostly avoided covering slasher releases between 1979–1982,[1] perhaps endeavouring to distance the genre (and horror fans) from the negative connotations surrounding slashers. Indeed, when one *Fangoria* reader observed that 'your magazine ignores films like *Prom Night*', the editor responded that 'you won't find every two-bit slash-em-up in these pages' (Martin 1981, 7), reinforcing the idea that the subgenre was unworthy of attention. As the 1980s progressed, the controversy surrounding the subgenre began to fade, and the accompanying derision became somewhat less vehement. Yet slasher films continued to be 'dismissed by most major publications, film journals, spectators and critics' into the late-1990s, this time for being 'too glossy, trendy and sleek to be considered worthwhile horror' (West 2018, 3–4). This broadly negative reputation continues to haunt the subgenre,

---

[1] The exceptions are articles on major box-office successes *Halloween* (1978) and *Friday the 13th* (1980), and some discussion of Tom Savini's FX work.

Note that throughout this book, titles unaccompanied by a parenthetical date will refer to the original film rather than identically titled features; so, for example, *Halloween* denotes the 1978 film. While all films are accompanied by their release date on their first mention in each chapter, other films with identical titles will continue to be accompanied by their year of release even in subsequent mentions, i.e. *Halloween* (2007) and *Halloween* (2018). When not clarified contextually, the original *Halloween* film will be distinguished from the overarching *Halloween* film series by adding a date to the film title: *Halloween* (1978).

manifesting in complaints that it now only or mainly consists of unoriginal remakes and reboots (see Clasen and Platts 2019, 26; Mee 2022, 4; Ménard, Weaver and Cabrera 2019, 622; Nowell 2012, 72). Nevertheless, audiences and filmmakers remain undeterred in their enthusiasm for the subgenre: just like slasher icons Freddy Krueger and Michael Myers, the slasher subgenre refuses to die.

As implied by this book's focus, the slasher subgenre is worthy of scrutiny. Scholars have been more charitable than critics in assessing the subgenre's significance. Some of horror studies' foundational texts – such as Dika's *Games of Terror* and Clover's *Men, Women and Chainsaws* – took the subgenre seriously. Even though the slasher has continued to receive attention from scholars, primarily in journal articles, book chapters, edited collections and monographs dedicated to single films or series (many of which will be cited within this book), much of that material deals with the subgenre's initial production boom-period from the late-1970s to the mid-1980s. Fewer sustained monographs have concentrated on the subgenre's development into the 1990s, and fewer still have accounted for recent generic shifts beyond the trend for remaking iconic properties. Consequently, the field has been left with a somewhat limited understanding of this highly popular subgenre in its present forms.

The Metamodern Slasher Film aims to address the latter problem by centralising a substantial body of contemporary slasher films. As a corrective to the idea that the subgenre has been monopolised by 'unoriginal' remakes since the early-2000s, this monograph argues that the slasher is replete with original films that continue to innovate within the subgenre. Such films are especially noteworthy, I argue, because when they are brought together, they are indicative of a change in the zeitgeist. That change is broadly summated as a move away from the cynical fatalism that epitomised postmodernism, towards sincerity, optimism in the face of crisis and an emphasis on felt experience. This turn has been acknowledged in recent scholarship via 'renewed interest in the concept' and value of postmodernism (Bentley 2018, 724), as well as the idea that postmodernism no longer speaks to the reigning cultural sensibility. The latter has been most pertinently captured in scholarly discussion by an alternative paradigm: metamodernism. Metamodernism illuminates important qualities that distinguish a body of slashers from their predecessors, thereby underlining salient developments within both the subgenre and the wider culture that situates these contemporary films. *The Metamodern Slasher Film* thereby offers readers new ways to understand the slasher film, the horror genre and also the sociocultural moment we find ourselves in. This book also contributes to the nascent scholarship on metamodernism and its application, being the first monograph to examine film in a sustained way using metamodernism, and the first academic work to analyse horror under a metamodern lens.

This very brief summation of the book's core contentions and contextual considerations will be fleshed out in greater detail below. The rest of this Introduction will also outline the book's rationale and the background assumptions that inform my argument. To initially contextualise the book's contentions about shifts within the subgenre, I will first define the slasher film. Doing so will delimit the kinds of films included and excluded from deliberation. Additionally, defining the slasher entails setting out key subgeneric tropes. Given that much of the book's analysis will be concerned with films that innovate by riffing on those tropes, this section will anchor key contentions that will be returned to throughout.

The Slasher Subgenre: Definitions and Tropes

Defining the slasher film is tricky, precisely because the subgenre includes movies that subvert (and therefore do not adhere to) characteristic tropes. Moreover, any bid to classify a subgenre is artificial in that it involves imposing boundaries of inclusion and exclusion upon it. The foundational slasher films were not created with the intention of founding a subgenre: the label was imposed after-the-fact, based on a perceived coalescence of shared features. Other scholars have underscored the difficulties of defining the slasher. For example, Rockoff (2002, 5) discusses difficulties in defining the slasher subgenre, even via its tropes. Elsewhere, Cherry uses the slasher to exemplify how subgenres are born from intertextual borrowings and filmmakers' attempts to innovate by introducing variations on established attributes (see Cherry 2009, 22–34). The category's coherence is further complicated by the coexistence of other adjacent terms circulated in critical, fan and scholarly discourses. Before 'slasher' became the prevailing nomenclature, these films were referred to as 'stalk and slash', 'slice and dice', 'teenie kill' and 'dead teenager' movies, for instance (see Jancovich 1992, 104; Leeder 2018, 65).

Such difficulties and ambiguities lead some to avoid categorisation altogether. For example, Schneider proposes that the label 'slasher' is 'little more than a catch-all' that lacks sufficient 'formal and historical specificity' (2000, 74). Yet, however imperfect the category might be, academics, critics and fans continue to use the term, behaving as if it does have coherent meaning. Contrary to Schneider's dismissal, it is possible to define the slasher subgenre as a cluster of characteristic conventions and narrative patterns, while also accepting that those conventions and patterns are not universally and consistently deployed in equal measure within each slasher film. Indeed, in her landmark study of the subgenre, Dika posits that the slasher is distinguished by a 'particular set of characteristics' and narrative structures that make the films 'intriguing to their audiences' (1990, 10; see also Rockoff 2002, 20). Muir concurs, noting that 'the joy of the slasher film arises in recognizing these components, and detecting how they are shuffled, subverted and reused in new and sometimes surprising' ways (Muir 2007a, 20).

For the purposes of this book, the slasher film is a narrative structured around emphasised moments of violence, committed by an individual (or individualised entity) who attacks and slays multiple protagonists across the film's duration.[2] The killer is either human or a supernatural version of a once-extant human (that is, the killer is not an alien, werewolf, vampire, demon or some other archetypal monster). The killer is obsessively compelled to eradicate a victim-pool. The victim base is usually a defined group, members of which exhibit a common identity trait (such as age or gender), belong to a specific social grouping (such as being college students or camp counsellors) or share a behavioural denominator (for instance, having committed some perceived wrong against the killer, or trespassed in some way). The slasher's antagonist typically picks off individual victims when they are isolated, although occasionally small groups such as couples are attacked simultaneously if they are vulnerable (for example, if they are engaged in sex).

The slasher film is commonly distinguished from (for instance) a serial killer film by being set around a specified location (such as a town or a wooded area) and/or a specified date (such as a calendar event or anniversary).[3] Filmic serial killers usually murder individuals who share a

---

[2] For example, *Scream*'s 'killer' is known as Ghostface – being spoken of as an individualised entity – even though the costume is donned by multiple characters across the series (as well as within single films). The same is true of *Gutterballs* (2008), in which three characters collaborate wearing an identical costume and mask. This part of the definition signals that slasher-adjacent films with explicit groups of killers – notably the *Texas Chainsaw Massacre* and the *Wrong Turn* films – will not be accounted for in this book.

[3] Drawing influence from *Black Christmas* (1974), *Friday the 13th* and *Halloween*, many slashers are preoccupied with killing on specific anniversaries and calendar dates. This fixation is reproduced in 1980s slasher titles such as *Mother's Day* (1980), *Happy Birthday to Me* (1981), *My Bloody Valentine* (1981) and *April Fool's Day* (1986). Of these, many are oriented around the winter festive period, encompassing films such as *Silent Night, Bloody Night* (1972), *New Year's Evil* (1980), *Don't Open till Christmas* (1984) and *Bloody New Year* (1987). The emphasis on dedicated dates helps to anchor the notion that the killers are obsessives who will ceaselessly pursue a goal.

certain trait, but those victims ordinarily do not know one another. In the slasher film, in contrast, the specified location usually yields victims who mostly know one another or are aware of each other's existence. Another convention of the slasher that separates it from the serial killer film is that the longest surviving targets customarily defeat the killer (at least temporarily) in the narrative's climax. This might sometimes occur in the serial killer film, but it almost always happens in the slasher film.

There are several other candidate tropes that further pin down the slasher film. Each recur with sufficient regularity that audiences might reasonably expect to see some or many of these in any slasher film, even if none of them are necessary or sufficient criteria for defining the subgenre. The following list is indicative rather than exhaustive, encompassing some of the more common attributes that will resurface in later chapters.

Frequently, the victim-pool is primarily composed of people in their late-teens and early-twenties (see Rockoff 2002, 10; Wood 2003, 173). Three implications follow. First, the cast of characters frequently corresponds with teen archetypes such as the jock, the popular fashionable young woman, the nerd, the prankster and so forth. Second, much of each film's runtime is spent following the protagonists as they engage in stereotypical teen behaviours, such as listening to music, swimming, playing pranks and so forth. Among the more common activities depicted are drinking, smoking marijuana and indulging in premarital sex. Third, the slasher's specified locations are often places where young people congregate. For example, college campuses are emphasised in 1980s titles such as *Prom Night* (1980), *Final Exam* (1981), *The House on Sorority Row* (1982) and *Sorority House Massacre* (1986), and these locations offer an abundance of young targets. The remote cabin or summer camp location was similarly popularised in early-1980s slashers such as *The Burning* (1981), *Friday the 13th* and *Madman* (1981). These locations isolate the victim-pool, distancing them from the civic authority structures one would usually turn to when facing grave peril. A related trend is that even where present, authority figures such as police, parents and teachers are ineffective, usually becoming victims if they try to halt the slasher (see Gill 2002, 17). The teen targets essentially fend for and defeat the killer themselves in these movies.

Of these targets, at least one – most commonly, a young woman – usually survives. This figure is often referred to as the Final Girl, following a term coined by Clover. Clover signals that the Final Girl is marked by her 'smartness, gravity, competence in mechanical and other practical matters', which help her survive (Clover 1993, 40; see also Dika 1990,

135; Muir 2007a, 25).[4] In rare cases such as *A Nightmare on Elm Street Part 2: Freddy's Revenge* (1985), a young man (a 'Final Boy') occupies this lead protagonist position instead. Occasionally, a couple or trio survive the onslaught, even if one of those characters – the lead protagonist – does the most to defeat the killer and save their peers.

The killer's identity is often obscured. Sometimes the killer is known, but is masked. That is famously the case in *Friday the 13th*'s sequels or the *Halloween* films, where masks metaphorically depersonalise the killer, connoting their emotional detachment. On other occasions, the killer is cast in shadow or the slasher's identity is hidden (at least from the viewer) using killer point-of-view shots, allowing the narrative to follow a 'whodunit' murder-mystery structure (on this, see Dika 1990, 54; Roche 2015).

Other trends were more common in early slasher films but became less typical as the subgenre developed. For instance, slasher killers reputedly wield sharp implements (hence the name 'slasher'; see Rockoff 2002, 7). While it is rare for slashers to carry guns, the reliance on blades quickly dissipated as the subgenre developed, perhaps simply because variety helped to keep the subgenre fresh. This is particularly true for sequels in longer-running series such as *Friday the 13th*, where an array of weapons and techniques (including bare-handed killings) are employed. Another trend that diminished as the 1980s progressed is the tendency to expound the killer's motivation via an opening (sometimes pre-credit) sequence, set prior to the narrative present (see Muir 2007a, 23; Rockoff 2002, 12–13). These tropes underline that the slasher subgenre is not static: its conventions adapt and alter over time. Although the slasher is a cohesive category with distinctive attributes, filmmakers are creative within those boundaries.

Extant criticism recognises that changes have occurred within the subgenre. Indeed, the subgenre is broadly acknowledged to fall into five major phases: the proto-slasher phase (the 1960s to the late-1970s); a production boom-period (the late-1970s to the mid-1980s); a phase of supernatural slashers and sequels (from the mid-1980s to the early-1990s); the postmodern phase (from the mid-1990s to the early-2000s); then a subsequent phase (up to the present), which has received the

---

[4] I intentionally avoid Clover's proposal that such qualities mean the Final Girl is 'boyish' and 'not fully feminine' (Clover 1993, 40), which makes a too-blunt connection between stereotypical social expectations and gendered identity. Clover's model implies that agency, resilience and strength are incompatible with femininity. That viewpoint has been the subject of much valid criticism, to the extent that the matter is no longer live in the field.

least scholarly attention to date. The temporal boundaries vary slightly according to different accounts, but this overall understanding of the subgenre's development is embedded in literature surveying the slasher (see, for example, Kerswell 2010; Leeder 2018, 66; Whitehead 2003). As is the case with defining the slasher, the picture is more complicated than this 'phased' story implies. If we accept that the boundaries of each phase are neither neat nor exclusive however, the phased model carries a kernel of truth: the subgenre has evolved over time, and those transformations follow broad patterns. Subgeneric rejuvenation does not merely and spontaneously emerge in a vacuum: descendants develop from their predecessors, and the phased heuristic can accentuate those relationships. Still, I concur with Nowell that when taken too literally, this model can lead to 'exaggeration' about 'breaks from convention' within each phase (Nowell 2012, 72). One such exaggeration is the idea that the most recent phase is an era of remakes. This book will complicate that notion by demonstrating that a considerable body of contemporary slasher films (including remakes) reflect the metamodern sensibility. To unpack that contention in greater detail, I will now turn to the book's structure.

The Structure of the Book

Chapters 1, 2 and 3 begin by mapping out relationships between metamodernism, knowledge and reality. Chapter 1 starts by introducing ('getting to know') metamodernism, addressing the ways metamodernism articulates a prevailing sensibility that is characteristic of the contemporary milieu. Chapter 2 considers epistemology, how knowledge is formed and the extent to which knowledge about others and the world is limited by subjective access. Chapter 3 then builds on that foundation by ruminating on how knowledge is derived from the way we exist in the world. This chapter's focus on ontology stresses that lived experience is crucial to how we understand the world and each other.

Chapter 1 delineates what metamodernism is according to the paradigm's main proponents (most notably, van den Akker, Vermeulen and Gibbons). I will also contextualise metamodernism by briefly outlining some alternative 'post'-postmodern frameworks (such as digimodernism and cosmodernism). These alternatives highlight pertinent concerns that inform my own take on metamodernism. The main content of Chapter 1, however, is devoted to delimiting the metamodern slasher's major distinctive features via comparison to the postmodern slasher. Most notably, the metamodern slasher rejects the postmodern slasher's ironic, inward-facing, fatalistic cynicism in favour of sincerity, outward-facing inclusivity and optimism about the possibility of subgeneric innovation. That said, metamodernism does not merely gainsay postmodernism: metamodern slashers build on the foundations laid by their antecedents. Metamodern slasher films echo the tenor of the zeitgeist, and so differences between postmodern and metamodern slashers manifest a wider drift in the dominant sociocultural mindset. Metamodern slashers continue to deploy irony, for instance, but do so as a conduit for sincere messages. Equally, these films retain the foci on stylistics, form and conventions that were foregrounded by postmodern slashers. In the metamodern slasher however, meditations on form are consistently married with tonal sincerity to convey that (for example) coherent meaning is possible. When conventions are unpicked, those examinations are naturalised because they are congruous with the metamodern slasher film's fictional world. Furthermore, these foci are intertwined with cogitations about the subgenre, which convey optimism about the possibility of innovation within the subgenre. This emphasis on optimism and future potentialities is also indicative of the metamodern outlook. These claims will become clearer as the book progresses, since the remainder of the book fleshes out Chapter 1's overview of themes via textual analysis of key contemporary slasher films.

Chapter 2 unpacks a contention that recurs throughout the book: namely, that the metamodern slasher's connotative deliberations on subgenre are integrated into its approaches to narrativisation and characterisation. As a foundation for that contention, this chapter will evince that metamodern slashers are invested in character positionalities. Chapter 2's case study films – *Shrooms* (2007) and *Triangle* (2009) – confirm that metamodern slashers employ epistemic alignment with lead protagonists to foster engagement with their situation as it develops, thereby placing weight on subjective experience. By investing in and foregrounding characters' subjective experiences, these metamodern slasher films intimate that subjective epistemic access is intrinsically valuable, because our experiences are the bedrock of lived reality. This emphasis exposes one way metamodern slashers build on and away from their postmodern antecedents. Postmodern slashers typically exploit epistemic alignment to withhold information from viewers (as part of a ludic 'trick'). Metamodern slashers instead use epistemic alignment to foreground the lead protagonists' experiences of existing in precarity. Because of the protagonists' limited, subjective perspectives on the events, we are not granted an objective stance on the narrative events. Consequently, several potential meanings are held in tension. Both films leverage their unresolved ambiguities in a productive manner, presenting a range of simultaneous live possibilities, from which multiple meanings can be freely generated. In this respect, both films reveal a further overarching characteristic of the metamodern slasher: viewers are invited to collaborate in making meaning out of the text's precarities, ambiguities and multiplicities.

This collaborative ethos informs the metamodern slasher's tone. Chapter 3 explores that aspect of the metamodern sensibility using coherence as a central theme. Chapter 3's first half presents a series of comparisons between postmodern slashers (such as *Wes Craven's New Nightmare* [1994]) and metamodern slashers (such as *Detention* [2011]) to demonstrate that where metamodern slashers utilise metafictional devices, they are integrated into the narrative, reinforcing other textual meanings (such as investment in the characters' experiences). That is, metafictional devices help to unearth coherent meaning. In contrast, where postmodern slashers point out their own fictionality by applying techniques such as metalepsis, mise-en-abyme and direct metafictional self-reflection in the script, those techniques are (supposedly) ontologically disruptive. Metamodern slashers eschew such ontological scepticism, instead expressing that authentic, coherent meaning is possible, even where the conduit for that meaning is fictional. Here, flagging fiction's construction does not disturb the boundary between fiction and reality: instead, it elucidates the authentic pleasures viewers can gain from engaging with fiction, despite understanding that fiction is not real. The underlying assumption is that viewers are sophisticated enough to accommodate such techniques into their narrative engagements without finding them overly disorienting or ontologically disruptive. Anchoring this implication, metamodern slasher films build and maintain ontologically coherent narrative worlds, taking the characters' experiences seriously (as per Chapter 2), even though the situation is contrived. Chapter 3's second half concentrates on a case study – *Happy Death Day* (2017) – to illustrate overt playfulness with narrative structure in a manner that embodies several intertwined metamodern qualities. *Happy Death Day* is again directly aligned with its lead protagonist (Tree), but here both the diegetic reality and narrative shape cohere with her personal development. Tree faces ontological disruption when she is subjected to the narrative's time-loop structure, and that disruption is resolved when she adapts as a person. Moreover, that resolution entails her gradual assent to a standard subgeneric character type: the Final Girl. This cohesion between narrative shape, diegetic reality, character and subgeneric typing is coloured by the film's tone, especially its optimism about the possibility of positive change (both for Tree and for the subgenre).

Postmodern slasher films customarily point out subgeneric conventions in a derisory fashion, although they also subsequently deploy those same conventions. Conventions are a trap for the postmodern slasher, not least since market saturation in the initial 1980s boom-period caused the subgenre's conventions to be consolidated, and then quickly led to repetition and overexposure in the marketplace. Chapters 4, 5 and 6 explore various ways metamodern slashers develop on and depart from the vision of convention as a form of restriction. Chapter 4 examines the ways metamodern slasher films provide new insights by viewing conventional situations from idiosyncratic perspectives. Metamodern slashers retain the reflexivity that was normalised in the postmodern phase, while also overcoming the postmodern slasher's self-consciousness about exploring conventionality. This case is illustrated via two case studies – *Behind the Mask: The Rise of Leslie Vernon* (2006) and *You Might Be the Killer* (2018) – which grant insight by taking unusual perspectives on the subgenre's standard events and tropes.

Behind the Mask follows an investigative reporter (Taylor) as she interviews Leslie, a slasher, while he prepares his homicidal campaign. The events play out via two main formal registers: a verité mode, capturing Taylor's 'behind the scenes' interactions with Leslie as he elucidates his methods, and a 'cinematic' mode, depicting Leslie enacting those tactics. The latter invites reconsideration of familiar conventions in light of Taylor's unfamiliarity with and Leslie's surprising explanations for the slasher's normative operations. *You Might Be the Killer* employs two notable perspectives. First, the film's lead protagonist (Sam) is an unwilling slasher who tries to halt his own murderous rampage. Second, Sam seeks advice on his situation by calling a film-nerd friend (Chuck). From outside the situation, Chuck guides Sam using her knowledge of horror film norms. This combination of two unusual perspectives yields new insights into well-worn conventions. Together, these case studies uncover three attributes of the metamodern slasher. First, conventions are naturalised because they are congruous with the characters and the fictional world. Second, conventions need not consistently and inevitably play out in normative ways; they are not fixed elements that 'trap' filmmakers and fatally constrain the subgenre. Third, in metamodern slashers, the expectations engendered by conventionality are opportunities to illuminate the subgenre's operations. In the metamodern slasher, meditating on conventions grants opportunities to innovate and surprise rather than purely trapping filmmakers and audiences in cycles of repetition.

Chapter 5 develops on Chapter 4's premise that re-envisaging conventionality cultivates opportunities for subgeneric growth. Chapter 5 uses three case studies to evidence how some metamodern filmmakers innovate by judiciously subtracting or compressing seemingly essential conventional elements. For instance, *KillerKiller* (2007) retains the slasher's formula of individuals being picked off within a defined location, but replaces the subgenre's expected protagonists (conventional teens) with a group of killers, who are eliminated by the film's 'Final Girl': a supernatural entity who stands in for the killers' previous victims. *Murder Loves Killers Too* (2009) adjusts the conventional slasher narrative's standard pacing, compressing most of its slaughter into the film's opening half-hour. Consequently, standard expectations about what will happen in the remaining hour of screentime do not apply in *Murder Loves Killers Too*, and that atypical structure is exploited to offer insights into the subgenre's usual operations. *I Didn't Come Here to Die* (2010) exemplifies a more substantial subtractive disruption, taking a standard 'teens camping in the woods' setup and entirely removing the slasher from its equation. The teens are still expunged one-by-one, but here they die because of their own recklessness or selfishness. Chapter 5's examples are indicative of contemporary slasher filmmakers' confidence in the subgenre's robustness, given that even seemingly essential facets can be amended and removed.

By evoking and adjusting conventional situations and character types, these metamodern slashers acknowledge that it is possible to cultivate new perspectives and surprises within the subgenre. In the metamodern slasher, the actualisation of convention is not cynically mocked, but instead is congruous with the in-film fictional world, the characters' motivations and so forth. Any foregrounding of aesthetics, form or convention is in keeping with the metamodern slasher's sincere tone, being part of the film's earnestness. That approach is most evident where metamodern slasher films amplify stylistic attributes, enjoying the absurdity of audiences becoming immersed in or having emotional responses to fiction, despite knowing that the fiction is only a construction. Addressing two case study examples – *Detention* and *Dude Bro Party Massacre III* (2015) – Chapter 6 examines forms of augmentation, which articulate the metamodern celebration of heterogenous abundance. As Chapter 2 proposes, idiosyncratic perspectives unveil unpredictable interpretive richness because each viewer is a collaborator in meaning-making. Metamodern slashers validate idiosyncratic perspectives, emphasise inclusivity, and ratify the productive potentials of variance. *Detention* and *Dude Bro Party Massacre III* both adopt abundant heterogeneity via what I call 'hypercoding': playful overexaggeration of formal elements and overt stylisation. In both films, the normative codes that characterise slasher filmmaking are amplified and embellished in an extreme fashion. The resultant incongruous, unexpected clashes might seem ridiculous at first glance, but they convey sincere reflections on the subgenre. In all three cases, realism is disrupted for the viewer, but not for the characters: the epistemic and ontological alignment with protagonists established in Chapters 2 and 3 prevails, since absurdism permeates the narrative world, the characterisation and the films' stylistics in equal measure.

The preceding chapters aver that metamodern slasher films innovate within the subgenre. Chapters 7, 8 and 9 examine the ways metamodern filmmakers forge connections between the subgenre's past, present and future. This understanding of the present as a temporal bridging point moves away from the defeatist forms of presentism that epitomise postmodernism, wherein 'the present is all there is' (Harvey 1989, 240). Consequently, in postmodern slashers, the past is misrepresented as passé, and the future is largely disregarded (given that innovation is considered impossible). Metamodern slashers begin from an alternative stance on the present. Chapter 2's emphasis on subjective perspectives underlines that our experiences occur in the present. Similarly, action can only be taken in the present. However, that does not mean (as per Harvey) that the present is 'all there is'. Because the subgenre's past can be distinguished from its present, some change must have occurred. Furthermore, since the subgenre has mutated in the past, it can also continue to adapt in the future. On this basis, metamodern slasher films recall and incorporate the past to facilitate meaningful development in the present and, ergo, to ensure the subgenre's continued development into the future.

Chapter 7 tackles these matters by probing how nostalgia operates in the metamodern slasher. Chapter 7's first half concentrates on 'throwback' slashers. Some are set in the present, but distil the slasher formula, stripping 'back to basics'. Others are (at least partially) set in the early-1980s or recollect the fashion, music and formal stylistics of the period. Both modes recreate 'old school' slasher thrills, thereby expressing nostalgic fondness for a clearly delineated past (the slasher's boom-period). Where contemporary throwback slashers conjure the past in the service of development in the present, they convey a metamodern sensibility. Nostalgic metamodern slashers acknowledge that fashions and aesthetic standards are remodelled over time, and that these modifications speak to changing values and concerns. In the metamodern slasher, such values, concerns and their stylistic manifestations are valued on their own terms, as opposed to being cynically dismissed as outmoded. Chapter 7's second half addresses a sustained case study – *Getting Schooled* (2017) – that encapsulates a different form of nostalgic engagement. Put bluntly, *Getting Schooled* is akin to a slasher iteration of *The Breakfast Club* (1985). Set in 1983, *Getting Schooled* rewrites the boom-period slasher according to a metamodern mindset, depicting seemingly typed characters growing and grieving in sincere ways. Nostalgic films illustrate that past and present are intertwined, but metamodern slasher films such as *Getting Schooled* can also figuratively recast the subgenre's past to illuminate its present.

Building on Chapter 7's discussion about the subgenre's past, Chapter 8 contemplates sequels to foundational slasher series, dissecting the ways they revamp narrative pasts and legacies. Two recent slasher films – *Scream* (2022) and *Halloween* (2018) – occupy ambiguous positions in relation to their host series, being (as is noted in *Scream* [2022]'s dialogue) somewhere between a sequel, a remake and a series reboot: thus, they are 'requels'. Chapter 8 explores the metamodern potentials of the requel, converging on productive continuities that can be engendered by selectively retaining, revising or erasing a series' core facets. These films play with the very notion of retroactive continuity that is fundamental to sequel series, abandoning or transforming established storylines. By not allowing antecedents to constrain subsequent iterations, metamodern requels defy complaints that sequels are 'lesser' works simply because they succeed an 'original'. Metamodern slasher requels redeem both the sequel (as a cultural form) and the slasher subgenre, which has become synonymous with sequelisation. To illustrate these contentions, *Scream* (2022) is first briefly inspected as a counterexample: despite the ambiguities inherent to the requel's status (as reboot/remake/sequel), the *Scream* series' continued adherence to postmodernism quashes its potential to recast the past from the present, thereby closing off productive possibilities for the subgenre's future. *Scream*'s unwillingness to depart from its established trajectories highlights how comparatively reckless the *Halloween* series is with its canonical story. *Halloween* (2018) is exceptionally severe in this regard, ignoring all films in the series bar the 1978 original. Attending to the film's direct evocation of Victor Frankl's thought, Chapter 8 indicates that *Halloween* (2018) is metamodern, being underpinned by a spirit of renewal, optimism in the face of tragedy and a desire to innovate rather than destroy. Finally, Chapter 8 bridges from past to present and future by retroactively recasting a pre-metamodern (indeed, pre-*Scream*) slasher sequel – *Freddy's Dead: The Final Nightmare* (1991) – as a proto-metamodern slasher. As the proclaimed *Final Nightmare*, *Freddy's Dead* actively extinguishes the series (both in cultural and narrative terms), by overhauling canonical lore and laying bare why the series had to end.

Thanks to chained slasher sequels, characters such as Chucky, Freddy Krueger, Michael Myers and Jason Voorhees metamorphosed from memorable killers into iconic slashers. Chapter 9 ruminates on contemporary slashers that either have the capacity to become or seem to be designed as new icons. Chapter 9 mainly zeroes in on the four-part *Hatchet* series as a case study, given that it has spawned more sequels than other comparable attempts to launch new icons, such as *See No Evil* (2006), *Laid to Rest* (2009), *The Orphan Killer* (2011) and *Terrifier* (2016). Metamodern new icon slasher films account for the possibility that the subgenre can attract new audiences who have not 'seen it all before' and who can authentically enjoy fresh iterations. More generally, these metamodern new icon slashers do not rely on references to the 'classics' but instead upcycle the properties and strategies that made the major icons 'classic' in the first instance. These films are informed by tensions that define the subgenre, combining past and present in a manner that is simultaneously future-facing (creating a new set of horror icons) and retrospective (nostalgically replicating what made the past classics so memorable and enjoyable). Chapter 9 closes with a final case study that more candidly cogitates on the present state of the subgenre and its icons. *Axe Murdering with Hackley* (2016) is set in an office context, presenting its killers as white-collar workers, and portraying its eponymous protagonist as an 'old school' slasher struggling to fit into the contemporary landscape. Its twist on the subgenre's formula yields opportunities to explicitly comment on the slasher's development from the boom-period to the present. *Axe Murdering with Hackley* primarily posits that innovation is required to maintain the subgenre's cultural relevance.

The book concludes by bringing together key insights from across the preceding chapters, weighing the slasher subgenre in light of metamodernism. The conclusion draws out extended implications for future work within horror studies and film studies based on the book's analysis. Finally, the conclusion will delineate the book's contributions to developing metamodernism as a theoretical model.

Aims and Caveats

Having summarised the book's content, this closing section will further clarify my objectives, and will underscore what the book is not aiming to do. Foremost, no book about a subgenre can be exhaustive. Digital production and distribution make it extremely difficult to track, watch and analyse all contemporary slasher films. Any book that tried to account for all contemporary slasher films would be both unwieldy and lacking in critical depth. I try to cover as much ground as possible within these pages, concentrating on examples that pertinently illustrate qualities and help me to explain the ideas. I am not claiming that these films are singular examples, but rather that they are indicative. Where space permits, I will briefly mention other similar examples to contextualise the discussion. However, case studies will allow me to provide detail and nuance as an alternative to simply offering unjustified, sweeping proclamations about how the metamodern sensibility is reified in contemporary slasher films. The present book offers a starting point for discussion. I encourage readers to deliberate about other films that are not mentioned, and to put the ideas to use in their individual engagements with the subgenre. After all, as will become apparent as the book progresses, metamodernism stresses that one's idiosyncratic engagements with the subgenre are distinctly valuable.

I have also tried to balance independent slasher features with more immediately recognisable, higher-budgeted titles. My inclusion of independent titles serves several functions. First, accounting for independent productions helps to counter the bias towards theatrical releases sustained by print press criticism. From an industrial perspective, the slasher's subgeneric phases are really concerned with theatrical releases and their profitability. The phased model suggests waves of market saturation and burnout, but these phases more accurately speak to the subgenre's prominence in the theatrical setting. Between each phase, the subgenre is sustained via straight-to-video releases and continues to develop in that sphere. A bias towards theatrical releases ignores these important contributions. That bias impoverishes understandings of the subgenre and its development. It also connotes that lower-budget productions are unworthy of critical scrutiny. Second then, addressing independent films alongside theatrical releases counters these negative connotations. The larger marketing and shooting budgets associated with theatrical releases do not automatically confer significance or guarantee richer expressions. Independent filmmakers might be liberated to take greater creative risks and may be less prone to interference from risk-averse executives anxious about their studio branding, for example. Third, the idea that the subgenre has been monopolised by remakes since the early-2000s is partially symptomatic of the print press's bias towards theatrical releases: those remakes have largely been theatrically released productions, and press coverage perpetuates the idea that nothing else of note has been happening in the subgenre. Fourth, the lines between theatrical releases and 'straight-to-video' releases are becoming less stark due to the rise of streaming platforms and (more recently) simultaneous theatrical and on-demand release strategies. In sum, only attending to larger theatrical releases would misrepresent the slasher film.

I only deal with slasher films in this book, since the subgenre is mainly associated with that medium. Nevertheless, various contemporary horror novels also exhibit metamodern traits. For example, Stephen Graham Jones's *My Heart is a Chainsaw* is a post-*Scream* slasher that exhibits a form of hypercoding (see Chapter 6), exaggeratedly amplifying the postmodern slasher's penchant for intertextual referencing (see Chapter 5): the lead character (Jade) thinks almost exclusively in slasher film references, understanding her experiences through the lens of the slasher's conventions. Jade's obsession also infects the book's form, since each chapter is named after an existing slasher movie. Yet the novel only makes intertextual connections to slasher films, underlining the subgenre's synonymy with that medium. Jade is occasionally reminded that she is not in a movie (and she is not; she is in a novel), but Jade is more concerned with a different separation: between the slasher's 'Golden Age' and the '*Scream* Boom of the late nineties'. A comparable division undergirds Adam Cesare's *Clown in a Cornfield*. Exaggerating the slasher's convention that adult authority figures usually fail to aid the slasher's teen victims, here the adult populace actively seeks to cull a township's younger generation. That setup figuratively encapsulates a split between the metamodern and the postmodern slasher; the town's adults reify the postmodern slasher's nihilistic disregard for the future (see Chapter 8), which is set in opposition to the metamodern slasher's forward-facing ethos (here, represented by the younger generation who strive to persist). Grady Hendrix's *The Final Girl Support Group* more directly renders that metamodern outlook by adopting an alternative perspective on a conventional situation. Raising similar themes to *Halloween* (2018) (see Chapter 8), the novel considers what happens beyond a usual slasher narrative, following protagonists who survived slasher attacks. Each is modelled on a famous cinematic Final Girl – for instance, Adrienne is a surrogate for Alice in *Friday the 13th*, while Julia is a stand-in for *Scream*'s Sidney Prescott – acting as a quasi-extension of those famous filmic slasher texts. Such novels are beyond the scope of *The Metamodern Slasher Film*, but I draw attention to them to underline that this book's findings are applicable to the horror genre (and to horror studies) in a wider sense.

Indeed, although this book concentrates on the slasher film, it is not the only subgenre in which the metamodern sensibility is expressed. Other horror subgenres include films that innovate in a metamodern way. For instance, *Pet* (2016) presents a reversal of torture porn's expected power dynamics, presenting its caged protagonist as having control over their abductor. *Intruders* (2015) similarly innovates by inverting the home invasion structure; the eponymous intruders are trapped and attacked by a homeowner protagonist who would conventionally be the film's victim. *Tucker and Dale vs Evil* (2010) upends backwoods horror by volunteering dual vantage points on the situation: urban teens perceive Tucker and Dale as archetypal killer 'hillbillies', and those stereotypes are undercut (to comic effect) via Tucker and Dale's perspective. In each example, a fresh take is afforded on a conventional subgeneric setup, triggering new possibilities within those frameworks.

Even more broadly, I do not proclaim that horror is the only genre to exhibit a metamodern ethos, or that the metamodern attitude exclusively emerges in film. The slasher film is my focus of study because it is an exceptionally apt and discernible iteration of this shift in sensibility. I will say more on the slasher's aptness as the book progresses, but for the moment it is worth noting that the slasher's robust conventions and structure make it flexible. As such, it can adapt to the ever-changing zeitgeist and readily accommodate turns in contemporaneous sociocultural mores. Such turns can be remarkably difficult to describe in the abstract, but items of popular culture provide snapshots of a moment's dominant cultural tone. Because of its responsiveness and mutability, the drift towards a metamodern mindset is apparent in the slasher film in a way that might be harder to perceive in some other subgenres or cultural forms.

To be clear, this book will not bluntly correlate individual films with specific political events. Rather, I contend that like other forms of horror fiction, slasher films are shaped by the tenor of the moment, speaking to prevailing fears, ambitions and collective interests that matter to its makers and contemporaneous audiences. This is not a novel position: for example, Cherry observes that 'horror films tap into the sociocultural moment by encoding the anxieties of the moment into their depictions of monstrosity' (2009, 11); Jancovich posits that 'the slasher subgenre uncovers feelings of vulnerability within contemporary society' (1992, 108); Clasen and Platts argue that 'slasher films reflect their sociocultural context, specifically . . . large scale shift[s] in values in American culture' (2019, 24) and so forth. This book will build on such extant work via its account of contemporary slasher films and the metamodern sensibility.

In sum, the central underlying claims of *The Metamodern Slasher Film* are that: (1) metamodernism describes the sensibility that has become prevalent since the mid-2000s; (2) the slasher films under examination are 'metamodern' insofar as they variously articulate the metamodern sensibility via the approaches taken to form, stylistics, tone, conventions, characterisation, character perspective, and viewership (as will be evinced via case study analyses); (3) since the early-2000s, a sufficient critical mass of metamodern slasher films has developed such that we can meaningfully refer to the metamodern slasher as a distinctive aspect of the subgenre.

All subsequent claims should be understood in this light. I am not claiming that every twenty-first-century slasher film is metamodern, but rather that a sizeable body of contemporary slasher films exhibits a shared sensibility. Subgenres develop in messy ways because filmmakers and distributors do not follow unified agendas. Even though I employ the term 'metamodernism' then, I am not suggesting that contemporary slasher filmmakers are aware of metamodern theory or intentionally set out to make 'metamodern slasher films'. Metamodern slasher films reproduce the tenor of the zeitgeist, and that is concretised in particular ways in each film. Metamodernism grants a conceptual lens that exposes both how these films capture the zeitgeist, and the broader implications of their operations. When analysing case studies, I will evidence how a film articulates the metamodern ethos through a combination of techniques.

Even so, that should not be taken as a claim that any one trait is exclusive to metamodern slasher films, or that every metamodern slasher will display that same property. That is, metamodern slashers are all demonstrative of the metamodern mindset, but they do not all present that mindset identically. As per my definition of the slasher film above, contentions about 'the metamodern slasher film' are to be understood as heuristics mapping dominant trends, not as rigid designations that must apply to every single film or serve a taxonomic function. The same applies to my discussion of postmodern slashers: not all slasher films of the mid-1990s to early-2000s are postmodern, and my contentions about a specific film are not implicitly applicable to every other postmodern slasher film. Postmodernism is drawn upon because of an intractable association forged between that term and a recognised trend within the subgenre. Postmodern theory will be utilised to highlight the postmodern slasher's characteristic tonal qualities. The same is true of metamodernism. This book does not aim to merely prove that a body of slasher films fits with the theoretical model of metamodernism. Instead, the theory allows me to delineate why a critical mass of contemporary slasher films operate the way they do, and to explain the significance of those operations, both in terms of their relationship with the zeitgeist and the subgenre's development.

While I compare postmodern slashers to metamodern slashers throughout the book, I am not proposing that one set of films (or the related theories) is superior to the other. I state this because one might justifiably assume that distinctions such as 'cynical' and 'sincere' are intended to draw value judgements. I have used such terms to articulate and distinguish between tones, but I do not necessarily mean to disparage postmodern slashers by insinuating that duplicity and cynicism are 'bad' features. Given that slasher films routinely portray homicide and suffering, it would seem reasonable for slasher films to carry a cynical tone. Also, if one were gunning for the slasher, a little duplicity is not exactly the subgenre's most damning quality. When I make claims about the postmodern slasher and its tone then, those claims should not be interpreted as expressing distaste for that phase; indeed, I consider many films of the era – including *Scream*, *Cherry Falls* (2000) and *Urban Legend* (1998) – to be among the subgenre's most important and enjoyable movies. I like these films for what they are: I do not feel the need to apologise for or deny their tone. Moreover, metamodern 'sincerity' could just as easily be read as 'naïveté', 'schmaltz' or trite sentimentalism; 'sincerity' should not be understood as positive per se. Furthermore, where I posit that metamodern slashers' reflections are more subtle or tacit compared with their postmodern antecedents, this is purely observing a difference in approach, not intimating that 'subtlety' is 'better'. Postmodern slashers' investigations of subgeneric norms are foregrounded because self-consciousness is integral to that very investigation. Metamodern slashers are frequently more ambiguous, and (as I will argue) that ambiguity is integral to the messages being conveyed. The main point of comparing postmodern to metamodern slashers is to illustrate an overarching and notable building away from the postmodern slasher's characteristic tone, and that observation offers an important way into understanding the metamodern slasher film's strategies.

Finally, this book centralises the slasher but that does not mean that the findings are aimed solely at understanding this subgenre. As MacDowell contends, the scholarship surrounding 'cinematic metamodernism' currently suffers from a dearth of 'detailed criticism' (2017, 26). MacDowell also rightly remarks that 'critical close reading . . . will improve not only our accounts of "metamodern" texts, but also our theorising of the metamodern itself' (2017, 27). This book's close textual analyses will demonstrate in detail how metamodernism materialises in contemporary film, and sustained engagement with one filmic subgenre will provide depth of focus. Again, my claim is not that slasher films are unique in capturing the metamodern sensibility, but rather that they are indicative. More broadly, the analysis that follows will contribute to the development of metamodern theory via its examination of a single subgenre. To date, most of the work on metamodernism has taken the form of single chapters and journal articles. Applying the nascent model in a sustained way will entail developing and refining the model.

CHAPTER 1

From Postmodern to Metamodern Slasher

This book's central contention is that a broad sociocultural turn towards a metamodern sensibility is reproduced in a substantial body of twenty-first-century slasher films. Alternatively, one might say there have been notable changes in the techniques and attitudes exhibited by many contemporary slasher films, and the reasons for and characteristics of those modifications are illuminated by metamodernism. Before engaging with specific examples to illustrate these transformations, this chapter will establish what metamodernism is.

The first part of this chapter will delimit metamodernism's key traits, which will be unpacked in greater detail via analyses of metamodern slasher films in subsequent chapters. I will then briefly sketch out some of the alternatives to metamodernism. These alternatives inform my own take on metamodernism and explain why I draw on metamodernism instead of another paradigm. Each alternative corroborates the case that the zeitgeist has shifted, such that the previous preeminent model – postmodernism – no longer captures the prevailing tenor of the moment. Metamodernism is not a complete break from postmodernism, however. As Toth avers, 'postmodernism . . . persists' insofar as 'what comes after postmodernism remains informed by postmodernism' (2010, 4). Accordingly, metamodernism builds on (and away from) the foundations laid by postmodernism.

The chapter then turns to the slasher subgenre, addressing a similar trajectory: delineating how metamodern slashers build on their immediate postmodern antecedents. To underline those developments, I first posit some high-level heuristics about the postmodern slasher, based on dominant critical and scholarly understandings. The subsequent section outlines core differences between metamodern and postmodern slasher films. Principally, the metamodern slasher replaces the postmodern slasher's inward-facing fatalistic cynicism with sincerity and innovations. Nevertheless, just as metamodernism does not simply gainsay postmodernism, metamodern slashers build on the foundations laid by the subgenre's previous phases. For example, irony continues to be a notable presence in the metamodern slasher, but here it is a conduit for sincere messages. Metamodern slashers also retain the foci on aesthetics, form and conventions that became decidedly pronounced in the subgenre's postmodern phase. In contrast to the postmodern slasher, these foci are not taken as disruptive problems in the metamodern slasher. Instead, form is consistently married with a sincere tone to convey that, for instance, coherent meaning is possible. Even where they are underlined, conventions are naturalised because they are congruous with the metamodern slasher film's diegetic worlds. Subjective experience is considered authentic and valuable in the metamodern slasher film, as opposed to being limiting, entrapping or misleading (as the postmodern slasher presented it). The rest of the book will subsequently unpack and evidence this chapter's high-level summary of positions via analysis of key metamodern slasher films. As such, this chapter furnishes readers with a primer for what is to follow.

Metamodernism (and its Alternatives)

There is no definitive consensus on what constitutes postmodernism (see Bertens 1995, 11, Currie 2011, 1; Pinedo 1996, 17). Regardless, there is greater agreement that 'postmodernism is rapidly becoming a thing of the past' (Rudrum and Stavris 2015a, xi; see also Gibbons 2015, 29; Hutcheon 2002, 165), or more specifically that 'we are now leaving the postmodern era with its essentially dualist notions of textuality, virtuality, belatedness, endless irony, and metaphysical scepticism' (Eshelman 2008, xi).

Much of the nascent body of literature grappling with what comes after postmodernism converges on the label 'metamodernism'. The term 'metamodern' is not itself new. For example, in 1975 Zavarzadeh used 'metamodern' to designate a relationship between metaphysical concerns and metafictional tendencies in American literary fiction. More recently, the term has been reinvigorated via the work of van den Akker and Vermeulen, who argue that postmodernism is characterised by 'plenty, pastiche, and parataxis', and that those approaches are inapt for articulating contemporary experience, which is shaped by 'material events like climate change, financial crises, terror attacks, and [networked] digital revolutions' (Vermeulen and van den Akker 2010, 2). As such, 'postmodern discourses have lost their critical value when it comes to understanding contemporary arts, culture, aesthetics and politics' (van den Akker and Vermeulen 2017, 3; see also Gibbons 2015, 30).

Rather than being a 'movement' or a 'philosophy', metamodernism is envisaged as a 'sentiment' (Vermeulen and van den Akker 2015).[1] That is, metamodernism speaks to the sociocultural moment's prevailing attitudes. Dember (2018) captures this sensibility as a drift away from 'the ever-present ironic snark that controlled the nineties', towards the 'express[ion of] unabashed feelings – joy, wonder, sadness, vulnerability, triumph'. Although this sounds like a full break from postmodernism, 'meta' (following Greek) is meant to indicate a state that is simultaneously '"with", "between" and "beyond"' postmodernism (Vermeulen and van den Akker 2010, 2; see also Bargár 2020, 3). Indeed, as we will see, metamodern slasher films carry forward and build on elements found in postmodern slashers, while the undergirding metamodern mindset shapes how those traits are employed.

Metamodernism should be understood as a continuation of postmodernism, just as postmodernism issues from modernism.[2] As an extension of both modernism and postmodernism, metamodernism implies that neither paradigm should be outright dismissed: both models have relevance and value inasmuch as they inform present understandings and outlooks. For some, this refusal to sharply break from postmodernism means metamodernism lacks conceptual distinctiveness (see Bentley 2018, 729–30; Rudrum and Stavris 2015c, 307). Yet, conceiving of modernism, postmodernism and metamodernism as mutually exclusive means disregarding continuities that provide richness. As Nealon contends, 'most continental political theory of the mid-to-late twentieth-century found itself trying to find a kind of "third way" between . . . binary oppositions' (2012, 120), and that ambition is paralleled by 'overt and constant critique of univocal meaning within literary theory' (2012, 129; see also Bargár 2020, 3). That foundational stance informs Vermeulen and van den Akker's conception of metamodernism as oscillating 'between hope and melancholy, between naïveté and knowingness, empathy and apathy, unity and plurality, totality and fragmentation, purity and ambiguity' (2010, 5–6; see also MacDowell 2017, 30).

I will return to the idea of oscillation (and its limitations) shortly. For the time being, it is worth observing that 'metamodernism' is but one label among many that seek to capture the dominant contemporary sensibility. It is unsurprising that disagreement should arise in the scholarship:

---

[1] Storm (2021) explicitly diverges from the majority of metamodern scholarship in this regard, attempting to create a 'philosophy' of metamodernism.

[2] Indeed, Zavarzadeh (1975) used 'metamodern' rather than 'postmodern' precisely to avoid implying that modernism had 'ended'.

as Hassan puts it, 'what lies beyond postmodernism? Of course, no one knows; we hardly know what postmodernism was' (2003, 199). However, there is agreement that a new model is needed, since 'the label postmodern . . . has exhausted its capacities to express the world now coming into being' (Lipovetsky 2005, 30). Each alternative model trying to describe this new state is distinguished by a primary point of emphasis. So, for instance, some wish to suggest that, far from becoming obsolete, postmodernism's features have intensified or accelerated. Such thinkers lean towards neologisms such as 'super-postmodernism, hyper-postmodernism, or . . . "late postmodernism"' (Nealon 2012, x). Some models are differentiated by adherence to a scholarly discipline and the media they thus attend to. Rudrum and Stavris (2015a, xxiv) observe that 'remodernism . . . is preoccupied with painting, while altermodernism foregrounds rather less traditional forms of the fine arts . . . Renewalism's principal emphasis is on narrative fiction . . . Digimodernism focuses mostly on audio-visual media', 'automodernism' is preoccupied with digital technology and so forth. Other divergences are based on sociopolitical or cultural emphases. So, for example, 'digimodernism' and 'automodernism' are not only interested in digital technology, but also the ways digital ubiquity shapes social lives and the production of texts (see Kirby 2009; Samuels 2008); 'hypermodernism' is concerned with a 'reign of urgency' in which temporal anxieties lead consumers towards nostalgia (see Lipovetsky 2005, 36); and 'cosmodernism' addresses globalisation and the repercussions of cultural blending (Moraru 2011).

Other scholars foreground relationships between modernism, postmodernism and the present moment. Shaw and Upstone eschew the '-modernism' suffix altogether, coining 'transglossic' to avoid 'a reductive association to the past which minimises . . . applicability to the dynamic newness' of the present (2021, 3). Others argue that the present state demonstrates the persistence of modernist values or a return to a more clearly defined set of modern (as opposed to postmodern) attitudes and techniques. Altermodernism and remodernism thus both seek to refine modernism in light of the contemporary milieu (see Smythe 2015, 365). Rudrum (2015, 345) suggests 'epimodern' captures 'the present cultural moment', and 'retrospectively . . . replace[s] the term postmodern', thereby creating continuity between modernism and the present situation, while 'dispensing with the need to envisage dramatic breaks between' those concepts. Another alternative – transmodernism – 'incorporates components of both modernism and premodernism while recognizing their shortcomings as identified by postmodernism' (Burns 2015, 68).

Transmodernism also carries pertinent tonal implications. Burns declares that transmodernism contrasts with 'the bleakness, loneliness and helplessness depicted in postmodernism' (2015, 68). Other models correctly identify pivotal tonal shifts that epitomise the cultural moment. For instance, remodernism and performatism herald 'the end of postmodern irony', which is replaced with 'a sense of sincerity or authenticity' (Rudrum and Stavris 2015b, 103). Dember volunteers a corrective to these theoretical frameworks with 'ironesty', which captures the idea that 'irony/sarcasm/sardonicness/snark' are now frequently 'employed in the service of making an earnest point or expressing a heart-felt emotion' (Dember 2018). That is, irony and sincerity are intertwined because sincere, emotionally honest messages are communicated via irony.

My preference for 'metamodernism' among these models is informed by several considerations. Foremost, 'metamodern' concentrates on prevailing sociocultural attitudes instead of a single medium, a specific discipline, or the relationships between modernism, postmodernism and political or economic matters. My model of metamodernism will encompass concerns about sensibility and tone raised by the various authors above. Second, although still nascent, metamodernism has thus far emerged as the axis for debates in this area. For example, despite capturing a ubiquitous mindset, 'ironesty' has not generated the scholarly momentum that 'metamodernism' has. I remain neutral on the semantics: each of the models mentioned in this section has its own value. Yet, as 'the most notable of these new post-postmodernisms' (Shaw and Upstone 2021, 576), metamodernism has stimulated a richness of discussion that some of the lesser-utilised models have not.

That said, the quantity of alternatives to metamodernism stresses that this is a live scholarly discussion. Accordingly, metamodernism is not a definitive or 'finished' paradigm. This section has briefly outlined the breadth of available ideas, themes and issues raised by those seeking to capture the present sociocultural moment. These alternatives offer inflections that can help to develop metamodernism. Accordingly, I will proceed to take metamodernism as a principal model, drawing on elements of these alternatives to refine that model. For instance, the underlying concerns raised by 'ironesty' chime with those elicited by other paradigms. Dember's framework usefully elucidates an aspect of the current cultural mindset that I take to be crucial – namely, tone – and I place greater weight on that aspect of metamodernism than van den Akker and Vermeulen do.

Whatever limitations 'metamodernism' has as a nascent theoretical structure, it articulates a broad drift in sensibility, building on (and therefore diverging from) postmodernism. Of course, given that this book focuses on the slasher subgenre, the most pertinent way to illustrate these transformations is to compare the postmodern slasher to the metamodern slasher. The rest of the chapter will map out that comparison, firstly by delineating the postmodern slasher.

From Postmodern Slasher Films . . .

The most significant phase of slasher film production preceding the metamodern slasher is the postmodern phase, which roughly spans from the mid-1990s to the early-2000s. Note that 'significant' does not necessarily mean prolific. The postmodern slasher phase – exemplified by high-profile movies such as *I Know What You Did Last Summer* (1997), *Urban Legend* (1998) and *Valentine* (2001) – is frequently referred to as a 're-emergence' or 'catalyst' for new horror (Perren 2012, 135). Some even refer to the postmodern phase as an 'avalanche' or 'surge' of horror production (West 2019, 10), despite the fact it consisted of only a dozen or so major theatrical releases. These slasher films seemed especially pivotal because they represented a moderate increase in the subgenre's box-office success compared with the declining returns of 1980s slasher sequels and early-1990s direct-to-video slasher movies. The high-profile postmodern slashers were subsequently slipstreamed by direct-to-video movies such as *The Clown at Midnight* (1998), *Lover's Lane* (1999), *Bloody Murder* (2000), *Final Stab* (2001) and *Halloween Camp 2: Scream If You Wanna Die Faster* (2004), which consolidated the postmodern slasher's reputation as an important new subgeneric phase. *Scream* (1996) is commonly understood as 'patient zero' of this trend (see Fenton 2016; Francis 2013, 71) and has been touted as 'fundamentally revitaliz[ing]' (Perren 2012, 132) and 'reinventing . . . the genre' as a whole (Rockoff 2002, 182). However hyperbolic these claims might be, they express the idea that the postmodern slasher is a distinctive production phase, encompassing slasher films that were greenlit in the wake of *Scream*'s box-office success. Consequently, the critical consensus is that the subgenre notably turned towards this 'postmodern' iteration in the mid-1990s (see Lockwood 2008, 41; Murray 2008, 1; Prince 2009, 283).

In the discourse surrounding these films, 'postmodern slashers' are commonly taken to encapsulate *Scream*'s three most conspicuous qualities, namely: (1) perspicuous discussion of genre conventions within the films; (2) direct references to other extant horror films within the script; and (3) deployment of metafictional devices (self-reflexiveness about film production and consumption). Therefore, *Scream* displays an explicit understanding of slasher film conventions in its script and depicts its protagonists watching and discussing slasher films (such as the original *Halloween* [1978]). These elements are not found consistently in every slasher film that has been grouped together under the 'postmodern' banner, even though *Scream* and its properties are 'regularly presumed to be emblematic of teen horror' of the period (Craig and Fradley 2010, 84; see also Clarke 2016).[3] For example, despite being a key 'postmodern slasher' film, *I Know What You Did Last Summer* does not incontrovertibly include the three attributes listed above. Nevertheless, where slasher films of the period flaunt one or more of these traits, that presence is sufficient to corroborate the discursive association between these components and the 'postmodern slasher' category.

These three conspicuous qualities are not exclusive to slasher films of the mid-1990s onwards, even if *Scream* was the first 'highly commercial (and therefore influential)' slasher to exhibit 'self-consciousness about genre convention' (Tudor 2002, 110). They are also evident in some slashers of the 1980s. For instance, *Student Bodies* (1981) pokes fun at the subgenre's conventions; *Friday the 13th Part VI: Jason Lives* (1986) includes self-reflexive humour about the *Friday the 13th* series; and *Return to Horror High* (1987) employs metafictional techniques. Intertextual referencing is a characteristic of Hollywood genre filmmaking generally (see Moine 2008, 102). None of these attributes are themselves sufficient to firmly separate the postmodern slasher from its predecessors. What is more notably distinctive about the films that followed *Scream* is their tone, which echoes a pervasive contemporaneous sociocultural outlook. To explain that tone, we need to inspect the postmodern slasher in greater detail.

As I have proposed, *Scream* plainly evokes the subgenre's conventions, and that evocation is shaped by its undergirding tone: as Church (2006) puts it, *Scream* 'announced the vacuity of 1980s horror formulas'. *Scream* achieved this by presenting conventional elements, pointing out that the elements were conventional, and connoting that these conventional elements were overplayed clichés. *Scream* is undergirded by dissonance, relying on and yet also criticising the subgenre's conventions. These tensions are symptomatic of what Hutcheon calls 'postmodernism's . . . wholesale "nudging" commitment to doubleness, or duplicity' (2002, 1). Such sardonic insincerity was prevalent in 'smart' films of the period (see Garcia 1996, 8; Harries 2000, 3; Holland 2013, 17). 'Smartness' here is a kind of hip self-awareness. *Scream* flaunts that self-awareness via its reflections

---

[3] Since it is commonly taken as initiating and epitomising the phase's most notable traits, *Scream* will be taken as a touchstone for the postmodern slasher throughout this book.

on conventions, and the jaded, flippant attitude exhibited by its key characters. For example, as West observes, 'almost all of [*Scream*'s] primary characters display a staggering disregard for their friends . . . arrogantly diffus[ing] . . . immediate threat[s] with one-liners and ironic detachment' (West 2019, 64 and 66; see also Duncan 2016, 112–13).[4] West highlights a ubiquitous smug self-assuredness among the characters, which manifests in, for instance, many of the town's teens attending a house party, thereby breaking the curfew imposed to protect them following a string of murders and attacks. These behaviours concretise a more expansive cultural sensibility – characterised by 'irony and cynicism' – that became the 'default setting' for American culture of the period (Turner 2015; see also Bargár 2020, 8). The teens act both as if their know-it-all savviness about horror film conventions protects them from literal harm, and as though their cynicism makes them emotionally invulnerable.

Scream's characters make unconcealed verbal references to extant slasher films (such as *Friday the 13th* and *Prom Night* [both 1980]) that *Scream*'s audience might have also seen. Two implications follow. First, by bridging between the diegetic world (*Scream*'s narrative content) and the real offscreen world (in which *Scream* exists as a cultural object), the intertextual references draw attention to *Scream*'s status as a constructed fiction film. Second, a parallel is drawn between the characters and subgenre fans who watch *Scream*, insofar as both groups consume the same films.[5] Indeed, *Scream*'s intertextual references – mainly name-dropped slasher film titles – are in-jokes for audience members who recognise those titles.[6] This mechanism rewards the cultural capital accrued by fans based on their familiarity with the subgenre. The mechanism also excludes anyone

---

[4] Perhaps influenced by Freddy Krueger's tendency to couple each death with a bon mot (see Conrich 2000, 227; Whitehead 2003, 38), numerous early 1990s slashers such as the killers of *Dr. Giggles* (1992) and *Funnyman* (1994) took up wisecracking in response to their victims' deaths. The postmodern slasher teen's ironic one-liners seem decidedly callous because of those extant connotations. Slasher killers treat victims as dispensable, interchangeable fodder, and these teens seem to have internalised that same attitude about their peers.

[5] Phillips' claim that 'the teenagers in *Scream* mirror precisely the young audience members who were its primary audience in the late 1990s' (2012, 89) requires some refinement here. *Scream*'s teens are representations, and the film's overarching sarcastic tone also shapes how the teens are portrayed. It is not that the characters 'mirror' the audience 'precisely', but rather that the characters offer a sardonic parallel of the audience, exaggerating traits for effect.

[6] Indeed, such inclusions come across as especially superficial in other postmodern slashers that add 'self-referential dialogue' as an 'obligation' (West 2019, 121), or part of a promise to audiences that the film will be 'like *Scream*' (see Hutchings 2004, 211).

who does not understand the references from partaking in the pleasures elicited by that form of communication. The protagonists' know-it-all smugness is mirrored in the 'knowing laugh' emitted when 'horror movies play to and feed upon the knowledgeability of their fans' (Kermode 2001, 60–61; see also Garcia 1997, 23; Scrutchin 1997, 6; West 2018, 8).

This mode of address is equally indicative of *Scream*'s ironic duplicity, since many of the series' characters – including arch horror film expert Randy – die despite their proclaimed savviness.[7] Subgenre knowledge is simultaneously prized and devalued here: such expertise does not help *Scream*'s overconfident protagonists to survive, and so the parallel between protagonists and fans implies that subgenre knowledge is of little practical use to fans. Instead of being a barbed attack on fandom however, this device is illustrative of what Hantke terms 'self-indulgent postmodern play' (2010, viii), underpinned by an apathetic attitude that nothing really matters because everything is merely a game.

By underscoring subgeneric production and consumption, films such as *Scream* also suggest that audiences take part in a ludic performance when consuming fiction films. For example, Tan and Visch consider absorption in film fiction to be a 'pretense game' in which filmmakers 'set the challenge of imagination' and enjoyment arises when viewers meet that challenge. Filmmakers can then 'optimize the playful element by manipulating the viewer's anticipations and rewards', while existing 'genre schemas' help to coordinate that interaction (2018, 237 and 242). *Scream*'s ability to generate suspense despite reminding the viewer of its fictionality speaks to both the allure of the 'pretense game' and how robust the subgenre's rules of engagement are. It is equally implied that filmmakers participate in this game, meeting audiences' expectations by adhering to subgeneric norms.

By transparently namechecking influential antecedents, *Scream* openly acknowledges that it mimics its subgeneric forebears, including the formulaic events and clichés those antecedents founded. *Scream*'s ploy was then mimicked by others (albeit in incohesive and/or superficial ways), to the extent that its distinctive qualities themselves became subgeneric clichés. This trend implies that the subgenre's well had run dry, having no original ideas left to impart. The postmodern slasher connotes that

---

[7] Indeed, it seems puzzling that the protagonists of *Scream 3* (2000) continue to defer to Randy's posthumous advice about horror movies when that knowledge did not protect him (he dies in *Scream 2* [1997]). The same is true in other films of the period; the protagonists of *Urban Legend* are not saved by their knowledge about urban legends, for example.

the only viable recourse is to repeat conventions while also openly and ironically acknowledging that repetition. Ergo, the postmodern slasher's playful tone is underpinned by fatalistic nihilism: subgeneric production and consumption are essentially futile because the subgenre is inescapably constrained by its conventionality.

Finally, this combination of ironic detachment, self-reflexivity and defeatism echoes the 'disengagement and psychological introversion' that was part of a 'national apathy' in the period (Briefel and Miller 2011, 2; see also Craig and Fradley 2010, 78; Hills 2005, 194).[8] This tonal inflection develops from modernist art's concern with 'alienation, anomie, solitude, social fragmentation, and isolation' (Gibbons 2017, 119). The horror genre was primed for such a move because of its turn to what Tudor calls 'paranoid' horror, which is based in everyday locations and features human (as opposed to alien or supernatural) threats (2002, 109; see also Budra 1998, 189). Postmodern slashers amplify that modernist inward focus via its metafictional techniques, which 'self-consciously embrace the problem of image creation': thus, postmodern fictions 'necessarily turn inwards upon themselves' (Harvey 1989, 323). When contextualised by an overarching tone of snarky cynicism and detached irony, this tendency for metafiction to 'withdr[a]w into itself' comes across as 'imprisoning' (Jeffries 2021, 275–9). Toth proposes that the 'paralysis' induced by metafiction either 'forces us to acknowledge the pointlessness of any narrative representation' or (worse still) 'represents "reality" as an ideological illusion' (2010, 121–2; see also Booker 2007, xvi; Gibbons, Vermeulen and Van Den Akker 2019, 174; Kaplan 1988, 4–5). The latter speaks to the latent nihilism that underpins the postmodern slasher.

. . . to Metamodern Slasher Films

Rather than being fatalistically resigned to the notion that originality is impossible, metamodern filmmakers innovate within the subgenre. As Cherry observes, inventiveness is potentially disruptive given that genres are 'based on sameness rather than innovation' (2009, 33). A subgenre is anchored by stable norms, which act as an unspoken 'contract between the producers of films . . . and their audiences' (2009, 33). Therefore, audiences might not simply feel dissatisfied if the subgenre's formula is modified: they might feel confused or betrayed if the implicit agreement Cherry refers to is contravened. Nonetheless, the slasher's evolution

---

[8] Arguably this 'navel gazing' was preceded in other areas of culture, such as grunge music, for instance (on this, see West 2018, 17 and 31).

to date helps to naturalise the metamodern slasher's innovations. The subgenre's core properties were swiftly established via rapid market saturation in the boom-period, offering a robust subgeneric identity on which to build. Market saturation also led to early experimentation and minor conventional deviations in the mid-1980s, priming audiences to tolerate experimentation. The subgenre's conventions and tropes were then laid bare via the postmodern slasher's overt self-reflexivity. *Scream*'s crossover success meant that knowledge about the subgenre's norms became part of the popular vernacular, especially when *Scream* and *I Know What You Did Last Summer* were parodied in *Scary Movie* (2000): the latter rearticulated slasher tropes and conventions to an even less generically-specialised audience. In this respect, metamodern slasher films are indebted to postmodern slashers for propagating knowledge about the subgenre's modus operandi. Rather than communicating to subgenre fans via in-jokes that rely on detailed subgeneric understanding to 'land' (thus excluding viewers with insufficient cultural capital), metamodern slashers work from the assumption that broad understanding of the subgenre's norms is commonplace.

Moreover, that broad knowledge is sufficient for noticing and comprehending the metamodern slasher's innovations. The importance of even minor innovations is illuminated by background knowledge of slasher films. Instead of seeking alternatives to the subgenre's standard plots and conventional actions, metamodern slasher filmmakers typically adopt fresh perspectives on formulaic situations by, for instance, modifying a key trope (see Chapter 5). Some metamodern slasher films still contain candid commentary on the subgenre's conventionality, as Chapter 4 will demonstrate. However, rather than reminding viewers that they are engaging with a fictional construction (as postmodern slasher films customarily do), metamodern slasher films either centralise narrative as the main source of pleasure, or playfully embrace the absurdity of the construction (see Chapter 6).

Metamodern slashers depart from the postmodern slasher's particular take on self-reflexivity. Dember (2018) proclaims that 'postmodern work' utilised 'self-reflexivity' to undercut notions of 'objective and universal truth' by highlighting 'that the author's own perspectives, flaws or belief systems may distort' meaning. Metamodern art instead 'repurposes' self-reflexivity 'to affirm [the consumer's] felt experience' (Dember 2018). By emphasising the consumer's 'felt experience', Dember underlines that metamodern art moves away from the postmodern preoccupation with authorship and construction, and towards the reader or viewer's experience of engaging with texts. The latter is pertinent to my analysis because metamodern slashers facilitate viewer investment in the characters' situations. By accentuating form, postmodern texts discredit sincere responses to their content. As I have proposed, postmodern slasher scripts constantly remind viewers that the text is purely a construct, and so viewers are encouraged to disown their emotional responses to characters' situations. Additionally, the characters are commonly apathetic about each other's emotional responses or treat displays of emotion with snarky disdain. Metamodern slashers take a different approach to self-reflexivity and 'felt experience', beginning with the supposition that viewers understand that the film is a fictional construction. Knowing that the events are fictional does not preclude viewers from experiencing genuine emotional responses. As subsequent chapters will illustrate, metamodern slasher films invite such emotional responses. For example, this is achieved by portraying characters sincerely caring about each other and taking each other's expressive reactions seriously (see Chapter 7), or employing limited protagonist perspectives to conjure subjective realism, exposing the significance of individuals' experiences (see Chapter 2).

This subjective focus unveils another crucial distinction between the postmodern and metamodern slasher. Metamodern slashers are anchored by a form of presentism: since subjective 'felt' experiences happen in the present, the past and the future are relationally deemphasised. That stance might seem to replicate a postmodern form of presentism, which is rooted in the idea that originality and progress are no longer possible (see Booker 2007, xv; Jeffries 2021, 98; Toth 2010, 128). In this view, the postmodern slasher's apathy and its sardonic, self-conscious replication of subgenre norms stems from this predisposition that innovation is impossible: the subgenre is thus trapped in the present, being doomed to repeat stale conventions that were forged in a now inaccessible past. From the postmodern slasher's vantage point, past 'classics' are viewed through a lens of lost innocence: one might recognise that *Halloween* was important in founding the subgenre's key ingredients and patterns, but that is not the same as experiencing the original *Halloween* as fresh or exciting, as some audience members might have when it was first released. That is, once the subgenre was recognised as such, and after *Halloween* was retrospectively understood as an instantiation of the slasher, it was no longer possible to experience *Halloween* in the same way its original audiences did. *Scream* inculcates that 'knowing', presentist viewing position, chiefly via its address to fans. Metamodern slashers take a contrasting stance on the present, which will be explored in detail in Chapter 7. Building from the postmodern position, it is taken as given that the past and future cannot be directly experienced first-hand. Yet, the present is conceived as a bridge from the past to the future. Innovating means advancing new elements that can be carried into the subgenre's future, but it also entails drawing on the subgenre's past (if only to distinguish the present iteration from antecedents). Since one can only ever act in the present moment, that is where any innovation must occur. The present is not fatalistically ensnaring, then. Rather, the present grants opportunities to act with the hope of instigating meaningful change for the future. Thus, metamodern slashers are presentist, but the emphasis shifts from a fatalistic to an optimistic mode.

This adaptation towards optimism will be exemplified via case study analysis (especially in Chapters 2 and 3), but more needs to be said about optimism before moving on. Admittedly, optimism does not seem to fit naturally with the slasher's subject matter. The subgenre revolves around depictions of young people being picked off, en masse, in the prime of their lives. On the face of it, the subgenre's staple plot structure befits postmodern cynicism, not metamodern optimism. To explain the metamodern slasher's optimism for the future, let us take a brief detour, turning to the wider sociocultural context surrounding metamodern slashers to clarify how irony is deployed in metamodern culture.

In an analysis of recent online political discourse, Griffin (2020) deals with 'funny memes featuring gallows humor'. On the surface, such memes seem to make light of matters such as 'the ascendancy of right-wing populism' (2020, 382), and so could be interpreted as the result of political disengagement. This might sound like a familiar tack, given that the ironic humour exhibited by postmodern cultural objects (such as postmodern slashers) has also been understood as symptomatic of a larger rejection of 'sincerity and seriousness', and disengagement from ethical and political responsibility (see Declercq 2020, 548). However, these memes utilise irony in a different way. The concerns raised within these joke memes seem to sincerely matter to those who create and distribute them. As Griffin remarks, laughter is expressive of an 'enjoyment-joy affect', even though the political situation arouses intensely 'negative affects like anger' in these individuals (Griffin 2020, 390). First then, Griffin's example illustrates that ironic humour can be employed to convey sincere political grievances. That approach is emblematic of metamodern irony, which is distinct from postmodern insincerity and disengagement. Second, Griffin makes sense of this combination of irony and sincerity by drawing on Tomkins's model of paired affects, such as 'enjoyment-joy . . . anger-rage . . . fear-terror' (2020, 383). These seemingly mutually exclusive affects go unresolved in Griffin's analysis: he does not unpack how these affects come together.⁹ Griffin describes these memes as hypostatising a 'politics borne of *oscillation*: between . . . anger and laughter' (Griffin 2020, 382, emphasis added). However, users do not 'oscillate' between mutually exclusive affects: these jokes express sincere fearful anger, and thus simultaneously evoke fearful anger and pleasure.

Griffin does not utilise the term 'metamodern' in his article, but his deployment of 'oscillation' appears to be influenced by the same background assumptions Vermeulen and van den Akker build into their model, with its 'oscillation between a typically modern commitment and a markedly postmodern detachment' (2010, 2). Most crucially for this book's purposes, Griffin's example reveals that oscillation does not convey the idea that Vermeulen and van den Akker refer to. Oscillation is a regular fluctuation across time. The amplitude (the degree of displacement) is equal above and below a baseline, meaning oscillation is a wave pattern that vacillates between two poles (the maximum amplitudes reached above and below the baseline). If we take those poles to be irony and sincerity (as Vermeulen and van den Akker do), the problem is apparent: it is not that metamodern texts regularly fluctuate between instances of sincerity and instances of irony as a text progresses. Rather, like Griffin's memes, metamodern texts are simultaneously ironic and sincere. Vermeulen and van den Akker directly employ the metaphor of 'a pendulum swinging' (2010, 6) to describe movement 'between two opposite poles' (2010, 8), but that metaphor suffers from the same problem Dulk identifies with 'new sincerity': that the relationship between irony and sincerity 'in the context of cinema has so far remained under-defined' (2020, 141) because it is conceived 'as a tension between two opposites' rather than a unified 'coherent' concept (2020, 141–4).¹⁰ A better analogy is that the metamodern text fosters superpositions: just as Schrödinger's cat occupies a seemingly contradictory superposition in being concurrently alive and dead, the metamodern text occupies a superposition in being at once ironic and sincere. When irony is implemented in the metamodern text, it delivers a sincere message. When one tries to pin down or assess a metamodern text, one might find that the superposition collapses: one observes either the irony or the sincerity. This is a natural growth from postmodern duplicity,

---

⁹ Griffin's analysis of memes also demonstrates that the metamodern sensibility is part of the zeitgeist: it is not only located within the narrative arts or (even more specifically) slasher films.

¹⁰ Konstantinou's 'post-irony' suffers similarly from its adherence to 'a confused sense of oscillating' when trying to pin down the 'betweenness' of 'transcending irony's limitations' without 'a simple return to sincerity' (2017, 88).

but metamodern films instead dwell in the coexisting multiplicity inherent to the superposition.[11]

Conceived this way, it becomes evident why horror aptly expresses a metamodern superposition-based sensibility. Horror fiction elicits seemingly incongruous affects, entailing taking pleasure in negative emotional states such as fear, disgust and anger.[12] In the slasher subgenre, furthermore, 'meaning is derived' from 'the binary oppositions generated by its stock characters', including their separations into 'valued/devalued . . . in-group/out-group . . . life/death' (Dika 1990, 134). That is, the slasher film's robust structure and normative conventions create binary oppositions. Even so, slasher films also continually bridge between those apparent binaries. For instance, the Final Girl is part of the victim-pool in-group, which is separate from the out-group of 'an old community': 'representatives of the "law" or of authority' (Dika 1990, 134). Simultaneously, the Final Girl stands apart from her peers by her capacity to survive: she is at once part of and an outsider to the 'in-group'. Her differentiation from the killer – ostensibly her binary opposite – is also less stark than it may first appear to be. The Final Girl is vulnerable as a would-be victim, but the narrative drives towards the moment she becomes a killer (slaying the slasher). As one who annihilates (not one who is stalked), the slasher seems to be positioned as an opposite to the victims, yet the narrative culminates in the killer's demise. Ordinarily, however, it also remains unclear whether the killer is finally defeated (whether they are dead or alive, to draw on another supposed binary): the slasher film's conventional 'sequel hook' hints that the killer's demise and the Final Girl's assumed conquest are only temporary. The Final Girl's triumph is also tempered by the numerous murders preceding it and any celebration of the survivor's victory is tinged by these prior defeats. In the postmodern slasher, these repeated structures involving irresolvable confrontations underscore the subgenre's inherent fatalism and futility. In the metamodern slasher, the emphasis is different. Although the subgenre is superficially rooted in simplistic core binaries – killer/victim,

---

[11] Shaw and Upstone (2021, 581) identify a comparable issue with metamodernism, using 'deep simultaneity' to describe 'the simultaneous occupation of multiple positions which is fundamental in its sustained expression at both formal and thematic levels within the text'. However, as with other aspects of their 'transglossic' model, that simultaneity is taken to articulate 'the text's relationship to . . . extratextual . . . social and political resonances'. I am less concerned with a text's political commitments or ability to instigate practical, real-world change.

[12] This issue has been the subject of much discussion in the scholarly literature on this topic (see, for example, Carroll 1990; Clasen, Kjeldgaard-Christiansen and Johnson 2020; Hills 2005).

alive/dead, win/lose – it is underpinned by complex, ambiguous relations. As this book will evince, metamodern slashers revel in forging superpositions, playfully bridging between supposed poles, thereby exposing similarities and continuities that are obfuscated by binary thinking.

This stance elucidates why metamodernism is not a return to modernism, but a re-envisaging of modernism's importance in light of postmodernism. It is not that 'metamodernism oscillates between the modern and the postmodern' (Vermeulen and van den Akker 2010, 5), but rather that it concurrently encompasses values from each. It is not simply that 'postmodernism is finished, passé', then (Hutcheon 2002, 66). As Hutcheon proposes, postmodernism's 'discursive strategies and its ideological critique continue to live on – as do those of modernism', and as such to ask whether postmodernism is 'dead or alive' is to ask the wrong question: it is simultaneously 'both' (2002, 181; see also Toth 2010, 2). That is, like Schrödinger's cat, postmodernism persists in a superposition. Metamodern slashers capture that notion by building on and also away from postmodern slashers; by being simultaneously akin to, yet divergent from those postmodern predecessors.

Metamodern culture thereby connects multiple facets of the past by understanding their continued relevance to the present. Thus, as James and Seshagiri contend, metamodernism entails 'a retrospective understanding of modernism' (2014, 88), in which artists draw from modernism's 'aspirational energies' (2014, 93) to 'mobilize innovations of their own' (2014, 94). Metamodern art then seeks to 'reconstruct', rejecting 'cynicism and despair' in favour of 'hope and optimism' (Abramson 2017; see also Bargár 2020, 6). The present bridges between multiple pasts and a future that is beyond our comprehension (I will return to this idea in detail in Chapter 8). Where postmodern art is founded on a pessimistic presumption that no future originality is possible and artists are inevitably fated to repeat from the past, metamodern art begins from the principle that innovation is possible. Metamodern texts are aspirational in this regard, even though they are simultaneously mindful of the past. Metamodern slashers recognise that the subgenre's future is suspended in ambiguity, encompassing a range of potentialities. Via their innovations, metamodern slashers embody optimism for future change within the subgenre.

A New Beginning

This chapter has briefly delineated what metamodernism is. Most notably, metamodernism (as I use it) is not a defined 'theory', but a way of articulating a sensibility. That sensibility, as I will go on to argue, is concretised in many contemporary slasher films. I refer to these as 'metamodern slasher films', but that does not imply their makers belong to a unified artistic movement. Rather, these films exhibit tonal qualities that are reflective of a metamodern outlook. More specifically, metamodern slasher films are characterised by optimism, sincerity and outward-facing inclusivity. They each volunteer subgeneric innovations, signalling hope for the slasher's continued future development.

To accentuate these qualities, I have outlined ways the metamodern slasher film builds on and away from its prominent antecedents: the postmodern slashers. That comparison is natural because metamodernism was conceived in response to postmodernism's inability to capture the contemporary milieu. The 'postmodern slasher' is not a perfect category, since not all slasher films that followed in *Scream*'s wake display exactly the same traits. Thus, when I employ the term 'postmodern slasher', I refer to a set of discursive associations, bringing together films that share recurring tonal qualities. Metamodern slashers represent a distinct move away from the duplicity, ambivalence and cynical fatalism exhibited by postmodern slashers, transforming those qualities into productive multiplicities and ambiguities. Comparisons between postmodern slashers and metamodern slashers will be drawn throughout the book to accentuate the metamodern slasher's innovations, since I anticipate that readers will likely be much more familiar with postmodern slashers than their metamodern counterparts.

This chapter's contentions have been limited to high-level heuristics about the subgenre, but a further aim has been to set up a key idea that informs the subsequent analysis: a film's narrative content, form, implied messages about the subgenre and overarching tone are all intertwined. For example, *Scream*'s characters might be reasonably described as sardonic, apathetic and insular, but *Scream*'s tone can also be conveyed via those same adjectives. Moreover, as I have proposed, *Scream*'s outlooks on the subgenre can also be seen as sardonic, apathetic and insular, both in its ironic communication to knowing fans (via intertextual references) and its defeatist connotations about the subgenre's prospects. The metamodern slasher offers a parallel set of intertwined components. As the following chapters will demonstrate, metamodern slasher films marry narrative content, form and implied messages about the subgenre, and each are shaped by the metamodern slasher's characteristic tone. So, for instance, metamodern slasher films contribute formal innovations (such as inventive takes on established norms) to the subgenre. Those innovations connote optimism for the subgenre's future, which is equally reproduced in narrative content (manifesting in, for example, hope for the lead protagonist's future).

The overview provided in this chapter is a foundation for what follows, and I will expand on these contentions as the book progresses. During this process, I will continue to refine metamodernism itself. Indeed, my own model of metamodernism developed as I engaged with extant cultural objects. My engagements with contemporary slasher films will expound merits and limitations of metamodernism as it is envisaged by its major proponents. In this chapter, I have already introduced one such development by replacing the commonplace, flawed concept of 'oscillation' Vermeulen and van den Akker baked into their model of metamodernism. As I have observed in this chapter, there are various alternatives to metamodernism, and each is epitomised by its divergences from postmodernism. Another way I will contribute to the development of metamodernism is by drawing on the strengths of comparable alternative frameworks. So, for instance, Chapter 7's analysis will make use of hypermodernism's emphasis on nostalgia, as well as digimodernism's preoccupations with digital ubiquity, the production of texts, and textual meaning. However, when I draw out these connections, I will not mention alternative neologisms: instead, I will directly build these concerns into my model of metamodernism. For the time being, this chapter has done enough contextualising: it is time to begin examining contemporary slasher films themselves.

CHAPTER 2

Investment (Epistemology)

Postmodern fiction routinely underlines its construction by highlighting formal qualities, structures and conventions. Slasher films were particularly prone to adopting that mode for several reasons. First, the slasher is anchored by a straightforward normative structure: 'sparse, streamlined plots' (Clayton 2020, 9), punctuated with regular murder sequences. Second, the enormous popularity of slasher films led to a production boom in the early-1980s (see Nowell 2011, 188), during which filmmakers borrowed core character-types and situations from immediate successful predecessors. For example, director Sean Cunningham openly admits *Friday the 13th* (1980) essentially purloins *Halloween* (1978)'s methods (see Grove 2005, 15). These foundations somewhat validate the commonplace criticism that the slasher subgenre is derivative, involving 'duplication of plots and circumstances' between films (Perkins 2012, 89). Thus, the slasher's formal qualities, structures and conventions solidified quickly in the boom-period, and repetition exposed those attributes for audiences and critics who saw multiple slasher films.

As the subgenre persisted into the mid-1980s and 1990s, filmmakers became increasingly self-conscious about audiences' and critics' (over)familiarity with the slasher's core components. The result was a continued reliance on those archetypal elements, flavoured with snarky duplicity about the subgenre's genericity. That duplicity is exemplified by the handling of character in postmodern slashers. As many have affirmed, the 'characterisations . . . tend to be more detailed and rounded' in films such as *I Know What You Did Last Summer* (1997), *Cherry Falls* (2000) and *Valentine* (2001) compared with earlier slasher movies, largely due to the casting of talented actors who cut their teeth in television drama (Hutchings 2004, 213; see also Craig and Fradley 2010, 87; Schneider 2000, 80). Postmodern slasher characters might be 'more detailed and rounded', but they are nevertheless conventional types – the jock, the nerd, the Final Girl and so forth – who are destined to die (or survive, in the Final Girl's case) based on their subgeneric situation. When contextualised by the postmodern slasher's self-consciousness about (sub)genericity, the combination of performative richness and stock character types takes on a critical tenor. That is, generic structures and norms seem to limit the postmodern slasher narrative's potential to flourish, in terms of fully leveraging both the actors' abilities and the characters' emotional depth.

The metamodern slasher develops from this state by foregrounding subjective experience and emotional resonance. Although it is taken for granted that the slasher's structure is built around sustained threat, the characters themselves are centralised and have resonance within metamodern slasher narratives. Metamodern texts lean into the precarity of the characters' situations. That precarity is informed by an underlying ethos of maintaining superposition potentiality: until or unless slaughtered, the characters are suspended between 'potential victim' and 'potential survivor'. It is unsurprising to find this metamodern spirit embodied by the slasher film. Whether metamodern or not, all slasher films follow protagonists who occupy a state of precarity insofar as the narrative situation imperils their survival. That tension precipitates suspense, which is amplified by the metamodern slasher's narrative investment in the characters' subjective experiences.

At first glance, these narratives are ostensibly anchored by a binary that has distinct moral orientations: 'bad' killer versus 'good' teens. However, the moral situation is less clear cut than it first appears to be. Stereotypically, the teen victims are taken to be legitimate targets because they violate moralistic norms (such as engaging in premarital sex or consuming drugs; see Shary 2002, 154). Even if some filmmakers arguably pass judgement on the follies of teenage freedom, slasher killers themselves are rarely motivated by the teens' violations of moralistic norms (on this, see Clasen and Platts 2019, 28). For instance, contrary to Muir's contention that the *Friday the 13th* series' homicides are motivated by 'bad teenage behavior . . . reinforcing cultural mores about drug use, premarital sex' (2007a, 98), Jason exterminates anyone who incurs on his territory (Camp Crystal Lake), irrespective of their age. His victims include Crazy Ralph, the middle-aged local harbinger of doom (*Friday the 13th Part 2* [1981]) and a group of non-teen paintballers who enter the surrounding woodlands (*Friday the 13th Part VI: Jason Lives* [1986]).[1] Outside of that terrain, he customarily fixates on victims who conform

---

[1] The same emphasis on territory extends across the subgenre, being reflected in location-based titles such as *Home Sweet Home* (1981), *Hospital Massacre* (1981), *Blood Theater* (1984) and *Nightmare Beach* (1989), and Michael Myers's obsession with his childhood home in the *Halloween* series.

to a 'type' (teenagers), regardless of what activities they participate in or refrain from. That is, neither drugtaking nor premarital sex are themselves necessary or sufficient conditions for murder in the series. Viewers might take *Friday the 13th*'s moralistic causality to be relatively straightforward then, but the 'on-the-ground' reality from the character perspective is far messier.

Character perspective is important to this chapter because it elucidates a significant shift between the postmodern and metamodern sensibilities. Where modern texts usually focused on structure, and postmodern texts commonly strived to stand apart from structure, scoffing at the absurdity of structure itself (see Bertens 1995, 4), metamodern narratives unveil the discordances generated by even simple structures. Metamodern slasher films convey subjective experiences induced by characters being trapped within precarious situations, and take the characters' experiences seriously, even though the situation is contrived.[2] In this way, metamodern slashers are more markedly invested in character positionalities than their postmodern predecessors were.

This shift illuminates another noteworthy divergence between the postmodern and the metamodern that informs this chapter's dissection of emotional investment in the metamodern slasher: the approach taken to epistemology (the theory of knowledge). Putting it crudely (for the sake of brevity), postmodernism casts epistemology as a problem. Epistemology presupposes that knowledge-generation is possible, but postmodernists commonly assume that our subjective perspectives are so intrinsically biased that knowledge claims cannot finally be verified. As Bertens argues, for postmodernists, meaning is 'inevitably local', yet 'contingent' (1995, 29): meaning is hopelessly curbed by our subjective limitations, being perpetually provisional and impossible to confirm. Thus, derived meaning is inauthentic, and any sense of epistemic progression – leading towards definitive knowledge – based on those derivations is illusory. At its most extreme, the postmodern position might even intimate that there are no facts in the world to access: that 'the world' is simply an amalgam of intrinsically unreliable subjective impressions.

---

[2] Much ink has been spilt over the supposed paradox of fiction: that is, the potential for fiction to stir genuine emotional responses in viewers who understand that a narrative is purely contrived (see Adair 2019; Denham 2020; Konrad, Petraschka and Werner 2018; Morreall 1985; Tullmann and Buckwalter 2014). Again, horror is exceptionally apt as a conduit for a metamodern approach to this issue, since horror film elicits genuine emotional responses (such as fear) in particularly visceral ways (on this, see Rust 2014, 551; Strohl 2012; Tamborini, Stiff and Heidel 1990).

These problems are not entirely abandoned or resolved under metamodernism. However, metamodern texts eschew postmodernists' rejection of epistemology. As Turner (2015) has it, the 'dominant cultural mode' is now characterised by 'a yearning for meaning – for sincere and constructive progression and expression'. As will be illustrated below, metamodern slashers continue to acknowledge that our epistemic access is limited. That limitation does not imply that there is no objective world beyond our subjective impressions: even if we cannot access it objectively, subjectivity does not preclude us from having individual experiences of a world outside of ourselves (a world shared by others), conveying our understanding of those experiences with others, or sharing in comparable experiences of phenomena, matter and events in that shared world. In this view, it is taken for granted that we cannot see the world objectively. However, objectivity can be utilised as an organising principle by which to orient and prioritise our subjective experiences.

This outlook is indicative of a pivot away from postmodernism's 'all-or-nothing' epistemic equations. It is recognised that even partial knowledge is nevertheless knowledge; incomplete access to the world is still access. Drawing on two case studies – *Shrooms* (2007) and *Triangle* (2009) – this chapter contemplates ways that metamodern slasher films present subjective epistemic access as intrinsically valuable, because our experiences are the bedrock of our lived reality. Instead of primarily associating subjectivity with epistemic limitations (which make objective reality essentially unknowable), emphasis is placed on epistemic access to the individual characters' (especially the lead protagonists') subjective experiences.

This understanding of subjective experience as the conduit for knowledge-generation is concretised in this chapter's case studies. Both *Shrooms* and *Triangle* are committed to and invested in their lead protagonists' subjective experiences. Narrative design fosters that alignment: *Shrooms*'s narrative perspective is shaped by the protagonists' use of hallucinogens, while *Triangle*'s events gradually unfurl via a time-loop structure.[3] Both films also embrace the ambiguities inherent to subjective

---

[3] To be clear, *Triangle* is not the only horror film to employ a time-loop structure (other examples include *Gruesome* [2006], *Haunter* [2013], *The House at the End of Time* [2013] and *Blood Punch* [2014]). It is not even the first slasher film to do so: *Timecrimes* (2007) also utilises a time-loop structure to tell a story about a masked killer, and its loops amount to a confined location for the action. However, as the analysis will evidence, *Triangle* uses the loop structure to convey metamodern concerns. Another metamodern time-loop slasher – *Happy Death Day* (2017) – will be examined in Chapter 3.

epistemic access. In both cases, the lead protagonist's subgeneric narrative role is uncertain: they are implicated as both Final Girl and killer. This dualistic superposition is engendered and sustained via alignment with the protagonists' limited epistemic vantage points: their (and, by implication, our) understanding of their position is restricted in both cases. Their positional precarity is leveraged to stimulate suspense, and ultimately horror.

The differences between these case studies unpack two key ideas sketched out in this introductory section. *Shrooms* emphasises that one's subjective perspective is the only available source of knowledge. Neither the viewer nor the characters have objective knowledge about the film's events because the narrative perspective is filtered through the characters' drug-addled vantage points. *Triangle* instead leans into emotional resonance, demonstrating that subjectivity is the bedrock of lived experience. The knowledge gained via subjectivity is so valuable to us precisely because it is deeply personal, being intertwined with our fundamentally emotional, experiential state of existence.

Are You Experienced?: Unreliable Perspectives and Ambiguity in *Shrooms*

Metamodern slashers typically prioritise the lead protagonist's perspective, presenting them as an unambiguously meaningful being, and expecting viewers to invest in their survival (at minimum, because perspectival alignment implies the narrative will cease if the lead protagonist dies). This alignment informs the metamodern slasher film's take on epistemology. In *Shrooms*, for example, the lead protagonist is the conduit for epistemic access, and any doubt regarding the veracity of information the viewer receives is in concert with her perception of reality. In *Shrooms*, the protagonists travel to Glengariff Forest Park, a remote woodland destination in Ireland, to trip on hallucinogenic mushrooms. The lead protagonist, Tara, accidentally consumes an exceptionally potent 'Death's Head fungi', which 'according to the ancient Irish druids', confers 'the ability to commune with the dead, uncontrollable ferocity, shape-shifting and . . . foresight . . . premonition'. Tara subsequently experiences vivid visions, and her fellow travellers are killed one-by-one.

Shrooms builds on established meanings of drug use in slasher films, which is usually deployed in two ways. First, in some cases, drug use is a defining trait for individual protagonists; that is, it is the behavioural attribute that distinguishes them as a type. So, in *Friday the 13th Part III*

(1982), for instance, Chili and Chuck are particularised as 'stoners'.[4] Second, even casual drug use is one way the teens exercise their freedom outside the restrictive purview of authoritative supervision. In both cases, drug use is incidental to the plot.[5] *Shrooms* takes an alternative route. All the protagonists consume hallucinogens, and the experience of drugtaking is centralised, being embedded in the film's aesthetic. Once the teens take the shrooms, techniques such as blurring, perspective skewing, pinching, warping and ghosting are employed to convey the teens' drug-induced experiences. Hallucinogenic effects shape many of the third-person 'objective' shots. For example, during her visions, Tara suffers from seizures, and external shots of her fits are over-cranked. Consequently, her movements are unnatural, conveying the experience of her seizures rather than a verité observational stance. Still, these hallucinatory effects are implemented most densely when rendering Tara's visions, which are often presented as point-of-view shots, enclosed in an eye-shaped iris. Thus, the film uses expressive stylistics to blur the lines between the characters' subjective drug-addled experiences and its portrayal of the objective world the characters occupy.

One impact of this combination is to facilitate audience investment in the characters, since our access to the narrative situation is inextricable from their interior subjective experiences. Here, narrative prioritisation of subjective experience makes it impossible to distinguish between the objectively 'real' and the hallucinatory within the fictional world. For instance, after taking the shrooms and drifting in-and-out of consciousness, Tara hears Jake and Lisa talking about Tara, Lisa warning Jake, '[if] you hurt her, I'll kill you'. However, we have no way of finally deciphering whether the exchange happened, or whether Tara just imagines the conversation during a hallucination. Furthermore, visual effects such as doubling and warping are wielded inconsistently. When Bluto

---

[4] In comparison to Shelly, for example, who is defined by another behaviour (he is *Friday the 13th Part III*'s 'prankster').

[5] That is, unless we accept the heuristic proposed by Randy in *Scream* that one can 'never drink or do drugs' because it is 'a sin', and so will be punished in the horror film context. Regardless of its inaccuracy (see Hernández-Santaolalla and Raya 2021; Ménard, Weaver and Cabrera 2019), the equation of substance abuse with death remains an entrenched stereotype in the discourse surrounding the slasher (for example, see Wood 2003, 173–4; Muir 2007a, 11; Petridis 2014, 77). As will become apparent, drugtaking is not plainly condemned as a mortal sin in *Shrooms*. Indeed, the activity is normalised within the protagonist grouping, even by the Final Girl. That is not to insinuate *Shrooms* is straightforwardly pro-drugs: there is a more direct causal connection between drugtaking and death here compared with the average boom-period slasher film.

wanders into the woods after taking shrooms, he is frequently blurred. That technique is abandoned as the sequence unfolds, and the inconsistency amplifies epistemic uncertainty for the viewer.

Shrooms's central mystery – the killer's identity – is complicated by this tack. That complication is accentuated by comparison with the postmodern slasher's standard ploy: cultivating epistemic uncertainty to defer the viewer's ability to identify the killer. Slashers are commonly 'whodunit' narratives, and it is typical for boom-period slasher films to 'hold back crucial information to generate shock and surprise' (even if viewers often 'have access to a wider range of information than characters do') (Clasen and Platts 2019, 35; see also Stewart 1982, 39). Nonetheless, as Balanzategui contends, postmodern slasher films foreground 'the whodunit game' for the audience,[6] tasking viewers with 'deploying their intertextual knowledge of the slasher formula in order to resolve the mystery of the killer's identity' (2015, 170). Although such manipulation is 'as old as the whodunit genre itself' (West 2019, 67), the ludic aspect is amplified by the postmodern slasher's ironic duplicity: filmmakers obfuscate the killer's identity but simultaneously encourage viewers to guess who the killer is regardless. This manoeuvre is in consonance with the tendency in postmodern fiction to 'create anxiety and irritation, confusion and annoyance' (Fjellestad 2021, 301) by not just withholding information, but also flagging that information is being withheld. In postmodern slashers then, multiple characters are cast as suspects, each is equally plausible, and viewers are made aware that the authors may be bluffing, double-bluffing or even triple-bluffing when casting suspicion. Multiple answers are advanced, but the viewer has no reliable means of deciphering which answer will eventually be revealed as correct. Moreover, the final reveal can be so left-field as to be essentially unguessable. Balanzategui suggests that 'usually' the postmodern slasher's killer is 'a seemingly harmless person who had been hiding in the community unscrutinized' (2015, 170). Conrich compares the postmodern slasher to 'Scooby Doo' in this respect (2015, 113), and although that might seem acerbic, the killers in *Scream Bloody Murder* (2003) and *Fraternity Massacre at Hell Island* (2007) are both school principals in latex masks in a turn that is expressly redolent of Scooby Doo cartoons. These two films perhaps exaggerate the postmodern slasher's approach to murder-mystery, but that exaggeration nevertheless highlights the flippant game-playing endemic to postmodern slasher films.

---

[6] The postmodern slasher's ludic mode amplifies an existing tendency within the subgenre; indeed, that leaning is evoked in the title of Dika's boom-period focused book, *Games of Terror*.

Shrooms offers an alternative take on the whodunit. Instead of casting doubt on most characters, only three possibilities are presented: the killer(s) might be the locals living in the woodland area, a supernatural entity (the 'Black Brother'), or our lead protagonist, Tara. In a superficial reading of the film, one might conclude that Tara is eventually outed as the killer. A series of ostensible flashbacks in the film's denouement re-envisage events that we previously witnessed, this time depicting Tara killing her friends while under the influence of the shrooms. *Shrooms* thus could be accused of tricking the audience in this regard. Tara is initially positioned as the film's Final Girl, being 'presented from the outset as the main character' and being characterised by her 'sexual reluctance' (Clover 1993, 39–40; see also Dika 1990, 135).[7] Lisa describes Tara as precisely that 'innocent' type early in the film. Lisa notes that she has 'never seen [Tara] take an aspirin', let alone a hallucinogen, and discloses that they both 'went to convent school'. Lisa then instructs Tara to 'for once in [her] life, let go'. Tara's rigid commitment to self-policing hints that she conforms to the subgeneric type. Given that Tara is positioned as the film's Final Girl, it might seem that the filmmakers follow the postmodern slasher's propensity to point to viable suspects – here, archetypal horror killer types (creepy rural locals or a malicious spirit) – only to then issue an unexpected 'twist'. Furthermore, by suggesting that Tara simultaneously occupies two (usually opposing) conventional roles – killer and Final Girl – it might seem like the filmmakers have merely misdirected the viewer. That interpretation neglects important aspects of *Shrooms*'s methods. Because of the text's epistemic ambiguities, the film ultimately provides no clear 'reveal' that verifies the killer's identity.

First, even if Tara were unambiguously the killer, the revelation is as much of a surprise to Tara as it is to the viewer. *Shrooms* would not be the first slasher film to have a 'Final Girl' who is revealed to be the film's killer: *Night School* (1981), *Sleepaway Camp* (1983), *Edge of the Axe* (1988), *Ripper* (2001) and more contemporaneously *All the Boys Love Mandy Lane* (2006) all pull that same switch. However, in those other cases, the killer's identity is presented purely as a 'twist' reveal. A comparison to *Shrooms*'s contemporary – *All the Boys Love Mandy Lane* – illuminates the distinction. Mandy Lane is painted as an 'untouched, pure . . . angel' by her peers. She conforms to Clover's Final Girl model, being the lead protagonist and rebuffing her peers' sexual advances. Viewers are given no reason to suspect Mandy inasmuch as we see that she is not present when the

---

[7] Even though this trait does not necessarily hold true across the subgenre, the connotations regarding sexual restraint remain entrenched in the Final Girl archetype.

first two teens (Marlin and Jake) are slain, and then Mandy's (supposedly) ex-friend Emmett is shown culling another teen (Bird). Emmett continues to menace the group, until only one remains: Chloe, who Mandy stabs. At this stage, it is divulged that Mandy plotted the murders with Emmett. Mandy then reneges on a planned suicide pact, executing Emmett. The twist that Mandy orchestrated the massacre simply entails withholding information from the viewer, and misrepresenting Mandy as the film's hero. Both Mandy and Tara are Final Girls in that they outlast their peers, but if we take Tara to be *Shrooms*'s killer, the narrative alignment with Tara's epistemic status is significant. We do not know Tara is the killer because neither does she. Moreover, Tara survives in this view because she is the source of the threat. Mandy Lane only pretended to be the Final Girl, whereas Tara genuinely occupies a superposition as killer and Final Girl in this interpretation.

Second, despite Tara's surprise, the final reveal is not an unguessable ludic turn. Hints that Tara might be the killer are scattered throughout *Shrooms*. Tara's visions are limned in irised point-of-view shots, but elsewhere in the film, grainy, desaturated, irised point-of-view shots are employed to denote the teens are being watched. In the context of slasher movies, such shots conventionally signal the killer's presence (see Cherry 2009, 132–3; Hart 2018; Modleski 1986, 16). Given these conventional associations, the deployment of irised point-of-view shots in stalking sequences and during Tara's visions hints that Tara might be the killer.

Even so, the situation is complicated by *Shrooms*'s centralisation of the protagonists' drug-addled experiences. Although there is a parallel between Tara's visions and what appear to be conventional stalker point-of-view shots, Tara is also captured in those same shots (see Figure 2.1). The blurry boundaries between interior, subjective viewpoints and the external 'objective' stance therefore present the viewer with a conflict: it is implied that Tara is the killer, yet she is also presented as one of the stalked victims. Usually, the latter would discredit the former, leading the viewer to discount Tara as a suspect and lending credence to the possibility that a malicious supernatural entity is attacking the teens. Here, the film's conflation of subjective and external viewpoints legitimates the possibility that Tara might 'see' herself during her visions as part of a drug-induced 'out-of-body' experience. This ambiguous superposition is maintained because of the film's epistemic alignment with Tara.

Third, Tara is not finally 'revealed' as the killer because the flashback 'memories' of Tara slaying her friends are tainted by the unreliability of her perspective. Those 'memories' are subject to the same desaturation and skewing that signify drug-fuelled hallucination sequences. If Tara

Figure 2.1 Tara is captured in an irised 'stalker' point-of-view shot in *Shrooms* (2007)

slaughters her peers, it is because she is so high that she does not know what she is doing. Nonetheless, if she is that high, we also cannot trust the climactic memory-flashbacks any more than we can trust Tara's earlier visions of the same incidents (wherein she was not the killer). Since the film contains clashing accounts, we know that some of the subjective images must be inaccurate. Still, we have no way of ascertaining which has greater veracity. One set of visions is not more reliable purely because it arises later in the text; in fact, the final flashbacks are positioned after a long chain of questionable accounts, compounding the notion that they amount to unreliable evidence.

Indeed, it is not obvious what kind of evidence could be bestowed by Tara's visions. She declares that the visions prove that she 'can see . . . the future', but the text offers ample reasons to doubt her claim. For example, although Tara predicts where Lisa can find Holly's corpse and the murder weapon, if Tara executed Holly, she would know where the body was (it would be a memory, not a premonition). In the final sequence, Tara re-envisages the incident by answering Lisa's question 'How did you know that [the axe was there]?' with the reply 'I put it there.' However, we also have reason to be sceptical that Lisa finds an axe or Holly's body at all: they might just be hallucinating.

Tara posits that 'we can't all be having the same trip', but she underestimates how susceptible to suggestion the hallucinating group appears to be. For instance, in an earlier scene, Tara believes she feels the presence of a hooded figure in the woods. Tara proclaims, 'There's somebody there!', even though a point-of-view shot (assigned to Tara) indicates that no-one is present. Lisa then confirms the absence ('Where? I don't see anything'), despite Tara's continued insistence ("They're right over there!'). In another point-of-view shot, we see a tree distort and then a hooded figure appears from the ether. The order of events suggests that Tara has conjured the figure in her mind, although she screams that she, Holly and Lisa should 'Run!'. Her friends then panic and follow Tara. Thus, Holly and Lisa assent to Tara's version of events, even though it does not concord with theirs. Once they stop running, Tara confesses that the figure was 'from the dream I had' and admits: 'I don't know what's going on in my head, what's real, what's not.' Regardless, she reaffirms her dubious conclusion that 'I'm seeing things before they happen.' Tara's certainty then seems to infect the others, given that they subsequently follow Tara's guidance even when they do not share or cannot confirm her proclamations about presumed threats in the woods. When Lisa supposedly finds Bluto's body, then, Holly's declaration that 'this isn't happening' seems reasonable. It is not wholly apparent whether they have found a corpse, or whether it is a hallucination the group projects onto a log or an animal carcass. To this end, Troy and Jake later also find Bluto's corpse in a seemingly different (more open) area of the woods. No external index is provided via which to verify or dispute their drug-addled perceptions.

It is not just that the characters cannot distinguish between fact and hallucination here. Instead, the boundary between the two is subject to slippage. The catalyst for Tara's hallucinations is the ostensible history of Glengariff Forest Park, and the extent to which that story is constituted by fact or myth is unclear. Tara encounters that history in a guidebook before she ingests the shrooms but hears the story again shortly after taking the hallucinogen. While she drifts in and out of consciousness in her tent, Jake tells the others a 'ghost story' about the location's supposed history. He recounts the tale of a 'religious order . . . the Black Knights' who ran a 'young offenders' centre' in the park's grounds. One sadistic 'Black Brother' tortured twin offenders, and one of the boys spiked the Black Brother's tea with the Death's Head fungi in return. During his hallucinatory state, the Black Brother massacred nearly everyone in the centre. As Jake recounts the tale, the film cuts to Tara, who frowns, pants, sweats and twitches restlessly. We also see grainy, monochrome, irised footage of the abandoned house, cut between shots of Tara's restlessness, implying that Jake's story is being incorporated into her drug-fuelled nightmare. She later refers to Jake's rendition of the story, hinting that she heard it. Although he later denies that the story is true – 'it was just a story' – Tara refuses to believe him (rebutting with 'you can't kid a kidder'). The tale forms the basis for her bad trip. When she sees a hooded figure in the woods, she concludes it is the Black Brother, because she believes the story. If Tara does murder her friends in a drug-addled frenzy, this story appears to trigger that trajectory.

Yet, if this is the case, Tara is susceptible to the story because it connects with her at a fundamental level. Jake's campfire 'ghost story' explains that the Black Brother was a fervent Catholic, presenting the massacre as a tale of 'sexual repression ... Catholic guilt and violence' being 'unleashed'. Notably, Tara too is presented as a self-repressing Catholic who takes shrooms to 'let go'. Thus, since Tara hears the story while under the influence of drugs, drifting in-and-out of consciousness, it seems plausible that Jake's story leads her to 'unleash' her repressed desires as violence. Notably, if Tara is the killer, it is because of precisely the self-policing and repressive innocence that also position her as an archetypal Final Girl. Nevertheless, the text maintains plausible alternatives to this explanation. One is that the final flashbacks are not remembrances at all, but rather a manifestation of Tara's Catholic guilt: that is, she may be suffering remorse not only from surviving, but from being unable to save her friends precisely because she 'let go' and took the shrooms. It is ambiguous whether the shrooms lead her to unleash her repressed Catholic guilt by exterminating others, or whether her Catholic guilt causes her to internalise responsibility for those deaths (in which case, the shrooms cause her to misremember the events). Both explanations are rooted in her character and the film's prioritising of subjectivity as the conduit for knowledge-generation.

Shrooms revels in these epistemic ambiguities, sustaining a range of live possibilities. Given that this chapter is concerned with investment in character, I have foregrounded the implications that follow from the protagonists' subjective experiences. However, this is a horror narrative, and so it is entirely possible that Tara does experience precognition, that a supernatural murderer slays her friends, that the Black Brother has possessed Tara or that the locals living in the woods (survivors from the youth offender centre massacre) are the killers. Within the genre and the fictional world, each of these accounts is plausible.

Any one of these possibilities would have resulted in a standard horror film that reiterates stock elements. Local rural killers are found in abundance in genre films such as *The Texas Chain Saw Massacre* (1974) or *Wrong Turn* (2003), for example. By balancing various conventional possibilities in simultaneity, *Shrooms* becomes more than the sum of its constitutive parts. As director Paddy Breathnach posits, his intention was to 'pla[y] with ... genre motifs and ... standard characters ... clichés ... the myths of horror stories ... getting them to behave in a slightly different way', and thereby exposing 'fault lines' between 'the language of the slasher film' and 'the supernatural'.[8] It is also notable that the filmmakers do not misdirect or present the viewer with the kind of 'gotcha' reveal that is representative of postmodern slashers' game-playing. Indeed, writer Pearse Elliott presumes that the horror audience is 'savvy', and Breathnach indicates that the 'real' horror of *Shrooms* lies in its 'uncertainty'.[9] Ambiguity reigns in *Shrooms*: the characters are just as uncertain as the viewer, and the film does not impart definitive answers because we have no objective access to the situation. Throughout, *Shrooms* underlines that knowledge is filtered via subjective perspectives. *Shrooms* thus submits that no final resolution is available. Since its ends – generating horror – are dependent on its ambiguities, *Shrooms* encourages viewers to relish precarity.

Three Sides to Every Story: Repetition, Reflection and Responsibility in *Triangle*

Triangle explores similar terrain to *Shrooms* in that the narrative's epistemic perspective is aligned with the protagonist's subjective experiential reality. However, *Triangle*'s structure reveals the lead protagonist's knowledge of her past actions in stages, foregrounding her struggle not only to survive, but to come to terms with her inner turmoil. *Triangle*'s plot follows Jess, who meets with Greg and his friends for a trip on Greg's yacht. When a storm capsizes the yacht, the group encounters and boards a seemingly abandoned vessel (the Aeolus). A masked killer attacks the group. The only survivor, Jess manages to push her assailant overboard, but not before hearing her attacker's warning: 'they'll return . . . you have to kill them . . . it is the only way to get home'. Moments later, Jess sees the group (including her) board the ship again. As the events replay, Jess intervenes, changing the course of action. Yet, she only temporarily delays some of the deaths. Desperate to leave the ship and be reunited with her son (Tommy), when the third cycle begins, Jess dons the mask herself. In a manner nearly identical to the first loop, Jess manages to cull everyone in the group apart from the alternate version of herself, and she is pushed overboard. Awakening on the shore, Jess runs home, where she witnesses herself snapping at and hitting her autistic son when he leaves his toy yacht outside and then spills his paint. The Jess we have been following executes this abusive version of herself, puts the body in the trunk

---

[8] Audio Commentary, *Shrooms* 2008 Region B Sony Pictures Home Entertainment Blu-ray release.
[9] Ibid.

of her car, and drives away with Tommy. Distracted by Tommy's distress, Jess crashes the car into oncoming traffic, leaving Tommy dead. Although Jess's body is also in the road, it is unclear whether the body is the Jess who was driving or the corpse that was stowed in the boot. The camera pans to another version of Jess, who understands that she only has one hope for changing what has happened: she returns to the harbour. The film ends where it began, with Jess meeting Greg's friends and boarding his yacht. When berating Tommy, Jess's counterpart declares that all she wants is 'just one fucking day off' to distance herself from her parental responsibility and go sailing with Greg. Jess's wish is granted in *Triangle*, but she then must live that 'day off' over and over again.[10]

This brief synopsis illuminates another reason *Triangle* is comparable to *Shrooms*: Jess occupies a superposition as the text's slasher and its Final Girl. Here, that duality is unveiled by 'replaying' events from alternative perspectives via the loop structure. Instead of being uncovered in the final act, *Triangle* exposes the killer's identity an hour into the film when Jess's second-loop counterpart removes her mask. While unconventional, this is not a 'gotcha' twist that wrong-foots the viewer. Jess's involvement is hinted at from the outset. For instance, Jess's sense of deja vu when they board the Aeolus (confirmed in her murmuring 'I feel like I know this place') foreshadows the forthcoming revelations about her relationship to the situation. The viewer is epistemically aligned with Jess here, sharing her sense of unease. Furthermore, Jess's superposition is expounded to Jess and the viewer simultaneously. It is not that Jess merely hides her murderous intent from others, as is the case in slasher films such as *Night School* and *All the Boys Love Mandy Lane*, where the Final Girl is eventually outed as a killer. The loop structure means multiple versions of Jess coexist: she is the killer and the Final Girl simultaneously, but separately. The version of Jess we follow is initially the Final Girl. She becomes the killer by the third loop. Then, she is defeated by precisely the same prior Final Girl version of herself. Here, *Triangle* is distinguished from other slasher films in which the Final Girl is the film's killer: Jess stalks and attacks herself, and this tension reifies Jess's inner conflict.

Jess is driven by regret over hurting Tommy, even if she does not fully remember what she has done until she returns home and witnesses her actions. *Triangle*'s loops are more than a structural gimmick. The loops gradually reveal Jess's turmoil to herself, as well as to the viewer. Consequently, the film is rooted in a complex and subjectively anchored set of

---

[10] This 'flawed wish' scenario follows in the tradition of W. W. Jacobs's horror story 'The Monkey's Paw' (1902).

motives. The subgenre's killers are typified by reasonably straightforward aims, such as simplified iterations of revenge or psychosis (see Hanich 2010, 34). Even the postmodern slashers – which reputedly advance a 'secular "anything goes" attitude of moral relativism' (Connor 2015, 32; see also Pinedo 1996, 17) – still conform to basic conventional goals. For example, the killers of *I Know What You Did Last Summer*, *Urban Legend* and *Valentine* seek forms of extra-legal justice that are indistinguishable from the conventional revenge-seeking that drives the killers of boom-period films such as *Prom Night* (1980) and *Graduation Day* (1981). Despite proclaiming that 'I don't really believe in motives', *Scream*'s Billy also has a customary impetus: Sidney's mother was having an affair with Billy's father, and that is 'the reason [Billy's] mom moved out and abandoned' him. Thus, *Scream* reiterates psychosexual 'mommy issues', duplicating a motive that was conventionalised by its subgeneric antecedents, including *Psycho* (1960), *The Eyes of Laura Mars* (1978), *Don't Go in the House* (1979) and *Maniac* (1980). In comparison, *Triangle*'s commitment to Jess's subjective perspective means her motives are much messier, chiefly since they evolve across the film. Initially, it appears that Jess seeks to escape the ship because she has a duty to her son; she avers, 'my world is waiting outside school for his mother to pick him up'. Once she returns home, however, it becomes apparent that she is driven by both the responsibility to protect her son and her failure to do so. That reassessment is triggered by the loop structure, which requires Jess to re-evaluate the events as new information is uncovered and her epistemic awareness adapts. The viewer is encouraged to share in Jess's reassessments because new information is divulged to Jess and the audience concurrently.

Triangle's metamodern sensibility is evident not only in its commitment to conveying the protagonist's experiential reality, but also in its use of structure as a means of illuminating her motivations from different angles. Jess's superposition as killer and Final Girl both amplifies and tests the limits of her responsibility. When she is confronted with a third-person perspective on how she treated Tommy, she comes to perceive her actions in the same way the viewer does. Ergo, it is not just that the viewer is aligned with Jess's epistemic position, but also that Jess is eventually aligned with ours.

These mutating perspectives add psychological depth to *Triangle*, replacing stereotypical, 'one-dimensional' motivations with Jess's overt rumination on her responsibility for the violence that ensues. This contemplation is especially discernible where Jess assesses her own actions as if they are someone else's. Throughout the initial loops on the Aeolus, Jess denies responsibly for the harms that befall others, continually insisting

'I didn't do this.' For the most part, she believes herself to be correct. For instance, when Greg is dispatched in the first loop, Sally accuses Jess ('you fucking bitch . . . he said you shot him!'), spurring Jess's refutation ('I didn't do it!'). At this stage, Jess's rebuttal appears to be justified: it is not clear to her (or us) that she can occupy the position of killer and survivor simultaneously. By the third loop, Jess dons the mask and 'becomes' the killer, actively choosing to sacrifice the others so that she can be reunited with Tommy. Therefore, she is unequivocally accountable for the homicides. Even so, Jess continues to deny responsibility. Before shooting Greg in the third loop, Jess explains that she is wearing the mask because 'I don't want you to see my face . . . because *this is not me*' (emphasis added). The mask does not hide her identity – Greg recognises Jess from her footwear – but nor does she intend it to. She only dons the mask to avoid third-personal judgement of her ethical character. Nonetheless, her continued denials are unsustainable: the mask cannot absolve her of responsibility.

Had *Triangle* only portrayed Jess in denial, or only portrayed her as someone with the propensity to snap and hit her child, the depiction of Jess would have been far less nuanced. Her denial is understandable. Her redemption arises both from eventually facing up to her actions and from re-entering the loop to change the situation. Her willingness to murder Greg and his friends to achieve that end only amplifies the complexity of her situation, certainly in comparison to the standard revenge motives or out-group targeting that are characteristic of the subgenre. Indeed, Jess only actively decides to execute the others on the third loop, after Victor has been mortally wounded. Knowing that the loop will begin again if they all die, she asserts to Victor that her actions are her attempt to 'save' (that is, resurrect) her peers. She then tells Greg that she plans to wait and prevent the crew from boarding on the next loop. Shooting Greg and his friends is, perversely, a means of rescuing them all. This seemingly paradoxical view of slaughter follows from Jess occupying two ostensibly diametrically opposed narrative positions (killer and Final Girl). The fact that her companions do all return unharmed is vital: otherwise, Jess's willingness to solve problems with homicide might cause viewers to resist the narrative's experiential alignment with Jess.

Above all, Jess is at war with herself, and that is most palpable when Jess exits the loops, arrives home and assassinates another version of herself (who will not return). This murder literalises the overarching symbolic suicide that permeates the film: Jess exterminates multiple versions of herself across the text (see Figure 2.2). This war is highly individualised, but it also speaks to a much broader subgeneric pattern. Slasher films almost always entail killers battling with Final Girls, and ordinarily end

Figure 2.2 'You're not me' – one Jess confronts another in *Triangle* (2009)

with a sign that the killer will be revived (see Bernard 2022, 55; Jess-Cooke 2009, 9). In many cases, the killer does reappear in a sequel, or the battle is replicated again (with variation) in a remake (on this, see Chapter 8). Across the subgenre, these archetypal figures are locked in repeating battles that are never finally resolved. *Triangle* revivifies that sense of endless combat between killer and Final Girl by having Jess occupy both roles – meaning the two are inextricably bound together in her – and by using the structure (three loops on the ship, contained in a narrative ouroboros) to suggest the perpetuation of that war.

In that light, *Triangle* could be misinterpreted as critiquing the subgenre: Jess initially appears to be doomed to repeat the same mistakes and, although she exits the Aeolus, she is seemingly trapped in purgatory. However, such a reading overlooks *Triangle*'s investment in Jess's experiential reality. Despite the repeated cycle, Jess does not relinquish hope that she can modify what is seemingly always-already 'done'. Jess affects the course of events in the second loop, meaning her in-the-moment choices are significant and that change is possible. That she transforms from Final Girl to killer as the narrative progresses also underscores the potential for reformation. *Triangle* is not a fatalistic tale of hopelessness. Even when she slays her counterpart at her home, Jess destroys the prior version of herself with the hope that she will be better in the future. Thus, *Triangle* holds a superposition, being at once tragic and yet simultaneously sustaining the aching hope that future change is possible.

The text itself underlines these overarching meanings. *Triangle* draws attention to its repeated structure by ending where it began (with Jess about to re-enter the loop). Even though the final sequence in which Jess re-boards the yacht is a direct replication of the opening (utilising the same footage), some of the edits are different. For example, the shot concentrates on Jess's face throughout, rather than cutting to show Greg's face or following Jess's eyeline to Greg's friends as it does in the opening. Moreover, *Triangle* rewards repeat viewing by containing details that carry new meaning once the entire context of Jess's impetus has been spelt out. Much of the dialogue takes on additional connotations that only become apparent on second viewing. For instance, early in the film Greg asks about Tommy, and Jess indicates that their life is built around routine, stating 'every day's the same . . . if I do one thing differently, I lose him'. The double meaning is only discernible after she traverses the loops and her impatience with Tommy has been laid bare. The loops on the Aeolus figuratively echo her daily inner frustration and guilt over that exasperation. The parallel between the oceanic time-loops and her repetitive daily life is corroborated by details that connect the two. For example, Jess recovers a capsized toy yacht from the paddling pool in her yard, mirroring the wrecking of Greg's vessel at sea. A painting of flying gulls on the wall of Jess's home is redolent of the gull that flies from the yacht's mast after Jess boards, shots of which are repeated at the film's start and end (signalling the opening and closing of the encompassing loop). Repeat viewing of the film yields a new epistemic vantage point that imbues these details with magnitude, stressing the potential for narrative reappraisal when elements recur. *Triangle* consequently intimates that there is value in repetition, and that there are opportunities for re-evaluation even when events are replicated exactly.

This stance on recursion is important because the subgenre has been widely condemned for being 'repetitive', and therefore unoriginal, uncreative and insubstantial. As Hutchings puts it, the slasher's 'cheapness, crudeness and formulaic repetitiveness' reputedly afford 'degrading experiences' to 'unsophisticated teenage audiences' (2004, 193). Such criticism was seemingly corroborated by the postmodern slasher's underlying presupposition that originality and subgeneric progress were no longer possible. *Triangle* counters the notion that the subgenre is simply repetitive by expressly playing with normative characterisations and archetypal positionalities. Although *Triangle*'s story entails seemingly endless recurrence, its narrative structure and its commitment to Jess's subjective perspective ultimately suggests that repetition results in opportunity, rather than being fatally limiting.

Centralising Subjective Experiences

Via these two initial case studies and this chapter's thematic foci on epistemology and investment, this chapter has delineated several important properties of the metamodern slasher that will be expanded on in subsequent chapters. First, *Shrooms* and *Triangle* leverage unresolved ambiguity in a productive manner, creating stimulating complexities that challenge established understandings of the subgenre: in this case, the subgenre's reputation for narrative and ethical shallowness (on the latter, see Ménard, Weaver and Cabrera 2019). In both films, ethical ambiguity is inextricable from the protagonist's subjective outlook and subgeneric position. These films draw on the subgenre's core antagonism between killer and Final Girl, reimagining it as a superposition: the lead protagonist is also partially cast as the lead antagonist. The viewer's understanding of the protagonist's subgeneric position (as killer or Final Girl) is aligned with the protagonist's view of themselves.

Second, then, both films are invested in the protagonists' subjective experiences. This second core attribute is tied into the third: metamodernism takes collaboration as a 'basic principle' (see Abramson 2017), and the metamodern slasher's tone is shaped by a collaborative (as opposed to separationist) outlook. In *Shrooms* and *Triangle*, these two qualities are imbricated because the collaborative outlook manifests via alignment with and investment in the protagonist's subjective experiences. A comparison to postmodernism and the postmodern slasher will help to disentangle and unpack these components. As proposed in this chapter's introduction, for postmodernists, our intrinsically subjective perspectives provide only partial, biased, fragmented access to the world. Epistemically speaking, this state is a fatal limitation, given that it means we cannot access and synthesise enough information with sufficient accuracy to make legitimate knowledge claims (see Kirby 2009, 139–40). One means of overcoming this subjective limitation might be to confer with others in order to yield consensus. However, communities are also incapable of forming unified knowledge according to this postmodern view, because one can only access another's thoughts when they are conveyed by language, and language is inherently unstable and ambiguous (see Gracia 1995, 25; Holland 2013, 17; Lyotard 1984, 9–10).[11] This inability to access a shared reality fosters distrust and paranoia, since we cannot know what others are thinking. Therefore, uncertainty is associated with 'crisis and despair' in postmodern fiction (Levchenko et al. 2021, 97). In postmodern slashers, that attitude is articulated via murder-mysteries in which most of the cast are implicated as suspects. I will revisit the postmodern slasher's paranoid

---

[11] Moreover, as Waugh contends, the postmodern stance that 'our knowledge of this world is . . . mediated through language' means that 'fiction . . . becomes a useful model for learning about the construction of "reality" itself' (1984, 3).

whodunits momentarily. For the moment, note that *Shrooms* and *Triangle* foreground the lead protagonists' experiences of existing in precarity: they are under threat, and they also occupy a dual position in the text. By prioritising subjective experience, metamodern slasher films build on (rather than ignore) the problems postmodernists raise about epistemic access. It is not that metamodern films impart a contrasting position, prizing objectivity. Instead, these films embrace the idea that the human condition is defined by our limited subjective perspectives. In this view, epistemology is shaped by our subjective experiences, and even when those experiences lead one to misconstrue objective facts (as they do for *Shrooms*'s characters), that does not invalidate or diminish the intrinsic value of subjective experience per se.

Postmodernists take the inability to access a shared, objective reality as a fundamental problem for human interaction. Resultantly, postmodernists privilege 'individualism and solipsism', and repudiate the value of 'communal bonds' (Toth and Brooks 2007, 4–6; see also Holland 2013, 17). Again, this outlook is reified in the postmodern slasher's paranoid whodunit narratives. Although viewers are goaded into guessing the killer's identity, postmodern slashers exploit the viewer's limited epistemic access. The final reveal is a surprise (or 'trick') that relies on the viewer's inability to access information the killer (and the filmmaker) has about the situation. Filmmakers intentionally withhold that information from the viewer to maintain the central mystery. As Levchenko et al. remark, in postmodern fiction, 'the author, the hero, and the text are united by certain integrity oriented on the interpretative playing with the recipient' (2021, 105). That is, the postmodern slashers' foundational logic is that filmmaker, protagonist and narrative are unified, but are separated from the viewer. The author is the meaning-maker, and viewers are precluded from collaborating in the generation of primary meaning.[12]

Metamodern slasher narratives – such as this chapter's case studies – take a different route, including the viewer, rather than creating a unity of filmmaker, protagonist and narrative that is separated from the viewer. As illustrated by *Shrooms* and *Triangle*, this is achieved by presenting a range of simultaneous live possibilities, from which multiple meanings can be freely derived. Those manifold meanings are held in tension: mutually exclusive interpretive possibilities are bestowed without final resolution. In *Shrooms*, it is not ultimately clear whether Tara is the killer. In *Triangle*, Jess's war

---

[12] Postmodern fiction's duplicitous game-playing is underscored by contradiction: the text signals that subjective meaning-making is inadequate, yet the author is also positioned as individualised meaning-maker.

with herself continues beyond the narrative because she re-boards Greg's yacht. Given our epistemic limitations, we might not be able to reach definitive consensus that amounts to objective knowledge. However, subjectivity's inherent limitations do not preclude us from trying to understand the world (and each other). Furthermore, if we accept that 'lack of certainty is . . . just a fact of being' (Stoev 2022, 96), we can embrace the richness that arises from bringing multiple viewpoints and possibilities into conjunction. As such, these texts are akin to what Fjellestad terms 'post-postmodern' fictions, which 'tacitly bestow praise on readers' for 'being highly competent co-players' (2021, 302). Rather than 'tricking' the viewer by withholding the 'truth' of events or lecturing the viewer (as Randy does in *Scream*), the metamodern slasher's viewer is invited to collaborate in generating meaning out of the text's precarities, ambiguities and multiplicities.

Finally, the mode exemplified by *Shrooms* and *Triangle* builds on the postmodern slasher's propensity to comment on the subgenre. Postmodern slasher films often glibly and self-consciously point out the subgenre's mechanics in their scripts. Frequently, the metamodern slasher's meditations on the subgenre are more implicit. Neither the subgenre nor its traits are mentioned in *Shrooms*'s or *Triangle*'s scripts: the connotative cogitations on subgenre are instead integrated into their approaches to narrativisation and characterisation. *Shrooms* and *Triangle* both re-evaluate the conflict between archetypes (killer and Final Girl) that drives the subgenre. *Triangle*, in particular, develops on this re-evaluation via its loop structure and its portrayal of Jess: *Triangle*'s narrative shape is redolent of the 'killer versus Final Girl' skirmishes repeated across the subgenre, while Jess's commitment to the possibility of mutability indicates that repetition is not a fatalistic trap (as is commonly implied by the postmodern slashers). Jess's desire for and optimism about change in the face of seemingly inexorable repetition allegorises *Triangle*'s relationship with the subgenre to which it belongs: *Triangle* itself is proof that rejuvenation is possible within established subgeneric limits.

These deliberations about subgenre are further elucidated by the way these films handle epistemic access. Given that postmodernists commonly reject the notion of collaborative knowledge generation, they also view subjective partial experiences as bringing about discordant accounts. In this view, bringing those accounts together results in noise that further distances us from attaining unified knowledge.[13] For instance, McHale

---

[13] More recently – and at a distance from postmodern thinking – Kahneman, Sibony and Sunstein reached similar conclusions about the problem of 'noise', defining noise as the 'unwanted divergence of judgments, the unreliability of the measuring instrument we apply to reality' (2021, 362).

suggests that under postmodernism, 'intractable epistemological uncertainty' gives way to 'plurality' (2004, 11). When we apply this stance to the slasher subgenre, the ostensible problem is that as more films are produced and more is written about the subgenre in response to those films, more 'noise' is created. According to the postmodern view, that noise hinders collective understanding and stalls the possibility of subgeneric progress: noise obfuscates shared premises about the subgenre and makes it impossible to form shared visions of the subgenre's development.

The metamodern perspective leads us in another direction. When conceived as 'noise', perspectival multiplicity is a hinderance to epistemology, but the same patterns can be productively reframed as variance. By validating subjective knowledge and emphasising inclusivity, metamodernism affirms that new perspectives and insights are possible. The variety of such perspectives amplifies (rather than dissipates) the subgenre's potential to develop. There is no shared aim for the subgenre, and it is not necessary to think of subgeneric progress as singular. Slasher filmmakers might borrow ideas and conventions from one another, but they do not act as a unified cabal with one vision for the subgenre. 'Progress' itself is multiple, being evinced by the introduction of new ideas and approaches to the slasher. After all, without the introduction of (even minor) idiosyncrasies and perspectival alterations to entrenched patterns, the subgenre would be constituted by identical films. Contrary to the postmodern position that 'the individual artist is no longer stable enough to be the source of a unique personal style', which results in 'borrowing styles from others via pastiche' (Booker 2007, xviii), even the most generic slasher film contributes some deviation from its predecessors.

Simultaneously, it is still possible to identify patterns within the variance. Indeed, subgeneric categorisation is contingent on heuristics; that is, noticing unifying factors. The next chapter will pick up these threads, attending to the ways metamodern slasher films highlight coherence. For the moment, it is worth underlining that metamodern slashers are markedly and positively disposed towards change, and this desire to enrich the subgenre by introducing variations is a distinguishing marker of the metamodern slasher film.

CHAPTER 3

Coherence (Ontology)

As the previous chapter argued, the postmodern outlook frames epistemology as a problem. This chapter explores a related 'problem': ontology. Whereas epistemology is the theory of knowledge (pertaining to knowledge generation and what can be known), ontology is concerned with the nature of being. Ontology and epistemology are connected by rumination on what can be known about that which exists in the world. What we know (or at least, believe to be true) about reality shapes how we conceive of what exists and what existence consists of. Chapter 2 examined ways metamodern slasher narratives are epistemically aligned with the protagonists' perspectives. Introducing ontology to this equation raises further issues that form the basis for this chapter's two sections. First, there are two layers or kinds of reality at play in film viewing: the audience's reality (in which the film is watched) and the diegetic reality (the storyworld in which the characters exist).[1] Second, extrapolating from that relationship raises additional considerations about what it is to exist within the fictional world: what it is to be a character, whose experiences are bounded and shaped by the narrative apparatus.

Before I begin, some additional context will help to flesh out the ways these sections engage with the relationship between epistemology and ontology, and how this chapter's theme – coherence – illuminates the metamodern aspects of these concerns. As Chapter 2 explained, many postmodernists express anxiety about the ways our limited subjective perspectives hinder the epistemological project. First, our perspectives are so limited that even if there were facts to discover in the world, we might not be able to access them. Second, our subjective experiential states colour our epistemological assessments. For example, as Elgin notes,

---

[1] This is not trivial insofar as the audience's engagement with fiction is frequently based on the characters behaving as if their existence is meaningful; that is, as if their motivations matter and their reality is comprehendible.

'emotions ... fix patterns of attention, highlighting certain features of a domain and obscuring others' (2008, 44).[2] In this view, our assessments about the limited facts we might access are mediated via this experiential lens. Third then, individuals might arrive at alternative interpretations of the facts. Fourth, as posited in Chapter 2, trying to achieve consensus on these facts involves further mediation. Communicating our claims to others entails employing language, and 'language is indeterminate' (McAdams 2013, 292; see also Bruner 1986, 24; Iser 1978, 24).

Worse still, these problems do not just apply to assessments of the exterior world, but also to the conduit for that access: the subjective self. As McAdams asserts, 'the concept of narrative is key in the psychological writings of postmodern thinkers' (McAdams 2013, 291). According to the resultant 'narrative self' model, we each collate our subjective experiences into a unified whole – a story – to cultivate 'some semblance of meaning, unity, and purpose' out of our moment-to-moment stream of experiences (McAdams 2013, xx; see also Habermas and Bluck 2000; Schechtman 1996). Two problems follow for the postmodernist. First, narrativising implies translating our experiences into stories, based in language. If language is indeterminate, narrating one's experiences to oneself entails introducing layers of ambiguity, undercutting the coherence that narrative is meant to provide. Second, our limited perspectives bias those narratives: according to this model, we customarily perceive ourselves as the lead protagonist in the story of our lives (see McAdams 1993; Storr 2017, 65), meaning we interpret events in the world and their significance in relation to our self-conceptions. Thus, according to this perspective, all knowledge claims are fatally unreliable, including one's claims about oneself (and even the claim 'all knowledge claims are fatally unreliable').

The prevailing postmodern response to this state is to reject the epistemological project as vanity or naïveté, treating knowledge claims as products of a futile game. In this view, constructing ontological knowledge is akin to constructing fictions, because knowledge claims are essentially fabricated stories about reality. That belief shapes the way postmodern fiction narratives are constructed, 'the primary purpose' being 'to unmask its own fictionality, to expose the metaphor of its own fraudulence, and not pretend any longer to pass for reality, for truth, or for beauty' (Federman 1981, 9). This outlook informs postmodern slasher films, which articulate scepticism about authentic expression via their ludic

---

[2] The relationships between epistemology and emotions are complex. Various approaches to that relationship are explored in Brun, Doğuoğlu and Kuenzle (2008) and Candiotto (2019).

trickery (see Chapter 2) and a pervasive ironic tone, which intimates that artificial communicative structures cannot yield substantial meaning.

Many postmodern slashers also implement metafictional devices to stress that the fictional world is purely a construction. In the postmodern context, such techniques imply that there is no substantive difference between the fictional world and the real world, because (in this view) our epistemic and ontological claims are fiction-like constructions. That similarity is flagged by metafictional devices such as frame breaks, which supposedly disrupt the boundary between the fictional world and the real world. Moreover, if epistemic and ontological claims are fiction-like constructions, and the content of those claims is too indeterminate to be reliable, the apparatus itself constitutes meaning. Much postmodern fiction uses self-reflexivity about construction processes to underline our inability to capture and convey substantive ontological or epistemological content.

Many contemporary slasher films instead follow a metamodern view that fictional constructions can generate valuable ontological or epistemological content. Even if ontological and epistemological claims are constructed, it does not follow – as implied by the postmodern perspective – that constructed claims have no value or that no insight can follow from such claims. Although our ability to access information is limited, we do have some knowledge of the world, which forms the basis of our epistemic and ontological claims. That knowledge is constructed out of extant ideas or information gleaned from others (such as educators, journalists, authors and so forth). We each encounter and construct such information idiosyncratically, depending on the sources we encounter, and which sources we trust. Our knowledge claims are tied to our individual experiential sphere since each person creates their worldview out of a unique combination of information. Consequently, our epistemic claims are inextricable from our ontological foundations: who we are and how we exist. For this reason, our epistemic and ontological claims might not be objectively accurate, but they are authentic and valuable to each of us. In sum, the metamodern position builds from the postmodern stance, accepting that epistemic access is limited, but subjectivity is taken to be a key strength, not a fatal flaw. Instead of critically hindering our endeavours, our subjective experiences are integral to knowledge-generation in this view. Consequently, it would seem outlandish to dismiss those experiences or ignore the amount of consensus we manage to forge.

These implications contextualise the chapter's first section, which probes fictionality, the processes of fictional construction and metafictional devices such as metalepsis. This section draws comparisons between postmodern slashers (such as *Wes Craven's New Nightmare* [1994]) and metamodern slashers (such as *Detention* [2011]) to evince a turn away from postmodernism's ontological scepticism, towards the metamodern slasher's underlying mindset that authentic, coherent meaning is possible, even where the conduit for that meaning is unreal (fictional). Once again, this approach evinces that metamodern slasher films carry forward and build on elements found in postmodern slashers, while the undergirding metamodern ethos shapes how those traits are employed.

The second section will zero in on a case study – *Happy Death Day* (2017) – in which coherent meaning is both discoverable and is integral to the lead protagonist's lived experience. *Happy Death Day*'s time-loop structure signals that the film is a construction. The time-loops disrupt lead protagonist Tree's existence without disturbing the boundaries between reality and fiction for the viewer. As with Chapter 2's examples, the narrative is epistemically aligned with Tree's perspective. Here however, *Happy Death Day* explores what it is to exist in the fictional world, connecting the character's experiential reality to the fact of her construction as a slasher film character. Across the narrative, Tree transforms into a more cooperative person due to her experiences. Her social adaptation is inextricable from a positional change: she becomes a Final Girl. That is, Tree's experiences are dictated by the artificial loop structure, and that combination simultaneously alters who Tree is as a person and as a subgeneric type. *Happy Death Day*'s coherence stems from bringing these elements together to stimulate meaning. Tree's modifications are coloured by optimism about future renewal that is indicative of a metamodern sensibility. Tree instigates slight variations in repeated loops, but those revisions precipitate positive progress. The connections between Tree's experiences, her subgeneric typing, and the narrative structure together reflect an underlying optimism about the potentials for positive change within the subgenre.

Pulp Friction: Metafictional Devices and Ontological Uncertainty

Metafictional devices are commonly associated with both modernist (Bentley 2018, 728–9) and postmodernist narratives (Currie 2013, 15). Metafiction 'self-consciously and systematically draws attention to its status as an artefact in order to pose questions about the relationship between fiction and reality . . . providing a critique of [its] own methods of construction' (Waugh 1984, 2; see also Prince 2013, 65–66; Scholes 2013, 29). Typically, this entails taking fictional construction as a theme within the narrative. By depicting fiction-making processes within fiction, viewers are given reason to contemplate the construction of the fiction they are consuming, and that correlation supposedly supplies a foundation for 'a contesting of "realism"' (Hutcheon 1980, 39; see also Waugh 1984, 18). As observed in Chapter 2, postmodern slashers ordinarily contain grounded, realist performances. That realism might initially seem to conflict with the reputedly 'anti-realist' stance necessitated by postmodern texts that 'construct fictional worlds only to expose them as artificial constructions' or 'thematise their own artificiality' to posit 'that both the fiction and the reality are, in the end, fictional' (Currie 2011, 2). However, realism is also an artifice: realist fiction inauthentically mimics the real offscreen world. Realism is also utilised to draw correlations between the diegetic reality (the world/s the characters occupy) and the real world the film's consumers and makers occupy. Many postmodern fictions wield ontological incoherence – uncertainty about the existence of or differences between ostensible layers of reality – to generate friction.

In postmodern slashers, such ontological friction is usually concocted in discrete sequences. One common ploy is the 'pullback-reveal', wherein a sequence is presented as if it belongs to the diegetic reality, then the scene pulls back to reveal that the sequence was contrived by characters within the narrative. For instance, *Urban Legends: Final Cut* (2000) opens with a 'pullback-reveal' sequence. The first shots are seemingly set on a flight during a storm. The scene continues until one character (Sandra) is surprised by a person unexpectedly appearing at the cockpit window. The unexpected figure is Toby, a film director, who yells for the scene to 'cut!'. The scene then pulls back to reveal that the flight was contrived, being part of a film shoot. By exposing the film-within-a-film as an alternative (constructed, artificial) layer of in-film reality, *Urban Legends: Final Cut* suggests that our ability to distinguish between layers of reality is deficient.

Another technique involves metalepsis, or seemingly impossible interaction between two 'ontologically distinct levels' of reality (Lash 2020, 8; see also Bertens 1995, 69; Currie 2013, 3). Again, *Urban Legends: Final Cut* offers an illustrative example, this time in the film's closing sequence. The film's end credits are interrupted by another pullback, which reveals the credits playing on a television set in a mental health facility. The television is watched by a male figure played by Hart Bochner, who portrays *Urban Legends: Final Cut*'s killer, Solomon. Rebecca Gayheart (who played the killer Brenda in the first *Urban Legend* [1998]) then arrives, dressed as a nurse, and looks directly into the camera with a smirk as she tells the patient that they 'have a lot in common' (see Figure 3.1). This moment is metaleptic insofar as the nurse seemingly acknowledges the audience's presence, signalling an interaction between onscreen and

Figure 3.1 Rebecca Gayheart's character breaks the fourth wall in
Urban Legends: Final Cut (2000)

offscreen realities. Her line seems to address the audience as much as it does the patient. This is Gayheart's only appearance in the film, and the character she played in the original film is not mentioned in *Urban Legends: Final Cut*.³ Breaking the fourth wall accentuates her presence, reminding the sequel's audience of the first film, and potentially hinting that the two villains could team up in future *Urban Legends* films.

According to some, these techniques are profoundly disruptive. For example, Cohn submits that metalepsis causes viewers to experience a 'feeling of disarray, a kind of anxiety or vertigo' (2012, 110) by causing 'confusion between distinct ontological levels' (2012, 106). Malina makes extremely bold claims regarding the power of metalepsis, proclaiming that the device has a 'fundamentally disruptive effect on the fabric of narrative, on the possibilities for achieving coherent readings, and on the very distinction between fiction and reality' (2002, 1).⁴ Nonetheless, it is worth heeding Lash's warning that 'it is easy to overstate the disruptive potential' of such techniques (2020, 28). If the aim is to cause ontological fracture, both *Urban Legends: Final Cut* examples are limited. First, Gayheart's character seemingly addresses the viewer in the final sequence,

---

³ Although implied by the casting and dialogue, since Gayheart is not credited, it is ambiguous whether this character actually is Brenda. The same is true of Bochner's character: it is not unambiguous that Bochner still plays Solomon in this final scene. The mental health facility might exist in another layer of reality (one where *Urban Legends: Final Cut* is shown on a television). However, neither ambiguity means the film disrupts the viewer's sense of what is real or what exists offscreen.

⁴ Similar claims abound in the discussion of metalepsis and postmodern fiction (for example, see Herman 1997, 135–6; McHale 2004, 226).

but that moment only entails the actor looking to camera (not at the audience itself). The camera is an invisible omnipresence throughout the film, and Gayheart looking towards the camera does not expose that apparatus: indeed, the idea that she interacts with the audience buttresses the camera's invisibility, further occluding the filmmaking process. Given that the moment is pre-recorded, it is not a genuine interaction between the in-film character and the offscreen audience, and neither layer of 'reality' is brought into conjunction any more than it is at every other point during the film. Second, the opening sequence cheats to pull off its transposition between layers. To surprise *Urban Legends: Final Cut*'s audience, the footage leading up to the reveal is presented as if it is the finished film product, not (as the narrative reveal suggests) the initial filming of those events. The footage consists of multiple shot setups edited together, and the footage has clearly been subject to postproduction manipulation (for instance, lightning effects have been added). Furthermore, the layer shift only applies to *Urban Legends: Final Cut*'s viewer, not to its characters. For example, when the camera pulls back to reveal the flight sequence was contrived, it is exposed that the approximation of cabin turbulence – which looked effective during the sequence – was created by Stan bouncing on a plank beneath the cabin. For the film's characters however, there was no illusion to shatter: there was only the crude plank mechanism. The viewer's ontological understanding is wholly undisturbed in both cases, because 'characters and action ultimately remain isolated from the sphere of the viewer' (Krzywinska 2002, 216; see also Tudor 2002, 110). The characters inhabit a bounded fictional world that is separate from the viewer's reality. At best, a film can mislead viewers into thinking that a set of contrived circumstances really occurred,[5] but it is a patent exaggeration to say that metafictional devices lead viewers to doubt their offscreen reality or their own existence.

The same is true even where transparent connections are made between the diegetic world and the real world. Of the postmodern slashers, *Wes Craven's New Nightmare* is the most explicit in forging such bridges. The film depicts the making of a new *A Nightmare on Elm Street* film, and key personnel who worked on the series – including actors Robert Englund and Heather Langenkamp, and New Line Cinema's then-CEO Robert Shaye – play themselves in *New Nightmare*. Parts of the film are shot in

---

[5] For example, some viewers apparently believed contrived events in *Snuff* (1976), *Cannibal Holocaust* (1980), *Ghostwatch* (1992) and *The Blair Witch Project* (1999) (to name a few famous examples) to be real. Many contemporary horror films also claim to be based on 'real events' to foster a similar dynamic (see Jones 2013, 67).

real-world locations such as the New Line Cinema offices. The narrative features several contrived earthquakes but employs footage of real-world buildings in Los Angeles damaged by actual tremors. The film overtly bridges between its diegetic world and the real world in a sustained way.

This setup insinuates that the series' antagonist (Freddy) is running amok in the real world. As Craven states in the film, Freddy has decided to 'cross over out of films, into our reality'. Still, it seems unlikely that viewers would mistake the dialogue for a declaration that Freddy is no longer a purely fictional entity. As Laidler (2005) demonstrates in his empirical work, even young children can distinguish between Freddy's existence as a filmic character and the idea that Freddy poses a genuine real-world threat. Recognisable personnel and relevant real-world locations might be used, but when Craven refers to 'our reality', he does so as a character in the film, and refers to a firmly bounded fictional world. Craven's onscreen presence as a fictional version of himself diverts attention away from the fact that *New Nightmare* is written by a real-world Wes Craven. Yet, that relationship is uncovered by the film's full title (*Wes Craven's New Nightmare*), as well as the end credits, which begin 'Directed by WES CRAVEN, Based on characters created by WES CRAVEN'. Despite the film's metafictional posturing then, it is quite apparent that the film is a work of fiction, and therefore that its storyworld is separate from the real world. Postmodern slashers present relationships between fictive layers or between the real world and the in-film fictional world, but that does not mean that viewers are seriously confused about ontological boundaries after watching films such as *New Nightmare*. The latter is proposed by Syder, for instance, who exaggeratedly conflates viewers' inability to distinguish between layers of reality within the narrative – 'we are left uncertain whether the scenes . . . are intended to signify the known, familiar world . . . or a dream world' (2002, 85) – with viewers' supposed confusion about their offscreen world: he asserts 'these films seem to suggest that distinctions between a "known" and an "unknown" world are somewhat arbitrary, that we can never truly know the world around us to begin with' (2002, 86).

Postmodern metafiction is not as ontologically disruptive as scholars such as Syder insinuate. That propensity further diminished as these ploys became commonplace in the popular cultural landscape thanks to films like *New Nightmare*. As Bentley contends, 'by the 1990s audiences had become so used to its practices of disorientation, metafiction, challenging of expected generic conventions, and the representation of prurient and transgressive subject matter that it had lost its power to shock' (2018, 727; see also Collins 1993, 248; Turner 2015). Subsequently, while relationships between author, text, consumer and world are treated as a problem that needs investigating in postmodern slasher films, metamodern slasher films largely abandon that project.

Therefore, metamodern metafiction has a different flavour. Metamodern slasher scripts do not plainly point out the film's status as artificially constructed fiction. It is assumed that viewers understand texts to be constructions. Thanks to postmodern metafiction, self-reflexivity has become so commonplace that it is akin to other artificial narrative-constructive techniques that viewers readily accept. For example, breaking the fourth wall is less common but is no less artificial than continuity editing. Both are contrivances, but both are quite normal aspects of conveying information to and stimulating viewers in contemporary fiction film. Where metafictional devices are implemented in metamodern slashers then, it is not to induce surprise. Manoeuvres such as breaking the fourth wall are treated as normative aspects of cultural engagement, and so such incidents are not punctuated as special or striking moments within metamodern slashers. For instance, *Detention*'s opening scene presents one character (Taylor) talking directly to camera. Within the first twenty-five seconds of the film, Taylor speaks to the audience in a way that indicates she is aware she is within a film ('by the time you actually watch this . . .'). However, her comment is brushed over – it is a throwaway moment – just as Taylor herself is discarded by the text (culled) within the first three minutes of the movie. *Detention*'s opening sequence sets the tone for the film to follow, in which such techniques are taken for granted rather than being noteworthy. Contrary to the enduring supposition that fourth wall breaking disrupts narrative absorption (see Brown 2012, x; Green, Brock and Kaufman 2004, for example), *Detention*'s opening naturalises the frame-break, implying that it is not inherently disruptive to remind viewers that they are watching fiction. Instead, it is presumed that viewers can be aware that they are watching a film, but can be absorbed in the story anyway.

'Pullback-reveal' sequences are largely abandoned by the metamodern slasher, but where the device is employed, its usage is adapted in line with the metamodern sensibility. For instance, in *Detention*, the teen protagonists believe they are being stalked by Cinderhella, a character from a slasher film series. When discussing the matter in Saturday detention, the teens elect to outmanoeuvre Cinderhella by downloading the workprint of *Cinderhella 3* so that they can anticipate Cinderhella's next moves.[6]

---

[6] *The Wisher* (2002) utilised this gambit several years earlier: lead protagonist Mary believes she is being stalked by the eponymous slasher from the film 'The Wisher', and downloads the film so that she can anticipate her stalker's next move. Mary becomes disoriented when she (mistakenly) believes she sees herself and her house in the downloaded content.

The clip of *Cinderhella 3* displays a parallel group of teens in Saturday detention. *Cinderhella 3*'s teens decide that 'the least we can do' as a response to being held in detention 'is download *Slashing Beauty 4* for free and watch it illegally on the Internet before it's released'. The footage is then substituted by the film-in-film-in-film (*Slashing Beauty 4*), which plays like a softcore porn movie. Apropos of nothing, *Slashing Beauty 4*'s teens pull out a VHS copy of *Beauty Beast 5*. The footage then cuts to the film-in-film-in-film-in-film, which is a horror porn movie. These layers are then quickly retraced, returning to *Detention*'s fictional world. Although there are immediate superficial similarities between the situations depicted (each layer is set in an analogous detention scenario), there are unmistakable boundaries between the layers. Rather than pulling back to reveal an unexpected layer shift, at each stage it is made clear that teens are watching another set of footage, because we see them engaging with devices (such as VHS players) to watch it. Each layer also has its own aesthetic. Compared with *Detention*'s glossy high-definition look, *Cinderhella 3*'s workprint footage is degraded (blurry and pixelated). Its characters' motives are similarly degraded compared with *Detention*'s: *Detention*'s teens seek information to aid their survival, whereas *Cinderhella 3*'s teens formulate an arbitrary rebellious response (illegally downloading a film for no discernible reason). These distinctions denote that the layers of reality are discrete.[7]

Detention's teens learn nothing from the ninety-six-second excursion through films-within-films, verifying that the ploy is little more than a stylistic flourish. I will revisit the significance of such flourishes within

---

[7] Readers might be reminded of the opening of *Scream 4* (2011), but the difference should be obvious: in *Scream 4*'s opening, no stylistic distinctions are made between the layers because (as per the postmodern slasher's ludic nature) the intention is to surprise (that is, trick) viewers by withholding and then revealing information. The supernatural slasher film *Killer Party* (1986) offers a precursor to this approach, opening with a multi-layered 'pullback-reveal' gag. Initially, a woman is shown attending a funeral, and is dragged into the coffin by her (un)dead mother. A pullback then reveals the footage was a movie playing at a drive-in. A drive-in attendee is attacked by zombies, then another shift indicates that the incident was contrived, being the opening for a music video set at the drive-in. A further pullback finally reveals our protagonist (Phoebe) in *Killer Party*'s diegetic reality, watching the music video on television. Each layer is presented as if it is *Killer Party*'s diegetic reality, but after this initial sequence, no further attempt is made to disrupt that final layer of reality. In *Killer Party*, the layering conveys that the audience should remain on its toes. It has no bearing on and is unconnected to the plot. That the 'pullback-reveal' is isolated to the opening suggests that the agenda is different to *Detention*'s: as Chapter 6 will argue, *Detention*'s multiple layering of 'pullback-reveals' is part of an overarching aesthetic approach.

Detention's context in Chapter 6. For the moment, note that the 'pullbacks' carry no narrative weight. 'Pullback-reveal' sequences are rare in metamodern slasher films because they are antithetical to the metamodern slasher's sincere investment in the protagonist's perspectives. In 'pullback-reveal' sequences, characters are either cognisant of the differences between layers of reality or remain entirely oblivious to the layering. The viewer, on the other hand, must acclimatise to layer-shifts. The metamodern slasher's nearest equivalent to this technique is based in the alignment of character and viewer perspectives. To illustrate, in *Shrooms* (2007), several versions of reality are presented, but neither the characters nor the viewer can finally distinguish between those layers. When Bluto wanders into the woods, he converses with a cow and is then seemingly executed. Tara then appears to wake up, implying that the preceding sequence was a premonitory dream. She then seeks Bluto and finds him talking to a cow (this time, the cow does not reply). Tara then ushers Bluto back to the camp so that he is not murdered. In the film's climax however, a third take on the situation is imparted. Here, Tara hides behind a tree, speaking to Bluto on the cow's behalf, then she slays Bluto. As per *Shrooms*'s modus operandi (see Chapter 2), the viewer is ultimately given no greater reason to trust the final iteration more than the previous two. The final retelling underscores how unreliable the film's perspectival stance is, yielding further doubt as opposed to clarity. That doubt is integral, reproducing the characters' hallucinatory experiences. While *Urban Legends: Final Cut*'s 'pullback-reveal' sequence connotes that the film is a fictional construction, *Shrooms*'s 'reveal' is concerned with divulging information about the characters and their situation.

Midnight Movie (2008) volunteers another metamodern take on metalepsis. Its plot centres on a screening of the slasher film-within-a-film *The Dark Beneath* at a small cinema. When one cinema worker (Kenny) refills the soda syrup in the theatre's cellar, he is stalked and assassinated by *The Dark Beneath*'s slasher. Footage of that murder is simultaneously projected as part of *The Dark Beneath*, signalling that there has been slippage between *Midnight Movie*'s diegetic reality and *The Dark Beneath*'s. Not recognising Kenny, the oblivious cinemagoers continue watching. Their belief that Kenny's murder is part of *The Dark Beneath* is indicated by the audience's comments; Sully urges 'I wouldn't go down there if I were him', and Mario complains that 'there's not that much blood'. That is, they treat a murder happening in their proximity as if it is unreal because it occurs onscreen, and so is interpreted as part of *The Dark Beneath*'s fictional world. When one of the protagonists (Sully) goes to the toilets, he too is murdered by *The Dark Beneath*'s slasher (see Figure 3.2).

Figure 3.2 The protagonists witness Sully's murder onscreen in *Midnight Movie* (2008)

Although his friends recognise him, they hail the incident as 'the prank of all pranks'. That is, they maintain that the boundaries between their world and the film-in-a-film remain intact despite what they see onscreen. As soon as they discover that Sully has genuinely been murdered, their attitudes transform: within minutes, one of the teens (Samantha) suddenly snaps from giggling 'it's not real', to yelling 'it's the killer from the fucking movie and he's here in this theatre!'. Ergo, in *Midnight Movie*, the metaleptic slippage does not cause ontological disruption, even for the characters. The characters' understanding of what is real expands to accommodate the supernatural murders occurring around them. As lead protagonist Bridget observes, 'what we're up against doesn't make any sense', but they 'need to start thinking' in line with their new ontological understanding. When conceived this way, the protagonists respond appropriately to the threats they face. So, Bridget notes that whenever one of them is stalked, the film footage shows the killer's point-of-view: 'Whatever the killer sees, that's what's on the screen.' Consequently, one of the teens watches the screen to locate the killer and warn the others of imminent danger. Metalepsis is not beyond the characters' sphere of awareness, nor is it deployed purely or primarily for *Midnight Movie*'s audience: the technique unveils new possibilities within a generic situation (teens being stalked in a confined location), and a standard stylistic mode (the use of stalking point-of-view shots in slasher films).

These metamodern slasher films build and sustain ontologically coherent narrative worlds, and the boundaries between the diegetic world and the offscreen real world endure, even where devices such as frame breaks are utilised. Films such as *Detention* and *Midnight Movie* are informed by the metamodern sensibility, moving away from postmodernism's ontological scepticism towards a metamodern belief that authentic, coherent meaning is possible, even where the conduit for that meaning is fictional. Implicit to this approach is a vision of viewers as collaborators in meaning generation, which manifests via the metamodern slasher's confidence about the viewer's sophistication. This setup provides opportunities to develop subtle interrogations of ontological coherence that work with (instead of attempting to disorient) the viewer.

Death Becomes Her: Structure as Catalyst for Growth in *Happy Death Day*

Happy Death Day embodies a metamodern approach to interrogating the relationship between the protagonist's existence within the storyworld and the character's existence as a fictional entity (as the viewer experiences them). As with the examples in the previous section, *Happy Death Day* overtly flags that it is a fictional construction, here through its time-loop structure. *Happy Death Day* follows lead protagonist Tree, who is murdered by a masked killer. She then wakes to find she is reliving the same day (her birthday). The pattern continues: she is murdered again and wakes on the morning of her birthday. As the narrative progresses, Tree endeavours to stop the masked killer, in the hope that she will be able to escape the time-loop.

Unlike techniques such as 'pullback-reveal' sequences or frame breaks, which postmodern slasher filmmakers use to disrupt the viewer's sense of what is real within the storyworld, *Happy Death Day*'s time-loops are only disruptive for Tree. That is, the loops lead Tree to question her grip on reality from within the text. In the second repeated loop, for example, Tree says 'I feel like I'm losing my mind, I don't know what's happening to me.' Still, the viewer's sense of the storyworld remains undisturbed thanks to *Happy Death Day*'s investments in Tree. Those investments take two forms. The first is emotional or experiential alignment. So, for instance, by the third loop, Tree's anxiety contaminates the film form. Waking to find that it is the same day that she has lived twice before, Tree scuttles across her college campus in a half-jog, breathing erratically. Her panic is conveyed formally via extreme closeups on Tree's face (see Figure 3.3). Shallow depth of focus simulates emotional intensity as well as centralising Tree in these shots. A slight RGB split effect is applied to the blurred background to create the sense of her world coming apart at the seams.

Figure 3.3 Tree's anxiety is emulated formally in *Happy Death Day* (2017)

Choppy editing and camera shaking matches her ragged breathing. This sympathetic emotional-experiential investment anchors the viewer during Tree's initial disturbance.

Second, then, as with Chapter 2's case studies, the narrative is epistemically aligned with Tree. Here, that alignment centres on the film's central mystery: the killer's identity. After Tree explains her situation to her future love interest, Carter, he suggests she follow a specific course of action: 'You have an unlimited amount of lives, so you have unlimited opportunities to solve your own murder.' From this point, she systematically works through a list of potential suspects. Tree's quest to discover who is executing her sharpens her resolve, allowing her to regain stability across subsequent time-loops. Her mission also anchors the narrative's epistemic alignment with Tree. That alignment is flagged when, for example, Tree wakes in a hospital bed, and in a blurry point-of-view shot, she sees the masked killer nearing. When her view snaps into focus, she realises that the figure is not wearing a mask: it is Carter. The sequence indicates that Tree suspects Carter could be the killer. Soon after, in the same hospital, suspicion is cast on a doctor (Gregory) when Tree finds the killer's mask in his office. Moments later, these men are redeemed when the masked killer murders them both. These instances build on the postmodern whodunit slasher's tendency to situate various cast members as the potential killer. Here, however, Tree's doubt is not sustained across the narrative. Indeed, her doubts are almost immediately undercut. Instead of fostering paranoia and distrust among the protagonists, *Happy Death Day* utilises Tree's doubt as part of its sincere investment in her experiential perspective.

The text's sincerity is equally conveyed via Tree's attitude towards her mission. Even though she is recurrently murdered and resurrected,

Tree does not lose faith in her ability to discover the killer's identity. Her commitment to that meaning-making end is confirmed when, in the eighth loop, she confronts the killer, asking 'what do you want? Why are you doing this to me? Who are you?'. Her ability to assess her situation is limited by the single day time-loop. Yet, via her actions, Tree hypostatises the belief that it is possible to glean facts from the world, generate meaning and alter her situation.

As she seeks to change her situation, Tree's epistemic goal becomes intertwined with ontological discovery. As she moves through the time-loops, she unearths more about herself, finds a sense of purpose and develops into a better person. Initially, Tree is an unpleasant or antisocial figure: she screws up her face and walks past a global warming campaigner; when a housemate smiles and waves, Tree blanks her; when Tree's roommate (Lori) gives Tree a homemade cupcake for her birthday, Tree drops it in the bin ('Too many carbs. Toodles!'); when Carter goes out of his way to return Tree's bracelet, she scowls at him and denies knowing him in front of her sorority sisters; she ignores her father's calls, leaving him waiting in a restaurant for over an hour and so forth. As she progresses through the loops, her demeanour is remodelled. In the second loop, Tree is distracted and unsettled by the repetition, so she is less aggressive when she asks Carter for Tylenol, and she mumbles 'Sorry, no thanks' to the global warming campaigner. In the third and fourth loops, Tree's demeanour mutates again: panicking because she is trapped in a cycle, Tree pushes past the global warming campaigner, for instance. These modifications are symptomatic of the narrative conveying Tree's emotional responses, rather than speaking to her personality. However, the loops eventually start to shape her in this respect too. That renewal is most notable in two parallel scenes set in the same diner. In the first, Tree compiles her list of potential suspects, which includes an Uber driver she spat on. She then justifies herself to a horrified Carter, exclaiming, 'What?! Nobody's perfect.' This admission and Tree's blasé attitude about the incident paint her in an unflattering light. The parallel scene in the ninth loop evinces Tree's personal growth. Here, she confesses 'I'm not a good person, Carter.' This revelation is directly tied into the loop structure. Tree reaches her conclusions because when 'you relive the same day over and over again, you . . . start to see who you really are'. In the earlier scene, Carter proposed Tree should find her killer. In the ninth loop, he suggests a parallel mission: 'Each new day is a chance to be someone better.' In loop ten, she embodies that ethos. In direct contrast to the first loop, Tree signs the global warming campaigner's petition with an encouraging 'You save that planet girl!'; she greets the housemate sat outside the sorority house with a cheery 'Morning!'; she apologises to Lori for being a 'loser' and a bad roommate; she breaks off her extramarital affair with Gregory, stating 'I can't change what I've done, but I can start trying to be a better person today'; she kisses Carter when he returns her bracelet; and she meets her father instead of standing him up.[8]

This journey towards becoming 'someone better' is affirmed by the text's alignment with her experiential states. For instance, Tree's first walk through the university courtyard is marked by Bear McCreary's subdued, sparse score, Tree's scowling and frowning (partially from squinting in the sun), and none of the individuals she interacts with bear a smile. Loop three – which represents the height of her panic – is ten seconds shorter than the first loop, rushing along with Tree in her flustered state. McCreary's sparse chords are accompanied by dramatic staccato strings in this loop, augmenting the scene's unease. The colour is significantly desaturated, and the golden sunlight that caused Tree to squint in the first loop is absent here, mirroring her despondency. By loop ten, Tree's transposition into the 'better' version of herself diffuses into the form. Tree has a beaming smile, holds her head high, and skips through the scene to the tempo of an upbeat extradiegetic pop song (Mother Mother's 'Love Stuck'). Although the lighting is less golden than in the first loop, the sequence is bright and airy. Wider shots are employed. This loop is eight

---

[8] This narrative shape draws from *Happy Death Day*'s influential time-loop predecessor, *Groundhog Day* (1993). *Groundhog Day*'s protagonist, Phil, begins the film as a sarcastic, bitter figure, who is described as 'egocentric' and 'a "glass is half empty" kind of guy' by those around him. His immediate response to being trapped in the same day is to double down on his established unpleasantness, becoming even ruder to others. When he realises he faces 'no consequences' for his actions because there is 'no tomorrow', he begins committing crimes, such as stealing money from an armoured car. He then uses the repeated loops to gather knowledge about his colleague Rita, attempting to seduce her by mimicking her idea of a perfect partner. When that fails, Phil tries to kill himself multiple times, but the loop always resets regardless. The loops amplify Phil's ingrained self-orientation and pessimism, and that combination ultimately cashes out in his futile attempts at self-destruction. On reaching this nadir, Phil undergoes a rebirth. In the last quarter of the film, Phil adopts a new attitude, seeking to make the most of his ostensibly immutable situation. He tries to better himself by reading and taking up new hobbies (such as learning to play piano), and then tries to help those around him. Phil engages in such activities for their own sake rather than with any ulterior motive in mind. The loops result in Phil's growth, helping him to find a sense of purpose and satisfaction. Unlike *Happy Death Day*'s Tree however, Phil never explicitly seeks to escape the loop (other than, perhaps, via his first suicide attempt). He simply submits to his chronological situation, stating 'There's nothing I can do about it.' Tree, in contrast, is presented with a clear purpose via her subgeneric positioning: because a masked killer targets her, she is impelled to save herself.

seconds longer than the first, and eighteen seconds longer than loop three, meaning it feels more open and relaxed. At each stage, Tree's outlook infects the scene, being shared by the mise-en-scène and those around her. When she flourishes, those around her and the scene itself flourish too.

Tree's development allows her to unearth coherent meaning from her otherwise incoherent chronological experience of enduring repeated time-loops. These implications are elicited via Tree's name: an abbreviation of Theresa, 'Tree' connotes both organic growth and the branching possibilities resulting from that growth. Tree's development is an exaggerated version of the narrative identity model introduced at the start of this chapter, which entails generating biographical, causal and thematic coherence out of one's experiences across time (see Adler, Wagner and McAdams 2007, 1182; Habermas and Bluck 2000), thereby anchoring the self with 'some degree of unity, purpose, and meaning' (McAdams and McLean 2013, 233). McAdams and McLean propose that 'integrative narrative identity' is developed 'through repeated interactions with others', which allow 'personal experiences' to be 'processed, edited, reinterpreted, retold' (2013, 235). Tree's rapid rejuvenation is consequently triggered by the loop structure's intensified repetition. Moreover, extraordinary events 'resist easy incorporation into one's narrative identity' and so 'the individual is faced with significantly revising his or her existing self-story' when unexpected events occur (Adler, Wagner and McAdams 2007, 1180). Tree's sudden, seemingly inexplicable propulsion into a time-loop is obviously a hyperbolic 'unexpected event', but it illuminates why the loop structure leads to Tree's rapid ontological overhaul.

So, Tree tries to generate meaning by discovering her killer's identity and also by self-making. These parallel objectives converge on the idea that she can save herself. Tree's arc is redemptive, and as McAdams observes, 'redemptive stories affirm hope for the future and a belief in human progress' (2013, 3). McAdams is critical of such stories, arguing that 'highly generative American adults' self-narrate their experiences as redemption stories, thereby rationalising their privilege and self-aggrandising (2013, xiv). Notably, Tree's redemption arc moves in the opposite direction, entailing her realisation that she is 'not a good person'. She does not deny or rationalise her previous behaviour in order to bolster her ego. Nor does she choose her redemption. Where *Triangle* (2009) deployed the loop structure to provide tragedy tinged with optimism (see Chapter 2), *Happy Death Day*'s loops push Tree away from her initial cynicism to unequivocal optimism about the future. Just as protagonist teens give voice to the postmodern slasher's cynical tone, Tree's renewal reifies the move from cynicism to optimism: a 'new yearning for meaning' that 'has found its expression in . . . metamodernism' (Bargár 2020, 4; see also Turner 2015). *Happy Death Day* is sincere about the possibility of human progress, which is encapsulated by Tree's journey across the text.

Tree develops into a 'better' person socially speaking, but that 'betterment' is also tied into the subgenre's norms: Tree's redemption means she concedes to a subgeneric heroic role. Ergo, Tree's personal rejuvenation is a conduit for commentary on the subgenre. Initially, her behaviour and attitude are indicative of a particular character type: the 'mean girl'. Yet, this typing is out of kilter with the subgenre's norms. As the lead protagonist in a slasher film, one would expect Tree to be the Final Girl. Traditionally, Final Girls are identifiable not only because they are positioned as the lead protagonist, but also because they are more sensible and prosocial than their peers. From the outset, Tree is situated as not fitting the archetypal Final Girl mould because she is a 'mean girl'; she might be 'popular', but her behaviour and attitude are fundamentally antisocial. As she traverses the loops, she instead becomes a Final Girl: the survivor who confronts and defeats the killer through her resilience. This capacity is what marks the Final Girl as the 'best' of the slasher film's protagonist types.

Tree's dual transformation reaches a crescendo just before her climactic showdown with Tombs (the serial killer she presumes to be the film's villain). Here, she fully accepts the subgeneric role the narrative has been pushing her towards: she becomes the Final Girl that the film requires. Just before this action-based climax, Tree reaches a personal, emotional summit. Finally meeting her father, Tree admits she was evading what she now recognises was the correct course of action: 'I guess I thought that if I avoided all of it . . . that somehow it would be easier. But it's not. It's been so much worse. All of this running and hiding has made me so miserable.' Here, Tree comes to terms with and openly communicates her emotional-experiential state, but the dialogue equally applies to her reformation into a Final Girl, tying the two arcs together. Furthermore, the narrative structure – the time-loop – pushes her towards that realisation: as Tree puts it, it took 'something totally crazy' to help her find her path.

Thus, Tree's personal betterment vis-à-vis social norms is interwoven with characteristic betterment vis-à-vis subgeneric norms, and both are triggered by the narrative structure (her journey through the repeated loops). Tree's three interlinked trajectories – stopping the killer, becoming a better person, becoming the Final Girl – are expressly ontological. From her perspective, they involve her experiences of being, which are conveyed via the film's formal foregrounding of her emotional states. From the viewer's perspective, they involve concerns about what Tree is (her subgeneric type). These perspectives parallel Bruner's 'two modes

... of ordering experience, of constructing reality' (1986, 11). Tree's experiences of being are akin to Bruner's 'narrative mode', which locates 'experience in time and place', while concerns regarding Tree's typology are akin to Bruner's 'paradigmatic mode', which 'employs categorization or conceptualization' to order experience (Bruner 1986, 13). *Happy Death Day* brings both modes together.

Happy Death Day's contemplation on the subgenre is embedded at its core precisely because the protagonist's character arc is a conduit for that deliberation. Accordingly, its cogitation is also shaped by the sincere tone that informs Tree's personal rebuilding, and which is representative of a metamodern sensibility. This perspective is a departure from the norm as Grant describes it: that 'the proliferation of teen-kill pics . . . through the 1980s and 90s' led to a subgeneric situation wherein 'one would be hard-pressed to find . . . even marginally interesting characters whose function is something more than target or wielder of ax, knife, or machete' (2004, x). Regardless of whether Grant is correct, his assertion captures the broad presumption about attitudes to horror protagonists proffered by critics since the slasher boom-period (which I will return to in Chapter 7). Metamodern films present an alternative view of characters' worth. Here, Tree's arc facilitates investment in her character despite the patent artificiality of the loop structure. The loop structure is seemingly arbitrary insofar as the cause of the looping is not explained in *Happy Death Day*'s narrative.[9] Nevertheless, the loop structure is clearly valuable in narrative terms because it dictates and defines Tree's experience, allowing her to discover who her killer is (and thus survive), as well as enabling her to grow as a person.

These connotations are further elucidated by the film's use of a time-loop structure. As we saw with *Triangle* in Chapter 2, the time-loop structure suits the slasher because of the subgenre's core 'killer versus Final Girl' conflicts, which recur across the subgenre. Whereas *Triangle* also recalled the custom of killers dying and returning across long-running series via Jess's dual status as killer and Final Girl, *Happy Death Day* replaces another normative subgeneric pattern: instead of portraying a group of teens being picked off by the killer, Tree is targeted repeatedly. Furthermore, in place of a killer who is reborn multiple times across a series, here Tree is continually resurrected. This pattern also riffs on another subgeneric trend. Watershed slasher films *A Nightmare on Elm Street* (1984) and *Scream* (1996) both draw from formative proto-slasher

---

[9] It *is* explained in the sequel, but the first film contains no indication that such an explanation will be forthcoming.

Psycho (1960) in initially presenting a character as if they are the lead protagonist, then undercutting expectations by eradicating that character (on this see Kerswell 2010, 33; West 2019, 20).[10] *Happy Death Day* plays with that now well-established fake-out pattern by extinguishing Tree, but then resurrecting her. *Happy Death Day* also upends expectations about formal character positions by setting up Tree as a lead protagonist who does not exemplify the qualities one would expect a Final Girl to have. Instead, she has the traits of a typical victim and, until she is finally reborn as the Final Girl, Tree is culled as a typical victim-type would be. Moreover, Final Girls usually learn more about the killer and their situation as the body count mounts around them, but here Tree's rebirths allow her to investigate the situation and ultimately defeat the killer. In these various ways, *Happy Death Day* advances alternative views on subgeneric norms, conveying that implicit commentary via its sincere investment in Tree.

Coherence and Meaning

This chapter's focus on ontology has highlighted some important distinctions between postmodern and metamodern slasher films that will inform subsequent chapters. Building on Chapter 2's epistemological concerns, the postmodern slasher raises ontological matters related to our inability to communicate accurately and authentically, or to create coherent meaning. That scepticism is notably expressed via metafictional devices that allegedly disrupt 'the constitutive boundary of a fictional narrative – the one between inside and outside, between story and world' (Malina 2002, 2–3; see also Genette 1980, 236; Pantaleo 2010, 12–14). The comparison between fiction and reality emanates from the postmodern notions that all meaning is constructed, that our assertions about existence are based in language, and so our ontological claims are inherently unstable. From this perspective, the world we inhabit is akin to a constructed text. Metafictional devices draw out that comparison by bridging between the fictional diegetic reality and the offscreen reality viewers inhabit. These techniques

---

[10] The same idea is riffed on in *Halloween: Resurrection* (2002), wherein the returning Final Girl, Laurie, is unceremoniously annihilated in the opening fifteen minutes. This execution is especially unexpected because the preceding film (*Halloween H20: 20 Years Later* [1998]) reverentially brought back Laurie as the series' centre. Another play on this approach is found in *See No Evil 2* (2014). Lead protagonist Amy is slain in the climax, shifting narrative emphasis to her colleague Seth. The move is surprising because of how late in the narrative that switch happens: Amy is dispatched only twelve minutes before the end credits roll, while the antagonist Jacob is (seemingly) defeated only six minutes after Amy dies.

are perceived as disruptive or disorienting by some critics, because they supposedly call into question whether there is any substantial disparity between constructed fiction and the stories we tell ourselves about who and what we are (for example, see Malina 2002, 8).

As this chapter's first section briefly delineated, metafictional devices are limited in their capacity to bridge between reality and fiction. In postmodern slashers, the boundaries between the real world and the film's fictional storyworld remain intact despite incidents where the fictional apparatus is exposed, where multiple layers of reality are brought into conjunction, or where the frame is 'broken'. This disruptive potential only diminished following the postmodern slasher phase because those techniques were overused in the period: viewers accustomed to the presence of such ploys are better equipped to integrate those strategies into their viewing processes. Metamodern slashers build from that foundation, assuming that such devices are familiar, and viewers are sophisticated enough to accommodate such techniques into their narrative engagements without finding them overly disorienting or ontologically disturbing. Minimally, as Abramson (2017) observes, metamodern texts acknowledge that we can have 'the feeling of understanding something, or at least thinking of it as "coherent", without being able to deconstruct it into its parts'. In metamodern slasher films, where metafictional devices are deployed, they are integrated into the narrative, reinforcing other textual meanings (such as investment in the characters' experiences). That is, metafictional techniques help to stimulate coherent meaning as opposed to being disruptive.

Happy Death Day then illustrated an alternative tack, implementing a transparently artificial structure (the time-loop) to cultivate coherent meaning that ties together characterisation, Tree's experiential states, and normative expectations about the subgenre. Tree's situation raises several interwoven epistemic and ontological concerns. These concerns include: (1) what Tree knows about her surrounding reality and how that differs from the viewer's understanding of the diegetic world as a construct; (2) the extent to which Tree is a reiteration of a subgeneric type, and the extent to which her typing dictates and limits her experiences; and (3) how the narrative structure expounds and shapes these elements. *Happy Death Day* evinces that, via their investments in characters' experiences, metamodern slasher films raise ontological questions – about what film is, what characters are, what the subgenre is – in more subtle ways than postmodern slashers customarily do. Furthermore, the metamodern slasher integrates these elements into a coherent, nuanced whole. The postmodern slasher, in comparison, is limited by an underlying desire to pull elements apart and a commitment to the notion that it is not possible to generate coherent meaning.

Chapters 2 and 3 have established various ways that the metamodern slasher builds on and is distinct from the postmodern slasher. Both chapters have outlined ways metamodern slasher films envisage viewers as collaborators in meaning-making. These chapters have also proposed that character and structure are wielded to both articulate characters' subjective experiences and to raise epistemological and ontological concerns that are central to the human condition (as envisaged through a metamodern lens). These chapters have also indicated that the metamodern slasher uses these concerns as a conduit for meditating on the subgenre by, for instance, marrying issues related to the characters (within their narrative situation) with implicit evaluations of the subgenre itself. Chapters 4, 5 and 6 will build on these premises, exploring different ways metamodern slashers resist a premise that undergirds the postmodern slasher: that subgeneric conventions fatally constrain the subgenre. To begin, Chapter 4 will examine the ways metamodern slasher films question that premise, providing new insights by viewing conventional situations from idiosyncratic perspectives.

CHAPTER 4

Conventionality

From the boom-period onwards, slasher films have ruminated on subgeneric conventions within their narratives. For example, 1980s films such as *Wacko* and *Pandemonium* (both 1982) poke fun at such conventions for comic effect, while films about making slasher films – including *The Last Horror Film* (1982) and *Return to Horror High* (1987) – draw on conventions to induce horror. This propensity was amplified in the postmodern phase following the success of *Scream* (1996), which candidly delineated stock subgeneric conventions. Contrary to Briefel and Miller's (2011, 2) claim that 'perhaps in response to *Scream*, other horror examples from this period steered clear of generic conventions', there is abundant evidence of genre convention playing out in the films that followed *Scream*. For instance, as Fordy (2018) argues, *Halloween H20: 20 Years Later* (1998) 'came as part of the 1990s post-modern [slasher] revival' and is 'more interested in being *Scream* than *Halloween* . . . spelling out the movie's own conventions'. Elsewhere, films such as *Bride of Chucky* (1998), *Urban Legend* (1998) and *Jason X* (2001) are just as intent on slipstreaming *Scream* by cynically illuminating subgeneric tropes.[1]

Scream does not merely expose conventions however, but also subsequently iterates those same conventions. As Church (2006) notes, *Scream*'s 'self-reflexivity operates to reinforce rather than subvert conventions' (see also Bernard 2020, 81).[2] To illustrate: in *Scream 2* (1997), protagonists Hallie and Sidney are trapped in the back of a police car and, in order to escape, both have to slowly crawl over the killer's unconscious body. The

---

[1] Many notable films of the period were greenlit because of *Scream*'s box-office success. See, for example, comments made by *Bride of Chucky*'s producer David Kirschner (in Rowe 1998, 22) and *Urban Legend*'s director Jamie Blanks in his Audio Commentary accompanying the 2004 Region 2 Columbia Tristar Home Entertainment DVD release of *Urban Legend*.

[2] I concur with Church's position, which diverges from Briefel and Miller's contention that *Scream* '*subvert*[s] and then reaffirm[s]' conventions (2011, 2, emphasis added).

suspense sequence is played straight, ratcheting tension across an agonising three minutes of screentime. When they escape, Sidney stops running and declares 'I'm going back . . . I want to know who it is.' Hallie points out Sidney's folly, (wisely) asserting 'Stupid people go back! Smart people run!'. Hallie's assertion is corroborated by *Scream 2*'s opening, echoing a criticism Maureen shouts at the cinema screen while watching *Stab* (the in-universe film based on the events of the first *Scream*): Maureen calls out to the onscreen protagonist, warning 'No, no, no! . . . Move! Go! . . . if that was me, I'd be out of there.' Therefore, the convention is pointed out before it arises in *Scream 2*, priming *Scream 2*'s audience to echo Maureen's exasperated pleas to the screen when, like so many slasher protagonists before her, Sidney ignores her friend's sage advice. When it plays out in *Scream 2*, the convention of slasher protagonists paying insufficient heed to the danger they face is not overtly scrutinised. That is, the convention is expounded, and then plays out in a conventional manner (as opposed to being subverted). This is typical of the *Scream* series, which reaffirms 'the object of its apparent mockery' because its 'high-points of horror-suspense are barely if at all distinguishable from the "straight" version' (King 2002, 109 and 125). Simultaneously, the earlier sardonic commentary on sub-genre conventions carries over, meaning subsequent 'straight' iterations of convention are underpinned by cynical eye-rolling, no matter how effective the suspense sequence is.

Ergo, postmodern slasher films have an uncomfortable relationship with genericity, relying on the very conventions that they deride.[3] This discomfort is redolent of a stance adopted by postmodern artists more broadly, who, as Hutcheon suggests, 'ironically abus[e] . . . conventions' (2002, 8). Such 'abuse' aims to unveil the text as a collage of conventions, all of which are purely constructs. As such, the notion that art can be original is disputed (given that artwork adheres to conventions). Conventions are fatalistically ensnaring according to this view. Even attempts to gainsay conventions implicitly verify the hegemony of such standards since they comprise the baseline that is being reacted against. That is, any bid to subvert or debunk entrenched conventions concretises their position as the normative standard. In this light, the incident of Hallie and Sidney trying to escape from their killer in *Scream 2* can be read metaphorically:

---

[3] An exception is *Wes Craven's New Nightmare* (1994), which diverts into 'art film' seriousness rather than reiterating conventions that made the *A Nightmare on Elm Street* series so popular. *New Nightmare* is not a slasher film in the conventional sense, and that perhaps explains its relative box-office failure (being the lowest grossing film in the series, having grossed only $18 million domestically according to Box Office Mojo).

just as the protagonists cannot escape the killer because their behaviour accords with convention, *Scream*'s subgeneric alignment means the series is trapped by necessary adherence to conventional norms. Established structures limit filmmakers and characters alike, and it is implied that neither can do anything to significantly modify those limitations.

Moreover, critics commonly dismiss the subgenre on the basis of its conventionality. To illustrate, Johnson (2007) offers a sweeping precis of the slasher's conventional components – 'large body counts, quick killings by superhuman bogeymen, and . . . the sex-means-death equation' – to insinuate that individual films comprising the subgenre are unworthy of contemplation. Such criticism arose in response to market saturation during the 1980s, wherein many films reiterated conventions. The self-conscious, snarky tone of postmodern slashers perhaps indicates that their filmmakers had internalised criticism regarding the subgenre's supposed repetitiveness.[4] That is, self-consciousness about subgeneric conventions is coupled with embarrassment about reiterating conventions, especially to savvy audiences.

Metamodern texts build on these premises, albeit in a different direction. Rather than treating subgeneric conventions as inescapable constraints that must be excused via self-conscious eye-rolling, metamodern filmmakers recognise that genre provides 'highly organised constraints on' both 'the production and *interpretation* of meaning' (Frow 2006, 10, emphasis added). As such, 'generic conventions are as much a property of [audience's] expectations as they are of works themselves' (Neale 2000, 29; see also Culler 2002, 17 –3). Instead of perceiving conventions as fixed 'rules' that belong to the texts, metamodern slashers attend to the pre-dispositional expectations that follow from subgeneric conventionality. Inherent to this mode is an outward focus, pointing towards the relationships between conventions, the subgeneric context and the ways viewers' expectations are shaped by the presence, absence or alteration of conventional elements.

By embracing conventionality, metamodern slashers retain the reflexivity that was normalised in the postmodern slasher phase, while also overcoming the postmodern slasher's self-consciousness about exploring

---

[4] That very criticism has a longer history: as Neale contends, 'most modern conceptions of genre derive from Romanticism, and Romantic attitudes to genre were largely hostile', associating genre with a 'lack of creativity, originality and individuality', and entrenching understandings of genre conventions as 'clichés, meanings as transparent and impoverished, structures as formulae, and characters as one-dimensional stereotypes' (2000, 195).

conventionality. Rather than flagging conventions such that the consequent iteration of convention seems awkwardly artificial (as the postmodern slasher usually does), metamodern slashers naturalise conventions by bringing them into congruity with the characters and the fictional world. Consequently, as we will see in Chapter 6, where conventions are absurdly unrealistic, so too are the metamodern slasher's characters and fictional world. Even when exploring conventionality, metamodern slashers usually emphasise narrative as the main source of pleasure. Postmodern slashers instead prioritise the pleasures derived from cogitating on genericity and fictional construction, not least when those pleasures conflict with the narrative.

Conventions are necessary for identifying and contextualising a film as belonging to a subgenre (see Grant 2007, 10), so they cannot be done away with altogether. Yet, that does not mean conventions are so inflexible as to preclude innovation per se. There are two avenues open to filmmakers who wish to innovate within a subgenre and still hold on to those conventions. First, adjustments can be made to conventions, thereby unveiling new possibilities. This option will be explored in Chapters 5 and 6. Second, conventions can be examined from a fresh perspective, so that they are no longer perceived as 'constraints'. This route will be exemplified by this chapter's case studies.

The first case study is *Behind the Mask: The Rise of Leslie Vernon* (2006), which develops on the postmodern slasher's techniques by devoting screentime to characters who are aware of and are seemingly fated by the subgenre's conventions. In contrast to the postmodern slasher, however, the actualisation of conventions is celebrated rather than satirised in *Behind the Mask*. That adjustment is achieved via its unusual perspectival conceit: an investigative reporter interviews a slasher as they prepare their homicidal campaign. Via a documentary mode, the killer rationalises repeated 'unrealistic' conventions; the film then presents those conventions in a 'standard horror film' stylistic register, asking the viewer to reconsider familiar conventions in light of the new perspective granted. *Behind the Mask* invites viewers to recall why those conventions were so successful in the first instance, underlining the joys conventional representations can arouse. The chapter's second case study is *You Might Be the Killer* (2018), which evaluates conventionality via an unusual perspective on the events. The film's lead protagonist unwittingly becomes a slasher and consequently tries to stop his own murderous rampage. The protagonist's unusual viewpoint is developed into a meditation on conventionality via his recurring engagements with a film nerd (an equivalent to *Scream*'s Randy) who imparts advice on the situation, based on her subgeneric expertise. This combination of perspectives yields new insights into well-worn conventions.

Many metamodern slashers evoke conventions implicitly, rather than having characters frankly discuss conventions. The implicit approach distinguishes metamodern from postmodern slashers. This chapter's case studies are more explicit, and so they are closer to the postmodern slasher in this regard. However, it is worth observing that where *Behind the Mask*'s characters discuss behaviours, types and attributes that are commonplace in the subgenre, they are not referred to as filmic conventions. Neither the subgenre nor its films are directly referred to in the script. *Behind the Mask* instead treats slashers as real entities. The parallels are clear, but viewers are left to connect *Behind the Mask*'s dissection of conventions to their own sphere of experience (in which slashers are purely fictional entities). *You Might Be the Killer* does refer to the subgenre and its films, but here the connections are forged to highlight ways its narrative events deviate from conventional norms. That is, the approach diverges from *Scream*'s technique of discussing then iterating conventions. Finally, even when conventions are discussed by characters in *Behind the Mask* and *You Might Be the Killer*, the connections between those conventional elements and each film's broader reflections on the subgenre still remain tacit.

These case studies illuminate three qualities of the metamodern slasher, namely that: (1) conventions are naturalised because they are congruous with the characters and the fictional world; (2) conventions need not consistently and inevitably play out in normative ways (they are not fixed elements that 'trap' filmmakers); and (3) metamodern filmmakers typically use the expectations generated by conventionality as opportunities to provide insights into the subgenre's operations.

Murder Will Out: Exposing Conventions in *Behind the Mask*

Although Petridis dubs *Behind the Mask: The Rise of Leslie Vernon* a 'pure postmodern narrativ[e]' (2014, 81), the film is on the cusp between the postmodern slasher and the metamodern, with much greater weight placed on the latter. The film follows a documentary crew led by investigative reporter Taylor, who interviews the titular killer. The film employs three distinct stylistic modes. The first mode – a documentary style – is confined to the film's opening moments. *Behind the Mask* begins with finished documentary footage that is displayed first-hand, in a 4:3 television ratio, complete with an onscreen 'WQHS 12' channel logo and polished voiceover. The scene then breaks, the aspect ratio changes to 16:9, and the film moves into its second (and dominant) mode: a more 'candid' version of the same documentary form, presented as if it is a set of raw rushes. As well as lacking the logo and voiceover that demarcated the 'finished' documentary sequence, the footage captures 'behind the scenes' incidents that would otherwise be edited out, including regular moments in which Taylor talks to the crew behind the camera. Therefore, just as the film-within-a-film (the documentary) promises to expose the killer 'Behind the Mask', the rushes expose the crew 'behind' the documentary. The third stylistic mode is redolent of 'cinematic' fiction film. Shot on 35mm, the footage is characterised by a mise-en-scène that encompasses deliberate camera setups, staged lighting, nondiegetic music (and so forth), thus contrasting with the 'behind the scenes' rushes' handheld verité style. These 'cinematic' sequences are interspersed throughout the film. When Leslie plans or talks through how he will stalk his target, the verité style is deployed. When he actually engages with his target, the mise-en-scène transfers to the 'cinematic' mode that is characteristic of normative horror fiction film. The final third of the film abandons the verité mode altogether in favour of the 'cinematic' mode.

The initial shift from documentary footage to 'behind the scenes' in the opening is not an equivalent of the 'pullback-reveal' technique popularised in postmodern film (see Chapter 3). Ordinarily, the 'pullback-reveal' is used to flag a metaleptic displacement between fictional layers, moving between the diegetic world and another fictional layer (a film-within-a-film), with the latter being presented as if it is the film's diegetic reality. That is, the 'pullback-reveal' is usually a surprise, given that the initial footage is presented as if it is the film's diegetic reality before it is revealed to be a fictional construct within the fiction. In *Behind the Mask*, the documentary footage's construction is self-evident. It is one window into the fictional world, and the transposition to 'behind the scenes' offers a differently stylised window. The shift is naturalised by *Behind the Mask*'s opening credits being imposed on the verité footage, signalling entry into *Behind the Mask* 'proper'. The vacillations between 'cinematic' and verité modes are more jarring; for example, any extradiegetic music applied to the 'cinematic' sequences drops out sharply (usually in the middle of a melodic phrase) when turning back to the verité mode. However, the initial switch from documentary to verité modes prepares the viewer for other such transitions. Also, these repeated sharp substitutions between the rushes and the 'cinematic' modes are unmistakable, drawing attention to form. Unlike the postmodern slasher then, the strategy does not attempt to 'trick' the viewer per se.

These formal devices set the ground for *Behind the Mask*'s engagement with subgeneric conventions. The stylistic changes prime viewers to expect that conventions will not purely be reiterated in a conventional manner. As with *Scream*, conventions are spoken about and then are confirmed. Nonetheless, there are notable differences between *Scream*'s and *Behind the Mask*'s approaches. First, *Scream*'s dialogue about conventions is sardonic, colouring its subsequent 'straight' demonstrations of those conventions. *Behind the Mask*'s explanations, in contrast, are just as sincere as its iterations of convention. Second, unlike *Scream*, where the discussion of convention and subsequent iteration are presented in the same formal register, conventions are expounded in *Behind the Mask*'s 'behind the scenes' rushes, and then subsequently iterated in the distinct 'cinematic' sections. Consequently, the explanatory sections are distinguished from the standard 'cinematic' mode that would usually condition iterations of subgeneric conventions. The register-shift accentuates the 'cinematic' sequences, even though they adhere to horror fiction film's conventions and stylistic norms (and so ought not to appear 'special').

The divergent stylistic modes precipitate the film's commentary on conventionality. The explanation sections naturalise conventions because they delimit Leslie's modus operandi. As the documentary's subject, Leslie's motivations and behaviours are central drivers in the fictional world. Still, Taylor's perspective is even more vital. Taylor is presented as having no prior knowledge of how a slasher behaves, so the explanations are aimed towards her. One implication is that *Behind the Mask* is inclusive in its contemplation about conventions. Since background knowledge of the slasher entered the popular vernacular following *Scream*, a majority of *Behind the Mask*'s viewers are likely to be broadly familiar with the subgenre's conventions. Yet Leslie carefully recounts tropes and conventions in detail, especially those that are so specific that a general audience with cursory knowledge of the subgenre might be excluded from understanding. Leslie also outlines even the commonest of conventions as if it is normal not to know about them. For instance, he refers to 'survivor girl' as an 'industry term'. Ergo, *Behind the Mask*'s rumination on conventions is accessible to even rookie slasher viewers.

Nevertheless, Taylor's 'novice' perspective serves an equally important function for those already familiar with the slasher's conventions. The explanations set up Taylor's expectations prior to the substantiation of those conventions in the 'cinematic' sequences. Her reactions defamiliarise the subgenre's accepted conventions and norms, or more precisely, the pre-dispositional assumptions that follow from those conventions. For example, following a standard 'cinematic' sequence depicting Leslie's first direct encounter with his proclaimed target (Kelly) at a library, the cut back to 'behind the scenes' finds Taylor jumping and whooping along with Leslie. Her excitement at seeing a conventional situation play out for the first time reminds the viewer of the pleasures conventions can arouse,[5] particularly for the neophyte slasher viewer. Taylor's experiential perspective as subgeneric 'novice' allow us to see the conventional sequences afresh. The register-shift formalises that suggestion because the convention is delineated, then is enacted from a different perspective (an alternative stylistic mode).

Elsewhere, Taylor's 'novice' perspective serves a more critical function. For instance, Leslie describes the 'pivotal moment when [the survivor girl] makes the transition from victim to heroine' as being 'visually manifested when she reaches for a big, long hard weapon'. He then clarifies that the moment is 'deeply symbolic. She's empowering herself with cock . . . she'll be taking my manhood and empowering herself with it.'[6] Although the sequence is played straight, Leslie's blunt description underlines how ridiculous the symbolism sounds in the abstract, leaving Taylor dumbfounded. This commonplace notion is laid bare via Taylor's fresh perspective, raising questions over the suppositions and expectations engendered by conventions. Even so, Leslie assures both Taylor and the viewer of the interpretation's broad acceptance – 'it's convention Tay, you have to respect it' – and this stance is upheld by the film. No matter how unrealistic they might sound, the subgenre's conventions are accepted facets of the fictional world, and the characters' behaviours adhere to those conventions. That implied acceptance is anchored by the verité mode. The interview is filmed for a factual documentary, and that context legitimates the explanation.

This technique is sustained throughout the film. When presenting subgenre conventions, *Behind the Mask* volunteers plausible explanations for even the most unrealistic tropes. Leslie reveals that the amount of cardio training he needs to do is 'ridiculous'. This regimen is required by a convention that dictates his behaviour: 'that whole thing of making it look like you're walking when everybody else is running their asses off'. His fitness regime rationalises a commonplace trope in slasher films (particularly the *Friday the 13th* series) that otherwise seems implausible. The convention itself is not criticised. Neither Leslie nor Taylor question why this behaviour is necessary. On the contrary, the explanation naturalises the convention despite its

---

[5] On this, see Buscombe (2012, 22).
[6] This explanation draws from academic theorisation, particularly psychoanalytic interpretation. *Behind the Mask* contextualises conventions by evoking factors surrounding the subgenre, not just the subgenre's films themselves.

outlandishness. Elsewhere, Leslie reads 'work related' manuals and textbooks on anatomy and escapology. He also demonstrates that he plans in advance to set up some of the ostensibly accidental or supernatural elements that are part of the slasher film's conventional field. For example, he has a cabin's 'main fuse rigged up to cut the power' with a remote switch, meaning he can produce what resembles a coincidental power outage; he saws through branches and weapons so that they will fall apart when utilised for escape; he wears a bulletproof vest to prevent injury from firearms; he ties transparent fishing wire to a door-prop so that he can cause the door to 'inexplicably' slam shut when he wants to scare his prey. That is, Leslie rationalises commonplace subgeneric tropes that, prior to his account, appeared unrealistic. Sometimes, a trope cannot be rationalised in this way. For instance, Leslie states that he nails ground floor windows shut in advance, and when Taylor asks if the victims would simply break the glass to escape, Leslie agrees that 'You'd think so. But you'd be surprised. No. And when they do smash it out, it is on the second floor or higher. And then they're out on the roof and they are screwed!'. Leslie seems as surprised as Taylor by his victims' panicked responses here, but nevertheless, the convention holds.

Furthermore, these fresh perspectives on familiar conventions are sources of humour within the film. As opposed to ironically mocking or overturning conventions, humour arises from the feasibility of its rationalisations, creating pleasurable surprises by unpicking the subgenre's accepted but seemingly implausible tropes. Conventions are thus anchored and celebrated. *Behind the Mask* does not merely lay out conventions and then corroborate them, then. Its rationalisations cast conventions in a new light. The direct discussion of subgenre conventions here implies that the same explanations for seemingly implausible, coincidental or supernatural events could hold true in all other slasher movies, therefore giving viewers reason to reassess their assumptions about these conventions whenever they are encountered across the subgenre. When conventions are deployed in *Behind the Mask*, they are presented via the 'cinematic' mode, mirroring the subgenre's standard stylistic register. The kinship between *Behind the Mask*'s 'cinematic' sequences and the subgenre's normative stylistic register invites viewers to take the newfound pleasures instilled by Leslie's explanations into their engagements with other slasher films.

Many of these explanations are groundwork for *Behind the Mask*'s finale. However, where earlier sequences adhere to Leslie's outlines, incidents diverge from Leslie's stated plans in the final act. At the centre of that divergence is Leslie's central target: his Final Girl. Throughout, Leslie indicates that his virginal 'survivor girl' opponent is a young woman named Kelly. In the finale, Taylor finds Kelly riding her boyfriend in bed, swinging her panties above her head. The documentary crew surmise that it is not Kelly's 'first time'. Taylor eventually realises that she has been his Final Girl all along, that Kelly was just a 'red herring' and that Leslie had planned the course of events 'before we even met . . . before we ever shot a frame'.

This revelation is not presented as the kind of left-field twist commonly found in postmodern slasher films, wherein the filmmakers trick the audience purely by withholding information (see Chapter 2). *Behind the Mask* forewarns that Leslie's plans might alter. When walking Taylor through the final act plans, Leslie asks Taylor to guess what he will do in the barn. As she talks through the situation in voiceover, we see the events she describes, conveyed in the 'cinematic' register. When Leslie points out that Taylor had forgotten to account for his 'Ahab' (Doc Halloran, who is tracking him), Taylor revises her understanding. The footage then rewinds and plays out differently to account for Halloran's presence. During the actual final act, some footage is replicated from Taylor's prediction. Where the footage deviates from her prediction, it is not an unexpected twist, but rather an equivalent of the 'rewinding' and remodelling we previously saw during their walkthrough.

Moreover, *Behind the Mask* hints that Taylor is Leslie's real target via its register shifts. The film establishes a pattern of moving to the 'cinematic' mode when Leslie engages with his supposed target, Kelly. The exception is when the climax begins. When Leslie starts enacting his plans, Taylor's crew's vantage point is retained along with its recurring verité 'rushes' mode. Eventually, Taylor decides to intervene to stop Leslie's murder spree, declaring 'It's over, the documentary is done.' Her assertion and her detachment from Leslie are confirmed by a final turn to the 'cinematic' register. The aesthetic alterations signal that Taylor has unwittingly stepped into the 'survivor girl' role prior to Taylor's own realisation that she is Leslie's true target.

Far earlier in the film, clues about Leslie's plans are relayed via double-coded dialogue. Leslie posits that the documentary crew have reached 'the point of no return', meaning they will have to commit to working with him or walk away. Taylor's assent is conveyed by footage of her following Leslie into the library, where he tries to murder a librarian (his first kill of the film). Taylor becomes a conspirator, deciding to enter a pact with Leslie. In the voiceover accompanying the footage, Leslie explains that the success of his plan depends on his survivor girl:

> I don't know that it will [work] . . . It's another test to see if we're on the same page. In fact, a lot of what happens from here on out, the success or failure of it depends on her, on what she does.

Taylor believes Leslie is referring to Kelly, and so does not realise that he is talking about Taylor's decisions, including her choice to enter the library with him.

This trajectory begins in their first sit-down interview. Taylor commences by accusing Leslie of 'terrorising innocent people', looking directly to camera, chin up, lips pursed, with an air of moral superiority. Leslie retorts, 'I can't just sit here . . . and explain it to you. It's got to come from your own understanding of the process.' The film's verbal explanations of conventions are thus coupled with the execution of those conventions because Taylor must experience Leslie's methods, and so Taylor's experiential development across the narrative is set up as a crucial explanatory mechanism. Consequently, when Leslie enlists Taylor to scare Kelly by slamming a door closed, it is not just that a convention is being enacted: the incident draws Taylor in, involving her with Leslie.

Taylor and Leslie are also co-conspirators insofar as he depends on his 'survivor girl' for meaning, even though (in accordance with convention) that relationship will culminate in his demise. The film presents the antagonistic killer-Final Girl nexus as a bond that confers mutual meaning. As Leslie discloses ahead of the climax, 'my fate . . . depends on what [the Final Girl] does', and the fact that he is trying to slay her is 'the paradox of what I do' (that is, it is inherent to their relative conventional positions). When Taylor surmises 'you love [the Final Girl]', Leslie looks down with the embarrassment of someone who fears rejection, stating 'I love the idea of her' before looking back to Taylor, continuing, 'of what I hope she'll find within herself'. When she adds to his reasoning, averring 'what doesn't kill you makes you stronger', she does so with the wry smile of understanding, evincing that she is no longer a 'novice'. At this stage, their bond is complete. Their connection is confirmed moments before the climactic confrontation begins: Leslie weeps with happiness, and Taylor empathetically places her hand on his.

Leslie talks of conventions as if they dictate his and the Final Girl's joint destinies, but *Behind the Mask* fosters a dualistic stance on the extent to which their trajectories are prescribed. Midway through the film, Taylor betrays Leslie's request to not speak to Kelly. He then demands that Taylor board her truck, grabbing her by the throat and causing her to well up with fear (see Figure 4.1). Although their bond is mostly jovial and they grow closer across the film, this moment underscores the threat he poses. When she comes back the next morning to continue filming, she rationalises that 'this is what I've chosen to do' and that she will therefore 'see it through'. In the climax, a parallel scene reminds us not only of the threat Leslie poses to Taylor, but also how their bond has developed because of her choice to 'see it through'. In the latter scene, Leslie again ushers the crew towards their truck, this time telling them to leave because he believes they will rescind their agreement to film without interfering. When Taylor implores him to halt his plans because he has 'elected to fulfil a destiny [he doesn't] have to fulfil', the earlier sequence is evoked in several ways. Taylor again wells up, but instead of grabbing her by the jugular, Leslie takes her face in his hands (see Figure 4.1). Where Taylor previously proclaimed that she has chosen to continue, here Leslie affirms

Figure 4.1 Parallel interactions between Taylor and Leslie in *Behind the Mask: The Rise of Leslie Vernon* (2006)

'I made a choice', following up with the more revealing confirmation 'This is what *we* were born to do' (emphasis added). Taylor and Leslie are 'fated' by their conventional positions as killer and Final Girl, but that does not imply fatalistic resignation: emphasis is placed on the characters' decisions. Both expressly declare their choice to continue, stressing the possibility that both could do otherwise. Conventionality is not a 'trap' here then, because even if Taylor and Leslie behave in conventional ways, that is because they opt to. This crucial element of the film's commentary on subgeneric conventions implies that slasher filmmakers too are not fated to reiterate conventions: they opt to do so and choose the ends they utilise conventions for.

Even though *Behind the Mask* exhibits a comedic self-reflexivity that is commonly associated with the postmodern slasher phase, its sincere tone is indicative of a metamodern sensibility. That tone is captured by the emotional closeness between Leslie and Taylor. Their bond underpins *Behind the Mask*'s discussion of subgenre conventions, because the killer-Final Girl relationship is itself so central to the subgenre. Situating Leslie and Taylor as co-conspirators presents that relationship in a fresh light. The sincerity that characterises their bond carries over into the film's investigation of the subgenre more broadly. By allowing Taylor to experience the subgenre's conventions, she has a richer understanding of her own existence within the fictional world. Her initial unfamiliarity with subgeneric conventions allows jaded slasher film viewers to perceive those conventions anew, and to carry that refreshed understanding or rationalisation of commonplace slasher conventions into engagement with other slasher texts. Rather than ironically mocking conventions then, *Behind the Mask* utilises conventions in an innovative way to provide insight, retaining the sincere tone and investment in character that are distinguishing features of the metamodern slasher.

Bad Advice: Unorthodox Perspectives and Positional Slippage in *You Might Be the Killer*

Behind the Mask's exploration of the slasher film is presented via the perspectives of a newcomer (a journalist-observer) and an expert (the slasher who lives within the subgeneric situation every day). Both actively choose to participate in the subgenre's conventions. *You Might Be the Killer* offers a different perspective via its central pairing: Chuck, a genre film aficionado who remains exterior to the events, and Sam, a 'newcomer' who has no choice but to participate in the subgeneric situation. *You Might Be the Killer* centres on a group of summer camp counsellors led by Sam. Sam outlines the history of Camp Clear Vista among a raft of other campfire ghost stories. Sam assures the group the tale 'is all true and happened right here on this very land': a 'dark, sinister' spirit was awoken by settlers, causing the settlers to murder one another in 'horrific ways' until a 'medicine man was able to trap the dark spirit in a dark red oak tree'. One hundred years later, a woodcarver who was 'known as the kindest person in his town' cut down the tree and made a mask. When he wore it, he 'killed everybody in the village, including his own family'. When one of the counsellors (Drew) finds the mask and puts it on Sam's face, he becomes possessed by the evil spirit and starts slaying the other counsellors. Sam only becomes aware that he is the killer during a telephone conversation with his friend Chuck (hence, the film's title).

Chuck works at a comic bookstore and is framed as a horror enthusiast. Sam rings her for help, suggesting that her expertise can help Sam. Chuck's advice is mainly based on her knowledge about horror conventions, meaning she talks about slasher norms in a manner similar to *Scream*'s Randy. Nonetheless, *You Might Be the Killer* highlights that it is not trying to replicate *Scream*'s strategies. In contrast to *Scream*'s Randy, Chuck's genre knowledge is insufficient to help Sam in several ways. First, Chuck is not Sam's first port of call. Chuck initially admits that she is not the best person to contact in Sam's situation, asking 'wouldn't you rather call the cops?'. Sam then reveals that he has already tried the police, but that the elderly local Sheriff 'doesn't really work nights anymore'.[7] A horror aficionado is Sam's 'last resort' as a source of help then, but it is still implied that Chuck's subgenre-based speculations might be of some use to Sam. Second however, when Chuck makes explicit comparisons to other slasher films, they are worthless to him. For example, Chuck asks if the killer is 'Freddy ugly or Matt Cordell ugly?'. When Sam fails to recognise that Cordell is the killer in *Maniac Cop* (1988), Chuck expresses her dissatisfaction in Sam's knowledge of police-based slasher films, but the question is irrelevant to Sam's survival. Third, Chuck's knowledge is not solely limited to horror or slasher films: she also bases deductions on knowledge about the occult and serial killers. When she employs those other forms of knowledge, she becomes an invaluable ally to Sam. So, when Chuck tries to help Sam work out who the killer is ('figuring out what they want could help you not die'), that line of enquiry illuminates Sam's situation. During the discussion, Chuck is again derailed into considering motives

---

[7] This situation is conventional, affirming the trope that police officers are mainly absent in slasher films.

from slasher films (asking 'Is it an old camper who was teased as a kid and is out for blood?'). Here, Sam hints that Chuck has wandered off course, tries to interject, and eventually impatiently cuts her off with 'It's nothing like that, I promise, okay?'. Chuck then returns to the facts of Sam's situation, asking 'Why didn't [the killer] kill you? . . . are you covered in blood? . . . is it your blood? . . . are you holding a weapon of any kind?'. These queries cause Sam to realise he is the killer. That is, where Chuck refers to slasher films and their conventions, it is a distraction, but when she concentrates on Sam's situation, drawing on other forms of knowledge, she genuinely helps him.

Thus, *You Might Be the Killer* evokes and then undermines the premise that reciting subgeneric conventions is useful or even applicable to the narrative situation, thereby implicitly disparaging the postmodern slasher's ploy of ironically laying out then substantiating conventions. Chuck's proclamations about subgeneric conventions are undercut throughout, and so her role as an equivalent of *Scream*'s Randy signals that when discussing and utilising conventions, *You Might Be the Killer* will not follow in the archetypal postmodern slasher's footsteps. *You Might Be the Killer* does not simply reify conventions, but instead interrogates the notion that those conventions must consistently and inevitably play out as they have done previously.

To illustrate, *You Might Be the Killer* regularly employs onscreen captions to tally the number of 'dead counsellors' accumulated across the film. The onscreen death tally recalls a conventional facet – the body count – that is commonly referred to in the name of denigrating the subgenre (and its fans). For instance, Crane decries the *Friday the 13th* series' 'spectacle of endless death', using his inability to count to double-digits as evidence of a supposed problem with the subgenre. He declares,

> the bodies piled up so quickly that I could never get an accurate head count . . . the fact that it was *impossible* to exactly total all the corpses without an inerrant adding machine made my point more effectively than a precise body count. (1994, 157, emphasis added).[8]

---

[8] Miraculously, others have since achieved this apparently 'impossible' feat (see Grove 2005, 231). The association between the *Friday the 13th* series and 'body count' was solidified by the trailers for *Friday the 13th* (which interrupted clips of its footage with a count from one to twelve, implying that thirteen deaths would be shown) and its sequel (which promised 'the body count continues', interrupting footage to count from fourteen to twenty-three). Since 2017, James A. Janisse has been tallying deaths in horror films on the YouTube channel Dead Meat (in a series titled 'The Kill Count'). Notably, the earliest videos in this series are devoted to the *Friday the 13th* movies.

Chuck uses the term 'body count' when trying to ascertain how many counsellors have died, and that phrasing ties the onscreen tally of 'dead counsellors' into this subgeneric discursive norm. Here, the captions are misleading. When Imani falls into a pit of stakes, the tally counts her as one of the dead. When she later wakes and climbs out of the pit, the tally is struck through and amended, decreasing by one ('H̶ 10'). This might appear to intentionally 'trick' the audience by withholding information, as is characteristic of the postmodern slasher (see Chapter 2). Still, the captions are not presented as definitive statements of fact. The first of these captions (forty-five seconds into the film) states 'dead counsellors (so far): a lot'.[9] From the outset then, the captions are flagged as being imprecise. Rather than being symptomatic of the postmodern slasher's cynical tone however, this initial caption undercuts the very notion of body count as a marker of value. If body counts are valued by fans such that higher body counts are 'better' (as the subgenre's critics insinuate), built into that notion is an implied comparison: an assessment of whether the present film's death toll is 'higher' than other extant slasher films' body counts. The quantity 'a lot' is too inexact to allow for such comparison. Furthermore, the ongoing count of dead counsellors is not a 'trick' on the audience because it is not aligned with the author's omniscient epistemic vantage point on the narrative events. Instead, the tally is aligned with the first-time viewer's perspective on the events.[10] Captions echo a viewer creating their own death tally, including revisions. So, when Imani is actually dispatched, the tally is amended again ('H̶ 1̶0̶ 11') as it would be if the first-time viewer were keeping count as the film progresses. The captions are not necessarily intended to lead the viewer astray so much as present information as it becomes available from within the evolving situation. Moreover then, the captions align the audience with the characters' perspective on the events. Indeed, when Imani emerges and startles Jamie, Jamie declares 'I thought you were dead!', and Imani explains that she intentionally concealed her status: 'I figured if [the killer] thought I was dead, I'd be off his list.'

Despite their apparent unreliability, the captions serve an important purpose in orienting the viewer. The narrative is primarily (although not exclusively) aligned with Sam's perspective. Much of the information is rooted in his limited understanding of the events. He is only portrayed as the killer once he realises he is the killer, for example. Most significantly,

---

[9] Presumably, Crane would be satisfied with this tally.
[10] A second-time viewer would be aware of Imani's return and ergo the tally's inaccuracy. The captions embed the first-time viewing position as the standard.

information is unveiled throughout in flashbacks as Sam relates his memories of the incidents to Chuck. Accordingly, the story events are presented out of chronological order, and the death tally orients the viewer as the narrative jumps to different points in the timeline.

Epistemic alignment with Sam grants a perspective on the events that is limited in some respects but abundant in others: he occupies a superposition, being simultaneously protagonist, antagonist and witness. Unlike a paranoid 'whodunit' narrative wherein the killer is exposed in a final act twist that could not be anticipated, the killer's identity is suggested in the title and is definitively expounded twenty minutes into the film. *You Might Be the Killer* parallels *Behind the Mask*, *Shrooms* (2007) and *Triangle* (2009) in that it investigates expected subgeneric roles via its unorthodox perspective on a conventional situation. As Chuck notes, Sam is 'definitely not the killer type', he is a 'nice guy'. In contrast to the emotive blankness slasher killers usually exhibit, Sam displays regret as he describes violent events to Chuck ('I know, I hate myself'). Simultaneously, the film complicates the idea that Sam can be a 'nice guy' and a killer. Overhearing Chuck's side of the telephone conversation, a customer in Chuck's comic bookstore proclaims that Sam is an 'asshole' who 'should kill himself', and that Chuck is an 'accomplice to murder' (see Figure 4.2). The film mainly sides with Sam, placing blame on the cursed mask, but the customer's damnation has some validity. *You Might Be the Killer*'s mixed perspectives open the possibility that the subgenre's conventional viewpoint is typically biased:

Figure 4.2 An eavesdropping customer berates Chuck for advising Sam in *You Might Be the Killer* (2018)

the killer's perspective is usually inaccessible. *You Might Be the Killer* provides an alternative vantage point, giving viewers reason to reassess the subgenre's typical events.

The film demonstrates that the expectations triggered by subgeneric convention can be reversed by adjusting the perspective. At the outset, Sam flees from the killer (not realising he is running from himself). Shortly after discovering he is the killer, Sam flees and hides again, this time from the remaining counsellors; as he asserts to Chuck, 'they're after me . . . I'm trying to stay alive.' Here, the subgeneric norm that teens are usually under threat is amended, but the film does not merely invert the conventional situation. It is usual for slasher films to contain sequences in which teens try to locate the killer. Killers customarily spend much of a slasher film's runtime offscreen, and so what they do during that time cannot be ascertained. As with *Behind the Mask*'s insights into the killer's unseen behaviours, *You Might Be the Killer*'s perspective shift fills in that gap, thereby depicting the killer in an unorthodox way: the subgenre's ordinarily impassive killers do not retreat and cower as Sam does.

As with many other metamodern slasher films that play with conventions, *You Might Be the Killer* focuses attention on the killer-Final Girl relationship. When Chuck explains that a Final Girl routinely defeats the killer, Sam's queries defamiliarise conventional expectations. Sam expresses some incredulity that he 'can kill some musclebound meathead' and yet will be slain by 'a sweet girl like Jamie'. Even though Chuck offers no justification for the discrepancy (simply responding, 'yup'), and Sam accepts the convention with a resigned 'Wow', Sam's doubt calls the convention into question. Similarly, when Sam notes that only 'the most pure [sic] person' will survive, he optimistically asks 'and that's never the killer?'. Again, he immediately concedes to Chuck's subgeneric knowledge (raising his hand in apology for even asking), but his question has legitimacy, not least since he does not fit the killer type.

Sam's questions raise uncertainty over whether the narrative will conform to or upend these conventions. Indeed, Chuck's convention-based speculation about the Final Girl – which is based on 'the thousands of hours we've spent watching horror movies' – is not straightforwardly borne out by *You Might Be the Killer*. Sam points out a potential loophole arising from his position as a reluctant killer. When Imani and Jamie lock him up, he proclaims 'I need you guys to stay alive so I can stay alive . . . as long as you two are alive' there is 'no Final Girl'. His gambit fails because Jamie executes Imani: after hearing about the trope from Chuck, the pair turn on one another. Imani claims to be better 'equipped to kill Sam' and tries to attack Jamie. Jamie then swiftly slays Imani with a shovel.

The incident is crucial for several reasons. First, Imani and Jamie are two competing images of the conventional Final Girl. Jamie stands for the traditional Final Girl of her namesake Jamie Lee Curtis: Sam paints Jamie as 'the sweetest girl on the planet'. Imani represents a more contemporary version of the Final Girl: a self-assured badass. It is not immediately apparent who will take the mantle when the two lock horns. Their tussle is a battle between two versions of the same convention. Their conflict hypostatises the fact that conventions are not fixed elements that inevitably play out in the same predictable fashion in every instance: they mutate over time. Second, Jamie wins by slaughtering Imani without hesitation. Jamie hits Imani in the head with a shovel while she is mid-sentence, then abruptly slices through her face with the shovel's blade. In doing so, Jamie becomes the last survivor, but she also undermines her erstwhile narrative status as 'pure and innocent': she becomes a ruthless murderer. Third, rather than burying the cursed mask in the final showdown, Jamie dons it and eradicates Sam. Jamie survives, walking away into the sunrise, but she does so as the film's slasher, not the Final Girl. In the end, contrary to Chuck's convention-based conjecture, Sam is the film's closest approximation of a hero. Fourth then, it is not just that the conventional Final Girl is undercut because the convention is inadequate or flawed. Imani and Jamie turn on each other because they learn about the convention. That is, the characters' knowledge of conventions does not help them to survive, it actively causes the normative internal order of things to fall apart.

Postmodern slashers iterate conventions via their dialogue and then confirm those conventions in their action, motioning that conventions are immutable and trap filmmakers into repetition. *You Might Be the Killer* instead indicates that conventions can be utilised not only to set up expectations, but also to yield surprises. This end is achieved by implicitly recognising that conventions are remodelled over time, and that evoking a particular convention does not necessary dictate what narrative consequences will follow from that evocation. These implications are underlined whenever Chuck's expertise on the subgenre is undercut by the narrative action, but especially where she proclaims that conventions are stable and inevitable. Whenever conventions are questioned, Chuck makes assertions to the effect that 'I'm not sure there's much . . . you can do to alter the course of these events. So it goes.' Her resignation encapsulates the postmodern slasher's cynical tone, chiefly since she is a movie expert-cum-advisor modelled after *Scream*'s Randy. Chuck's description of conventions playing out in inexorable ways makes conventions sound like the stereotypical slasher killer: fixated, unerring and relentless, moving through a routine of carving up teens until being defeated by the Final

Girl. *You Might Be the Killer* undermines that view of the killer via Sam's multifaceted position. Sam may be unconscious, mindlessly killing under the mask's influence, but when he can remove the mask, he deliberates on and rejects that behaviour. The movements between Sam-as-killer, Sam-as-witness, Chuck's assessment, and even the comic bookstore customers' criticisms of what they overhear, afford distance for judgement. As such, *You Might Be the Killer* embodies a critique of slasher films that 'thoughtlessly' go through the motions. Its dissection of conventionality takes the 'self-awareness' of the postmodern slasher and translates it into a kind of awareness-raising through critique. As with the other metamodern slashers, *You Might Be the Killer* innovates by tweaking the subgenre's conventional aspects, conferring new perspectives on entrenched tropes. Even where iterating well-worn conventions, the film roots its narrative in characters' experiences, leaning into sincere appraisal of the subgenre that is coloured by an ambition to offer something fresh.

Conventional Wisdom

Slasher films have a history of contemplating conventions onscreen. Yet, those ruminations transform over time, being shaped by the subgenre's development. In the boom-period, such reflections identified common tropes, thereby helping to pin down conventions as conventions, and anchoring the slasher film as a subgeneric category. Later, such cogitations were instead shaped by the postmodern slasher's flippant cynicism. Postmodern slashers' self-conscious meditations on conventionality imply that filmmakers were critical or perhaps tired of the subgenre's tropes, although they were stuck reciting them regardless. Delineating then demonstrating tropes reaffirmed the persistence and power of such conventions. As this chapter's case studies illustrate, it is possible to take an alternative stance on conventionality. In the metamodern slasher, transparently reflecting on conventions grants opportunities to innovate and surprise rather than purely trapping filmmakers and audiences in cycles of duplication. Indeed, as demonstrated by Chapters 2 and 3's time-loop case studies – *Triangle* and *Happy Death Day* (2017) – repetition can provide opportunities for renewal and growth. That ethos is further accentuated by this chapter's case studies, which candidly educe conventions, and so are emblematic of the sincerity and desire to innovate that epitomise the metamodern sensibility.

Three further observations will refine this position. First, subgeneric innovation does not require abandoning all conventions and tropes. Doing so would make the resulting product unrecognisable as a slasher film. As Moine argues, genre is 'a communication pact . . . an interpretive contract' between creator and consumer, offering 'a familiar structure that is identifiable because of its play of conventions' (2008, 88). Minimal adherence to conventions and subgeneric expectations is required so that deviations or innovations are recognisable as such. Second, this chapter's case studies underscore that although subgenres are identifiable via their conventions, alignment with a subgenre does not intrinsically result in 'a thoroughly predictable string of stock situations and images' generated by filmmakers who 'slavishly cop[y]' ingrained conventions (Buscombe 2012, 23). Subgeneric conventions 'furnish the audience with a context for the interpretation of the film', meaning they are not simply constraints: 'genre both opens and shuts various possibilities for appropriation and comprehension' (Moine 2008, 88). One key difference between the postmodern slasher and the metamodern slasher is that the former tightly 'shuts possibilities for appropriation and comprehension', and the latter does more to open those possibilities.

Third, this chapter's case studies both foreground convention, meaning they are more akin to postmodern slashers than many of the other examples covered in this book. That kinship illustrates that the metamodern slasher is an organic development within the subgenre, building on preceding phases. The importance of that progression is stressed by comparison to Schatz's four-stage model of generic development, which consists of

> an experimental stage, during which its conventions are isolated and established, a classic stage, in which the conventions reach their 'equilibrium' and are mutually understood by artist and audience, an age of refinement, during which certain formal and stylistic details embellish the form, and finally a baroque (or 'mannerist' or 'self-reflexive') stage, when the form and its embellishments are accented to the point where they themselves become the 'substance' or 'content' of the work. (1981, 37–38)

Up to and including the postmodern phase, the slasher neatly conforms to this model. However, rather than burning out and requiring a new form to take its place (as per Schatz), the metamodern slasher illustrates a potential fifth stage that combines the preceding modes. The metamodern slasher both experiments and embellishes, while retaining and verifying core conventions and normative structures in order to elucidate those renovations. As this chapter's case studies exemplify, the combination of experimentation and reaffirmation can be overtly highlighted, but self-awareness need not necessarily lapse into paralysing, insular self-consciousness.

Schatz's model suggests that conventions become stable in the 'refinement' stage and are then foregrounded in the 'self-reflexive' stage; as Neale remarks, 'each and every genre film is "predetermined" by convention' for Schatz, who perceives genres as 'closed and continuous rather than open and intermittent systems' (2000, 199). The potential 'fifth' stage offered by metamodern slashers reintroduces some degree of precarity to Schatz's model. Fixed conventions provide a stable context for creation and interpretation, and so modifying conventions necessarily causes some instability. More concretely, *Scream*'s gambit is to point out that subgenre conventions are artificial, but also to prove that those conventions work because they are expected facets of the narrative context. This chapter's examples question the fixity of those conventions. In *Behind the Mask*, the shifts between 'cinematic' and 'behind the scenes' registers produce a gap between rumination on and articulation of convention, introducing the possibility of disjuncture between the two. Even though it is the standard mode via which we would normally encounter subgenre conventions, *Behind the Mask*'s stylised 'cinematic' sequences come across as artificial compared with the 'behind the scenes' sequences. That is because the latter's verité aesthetic implies unfiltered immediacy, and the rationalisations have an explanatory force that the 'cinematic' sequences lack. Both sets of sequences concentrate on the same conventions but convey different information about those conventions, thereby indicating that there is no one fixed view on a convention, or one stable interpretation of the convention's meaning. The 'behind the scenes' sequences volunteer fresh perspectives on core conventions, and the explanations raise doubts over their presumed fixity. Yet, the 'real' story – the revelation that Taylor is Leslie's actual (and conventional) target – is revealed when the film abandons the verité mode altogether, entering into a conventional 'cinematic' register. That move signals that the film is primarily concerned with that conventional mode and the expectations that follow from it. *You Might Be the Killer* generates the same precarity by undercutting subgenre expert Chuck's convention-based explanations of the narrative events. Chuck's guidance assumes conventions are fixed and stable, but the opposite is illustrated by Sam's inability to apply her advice, and the undermining of killer and Final Girl types that ensue. *You Might Be the Killer*'s various perspectives – including Sam's polyvalent position as protagonist, antagonist and witness – further attests to the potential for mutability.

Therefore, these films prove that the subgenre's conventions were not fixed in the subgenre's mid-1980s 'refinement' stage. The slippages described above flag that conventions continue to develop and, in turn, so does the subgenre. New perspectives on subgenre conventions continue to be advanced by filmmakers, and those articulations have the potential to enrich the subgenre, particularly by adjusting audience understandings of and expectations that follow from conventions. This is noteworthy because, as these metamodern films disclose, meaning-making is collaborative. The subgenre is amended according to changing audience expectations, while transformations within the subgenre also modify audience expectations. However, openly discussing conventions is not the only way to make such changes. The next two chapters will address two other methods of playing with convention, thereby adjusting audience expectations: subtraction and augmentation.

CHAPTER 5

Subtraction

Chapter 5 develops on the premises delimited in Chapter 4: of re-envisaging conventionality as an opportunity for development, not a trap that dooms filmmakers to repeat. Chapter 4's case studies were films in which subgeneric conventions are candidly discussed within the script. Such evaluation remains implicit in this chapter's case studies, being based on shared knowledge of the subgenre's conventions. This is not a novel gambit. Postmodern slashers also draw on assumed knowledge by including intertextual references – such as dialogic references to other extant slasher films – that are accessible to viewers who have sufficient subgeneric acumen. Metamodern slashers build on that preceding trend but take a different approach. As with other comparisons between metamodern and postmodern slashers outlined thus far, the distinctions are related to tone and purpose. As I will go on to detail, postmodern slashers' intertextual references separate slasher fans from casual viewers who lack the subgeneric knowledge required to catch the in-joke. That is, postmodern slashers' intertextual references contain an extra layer of meaning that is accessible only to those who have the requisite subcultural capital, excluding those who lack that detailed knowledge.

The metamodern slashers under consideration here take an inclusive stance, moving away from the particularities of intertextual references that exclude or divide audiences according to subcultural capital, and instead recalling conventional shapes and structural norms that do not require detailed knowledge of the subgenre. Thanks to *Scream* (1996)'s success with a crossover audience (see Hills 2005, 193; Leeder 2018, 154; West 2019, 48), broad knowledge about the subgenre has been anchored in the cultural imagination. Although Grant (2007, 21) and Moine (2008, 103) both associate detailed genre knowledge with increased ability to engage with and appreciate modifications to standard formulae, the adjustment of conventions we find in metamodern slasher films is accessible to anyone with even a rudimentary understanding of the slasher film. Nonetheless, because the commentary is implicit (rather than being explicitly flagged via dialogue, for instance), viewers are required to remain attentive, taking an active viewing stance in order to perceive the film's contemplation on and remodelling of subgeneric norms; that is, viewers collaborate with metamodern slasher films to kindle insight.

Here, the cogitation on subgeneric conventions manifests by renewing core, normative structural elements, and those alterations afford new perspectives on what the slasher film can do. More specifically, the films deliberated in this chapter are innovative because the filmmakers judiciously subtract or compress seemingly essential conventional elements. This is not to say that these films remove all conventional elements. Indeed, if that were the case, the resultant film would no longer be recognisable as a slasher film. The subtle adjustments administered in these films are thrown into relief by the retention and co-presence of standard conventional elements.

Subtraction is an unorthodox strategy because innovation is synonymous with addition. As Adams et al. observe, 'people systematically default to searching for additive transformations' and routinely 'overlook or undervalue subtraction as a way to improve objects, ideas or situations' (2021, 258). The concepts of enhancement, innovation and progress are associated with adding new elements, not removing (see Meyvis and Yoon 2021). Concepts such as growth, accumulation, creation, invention, progress and evolution have become inextricable from the idea of innovation (see Adolf, Mast and Stehr 2013, 28). Subtraction is an antonym for innovation in this discursive context. To illustrate, in his description of how innovation happens, Hitcher (2006, 86) submits that 'a method or approach . . . provides exponential growth until the method exhausts its potential', at which point it becomes defunct, and innovation is needed. Still, rather than acknowledging that the previous 'method or approach' must be removed or rescinded, Hitcher instead skips straight to the addition of a new element: a 'paradigm shift' that 'enables exponential growth to continue'. Major monographs (see Berkun 2007; Godin 2017; Jacobs 2014) and edited collections about innovation (see Adam and Westlund 2013; Pratt and Jeffcut 2009), abound with 'addition'-based discussion, while words (and derivations thereof) such as 'delete', 'remove', 'edit', 'strip' (back/out) or 'subtract' are not used. Consequently, when metamodern films innovate by removing or compressing conventional elements, they grant new vantage points on the slasher film, but they also amount to an unusual perspective on innovation itself.

In the context of subgenre filmmaking, the risk of removing core conventional elements is high because audiences rely on those structural elements. According to Beasley and Brook, 'film genres by definition offer familiar narrative stories and stock characters, enabling audiences to view them with reasonably predictable expectations' (2019, 29; see also Carmona 2017, 9; Cutting 2016, 17). Frow goes as far as to suggest that 'generic structure . . . is a basic condition for meaning to take place' (2006, 10), and Pagel proposes that film viewing both 'requires audience familiarity with the technical procedures utilised in narration, genre', and trains 'viewers to expect that a film will include accepted film-making conventions' (2014, 185). Filmmakers do not merely subvert conventions: conventions are adjusted to destabilise audience expectations, which are fostered through 'training'. From this perspective, audiences are envisaged as collaborating with filmmakers to generate meaning.

This chapter's first section will evince the metamodern slasher's approach to innovation. The section will begin by outlining the postmodern slasher's deployment of unexplained, particularised intertextual references. As I will demonstrate, this ploy is symptomatic of the phase's closed insularity, and connotes that innovation is not possible. This postmodern iteration will highlight the metamodern slasher's contrasting route into implementing subgenre knowledge, which is inclusive, collaborative and, most significantly, points towards the possibility of subgeneric innovation. Three illustrative case studies will then be examined to evince how metamodern slashers innovate using subtraction and compression. *I Didn't Come Here to Die* (2010) exemplifies a substantial subtractive disruption, taking a standard 'teens camping in the woods' setup and entirely removing the slasher from its equation. The teens are still expunged one-by-one, but here they die because of their own recklessness or selfishness. I will contend that this tack raises and interrogates a critical complaint that the subgenre's victims 'deserve' to die. *Murder Loves Killers Too* (2009) applies compression by amending the conventional slasher narrative's standard pacing structure: aside from the lead protagonist, all the teens are dispatched within the film's opening half-hour. That adjustment leaves the audience without an expected formula to lean on for the film's remaining runtime. That context means even conventional events come across as surprising because they occur outside of the subgenre's typical narrative structure. *KillerKiller* (2007) retains the slasher's formula of individuals being picked off within a defined location but replaces the subgenre's expected protagonists (conventional teens) with a group of killers. The group are eliminated by the film's Final Girl-cum-slasher; a supernatural entity who stands in for the killers' previous victims. *KillerKiller* eschews the dynamic that usually dominates a slasher film's runtime – an individual slasher stalking a victim-pool – replacing it with a reversal of the usual climactic moment in which the Final Girl confronts and dispatches the antagonist.

By removing or compressing conventional elements, these metamodern slasher films acknowledge that even if only by subtly adjusting conventional situations and character types, it is possible to generate new perspectives and surprises within the subgenre.

Leveraging Subgenre Knowledge: From Postmodern Exclusion and Unoriginality to Metamodern Engagement and Innovation

Postmodern slasher films commonly appeal to viewers' subgenre knowledge by including a litany of intertextual references. That trend is epitomised, for example, by the many references included in *Halloween H20: 20 Years Later* (1998) (see Petridis 2014, 18). Such referencing ostensibly signals the author's familiarity with subgenre 'classics' and the debt the author owes to those influences. As Crane has it, these films trade 'on "insider knowledge", a fan's familiarity with the rules of the game' (2004, 148). It is not just that these references are 'addressed to a specific segment of the audience: fans' (Nelson 2015, 83), but that filmmaker and fan belong to an in-group based on shared subgenre knowledge. As proposed in Chapter 1, this manoeuvre encourages fans to distinguish themselves from non-fans because they have a different kind of access to the material on offer. Such a response is intimated by Schneider's comment that *Scream 2* (1997) contains numerous 'horror references for fans of the genre to grin knowingly about' (2000, 83). Here, 'grin knowingly' implies that there is smug glee to be found in having access to knowledge that the non-fan is excluded from. Indeed, fans who recognise the filmmakers' textual allusions might perform access to insider knowledge via laughter, treating the references as 'in-jokes', even though such allusions are rarely set up as jokes: they are usually just verbal, audio or visual cues that acknowledge the existence of other films, but which do not have any substantial bearing on the narrative events. These references are frequently limited to 'name-checks' alone. In contrast to Currie's description of 'postmodern fiction' displaying a 'deep involvement with its own past' and being in 'constant dialogue with its own conventions' (2013, 1), the postmodern slasher's intertextual allusions recall the past at a surface level, but do not critically explore or yield substantial meaning from those connections.

This take on intertextuality is influenced by the postmodern position that 'the world cannot be known outside of mediated structures', and so the world 'possesses no intrinsic, unmediated essence' (Syder 2002, 86; see also Rust 2014, 552). This 'lack of faith in the viability of any messages' arguably results in 'vapid . . . half-heartedness' (Booker 2007, xiv;

see also Holland 2013, 1). In this view, intertextual references are hollow because there is nothing outside or beneath the chain of mediated representations such references point towards. This explains why postmodern slashers contain so many intertextual references, despite how little work those references do for the narratives. As Prince observes, 'the explanations they supply' are often 'trivial' (2013, 66). If the main insight such allusions impart is that the fictional text is a work of fiction among many others, the technique seems quite vacuous. Presumably, most viewers are already aware of that fact.

A more charitable interpretation is that postmodern texts foreground or transparently flag intertextual allusions to 'breakdown' the boundary between the fictional diegetic world and the offscreen reality in which the referent texts exist. Yet, as I indicated in Chapter 3, that strategy is limited in its disruptive efficacy. A further possible implication is that originality is impossible: every text is the product of preceding influences, and the self-conscious inclusion of pre-existing elements within a text highlights that the work is neither unique nor original (see Jameson 1991, 16; Toth 2010, 22). In this view, postmodern slashers would be akin to what Scholes sees as a problematic 'fiction of forms', in that they contain within them the notion that the subgenre 'repeats the forms bequeathed it, satisfying an audience that wants this familiarity' even though those 'derivative' articulations signal the form's 'atrophy and decay' (2013, 25). There is certainly some truth to the ideas that works of art are influenced by their predecessors, and that established codes and conventions shape both the ways fiction is constructed and received. However, the postmodern outlook on this state is coloured by fatalistic pessimism: intertextual allusions imply that innovation is impossible because creators are doomed to repeat extant ideas.

Metamodern texts take a divergent stance on the same scenario. Metamodern films acknowledge that even if only by recombining elements and illuminating conventions in unexpected ways, innovation is possible. These possibilities pull metamodern slasher films away from the cynicism that characterises postmodern equivalents. Even if there were no way to escape chains of representations, every additional representation contributes to the chain, appending a new point of influence that could inspire others. In the postmodern context, intertextual references constitute the discourse; as Hutcheon observes, 'ironic quotation, pastiche, appropriation, or intertextuality – is usually considered central to postmodernism' (Hutcheon 2002, 93; see also Currie 2011, 3). The metamodern outlook instead conceives of intertextuality as dialogue, a contribution to ongoing discourse.

Metamodern slashers typically avoid the postmodern ouroboros by leaning away from direct references or allusions to other individual texts. Even where this occurs, the inclusion is usually part of a focus on the subgenre's norms. To illustrate, *You Might Be the Killer* (2018) includes direct references to slasher films such as *Halloween* (1978), *Friday the 13th* (1980) and *Sleepaway Camp* (1983), mentioning the titles of these films, the names of their killers or quoting lines of dialogue. For example, Chuck drinks from a mug bearing the line 'we all go a little mad sometimes' from proto-slasher *Psycho* (1960). The camera pans up from a closeup of the mug on its first appearance so that the slogan is readily legible. At first glance, the mug's inclusion echoes the shallow intertextual referencing deployed in postmodern slasher films.[1] However, in *You Might Be the Killer*, these references are limited to one character: Chuck. As such, the references serve two distinct functions. First, they help to define Chuck's character. Given that Chuck is only shown inhabiting the comic bookstore where she works, and that kind of film-related paraphernalia is sold in such stores, the mug acts as shorthand to establish the location and Chuck's typing as a comic-book enthusiast. Second, the references form part of a larger critique. As I have argued, Chuck's detailed subgenre knowledge is insufficient to help Sam when he has to navigate the subgenre's conventions in his own life. In other words, Chuck's supposed expertise is undercut because it is ineffectual; it does not reveal anything meaningful about the (subgeneric) situation at hand.

More commonly, metamodern slashers engage with the subgenre's structural norms rather than making direct references to specific texts. Metamodern slasher films work from the principle that most viewers will already be familiar with the slasher's general tropes, structures, conventions and normative subgeneric situations, and that familiarity will be sufficient to allow viewers to understand deviations from expected norms as innovations. The revision to how intertextual references are employed is shaped by the surrounding media context that situates metamodern filmmaking. *Scream*'s intertextuality is part of a wider cultural movement characterised by, for instance, Quentin Tarantino's pastiches and homages to the cinematic past. During the mid-to-late 1990s, it became something of a convention within popular culture to include allusions to prior cultural touchstones. By the 2010s, mainstream

---

[1] This particular reference might also allude to *Psycho* to set up Sam's situation: like *Psycho*'s Norman Bates, Sam is (initially) unaware that he is the film's killer. That said, the reference seems unnecessarily oblique if the aim is to make that comparison, especially given that *You Might Be the Killer*'s title is blunter about Sam's dual status.

audiences had become accustomed to the presence and implied meanings of intertextual allusions. In other words, allusions are no longer the province of specialist fans but are part of blockbuster outputs such as Marvel's 'cinematic universe' movies. Furthermore, the Internet also allows non-fans to more readily and easily decode allusions that they would otherwise remain oblivious to without the fan's knowledgeability (or the effort implied by attaining such knowledge).

As the previous chapter outlined, instead of just pointing out generic traits as an endpoint, metamodern slasher films expand on or develop from subgeneric conventions, even if only by recombining anticipated elements in unusual ways. While such modifications are often surprising, they are inclusive, guiding the audience (not just knowledgeable fans) at the level of narrative. Although it is assumed that viewers will be familiar with the subgenre's structural norms, metamodern texts avoid excluding the non-fan from apprehending the film's innovations.[2] The metamodern approach can be elucidated by comparison to meme culture. Memes induce humour by expressing a current sociocultural or political event or attitude, usually by juxtaposing images and text. The meme is then adapted by other creators based on a foundational template, using the same image with different text or altering the image to create new meanings. Images become memes via this process of distribution and variation. One may find a single instance of the meme to be funny without encountering any other variations. Even if one encounters multiple variations, each generates humour in its own right. Memes do not customarily rely on prior knowledge of another variation, because memes are distributed in inconsistent, unpredictable ways (depending on, for example, how the meme is shared among social media users). Regardless, one may find additional layers of humour based on one's prior encounters with variations on a meme; for instance, one might find a variation in the imagery itself funny because of one's familiarity with that image across multiple memes. An individual encountering the image for the first time would not share in that secondary form of amusement, but that would not exclude them from enjoying the meme's primary generation of humour in any one instance. Additionally, researching the history of a meme's development (via, for example, knowyourmeme.com) would not intrinsically make a particular instance of a meme funny in the secondary way. Humour is generated experientially by encountering the variations

---

[2] Arguably, if a viewer is not familiar enough with subgeneric norms to understand why the adaptation is significant, that viewer would consider even the mere playing out of conventions to be innovative.

themselves. The analogy to metamodern slashers is thus: one can enjoy a metamodern slasher film in its own right because of its innovations, even if one is not aware of the specific, preceding influences that led to the present iteration. Enjoyment might be amplified by awareness of other comparable variations, but primary enjoyment of any one instance is not contingent on such knowledge.

This ethos is enacted in *Behind the Mask: The Rise of Leslie Vernon* (2006). The opening documentary footage refers to Jason Voorhees, Freddy Krueger and the events of *Friday the 13th* and *A Nightmare on Elm Street* (1984) as being real within *Behind the Mask*'s fictional world. Footage portrays the actual shooting locations used in these films as sites of genuine homicide. Kane Hodder (the actor who played Jason in the seventh through to the tenth *Friday the 13th* films) is briefly seen entering 1428 Elm Street, a central location that reappears throughout the *Elm Street* series. This mixing of the two horror properties is made only in passing in *Behind the Mask*: as with postmodern slashers, the detail is an in-joke for subgenre fans to notice. However, this level of direct intertextual referencing is mainly confined to *Behind the Mask*'s opening minutes, gesturing that it chiefly serves an establishing function. In the narrative sense, these nods to *Friday the 13th* and *A Nightmare on Elm Street* build the fictional world Leslie operates in. Nonetheless, it would not be necessary to employ the authentic shooting locations to convey that idea, so something more is connoted in this opening. Being on the cusp between the postmodern and metamodern slasher, *Behind the Mask* begins self-consciously, assuring fans that its subsequent unpicking of conventions is delivered in good faith rather than aiming to mock the subgenre or to suggest that *Behind the Mask* is superior to its predecessors. Notably, that same meaning is conveyed to non-fans by positioning Leslie as an aspiring slasher who seeks to join a pantheon of recognised killers. Retired slasher and Leslie's mentor Eugene dismisses nameless 'hacks' and 'one hit wonders' (those slashers who 'get killed or arrested'), but he acknowledges that 'Jay, Fred and Mike' are 'legends' who 'lifted [slashing] to a whole other level . . . changed the whole business' of slashing. These three long-running franchises are prominent, canonical slasher properties and were reasonably 'current' in 2006 when *Behind the Mask* was released. Therefore, it is reasonable to suppose that most viewers would be familiar with these filmic villains, even if they had not engaged with the original films. No detailed knowledge of these figures or the films is required to access *Behind the Mask*. In fact, one could still readily access the narrative meaning without understanding that 'Jay, Fred and Mike' are characters from other extant films. In context, Eugene explains that they are famous slashers. As opposed to ruminating on individual texts, *Behind the Mask* principally attends to the subgenre and its norms, and beyond the opening minutes, its full meanings are accessible to all viewers. Indeed, as noted in Chapter 4, Leslie explains even the broadest of conventions as if it is normal not to know about them.

Postmodern slasher films can also be enjoyed by those unfamiliar with the slasher subgenre, but those individuals are broadly excluded from enjoying oblique intertextual references to specific texts (or at least those that are not explained directly), and the deployment of such references is much more prominent and sustained than it is in metamodern slashers.[3] Reflection on subgeneric norms commonly operates separately to (or 'above') the postmodern film's narrative, having little or no bearing on the character's situations, generating a separate set of pleasures. In the metamodern slasher, deliberation about subgeneric norms is intertwined with the narrative, yielding concurrent pleasures. Metamodern slashers simultaneously evoke and adjust conventional situations, tropes and character types to yield fresh vantage points on the subgenre. Instead of being fatally limiting, the subgenre's norms afford opportunities for innovation here. Key to this innovation is the use of structure to renovate the subgenre's expected operational norms. The following subtractive case studies will illustrate that modus operandi.

No Killer, No Cry?: Subtracting the Slasher in *I Didn't Come Here to Die*

In *I Didn't Come Here to Die*, teens die one-by-one while out camping in the woods. This traditional slasher setup was founded in the subgenre's 1980s boom-period via films such as *Friday the 13th*, *The Burning* (1981), *Madman* (1981) and *Sleepaway Camp*. Here however, the conventional narrative circumstance is troubled by *I Didn't Come Here to Die*'s key

---

[3] Hills claims that *Scream* mainly works 'without alienating non-fan, genre audiences who can still participate in the ride' (2005, 192). To illustrate, Randy essentially lectures the audience on relevant subgenre tropes so that all viewers can access some of the main jokes about conventions. However, many of the in-jokes are limited to simply name-checking films without any further explanation. Others are also reliant on detailed sub-textual knowledge. For example, *Scream*'s director Wes Craven has a fleeting cameo as a janitor named Fred who wears a distinctive red and green striped sweater, but his presence is not explained to the crossover audience, nor is the overt similarity to Craven's most famous horror creation, Freddy Krueger. Especially pre-Internet, one required reasonably detailed knowledge of the subgenre to recognise Craven and so to access that aspect of the in-joke.

innovation: subtracting the slasher. Prior to any of the deaths, the narrative delineates its kinship with the slasher film. The film's opening sequence offers a flashforward to the very end of the story: the local Sheriff finds the vicinity littered with corpses, then a bloodied, eyeless figure appears to pursue him through the woods. The implication that a slasher inhabits the area is seemingly confirmed early in the narrative. Sat around a campfire, Sophia unveils the location's backstory to the other teens: a girl was murdered in the area, and her wealthy family donated the land so that a 'summer camp . . . for underprivileged youth' could be built there. One of the teens (Julie) jokes that 'maybe she roams these very woods seeking revenge'. The campfire story and the conventional plot situation connote that the eyeless figure seen in the film's opening is a slasher, and that she massacred the protagonists. As the narrative plays out, it is revealed that the eyeless figure is one of the teens (Miranda), who is blinded by walking into branches on two separate occasions. This reveal is only confirmed in the film's final shot when Miranda loses her remaining eye just before encountering the Sheriff. Consequently, Miranda screams at him because she is terrified and in pain. Without that narrative explanation and with only the subgenre context as an index, the opening implies that the eyeless figure instead pursues him with malicious intent.

Miranda's misfortune is representative of the film's method: there is no need for a slasher here because the teens injure and exterminate themselves or one another. Early in the film, Miranda loses her (first) eye, and while the volunteer-group leader Sophia drives Miranda to hospital, Julie messes around with a chainsaw, thrusting it through the air as she pretends to fight off zombies. Despite a warning from her peer Steve, she refuses to wear protective headgear, and so when the chainsaw slips, it lodges into her face. Steve attempts to aid her by dislodging the chainsaw but instead manages to split her head in two, inadvertently ensuring that she does not survive the incident. Racked with guilt, Steve hangs himself. Chris then confesses that he is volunteering as part of his court mandated 'community service', and fears that the situation seems so unbelievable that it will appear as if he murdered the others. He decides to cover up the incident, but Sophia returns as Chris is burying Julie's body. When she attempts to call the police, Chris slays her in desperation. He then pursues fellow volunteer Danny (the only surviving witness), who dispatches Chris in self-defence. Danny is then accidentally run over and killed by Miranda who, only having one eye, lacks the depth perception required to drive safely. Miranda then discovers the other bodies, panics, turns to flee and impales her remaining eye on a branch.

The idea of a slasherless slasher film might seem absurd since the slasher ought to be a necessary facet of the subgenre. However, *I Didn't Come Here to Die* remains recognisable as a slasher text, and the removal of the slasher demonstrates that the subgenre's normative framework is so robust that it can survive even after subtracting that central figure: violence and bloodshed ensue regardless.[4] Moreover, this core subtraction flags that the film is playing with the expected structure, thereby priming viewers to notice other ways the film disrupts associated subgeneric norms. For instance, the summer camp slasher's murderous campaign is usually triggered by a traumatic event that previously occurred at the camp: in *Friday the 13th* for example, Jason's mother holds neglectful camp counsellors responsible for her son's (ostensible) death by drowning, leading her to target subsequent camp counsellors. *I Didn't Come Here to Die* takes a further step back. Here, the teens are building a summer camp from scratch, and so the camp has no such traumatic history. It is implied that the events of *I Didn't Come Here to Die* will become the stuff of campfire legend: that once the camp is built, counsellors will tell the story of teens dying and an eyeless figure roaming the woods, seeking revenge. The rationalisation of how Miranda lost her eyes is destined to be replaced by myth. That implication manifests in the film's opening where, because the incident is decontextualised, Miranda seemed to be the film's slasher. Yet, in contrast to the blunt, personalised trigger events of films such as *Friday the 13th*, the area is also revealed to be a site of prior violence (a murder), which is translated into a campfire legend. *I Didn't Come Here to Die* thereby implies that such locations may have even deeper histories as sites of death and bloodshed that are erased from (or at least neglected by) conventional summer camp slasher films.

I Didn't Come Here to Die's rumination on conventional summer camp slashers is not only based on its structure and location, however: it is also evident in the film's approach to characterisation and causes of death. Once the killer is subtracted, the teens (who are usually victims) fill that narrative void, coming to slay themselves or each other. This alteration allows *I Didn't Come Here to Die* to interrogate the prevalent critical notion that

---

[4] *Bodies Bodies Bodies* (2022) employs a similar approach. It is concerned with teens in a remote location who play a game of 'murder in the dark'. After one of the party is seemingly violently slaughtered, they assume they have a genuine murderer in their midst and so turn on each other. Eventually it is revealed that the first death was an accidental suicide. The ludic setup draws on the postmodern whodunit's paranoia, but the film is not unambiguously aligned with the slasher subgenre. *I Didn't Come Here to Die*'s overt evocations of slasher norms highlights its subgeneric innovation.

slasher teens are selfish, 'never learn', and are 'too stupid to live' (Whitehead 2003, 7–9), or are 'so unlikable that you don't empathize with them' (Muir 2007b, 441), meaning 'we're supposed to think they deserve' to die (Muir 2007b, 652). This complaint seems to emerge out of the slasher's normative structure, insofar as a cast of characters are introduced and then die as the narrative ensues. This pattern seems to lead some critics to divest from the teens, perceiving them as just fodder, as victims-to-be, and linking anticipation of their destinies to postulations about the filmmaker's intentions (suggesting that these characters are insufficiently fleshed out so that viewers are encouraged to divest). For instance, Di Muzio sweepingly proclaims that 'writers and producers of horror films . . . often work dislikeable [sic] characters into the script, so that the audience can cheer the killer on as he pursues and murders them' (2006, 287). Rather than merely gainsaying these associations by presenting cooperative, virtuous teens, *I Didn't Come Here to Die*'s revised context literalises and rationalises the teens' self-orientation, and then problematises the supposed connection between self-orientation and the teens' fates.

The film's teens volunteer to help build the camp, and Sophia reminds them (and the viewer) that 'helping others' is the credo of the volunteer corps: 'none of you should be here for the benefit of yourself'. When she subsequently asks why they signed up, their answers are decidedly self-motivated: for Steve it is 'a cool way to travel and meet some people'; Miranda thinks 'having a national service experience . . . on my resume will look really great'; Chris states that he 'came here to get laid . . . easy poon, free food'; Julie remarks that 'it just seemed better than staying another year at home, I guess'; Danny speaks of 'not really knowing what to do' after his close friend drowned. The teens thus seemingly conform to the type sketched by critics such as Whitehead and Muir, inasmuch as they are focused on personal, experiential benefits to themselves. Although they are volunteers, none of the teens prioritise helping others.

Still, their versions of self-orientation differ from the critical norm in important ways. It is not simply that the teens are obnoxious and therefore deserve to die. As with other metamodern slasher films, *I Didn't Come Here to Die* is sincerely invested in the protagonists, meaning the events arise out of characterisation and character motivation, not because they are types who behave in stock ways. As the film's title submits, the characters are not just 'victims-to-be', present only to be executed. Instead of purely condemning the teens, the film mainly presents them as lacking foresight or underestimating the negative consequences of their actions. For example, Miranda is ambitious and overly keen. She talks of how useful the experience will be '*when* [she] come[s] back next year as a team leader' (emphasis added). That impetus explains why she rushes back to the camp despite her optical injury. She accidentally causes Danny's death because she wants to protect her self-image as someone eager to fulfil a designated role (here, as future volunteer leader). The accident is caused by her inability to calculate the consequences that might follow from her behaviour. The same is true of the other characters, who do not act out of malice or absolute disregard for others. Steve's motive for joining the group might be self-oriented (being about his experiences), but his desire to 'meet people' speaks to his interest in others. He may lack foresight when he powers up the chainsaw to dislodge it from Julie's face, but he subsequently internalises responsibility for her death to the extent that he commits suicide. Julie is irresponsible because she is fixated on the present, paying insufficient attention to the future.[5] Her motive for joining the group is based in her boredom at home, but she does not sufficiently assess the work involved in volunteering and so complains about the effort required. For instance, when told the group will need to carry their gear to their campsite on foot, she whines 'please, no', slumping her shoulders forward and stroppily shuffling back down the track. She implores Chris to 'bus[t] out . . . booze tonight' despite his warning, 'Are you kidding? We've got to work tomorrow.' Her prioritisation of immediate pleasure results in a hangover, meaning her head 'hurts too much' to wear protective headgear. She then plays around with her chainsaw, failing to account for the dangers of doing so, as is symptomatic of her desires to avoid the immediate displeasure of expending effort and to quell boredom by seeking amusement. Whether Julie deserves to suffer or die because of her irresponsibility is another matter, but any assumed connection between her attitude and her demise is upended by Steve's intervention. Her irresponsibility causes a self-inflicted severe facial wound (see Figure 5.1). Had she survived, that grave injury might have transformed her outlook. Regardless, she dies because of Steve's attempt to help her. Disconnecting her behaviour from her demise disrupts the conventional stance that the victims 'deserve' their fates merely because they are annoying.

Another disconnection is evident when comparing the only characters who intentionally extinguish another person in the film: Chris and Danny. As 'types', Danny is the narrative's closest approximation to a hero, while Chris is more akin to an antagonist. Danny kills Chris in self-defence, and presumably most would accept that motivation as sufficient to justify his

---

[5] Insofar as it results from her insufficient attention to the future, Julie's attitude is redolent of postmodernism presentism (which will be explored in Chapter 7). As such, her death can be read as hypostatising the futility of that postmodern viewpoint.

Figure 5.1 Julie pays a high price for her lack of foresight in *I Didn't Come Here to Die* (2010)

actions.[6] However, Chris too is motivated by self-preservation. Realising that he is unlikely to be believed because he has a criminal record, and panicking because of the situation's apparent implausibility, he acts rashly in his bid to resolve the circumstances. Chris's response indicates that the characters are unmoored by the situation: the conditions imply a killer is present, and Chris is compelled to fill that void. Furthermore, just as Chris endeavours to bury the bodies out of fear that the police will find them, Danny bundles the bodies into the camper van and flees the scene. When he is pulled over by the local Sheriff, he contemplates assassinating the officer (pointing a gun at the cop when his back is turned) in order to cover his tracks. That Danny's behaviours echo Chris's so closely should give the viewer pause in condemning one but not the other, casting doubt over their approximations to conventionally opposed narrative types.

Although the two are as close as the film comes to providing a hero and a villain, both are intrinsically flawed, and their motives (rooted in their characters and the situation) are sufficient to comprehend their behaviours. That emphasis on characterisation matters because it helps *I Didn't Come Here to Die* to avoid insinuating that the characters are principally motivated by their status as conventional stock archetypes. Just as the Final Girl might be expected to be cautious, insightful and resourceful by proxy of her position as lead protagonist, one might expect other teens to be

---

[6] On justifications for killing in self-defence, see Leverick (2006) and Steinhoff (2017).

reckless, unaware and inept by distinction. Indeed, postmodern slashers amplified that distinction by juxtaposing lead protagonists with knowledgeable but overconfident (even arrogant) teens who behave recklessly despite their supposed nous.[7] *I Didn't Come Here to Die* instead fleshes out the protagonists by giving them psychologically realistic motivations. They respond to the immediate pressures of the moment in understandable ways, at least given their (very human) flaws. This combination of investment in character and serious disruption to the stock narrative situation – subtracting the slasher – allows *I Didn't Come Here to Die* to interrogate and revise expectations that surround the subgenre.

Structural Compression in *Murder Loves Killers Too*

Subtraction does not necessarily just mean removing entire figures from stock situations. Another reduction-based tactic is compression. As with other metamodern techniques, here we see metamodern slashers building on (as opposed to gainsaying) the concerns that informed their postmodern-influenced predecessors, while the distinction between metamodern and postmodern is evident in approach and tone. From the postmodern perspective, one initiating cause of wider 'crisis' or 'collapse' is the intense compression of space and time caused by globalisation (see Bertens 1995, 218; Francese 1997, 3; Malpas 2005, 1; Smethurst 2000, 87–88). This understanding of compression as producing 'volatility', 'annihilation' (Harvey 1989, 286 and 293), upheaval and uncertainty, is undermined by the filmic medium. Spatiotemporal compression is one of cinema's essential facets (see Cutting 2016, 16; Dudai 2008, 30). Framing entails selecting focal points within a space, and editing involves eliminating moments that do not contribute to the film's narrative or thematic development. Contrary to the postmodern characterisation of spatiotemporal compression as disorienting, metamodern film naturalises compression, given that it is intrinsic to how film communicates.

Nevertheless, that naturalisation means film's compression frequently goes unnoticed: indeed, the intention is for the compression to remain 'invisible' in much mainstream fiction filmmaking because the purpose is to convey the narrative rather than to distract from it (see Bordwell and Staiger 2005, 3; Fairservice 2001, 300; Gallese and Guerra 2020, 92).

---

[7] For example, following *Urban Legend* (1998)'s opening murder, Paul alerts '3,500 students' to the possibility of a 'lunatic on campus' via his front-page newspaper story. Despite that warning, the film's teens do not seem well prepared for or vigilant about imminent danger.

Accordingly, we might not notice the ways filmmakers routinely shape narratives by applying compression. For example, Cutting (2016) observes that discussions of narrative structure ordinarily orient around plot blocks – dividing the film into acts – paying little heed to how pacing operates within these acts. Cutting argues that changes in pacing between and within acts are normalised for audiences, because such fluctuations are repeated across a range of prominent films. Those repeated patterns shape viewers' expectations, forming the status quo against which deviations in pacing are assessed. Consequently, filmmakers can push against expected structural norms by adjusting pace.

In the case of *Murder Loves Killers Too*, compression is utilised to disrupt the slasher film's standardised pacing, thereby reinvigorating a highly conventional situation: five teens vacation in a woodland cabin and are eradicated one-by-one. A standard slasher narrative is punctuated by regular slayings that are spread out across the first three acts, with the final act (the climax) being reserved for the Final Girl's confrontation with the slasher. Since the potential victim-pool consists of only five teens, it would be reasonable to anticipate that *Murder Loves Killers Too*'s murders would be spread quite far apart during the first hour of the runtime, ensuring that peaks of tension – stalking and/or murder sequences – are distributed so as to sustain the viewer's attention. However, one teen (Lindy) is abducted almost immediately. An unbroken three-minute shot follows the teens from the moment they set foot in the cabin, moving with them as they explore its layout, ending with Lindy being grabbed by the film's killer (Stevie). Given that the sustained take is the first interior shot of the cabin, it solidifies the impression that the group has only just arrived. Two minutes later, Lindy's boyfriend (Kyle) is abducted too. By the thirty-minute mark, all the teens bar Aggie (the Final Girl) have been slain.

It is evident that *Murder Loves Killers Too* condenses diegetic time during this opening half-hour. While Kyle and Lindy are butchered by Stevie, the other teens drink and play pool. Their entire day (until nightfall) is conveyed in three minutes of screentime. Time is evidently compressed during this sequence, but the compression is made most obvious via a jump cut: Tamra drinks too much and passes out fully clothed, then suddenly she is seen in the same position in just her underwear, indicating that her boyfriend (Bryan) has removed her clothes as she slept. Instead of spending time with the teens to space out the slaughter, that conventional aspect of the slasher film structure is subtracted.

This compression is striking because it undercuts the norms repeated across preceding slasher movies, which shape audience expectations. We are left with a direct confrontation between killer and Final Girl that would typically occupy around fifteen minutes of a slasher film's runtime rather than nearly two-thirds of its duration (as it does in *Murder Loves Killers Too*). Once the victim-pool (bar Aggie) has been wiped out, the pace slows dramatically. For instance, ten per cent of the film's runtime is expended in a single room as Aggie hides from Stevie. That sequence is part of a longer section (one quarter of the film) that has no dialogue, making the pace feel even slower. During this section, and in direct contrast to the three-minute compression of an entire day of drinking and fun, Aggie spends an excruciating three minutes of screentime trying to retrieve a key from the other side of a locked door using a wire hanger. This acute deceleration underscores just how compressed the first act was, illuminating the film's unusual structure. Without the conventional structure to rely on, the viewer's expectations are unmoored: it is difficult to anticipate what exactly might happen and when. The torpid pace affords space to meditate on the significance of structure and the relationship between pace and expectation.

The film invites such contemplation by priming the viewer. The film's opening moments are its most unusual, headlining its subtractive methods in several ways. The first shot (post-credits) is of a road running through a wooded area. A caption reading 'some years ago' materialises, followed by a blue jeep full of teens driving at speed along the road, with one hanging out of the passenger side, whooping as they traverse the shot. The shot lingers uninterrupted, and a new caption indicates that we have jumped forward in time to 'now', and a different group of teens – this time in a blue car, but still with one of their party hanging out the passenger side, whooping – drive along the same stretch of road. The latter are our protagonists. The former teens are not seen or referred to again in the movie. The shot carries three implications. First, the similarities between the anonymous teens from 'some years ago' and our protagonists – both groups driving along the same road in a blue vehicle, with one hanging out the window whooping – signal kinship, connoting that our protagonists will follow an entrenched (conventional) pattern. Second, the juxtaposition of the two teen groups suggests that the teens from 'years ago' have some bearing on the present action, even though they are not referred to again. Third, there is a gesture towards the kind of lore contained in numerous woodland slashers, such as the fireside song and tale in *Madman*'s first scene (which outlines the film's plot), or the dream sequence and fireside tale that recap salient aspects of the series' ongoing plot (both for the protagonists and the viewers) in *Friday the 13th Part 2*'s (1981) opening act. In *Murder Loves Killers Too*, the fleeting presence of teens from 'some years ago' sets up an expectation of lore.

When that backstory is not volunteered in the film, its absence is conspicuous. This oddity is unsettling and may even cause some viewers to wonder if they have missed a prequel film: it is feasible that *Murder Loves Killers Too* could be a titular riff that stands in for *Murder Loves Killers Two*. That is not in fact the case, but the opening's unusual juxtaposition of teen groups instructs viewers to weigh the relations between the past ('some years ago') and present ('now'),[8] as well as the relationship between our protagonists and the conventional types that usually occupy slasher films. It also hints at the film's compression-based strategy: the fleeting glance of teens enjoying themselves in a rural area is sufficient to understand their fate. Given the subgeneric context, the juxtaposition intimates that the members of the prior group were murdered, and our protagonists will also be massacred. The teens from 'some years ago' are a condensed symbol that stands in for an absent story, and their fate is relayed solely by the subgenre context. Consequently, their presence flags that the film intends to play with the context and the expectations that context generates.

It is not only the abrupt juxtaposition of 'some years ago' and 'now' that prepares viewers to anticipate that *Murder Loves Killers Too* will challenge convention. The sequence is the only one in the film accompanied by a narrator's voiceover, in which the narrator imparts such musings as,

> the friends lived in such a way as to defy boredom, refusing all proposals of responsibility and swimming upon the high tide of youth . . . they were poised to enjoy their summer escape, free of care, at the idyllic mountainside retreat . . . and, no doubt, they would have, had they not all been brutally murdered, one by one.

Although the narration is apt inasmuch as it describes events one would anticipate in a slasher film (and indeed, the core plot of *Murder Loves Killers Too*), because the narration is interrupted by the two groups traversing the shot, it is not clear to whom the narrator refers: one of the two teen-groups we see, both groups, or teens in general. The narration's tone is anachronistic to the film's contemporary setting. So, the voiceover also implies that tales of exuberant teens naïvely wandering into peril are as old as the narration style, older than the slasher subgenre. The voiceover is also conspicuous in its incongruity, being too literary for the subgeneric context. This point of entry elucidates that *Murder Loves Killers Too* intends to play with convention, even though the intended meanings of this situation remain ambiguous.

---

[8] Past-present relations will be explored in detail in Chapter 7.

This playfulness is stressed across the film's first act via other unusual formal choices. For example, when Tamra is executed, the shot of her being stabbed in the abdomen and then the mouth is presented from the knife's point-of-view. This unusual perspective is more than a moment of idiosyncratic visual flair because, as outlined in Chapter 2, the point-of-view shot is a distinct part of the slasher's language that conventionally connotes killers stalking unwitting victims (see Dika 1990, 19–20; Hutchings 2004, 195; Jancovich 1992, 106). Presenting the knife's point-of-view during the attack on Tamra at once literalises the threat that is usually implied by point-of-view shots (signalling the killer's presence) and also reduces the killer to their instrument. This choice underlines that where point-of-view shots imply the killer's presence, the killer is absent (is not depicted onscreen).[9] The relationship between the killer's role and this conventional shot-type is made strange by the unusual implementation here.

This setup cashes out in the second act, when Stevie stalks Aggie. Beginning in the same room where Tamra died, Aggie hides from Stevie as he prowls the area. Point-of-view shots are employed, but here they are assigned to Aggie, not Stevie. Point-of-view shots are again used when Aggie subsequently hides in a locked room, spying on Stevie through a keyhole (see Figure 5.2). This reversal of the conventional setup – in which the killer would usually stalk the Final Girl from a

Figure 5.2 Aggie spies on Stevie through a keyhole in *Murder Loves Killers Too* (2009)

---

[9] That absence can be used to trick the viewer; on this, see Jones (2013, 76).

distance without her knowledge – is imparted by Aggie brandishing a knife during the latter sequence. Ergo, Aggie occupies a formal position usually reserved for the killer.

The reversal is further consolidated by the insights that adjusted perspective provides. As with *Behind the Mask* and *You Might Be the Killer*, the unorthodox perspective reveals behaviours that are usually occluded by the slasher film's standard structure. Killers are only usually portrayed stalking and murdering in the slasher film, whereas teens are frequently depicted engaging in banal activities (such as dancing, drinking and swimming).[10] *Murder Loves Killers Too* undercuts that norm: through the keyhole, Aggie watches Stevie eating ice cream and blowing his nose. By compressing the victim slayings into the first act, the protracted 'killer versus Final Girl' remainder includes details about the killer's behaviours that are usually subtracted from the slasher narrative. Elsewhere, Stevie nonchalantly tidies up the cabin after the teens. His flat demeanour in these sequences highlights that he also has the same dispassionate affect during the murder sequences. Stevie remains in his bathrobe as he impassively drills into and stabs Kyle, for instance. Without the compression of the homicides and the consequent perspective substitution, Stevie's unemotional disposition during the kills would be reminiscent of, for example, Michael Myers's mechanical blankness in the *Halloween* series (see Bernard 2020, 15). The adjusted perspective on Stevie's behaviour leads to a different implication: it seems like he is 'going through the motions', that murder is as much of a tedious chore as tidying the cabin is, or that murdering the teens is a form of 'cleaning'.

These deviations ultimately pay off in the final scene. Having captured and strangled Aggie (ostensibly eradicating her), Stevie ensconces her body in his car's trunk, and returns home to his wife and daughter. His humdrum life continues the next morning when he leaves for work, at which point Aggie springs out of the trunk and bludgeons Stevie, ripping out his tongue and forcing him to choke to death on it. While this incident is conventional insofar as the Final Girl defeats the killer here, Aggie once again occupies a position conventionally reserved for the

---

[10] These mundane activities are important to the slasher's standard narrative structure. First, they highlight that the kills are (by comparison) peaks of narrative excitement. Second, these activities indicate that the teens are just living their normal lives and do not anticipate eruptions of extraordinary violence. Critics might suggest the teens are unobservant and so deserve to die, but that complaint does not adequately account for what the situation looks like from the characters' perspectives.

killer: she jumps up apparently back from the dead for one final surprise scare.[11] This positional slippage elucidates that the Final Girl is also a killer, not least since the mode of killing (ripping out Stevie's tongue) extends beyond a level of force strictly necessary for self-defence, and into the terrain of gory overkill that is more usually associated with slasher killers.

Murder Loves Killers Too begins from a highly conventional setup, compresses the expected structure into the first act, then implements perspectival shifts to fill the remaining time. In doing so, it plays with conventions, calling into question the Final Girl's role, in particular. It is worth revisiting the title in this light: *Killers* gestures that the film is concerned with more than one murderer. The film certainly contains two people who commit homicide – Stevie and Aggie – but one would not normally refer to the Final Girl as a killer because Final Girls usually act in self-defence. Nevertheless, *Murder Loves Killers Too*'s playful manner hints towards the possibility that Aggie's excessive violence – especially ripping out Stevie's tongue – is primarily (perhaps only) legitimised by her narrative position as Final Girl. Although such films do not reinvent the slasher narrative, they supply fresh perspectives, demonstrating that tired narrative setups can still yield surprises.

'Every-Victim', Every Slasher: *KillerKiller*

KillerKiller offers a combination of the subtraction-compression techniques exemplified by the preceding case studies. The film begins again with a standard slasher plot setup, being based in a defined location (here, a prison facility) in which the protagonists are eliminated in succession by a homicidal supernatural entity. Rather than subtracting the slasher as *I Didn't Come Here to Die* does, the usual innocent teen victim-pool is removed. *KillerKiller*'s protagonists are instead all murderers who are imprisoned together in a high-security facility. Indeed, each protagonist is the kind of killer who could be an antagonist in a conventional slasher film. Prior to their imprisonment, each targeted a stereotypical slasher victim group: campers, sex workers, cheerleaders, students and so forth.

---

[11] The surprise return of the killer (seemingly from the dead) became a convention within the slasher subgenre following *Friday the 13th*: the series spawned from Jason's surprise appearance in the original's denouement (which emulated *Carrie* [1976]'s final jump scare). The subgeneric convention is explicitly flagged in the *Scream* series, beginning with Randy's warning that 'the supposedly dead killer' will come 'back to life for one last scare' at the end of the first film.

The narrative's homicidal supernatural entity visits each prisoner in visions, dressed as their preferred victim-type. The entity is played by one actor (Danielle Laws), and three implications follow from that choice. First, having one actor play all members of the conventional victim-pool underlines the absence of an expected group of teens. In the wake of that subtraction, a disanalogous group – the imprisoned killers – fills that structural void. Second, having one actor play each teen victim draws attention to the superficial stereotypical outfits that signal these types. From the prisoners' perspectives, that is precisely how they perceived their former victims: purely as undifferentiated 'types', as opposed to individuals. Third then, Laws's 'every-victim' also recalls the reputed homogeneity of supposedly 'interchangeable' victims that populate the subgenre (on the latter, see Rafter 2006, 89; Russo 1992, 39). The entity is a compression of both the film's expected teen victim-pool and the subgenre's victim types.

The typing at hand is undercut by reversing the slasher's normative position: in each vision, the prisoner attempts to vanquish the entity as if she is a typical victim, but she instead slaughters them. When she does, they spontaneously die in the prison. The film's title might initially strike one as referring to the multiple killers in the prison (*Killer[,]Killer*), but it actually refers to the entity (*Killer[of]Killer[s]*). Amplifying the questions *Murder Loves Killers Too* raises over Aggie, *KillerKiller* spotlights that the Final Girl is also a killer, not just a victim. Here, the entity is the film's slasher, but she simultaneously stands in for the Final Girl, given that she confronts and kills the prisoners (who are slasher 'types'). *KillerKiller* thus compresses what would usually be a series of 'killer versus Final Girl' climaxes from across a series or across the subgenre into a single film. Here too, the title *KillerKiller* is pertinent, evoking sequenced repetition (*Killer[.]Killer*). In sum, the entity is a complex compression of multiple character positions that are core subgeneric ingredients: she represents the subgenre's usual victim-pool, she is the film's slasher and the film's Final Girl.

Yet, *KillerKiller* is equally playful with the conventional notion of the Final Girl as an innocent protagonist who outlasts her peers. Out of the victim-pool, one prisoner – Rosebrook – is ostensibly the closest equivalent to a Final Girl. It is eventually revealed that Rosebrook summons the entity 'so that those who have taken lives will be punished'. Rosebrook is assured of his own safety ('she's not going to come for me') since he believes that he was imprisoned after being 'wrongly accused' of murder. However, the declaration that he is 'innocent' is undercut in the film's final moments when Rosebrook realises he is suffering from alcohol-fuelled amnesia and is also in fact a murderer.[12] Therefore, he too is dispatched by the entity. Regardless of his past, however, Rosebrook would still be a killer. Rosebrook indicates he is incapable of murder, but he is responsible for his fellow prisoners' deaths: he summons the entity with the sole intention of causing fatalities. Rosebrook positions himself as a 'Final Boy', but the clash between his proclaimed innocence and the deaths he incites underscores that murder is usually a prerequisite for surviving the slasher film.[13] As with the previous examples, the narrative's rumination on subgenre norms is elucidated by its core subtraction-compression.

KillerKiller's playfulness is also evident in its narrative situation. The plot proper begins when the prisoners wake up to find their cell doors are open, the guards are missing and the building is in a state of decay. Rosebrook flags that the situation is abnormal (given that we have not seen the prison previously), asserting that 'this place looks ill. It didn't look like this last night.' The unnatural aspect of their situation is anchored by the presence of an impenetrable freezing mist around the prison. One prisoner (Perry) describes it as a mist that 'bites', and Lawrence's failed attempt to traverse the mist proves that they are trapped. This situation leads Lawrence to theorise that their situation might not be as literal as it seems: he wonders 'What if we're dead and in limbo?', noting that this is the explanation for similar events in 'so many movies and so many books'. His hypothesis anticipates that *KillerKiller*'s viewer might reach the same conclusion. Postmodern slasher films prepared viewers for second-guessing how slasher narratives would unfold. This anticipation of plot twists is part of the ludic tack that became synonymous with the subgenre's postmodern phase. However, Lawrence's proposal is not an ironic wink to its viewers, but is instead raised to close off that possibility: Lawrence admits that his theory 'sounds stupid', and Rosebrook confirms that the 'theory is bollocks'. This pattern repeats throughout this film: clichéd narrative turns are anticipated so that they can be dismissed. Instead of reifying overplayed conventions, *KillerKiller* raises explanations, then rejects them. The film thereby motions towards sincerity, even when playing with subgenre norms. The objective is not to trick viewers.

---

[12] This eleventh-hour reveal is distinguished from the postmodern slasher's 'gotcha' twists via its epistemic alignment with Rosebrook. The twist is based on information that is withheld from both Rosebrook and the viewer until the film's closing moments. In this regard, Rosebrook occupies an ambiguous position akin to Tara's in *Shrooms* (2007), Jess's in *Triangle* (2009) or Sam's in *You Might Be the Killer*.

[13] This was not one of Randy's 'rules' for surviving a horror movie in *Scream*.

Indeed, *KillerKiller* is upfront about the intention to modify norms. The first materialisation of the film's homicidal supernatural entity occurs before the prison location is introduced. A babysitter is stalked through a house by a masked killer. As he raises his knife to strike, the victim-to-be spins to look at the killer coldly, the naturalised aesthetic sharply snaps to harsh, high-contrast lighting and she suddenly hacks back with two knives of her own.[14] Her victory is signalled when she licks blood from one blade. During the opening, no context is volunteered for who the babysitter might be. When Laws emerges again as a different 'victim' type who dispatches Harris, it substantiates her status as the film's supernatural slasher. Lawrence only comes to understand what the entity is thirty minutes after her status has been exposed to the audience. *KillerKiller* plays with conventions then, but it does not do so to trick the viewer. *KillerKiller*'s playfulness relies on viewers' prior knowledge of the subgenre to illuminate the fresh perspectives afforded by its adjustment of conventions.

Loss Aversion, Forward Momentum

This chapter's case studies each offer fresh perspectives and reflections on the slasher's norms by removing and/or compressing subgeneric elements, thereby evincing that it is possible to innovate within the subgenre. This strategy is even riskier than remodelling conventions. As Chapter 4 made clear, viewers draw on subgeneric conventions as orientation points. Filmmakers equally rely on subgeneric norms. As Grindon argues, genre conventions 'allow filmmakers to build narratives around patterns that have satisfied audiences in the past' (2005, 200). Removing core elements might not only result in a failure to satisfy audiences, however. Compressing or subtracting normative components that designate subgeneric affiliation potentially jeopardises a viewer's ability to appropriately contextualise a film and so decipher its innovations. That is, viewers need to recognise a film's subgeneric affiliation in order to comprehend its deviations from the norm.

Of importance here is the phenomenon of reference dependence: once a state has been discursively established as the status quo, that state is

---

[14] The short film *Slasher Squad* (2022) uses a similar scenario, in which a slasher stalks a young woman as she showers, before revealing that the situation is contrived to trap the killer. *Jason Goes to Hell: The Final Friday* (1993) is a precursor to both, but in that case the young woman is interrupted before entering the shower and then flees her cabin, leading Jason to a clearing where her fellow armed federal agents execute Jason.

taken as a baseline against which the outcomes of revision are assessed (see Kleinberg, Kleinberg and Oren 2021).[15] This phenomenon is pertinent in the present context of subtraction and innovation. As Eidelman and Crandall observe, 'because the status quo operates as a reference point from which change is considered, the costs of change carry more weight than potential benefits', and consequently decision makers tend to be loss averse (2012, 271; see also Moshinsky and Bar-Hillel 2010). The combination of reference dependence and loss aversion amplifies the perceived risks of remodelling proven ideas and components, so it is unsurprising that for many filmmakers and distributors, maintaining the status quo seems far preferable to removing ingrained subgeneric elements. Indeed, some have proffered that this inclination towards perpetuating the status quo is the prevailing norm among horror filmmakers. For instance, Fortuna (2018, 124) indicates that 'American horror film producers and directors do not [need to] search for new ideas' because 'scary movies seem to be lucrative and prolific nonetheless'. This pessimistic view suggests there is little impetus to take risks in the name of innovation.[16] Postmodern slasher filmmakers – especially those mimicking *Scream*'s success – seemed to double down on that pessimism. By self-consciously reiterating more than expressly modifying conventional setups, postmodern slashers submit to the notion that the subgenre is repetitious and plagued by unoriginality. This manoeuvre confirmed a baseline founded by critics; Fortuna goes on to proclaim that 'in many popular articles about contemporary American horror, the lack of fabular originality is presented as the biggest problem of these films' (2018, 125).

Filmmakers need not perceive conventions and structures as traps that prevent innovation. This chapter's case studies reframe the 'problem' as

---

[15] This phenomenon also explains the persistence of negative critical assessments about (for example) the relationship between sex and violence in the slasher, despite empirical evidence to the contrary (see Cowan and O'Brien 1990, 187; Ménard, Weaver and Cabrera 2019, 634–5; Sapolsky, Molitor and Luque 2003): the discourse can act as the baseline, regardless of its empirical veracity.

[16] One might protest that Fortuna's pessimistic view does not adequately account for a seemingly pervasive desire for novelty. However, in their overview of innovation research, Pratt and Jeffcut (2009, 266) aver that novelty is 'a much-derided version of innovation', implying that it should be considered a separate concept. Moreover, Eidelman and Crandall note that novelty is limited by reference dependence and loss aversion, because 'the pursuit of novelty often occurs in the context of what is familiar, established and comforting', meaning 'updated' forms are sought over 'entirely new' forms (2012, 277). This balance of familiar and novel is also illustrated by the popularity of sequels, remakes and reboots (see Chapter 8), and the development of new slashers based on previous icons (see Chapter 9).

a challenge, and experiment by subtracting one or more of those limiting factors, thereby freeing up space to innovate and to evaluate the subgeneric status quo. Contrary to the reputation Fortuna refers to, the subtractive mode befits the slasher, because it is naturalised by the subgenre's modus operandi. First, as Stewart avers, 'manipulation of narrativity' is particularly vital to horror, where 'narrative sequencing' is necessary for building tension, for example (1982, 33–4). Thus, the manipulations of narrative structures exhibited by this chapter's case studies extend from horror storytelling's intrinsic preoccupations. Second, the emphases on subtraction and compression illustrated by these case studies are naturalised by the slasher's core narrative operations. In slasher films, a victim-pool is introduced, and then individuals are removed from that group as the story progresses. This trajectory can be viewed as a kind of distillation or refinement, eliminating those who cannot withstand the killer, driving the narrative towards the climax in which the Final Girl defeats the killer. In this light, the slasher's narrative design is to subtract in order to progress the plot, and in that sense the movement towards the climax (in which the killer is defeated) is forward motion. This might sound counterintuitive because death carries negative connotations. In fact, the latter is perhaps the main reason some critics disparage the subgenre. For instance, Di Muzio insists that slasher films are immoral because they are 'devoted primarily or solely to representing violence and death' (2006, 281), and others vilify this narrative strategy, characterising these horror films as 'celebrating' death (Freeland 2000, 243; Weaver 1991, 385). Loss aversion again helps to make sense of these criticisms: after all, death is the ultimate form of loss. Belshaw (2021, 81–2) captures this idea in his 'deprivation account': life is presumed to be intrinsically good, and so death is equated with subtracting goodness from the world. Ergo, one might reasonably posit that awareness of mortality is a strong candidate for explaining the pervasiveness of loss aversion and the negative associations surrounding subtraction.

My aim is not to defend the centralisation of death in slasher films per se, but to point out that by using death to progress plot, the subgenre's conventional narrative structure complicates the idea that subtraction is incompatible with forward momentum. The observation that slasher narratives are based on a series of deaths helps to elucidate why subtraction is naturalised as a path to innovation in this context, even though subtraction is not commonly perceived as a conduit for innovation. As we have seen via this chapter's case studies, it is possible to wield subtraction to deliver fresh perspectives on the subgenre's operations, including raising questions over the status of the Final Girl as a killer (not just a hero). The forward motion resulting from subtraction is not just confined to narrative progress within a particular film then, but also applies to the subgenre's forward momentum. Subtraction is only one strategy among many however, and this chapter should not be taken as claiming that metamodern filmmakers ignore the possibilities afforded by addition and augmentation when innovating within the subgenre. Indeed, that approach is the subject of the next chapter.

CHAPTER 6

Hypercoding

Chapters 4 and 5 dissected different approaches to subgeneric conventions within the metamodern slasher film; namely, openly reflecting on or subtracting core conventional elements, thereby highlighting the subgenre's operations and how expectations are shaped by conventions. In both cases, new insights are offered, flagging that conventions do not prohibit subgeneric innovation. In contrast to the subtractive mode, some metamodern filmmakers instead augment, using a technique I call 'hypercoding'.[1] Before I explain the 'hyper-' aspect, I will first clarify what I mean by 'coding'. Here, 'coding' refers to the subgenre's standardised means of enciphering narrative events. The coding provides a context that calibrates audience expectations and allows viewers to decode the content appropriately. The coding acclimatises events – such as a seemingly indefatigable masked assailant regularly slaughtering teens – that would be startling in another generic context (such as romantic comedy). I have already observed that the cumulative presence of character archetypes, conventional events, stock locations (such as summer camps), an expected narrative structure (and so forth) indicate a text's alignment with a subgenre. The subgeneric context is crucial because, as Walton posits, the ability to identify which 'category' a work belongs to allows recipients to perceive when the work evokes norms, when variations on norms are offered, and when a norm is being opposed (1970, 356–7). For Walton, categories (such as subgenres) also enable consumers to recognise (or accurately decode) a work's 'aesthetic properties' (1970, 363). Although I have addressed conventions in the previous two chapters, I have not yet contemplated aesthetics or 'style'. These too are vital aspects of the subgenre's coding, enciphering narrative events in relation to expected responses; for example, informing viewers whether the

---

[1] Since I regularly refer to postmodernism in this book, it is worth clarifying that the term 'hypercoding' is unrelated to Nealon's 'overcoding' (2012, 22), which is expressly tied into a Jamesonian socioeconomic stance.

events are meant to be interpreted as serious or funny. Aesthetic coding customarily naturalises events by corroborating a film's adherence to a subgeneric context, and the expectations that follow from that contextualisation. The metamodern films under scrutiny in this chapter take a different route, overtly exaggerating the subgenre's normative aesthetic or stylistic codes.[2] This is what I refer to as 'hypercoding'.

Here, 'hyper-' is intended to capture two aspects of the technique as it is employed in these metamodern slasher films. First, hypercoded films include a surplus of aesthetic information, at least in comparison to the subgenre's norms. 'Hyper' suggests stylistic amplification, such that the film's formal properties are constantly accentuated across the text. Second, that stylistic abundance shifts the subgenre's expected coding parameters, cultivating a new context. In this regard, 'hyper' denotes expansion, in the sense that the augmentation of style stimulates new possibilities within the subgenre. Whereas subgeneric coding usually conveys information about how to decipher a text, hypercoding revises the cipher itself, because: (1) normative codes are exaggerated to the extent that they are ineffective in their usual naturalising function; (2) the standard subgeneric cipher fails to decode the hypercoded text; and/or (3) too many code cues are delivered – the text is flooded with stylistic information – hindering one's usual decipherment strategies.

Hypercoding is not the result of like-minded filmmakers intentionally working towards a shared goal. In the context of the slasher subgenre at least, hypercoding seems to be the product of an organic drift away from the postmodern slasher's prevailing sensibilities. This claim requires some clarification since hypercoded texts might sound reminiscent of the postmodern slasher's metafictional gambits, insofar as they foreground formal structures and are ostensibly disruptive (see Chapter 3). The postmodern slasher is double-coded (as opposed to hypercoded). Postmodern double-coding manifests in several ways. For instance, as Chapter 4 evidenced, postmodern slasher characters often express that the subgenre's conventions are predictable (even passé), but the films simultaneously deliver those same conventions in standard ways, confirming how effective those conventions are. The postmodern slasher's governing ironic tone facilitates this double-coding: ironic communication is duplicitous in that two divergent meanings are conveyed simultaneously.

---

[2] Stylistic augmentation is distinct from just amplifying narrative elements. Hanich proposes that 'horror is easily intensified' (2010, 84) via narrative adjustment: 'by strong character allegiance, along with exceptional immorality and brutality' (2010, 158), for example.

The postmodern slasher's messages regarding the efficacy of subgeneric conventions, the pleasures arising from engaging with the subgenre, and the subgenre's future are all double-coded because of its pervasive irony. Ultimately, that double-coding comes across as ambivalence because of the overarching noncommittal, apathetic, fatalistic outlook that informs the postmodern slasher.

In contradistinction, hypercoding is informed by the metamodern slasher's sincerity and inclusivity. First, aesthetic amplification is foregrounded and is immediately apparent; it is a dominant mode, rather than being contained in discrete sequences as per the postmodern slasher's 'pullback-reveal' scenes (see Chapter 3). Second, the hypercoded slasher's stylistic amplifications are combined with exaggerated narrative content. These films contain absurd events and actions that are incongruous with the subgenre's norms. Third, even though the events are absurd, these films maintain the metamodern slasher's characteristic investment and alignment with characters (see Chapter 2). Hypercoding disrupts realism from the viewer's perspective, yet the characters behave as if the diegetic world is coherent. Absurdism permeates the narrative world and the characterisation in equal measure. Aesthetic flourishes and exaggerated performances convey valuable information about the characters' world that explains their motivations (and thus their heightened emotions, attitudes and behaviours). Together, exaggerated aesthetics, absurd narrative events and amplified characters form a cohesive style.

Although hypercoding might sound as if it will undermine the naturalising effect of subgeneric contextualisation, the purpose of that contextualisation is to set audience expectations, offering viewers an appropriate framework for deciphering the content. In the hypercoded slasher, that end is achieved through stylistic consistency and its harmonisation with narrative events and characterisation. The narrative unpredictability created by hypercoding remains grounded because the approach is consistently deployed in an unconcealed way in these films. Even when presenting surprises, viewers are always 'in' on the joke, and subgeneric incongruities are naturalised by the new hypercoded context.

Again, these metamodern slashers build on and away from procedures that typify postmodern slashers. As Chapter 3 posited, postmodern slashers are predominantly realist, but often implement interruptive metafictional techniques to denaturalise realism. By revealing that the fiction is a construct, postmodern slashers illuminate a relationship between the diegetic storyworld and the offscreen world (the viewer's own reality). Hypercoded metamodern slasher films instead proceed from two background principles. First, in fiction, what is realistic is naturalised by the subgeneric context (see Liao 2016, 2), and that context is established via the text's coding. Second, viewers already understand that fiction films are constructed,[3] and that knowledge does not prevent viewers from readily investing in fiction. Hypercoded metamodern slasher filmmakers lay bare how absurd it is that viewers routinely invest in fiction despite knowing it is contrived. Hypercoding invites rumination on that situation by offering patently unrealistic characters and situations, stressing the contrivance via stylistic amplification. Simultaneously, the viewer-film interaction is harmonised with the hypercoded slasher film's pervasive stylistics, characterisation and narrative events: all are perspicuously exaggerated, and that amplification yields further pleasures.

Below, two case study examples will illustrate ways hypercoding materialises in the metamodern slasher. In previous chapters, I have proposed that metamodern slashers validate idiosyncratic perspectives, emphasise inclusivity and ratify the productive potentials of variance. Here, the hypercoded case studies celebrate heterogeneous abundance via their stylistic amplifications. That abundance is employed to highlight new perspectives on the subgenre's norms. *Detention* (2011) and *Dude Bro Party Massacre III* (2015) both adopt abundant heterogeneity via playful exaggeration of formal elements and overt, heightened stylisation, combined with absurd narrative events. In both films, slasher filmmaking's normative codes are amplified and embellished in an acute fashion. The resultant incongruous, unexpected clashes might seem ridiculous at first glance, but they convey sincere deliberations on the subgenre.

Amped-Up '80s: Pleasurable Absurdism in *Dude Bro Party Massacre III*

An example will more clearly demonstrate how hypercoding works. The plot of *Dude Bro Party Massacre III* (hereafter, *Dude Bro*) broadly follows a conventional slasher film outline. *Dude Bro* opens with a montage recap

---

[3] Indeed, it seems reasonable to presume that such knowledge is a prerequisite for many viewers who derive pleasure from slasher films. Numerous bloody murders are depicted in any given slasher film, and the subgeneric context provides functions and meanings to those killings. Homicide has vastly different meanings outside of the fictional context, being likely to elicit distress and disturbance. I would hope the latter was obvious, but as I observed at the end of Chapter 5, some critics conflate the two.

of the two (non-existent) preceding movies in the series,[4] narrated by surviving protagonist Brock. Brock is then murdered before the film's title card. Focus transfers to his twin brother Brent, who seeks to uncover and avenge his sibling's death by joining Brock's fraternity. The action takes place in conventional slasher locations: initially on the college campus, then the remote cabin where the fraternity spend spring break. There, the film's killer (Motherface) eliminates the protagonists.

Within this framework, the filmmakers deliver what they describe as 'a satirical twist on the gory and sexually charged 1980s slasher'.[5] That 'twist' emerges via multiple bizarre plot turns. For example, the film's subplot follows police Officer Sminkle, who is instructed by his Chief to track down the Dude Bros, and 'bop them on the nose' to 'turn them back into their actual forms . . . bags of oranges'. Unbeknownst to Sminkle, the Chief's ruse is to sacrifice 'that idiot virgin Sminkle' in a satanic ritual, so that Motherface will have 'the power to defeat' the fraternity. In the denouement, Sminkle's partner (Officer Buttiker) confesses that she is in fact a stack of oranges. Until this point, she is shown as a human, but in this sequence's flashbacks, she is replaced by a person-sized stack of oranges instead. Here, another pair of officers look on in disdain declaring, 'look, he's talking to that bag of oranges again', confirming that the narrative perspective previously shared Sminkle's delusion. When he bops Buttiker on the nose, she transforms into oranges, and oranges rain from the sky across the city.

Although outlandish, this subplot is nevertheless rooted in slasher conventions, and unpicking that connection will elucidate *Dude Bro*'s take on hypercoding. A lack of dependable adult authority figures is a slasher trope (see Dika 1990, 138; Muir 2007a, 24–25; Rockoff 2002, 11–12), and the 'bumbling cop' is a conventional type epitomising that absence. The unreliability of law enforcers plays out in earlier slasher films in unusual ways. For example, in the climaxes of both *Edge of the Axe* (1988) and *Death Screams* (1982), a Sheriff arrives to 'save the day' by shooting who they believe to be the killer, even though neither law officer has sufficient

---

[4] Although the film is named as if it is a sequel, there are no preceding films in the series. The same approach has been employed by subsequent films such as *Camp Death III in 2D* (2018) and *Deathblood 4: Revenge of the Killer Nano-Robotic Blood Virus* (2019). These titles operate as jokes about the proliferation of horror sequels in the 1980s. In *Dude Bro*, those connotations are anchored by the narrative's 1980s setting. Several slasher films made during the 1980s utilised the same joke, including *Return to Horror High* (1987) and (more overtly) *Unmasked Part 25* (1988).

[5] Stated on the film's official website (http://www.dudebropartymassacre3.com/).

information about the circumstances to make an accurate adjudication of guilt. In *Edge of the Axe*, Sheriff McIntosh arrives on the scene and hastily culls Gerald (assuming he has correctly identified the killer), leaving the actual killer (Lillian) alive. In *Death Screams*, Sheriff Avery blunders around trying to find a missing person and accidentally discovers a corpse in a garage. Later, he somehow happens upon the woodland location where the killer is eliminating victims, sees an individual – Marshall, who happens to be the killer – fall out of a window, and then simply shoots the man in the face five times. Avery executes someone who has committed crimes, but Avery has no unambiguous proof connecting Marshall to the corpse he previously discovered, no awareness of the subsequent slaughter, and no reason to consider that (the now seriously injured) Marshall poses any continued threat. The town Sheriff is just as dangerous as the film's killer, then. Such portrayals inspire little confidence in the police. Yet *Death Screams* naturalises Avery's version of 'upholding the law' by conflating the viewer's understanding of events with the Sheriff's: the killer's identity is confirmed for us, so we might not immediately notice that Avery is not privy to that same information.

Elsewhere in the subgenre, police ineptitude is unmistakably flagged. *Scream* (1996)'s Dewey is born of the 'bumbling cop' trope, leading to incidents such as responding to Sidney's 911 call, and inadvertently frightening Sidney as she tries to escape by appearing at her front door holding a 'Ghostface' mask. When she responds with a startled yelp, Dewey recoils and screams in terror. Dewey is positioned as incompetent and cowardly here, signalling that Sidney is better off defending herself than involving the police.[6] An earlier example even more plainly utilises the trope for comedic effect: in *Halloween 5: The Revenge of Michael Myers* (1989), the officers are heralded with a ridiculous tuba oompah theme, accompanied by assorted extradiegetic silly sound effects. When the officers are sent to stake out a party, they directly admit that they are 'lousy cops', and that confession is accompanied by an extradiegetic whistle and horn honk.

---

[6] These traits were parodied in *Scary Movie* (2000)'s exaggerated version of Dewey (Doofy), who is eventually revealed to be the film's killer. Elsewhere in the period, *Bloody Murder 2: Closing Camp* (2003)'s Sheriff is also the film's killer.

  Lucky (2020) extends this line of thought to all officials – police, paramedics, psychiatrists, social workers – who fail to aid the film's protagonist, May, as she is attacked every day by the same masked killer. Each ignores May's concerns, foisting their own explanatory framework onto the situation instead. Thus, the lead detective is preoccupied with May's husband's absence, repeatedly referring to May's situation as a 'domestic dispute', for example. May is left to fend for herself.

The absurd sound effects evince that the cops amount to comic relief, and so the film itself concords with one officer's complaint that the teens have 'no respect for authority anymore'. *Dude Bro* amplifies that established subgeneric trend via its ultimate 'bumbling cops': a delusional investigating officer and his partner, a mound of fruit. The underlying notion – that authority is to be distrusted – is further underlined via their Chief, who aids the killer and tries to sacrifice Sminkle in a satanic ritual.

The citrus metamorphosis incident might first appear to be incongruous because it seemingly does not belong within the normally realist slasher film context. By definition, incongruities are elements that defy preconceptions about what belongs within a specific context. However, *Dude Bro*'s fruit transformation does belong to the subgeneric context: it is not an unrelated novel interruption, it is a hypercoded exaggeration of a subgeneric attribute. Here, hypercoding subgeneric norms serves a distinct purpose, being the conduit for the film's 'satirical twist'. Rather than foregrounding conventionalities as *Scream* does (see Hills 2005, 190; Leeder 2018, 73; Miller 2014, 110), *Dude Bro*'s absurdism consequently acts as a metacommentary on the relationship between subgeneric conventions, the expectations that follow from that conventionality and audience tolerance for deviation from norms.

Although *Dude Bro*'s absurdist occurrences might be unrealistic, they are not antithetical to the subgenre's normal operations. Multitudinous incongruities are present across the subgenre, such as Freddy's resurrection being catalysed by a dog urinating fire in *A Nightmare on Elm Street 4: The Dream Master* (1988), Jimmy's attempt to impress his beau with eccentric and highly erratic dancing in *Friday the 13th: The Final Chapter* (1984), the inclusion of a song-and-dance number – the Driller Killer lip-synching to John Juke Logan's 'Let's Buzz' as he attacks the cast – in *Slumber Party Massacre II* (1987), or *Pieces* (1982)'s extraneous 'kung-fu professor' sequence, which emulates the high-kick to camera shots made famous by *Way of the Dragon* (1972)'s climactic Coliseum fight. Such odd, unexpected incidents are usually isolated digressions, and the slasher's robust formula ensures that the narrative is not derailed by these occasional ruptures. As part of its hypercoding, *Dude Bro* compiles a banquet of such incidents into one film. Moreover, instead of being notable or memorable because they are discrete disconsonant incidents, these occurrences are fashioned into a coherent whole. *Dude Bro*'s qualitative and quantitative amplification of such incidents within one film not only submits that such discordances are part of the slasher's charm (they are a semi-conventional part of the subgenre), but also that – contrary to complaints that the slasher is repetitive and one-dimensional (see Muir 2007b, 777; Perkins 2012, 89; Petridis 2014, 83) – the subgenre's generic formula is a key strength. *Dude Bro* proves the subgenre is durable and can readily assimilate numerous eccentricities.

Dude Bro's narrative oddities are naturalised by a host of surrounding incongruities and unrealistic amplifications that together form a cohesive style. For instance, when Samantha talks to Brent indoors, her hair (and only hers) blows as if in wind; when Derek inexplicably utters a single line of dialogue in French, it is accompanied by a subtitle that reads 'Help! I'm trapped in a basement and forced to write subtitles!'; when Turbeaux sharply turns his head in Derek's direction, the movement is accompanied by a cartoon 'whoosh' sound; when Brent is intimidated by Turbeaux, his t-shirt is thoroughly soaked with perspiration, and is dry again in the next shot and so forth. These formal interventions pervade the film, including its dialogue and performances. For example, Todd hyperbolically screams 'YOU'VE RUINED MY LIFE' at Samantha, tearing off his t-shirt for emphasis. When Turbeaux mimics the same action later in the film, that inappropriately augmented anguish is marked as even more farcical than Todd's, because Turbeaux is bare-chested at nearly every other point in the film; Turbeaux only dons his vest moments before ripping it off, meaning he only wears the garment so this ludicrous display can occur. This ubiquitous amplification is illustrative of *Dude Bro*'s hypercoding.

Another stylistic device is especially prominent in *Dude Bro*'s aesthetic design. An opening caption presents *Dude Bro*'s overarching conceit: that the only known surviving copy of the film was captured by 'a local teenager who stayed up to record it on his VCR' when it was broadcast 'at 4AM on a public access show ... The Midnight Morning Movie'. *Dude Bro*'s aesthetic is presented accordingly, sporting artefacts associated with VHS recording throughout, such as time base skew error at the bottom of the screen. This conceit is the basis for *Dude Bro*'s most candid formal interjections: the flow of the narrative is regularly interrupted by contrived advertisement breaks.[7] These interruptions are presented as the result of not pausing quickly enough to 'edit out' the adverts while recording, or slipping from 'pause' during a commercial break. Consequently, only disjointed fragments of the adverts remain. For instance, a person screams 'all these BILLS' at the start of one advert, but that immediately blurs into the closing shot of an advert for 'Wallwashers feminine products'. Both the VHS aesthetic and these advert fragments are overt

---

[7] Other films have previously utilised the same technique, including *WNUF Halloween Special* (2013) and *Lake Nowhere* (2014).

stylistic choices that draw attention to the film's formal construction. In particular, the adverts halt the narrative, regularly pointing away from the ongoing slasher tale and towards another story about the video's genesis and the recorder's process.

Rather than being wholly disruptive however, these incidents are in concert with the other forms of hypercoding exhibited by the text. Indeed, the narrative content eventually blurs with the 'incidental' juxtaposed commercials, imparting that both belong to the same framework, and are equally part of the same bounded viewing experience. The final advertisement break concentrates on a contrived programme ostensibly scheduled after *Dude Bro*: a talk show called *KTRP7*. As the hosts outline what is coming up in the programme, *Dude Bro*'s Brett wanders behind them. That is, the borders between *Dude Bro*'s main fictional world and *KTRP7*'s separate fictional world leak into one another. Brett's presence is not acknowledged by the *KTRP7* presenters, implying that the blurring could be the result of VHS ghosting or bleed-through. Brett's presence thereby marries the narrative content, the visual artefacts associated with VHS recordings, and the commercials as another kind of artefact brought about by the recording process.

In contrast to the discrete incongruous moments found in non-hypercoded slasher films then, hypercoding harmonises what might otherwise be considered disruptive elements into a cohesive whole. Although the ad breaks interrupt the narrative flow, they are not especially unsettling given that the film's absurd performances and incidents prevent suspension of disbelief in any case. The film's immersive qualities mainly stem from its hypercoding. *Dude Bro*'s stylisation captures the experience of rewatching a film taped from television onto VHS. The presence of advertisement breaks (or the imperfect editing out of such breaks) is as much a part of that experience as the narrative itself is. Such juxtapositions are unique to the individual recorder's experience of the film since it results from their idiosyncratic use of the pause function. An individual might have fondness for such a VHS-taped copy of a film because the recording bears the unique markers of their interaction, including pauses and even the tape wear that arises from repeat rewatching. The individual who recorded the footage is consequently intimately linked into their own later re-viewing experience. *Dude Bro*'s aesthetic is redolent of this powerful connection between the individual viewer and their idiosyncratic viewing experience.

Dude Bro's mode will therefore be exceptionally meaningful to a demographic who regularly consumed films taped from television onto videocassette. Given that VHS's commercial and technological dominance was in the 1980s, such a demographic is likely to have been alive during the slasher boom-period. Furthermore, it seems likely that the kind of person who rewatched films multiple times and recalls that experience fondly would be a film enthusiast. As a hypercoded slasher film, *Dude Bro* seems to be primarily pitched towards the subgenre's fans. Yet *Dude Bro* does not try to replicate the fan's experience of enjoying a particular slasher film, which would entail making intertextual references to a single property or mimicking distinctive events from individual films (as *Scary Movie* does with *Scream* and *I Know What You Did Last Summer* [1997]). Instead, *Dude Bro* draws on a more expansive experience of the subgenre as a whole: aggregated memories of encountering dozens of slasher films in the aisles of video rental stores or late-night television broadcasts. That cumulative experience is conveyed via the hypercoding. The absurd events and performances are redolent of memorable moments that standout in one's total subgeneric consumption because of their outlandishness, while the amplified aesthetics foreground the process of engaging with and (re)watching VHS recordings per se.

Regardless of whether one was alive during VHS's golden era, *Dude Bro*'s stylisation grants a particular viewing perspective that incorporates pleasures fans derive from the subgenre (including its occasional, seemingly bizarre incongruities). This pitching contextualises *Dude Bro*'s exaggerated humour. In isolation, its exaggerations might sound as if they are spoofing or mocking the subgenre, pointing out how ridiculous and contrived slasher films are. When contextualised by the film's amplified aesthetics however, it is evident that the film laughs with, not at, the subgenre. This leaning is implied by *Dude Bro*'s framing device. The film's opening caption not only explains that the film was recorded from early morning cable, but also proclaims that the film was 'almost lost forever' because 'all known copies were banned and destroyed under an executive order by President Reagan'. Two implications follow. One is that the film is a maligned object, being so abhorrent that the US government mandated its eradication. The technological desuetude of VHS underscores that the film is also obsolete: it has supposedly been forgotten, even by the subgenre's most ardent devotees. Second however, from the fan's perspective – and this is the perspective inculcated by *Dude Bro*'s stylistics – these negative connotations are reversed: obscurity is what makes such a film a prized object for a fan collector. Rather than being culturally worthless detritus, such a film is a lost gem waiting to be rediscovered. *Dude Bro* thereby acknowledges that slashers have been culturally derided, while recognising that fans value these films. *Dude Bro*'s exaggerations volunteer a highly amplified version of the pleasures fans derive from slasher films, and its comedy invites viewers to experience those pleasures through laughter. *Dude Bro*'s manoeuvre of building the fan perspective into the form thus distinguishes it from *Scream*. Where the latter included the fan perspective by representing fans in the narrative (see Leeder 2018, 154; Smith 2007, 84), *Dude Bro* is more invested in experiential replication, using hypercoding to convey ways in which even the slashers' 'worst' elements can be pleasurable (amusing, entertaining). This combination offers a stimulating vantage point on the subgenre.

Any Time Now: *Detention*'s Heterochronic 'Stylish Style'

Detention's hypercoding is multi-layered, and so needs to be unpacked in stages. In contrast to *Dude Bro*'s replication of VHS aesthetics, *Detention* is a hyper-stylised, contemporary affair. *Detention* draws on what Bordwell calls the 'stylish style' that dominates 'American mass-audience films' (2006, 120). Shots are usually bathed in golden light, producing lens flare. The editing is typified by very short shot durations. The camerawork is characterised by dynamic angles and constant flux (zooming in or out, panning, focus pulling). When the camera is static, dynamic movement usually occurs within the shot. For example, a floor-level camera remains stationary as lead protagonist Riley falls to the ground, then the film's slasher also drops into the frame between Riley and the lens. *Detention*'s glossy, kinetic style exemplifies Bordwell's model of 'intensified continuity' (2006, 137–8); a concentrated version of Classical Hollywood's visual language that intensifies the viewer's affective experience.

Being hypercoded, *Detention* amplifies this 'stylish style' by adding a barrage of exaggerated, conspicuous aesthetic variations and stylistic flourishes throughout. For instance, while *You Might Be the Killer* (2018) implements attention-grabbing onscreen captions to tally 'dead counsellors' (see Chapter 4), onscreen motion graphics are employed with even greater regularity and in even more distracting ways throughout *Detention*.[8] To illustrate, when Riley declares 'life sucks' early in the film, her sentiment is confirmed by a computer-generated onscreen caption. Riley looks in the caption's direction with a puzzled expression. In a reverse shot, the caption is still visible in the distance, inverted and out

---

[8] This approach is so deeply infused in the film that the DVD feature 'Cheat Mode: The Unbelievably Mind Melting Making of *Detention*' takes the form of motion graphic captions and screen-in-screen video bubbles – spotlighting behind the scenes photos, audition footage, talking head interviews with cast and crew – superimposed over the film. Any further reference to this 'making of' feature will be cited as 'Cheat Mode', which accompanies the 2012 Region 2 Sony Pictures Home Entertainment DVD release.

of focus compared with Riley's hand in the foreground (see Figure 6.1). Riley does not directly comment on the caption's presence, and it is not entirely clear whether she sees it.[9] Nevertheless, these stylistic choices are accentuated for the viewer. Intertitle captions are also used throughout the first half of the film, and each is a hyperbolic rendering of the characters' situations: for example, one caption refers to Billy's backstory as 'The Lonely Ballad of Billy Nolan'. The presence of such captions is unusual for a slasher film, and their inflated tone is emblematic of hypercoding. However, these captions also begin to elucidate how *Detention*'s hypercoding conveys its metamodern sensibility. Although these title cards are 'melodramatic' and thus comic, director Joesph Kahn explains that they are also 'very, very serious'. Kahn proposes that the title cards

Figure 6.1 Shot and reverse shot indicating that the caption 'life sucks' is present within the diegetic world of *Detention* (2011)

---

[9] Riley sports a disconcerted expression, which might be caused by the sudden presence of the wording, but it might equally be induced by the pasta sauce she discovers under her duvet at that same moment.

capture 'gigantic teenage ways of describing the world' that follow from having emotional experiences 'for the first time' as a teenager, meaning 'they are the most intense feelings you'll ever feel in your life'.[10] This combination of comic exaggeration and sincerely capturing felt experience is exemplary of a metamodern tone. As with other metamodern slasher films, the technique is underpinned by investment in the characters' subjective experiences.

Detention's stylistic exaggerations are not limited to conveying heightened teenage emotions, however. Additional layers of *Detention*'s hypercoding are uncovered when the film's plot is accounted for. When the protagonists are in Saturday detention, one student (Elliot) calculates that their existence is threatened by an explosion that will devastate the school in the past. The protagonists use their science project – a time machine made from the school's taxidermied bear mascot – to travel from their present to 1992, where they discover that the killer is among them: one of the teens (Sander) travelled to the past to goad a student (Verge, who grew up to be their school principal) into destroying the school. The relationship between past (here, always defined as the 1990s) and narrative present (2011) encapsulates the 'heterochrony' or 'intermixing of temporal chronologies' commonly found in metamodern works (Gibbons 2015, 33).

This heterochrony is crucial, since it illuminates multiple implications emanating from *Detention*'s hypercoding. Initially, the film's temporal setting is somewhat hazy because of the co-presence of various cultural objects in the storyworld. For instance, smartphones are visible from the opening scene onwards, imparting that the film is set after 2007 (when the first iPhone was released). Still, other elements are transparently incongruous with the film's temporal setting. At cheerleading practice, Ione produces a small boombox and dances to a cassette recording of C+C Music Factory's 1990 hit 'Gonna Make You Sweat (Everybody Dance Now)'. None of the characters pass comment on this cultural or technological anachronism, leaving the viewer with conflicting evidence for *Detention*'s temporal setting. That tension appears to be resolved when lead protagonist Riley later questions Ione's use of the dated idiom 'eat my shorts'; Clapton rationalises Ione's anachronistic cultural interests by describing her as 'an old soul trapped in a painfully hot cheerleader body'. Nonetheless, it is not until much later in the narrative that Ione's '90s obsession' is explained. It is revealed that Ione and her mother Sloan have swapped bodies, meaning Ione travelled back in time to inhabit Sloan's body in 1992, while Sloan

---

[10] Kahn in 'Cheat Mode'.

inhabits her daughter's body in 2011. Therefore, Ione is not just obsessed with 1990s culture: she reifies an 'intermixing of temporal chronologies' because she belongs both to the past and the present. Consequently, the initial temporal ambiguity was actually evidence of temporal blurring.

Ione's fixation on 1990s culture has broader significance within the narrative, however. Both Ione and Sloan are happy with the body swap, given that Sloan has the opportunity to relive her youth and Ione finds 'be[ing] cool in 1992' effortless. The swap is effective for both parties because *Detention*'s 2011 setting is inherently heterochronic, thanks to a contemporaneous nostalgic interest in 1990s culture. Leading man Clapton embodies that cultural trend. Clapton dresses in neon 1990s clothing and he bonds with Sloan (in Ione's body) over their shared knowledge of 1990s culture; for example, Clapton agrees with Sloan's proclamation that 'Sting is the Bruno Mars of 1992'. Clapton is not alone in these interests. In the opening scene, 'popular girl' Taylor Fisher asserts that 'the 90s are the new 80s' in her 'Guide to not being a Total Reject', suggesting that an interest in 1990s culture is mainstream as opposed to niche. Lead protagonist Riley is also contaminated by this interest in the 1990s. She attends Sander's 'costume party' dressed as Angela Chase of the hit teen soap series *My So-Called Life* (1994–1995). Although she berates Sander because they are the only two in costume (so she believes she has been misinformed about the nature of the party), it is not evident to anyone else that her authentic 'vintage 1994' overalls are a costume because most of the other teens also wear 1990s-style clothing.

This cultural heterochrony translates into a more literal temporal intermixing for Riley as the film progresses. When she is first seen, Riley contends that she is 'only the second biggest loser to walk Grizzly Lake High. First place goes to the drunk slut who screwed the dead mascot in 1992.' As a reminder of that status, she owns a poster of the 'drunk slut' who is photographed from behind, bent over under the school's Bear mascot. Later, it is disclosed that the individual in the photograph is in fact Riley: unbeknownst to her, the photograph was taken when she travelled back in time. Her initial assessment that 'the 90s are history, and so am I' is portentous, indicating that the past is not inert, since it is thoroughly intertwined with the present.

That outlook is also articulated by Clapton, who argues that 'now's all we got . . . I think now's pretty rad'. Again, the sentiment manifests temporal slippage because the slang term 'rad' was associated with West Coast surf culture in the early-1980s and was reinvigorated in the early-1990s following the phenomenal cultural prominence of *Teenage Mutant Ninja Turtles*, which adopted that 'surfer dude' vernacular. Clapton's repurposing of dated slang is again echoed by 'popular girl' Taylor, who also uses 'rad' in the opening scene, juxtaposed with more recent text speech slang 'rawr'. These terms are displayed onscreen via a standard smartphone SMS bubble, but Taylor's texts are presented in a pixelated font redolent of the pre-smartphone era. These heterochronic juxtapositions blend past and present, even though the medium (texting) emphasises the present.

The same emphasis on 'now' is borne out by *Detention*'s aesthetic. In fact, *Detention* is so heavy-handed in its amplified contemporaneous style that even when watching in 2011, it felt as if the film dated within its own runtime. Although *Detention* ruminates on the teens' present experiences and connects them to short-term cultural heritage (lineage from the 1990s), *Detention* also stresses the fleeting nature of stylistic trends. In the film's opening lines, Taylor introduces herself as 'a bitch: Beauty, Intelligence, Talent, Charisma, Hoobastank'. The latter refers to a band who formed in 1994, but who reached the peak of their success in 2003 (with the album and single 'The Reason'). Taylor pre-empts the viewer's disagreement ('What? They're good') and acknowledges that viewers might not understand the slightly dated reference point ('indie rock trends do move fast'). Moments later, Taylor complains that 'stalkers are so 2011', submitting that even 'live' trends in the narrative present are 'over'. The same outlook is captured when Elliot explains he has been in detention for nineteen years: that time span is articulated via a montage of periods between 1992 and 2011. Each era is punctuated by a pop music hit of the period, such as the 1997 single 'Everybody (Backstreet's Back)', and the teens in detention are dressed in styles that correspond to each era. This montage underlines that teen fashion and pop culture is subject to swift and constant remodelling. The narrative present is implicated as yet another fleeting cultural moment.

Fleetingness is not disparaging here, however. Just as the melodramatic intertitles accentuate subjective experiences, the present is important and urgent to the characters, even though the film suggests that what is important or urgent shifts rapidly in the scheme of history. Accordingly, when Elliot calculates that a bomb will explode eradicating 'everyone you know . . . in nine minutes . . . in 1992', emphasis is placed on the present: they have minutes to act. That urgency underscores the unusual causal relations triggered by their situation,[11] but it also conveys that the narrative privileges the as-experienced present.

---

[11] I will return to these retrocausal implications in Chapter 8.

That presentism has greater significance to the narrative whole than is initially apparent. In the closing voiceover, Riley delineates the story's moral: 'Sander [the killer] saw no future for us because he lived in the past. So, his experiment was to end time itself . . . the only way to change the past is to change the present.' This sentiment is coupled with a montage of character arcs being completed. For instance, Riley stands up to the bully who stole from her in the opening scenes, a budding romance between Toshiba and Mimi is realised when Mimi takes Toshiba's hand and so forth. As Riley has it, this is 'just a start. A beginning not an end'. So, when Riley and Clapton see a television news broadcast announcing that aliens have invaded Grizzly Lake in the film's final shots, optimism endures despite the immediate threat. As Riley has it, 'it's not the end of the world'. That is because, according to *Detention*'s message, there is hope for future adaptation when working forward from the present.

The specific meaning of that message is elucidated by the film's idiosyncratically persistent emphasis on the 1990s as 'the' past, even though that period seems too close to 2011 to be considered 'ancient history'. The emphasis on the 1990s stems from *Detention*'s core identity as a slasher film. First, as I have proposed, *Detention* underlines the fleeting nature of stylistic trends, indicating that cultural objects fall out of (and back into) fashion very swiftly. Slasher films are susceptible to imminent cultural obsolescence because of the subgenre's prevailing centralisation of teens. Those teens carry with them youth-oriented cultural signs such as fashion, hairstyles and music, that mark a slasher film as belonging to a defined era.[12] Given that such films are ordinarily thought of as being marketed to a teen demographic (see Cherry 2009, 39–40; Clover 1993, 6; Muir 2007b, 610), they are usually steeped in the normative aesthetic standards of the moment (that is, they are 'on trend'). As such, slasher films made only a decade ago are vulnerable to being perceived as relics by anyone who did not experience them first time around. Second, the immediate cultural past that contextualises *Detention*'s operations is the postmodern slasher phase, which flourished in the mid-to-late 1990s.

Indeed, although various aspects of 1990s culture are referred to, the postmodern slasher is specifically implicated when the killer is discussed. For example, when Riley tries to describe the killer to the police, Officer McNally explicitly compares the situation to *Scream*. Riley denounces the comparison ('I'm not . . . Neve Campbell, okay?'), then theorises that the

---

[12] The fact that slasher films date quickly facilitates the negative critical appraisal of such films as disposable culture.

use of a Cinderhella mask is 'so obviously a conspiracy to get everyone to think I'm a total loser making pre-emptive mid-90s pop references'. The postmodern slasher is recalled chiefly to flag its pastness, particularly from the perspective of Riley's generation: it is as dated as Officer Randazzo's reference to 'rave drugs', which Riley rebuffs by asking 'what is this, 1996?' (notably, the year of *Scream*'s release).

That outlook is consolidated in the climax when Sander is unmasked as the killer. Here, Riley denigrates Sander's decision to murder wearing a Cinderhella mask. Sander claims that referencing a horror movie villain while acting as one exemplifies 'post irony', but Riley sarcastically dismisses his efforts as being 'so original'. At these key moments, Riley dismisses Sander's gambit as outmoded because it replicates the postmodern slasher's modus operandi. This judgement informs Riley's final dismissal of Sander as 'liv[ing] in the past'. Sander personifies the postmodern slasher's key elements: omitting the possibility of a productive future; referencing prior slasher films (as one manifestation of a myopic attitude towards the past); and using irony to rationalise his cynical insularity. Since Sander embodies these traits and is also the film's antagonist, Riley's criticisms of Sander also target the postmodern slasher film. Riley implies that ironic reflexivity and making direct intertextual references to slasher films is the equivalent of Sander's attempt to 'end time itself': wallowing in the past instead of moving towards a future. Her own character arc, in contrast, turns from insular cynicism – her opening motto, 'life sucks' – to a forward-facing perspective that is live with possibility: 'it's just high school, it's not the end of the world'.

Moving towards that future does not entail dismissing or gainsaying the past, but rather building on the past. As *Detention*'s heterochrony suggests, the past is intertwined with the present. Although Riley expresses a desire to remodel the subgenre by deriding the postmodern slasher's irony and 'mid-90s pop references', the film tells a slightly more nuanced story: after all, it is ironic that *Detention* makes dozens of references to mid-1990s pop culture. Riley's dismissal draws attention to those references, and her critical tone motions that the function of such references ought to be questioned.

As Chapter 5 outlined, the postmodern slasher's intertextual references typically do little for the narrative. One way *Detention* builds on the technique is to employ such references to uncover information about the plot and characters. For instance, until her body swap is revealed, Sloan's references to outdated culture seem arbitrary. For example, she tells the football coach that he is 'as funny as Bronson Pinchot', and an onscreen caption explains that Pinchot was famously the co-star of sitcom *Perfect*

Strangers, which was cancelled in 1993. The caption indicates that despite the sitcom's success at the time, the cultural reference point will be lost on most of *Detention*'s viewers. As such, it appears to be an arbitrary intertextual reference that signals how fast-moving popular culture is. However, it gradually becomes clear that such references develop towards the revelation of Ione and Sloan's body swap. One need not know anything about *Perfect Strangers* to understand the reference's purpose: one need only know that the reference is dated, and that is conveyed by the caption's presence and content. The fact that some of Sloan's cultural references mistranslate between generations conveys information about the characters and story.

That is just one way *Detention* builds on the intertextual referencing technique. Where the previous example depended on *Detention*'s visual hypercoding strategy (using onscreen captions), another mode is informed by hypercoding's more general augmentation and excess. The postmodern slasher's hollow name-checking is amplified into an abundance of reference points, brushed past at breakneck pace. In this mode, *Detention*'s intertextual onslaught is seemingly arbitrary, ranging from dated, niche cultural items to recent, well-known blockbusters; for instance, many films are mentioned in passing, including *Freejack* (1992), *Volcano* (1997), *Torque* (2004) and *Iron Man* (2008). Where postmodern slasher films connect intertextual referencing with (sub)cultural capital by referring to 'classic' horror films, *Detention*'s capricious referential whirlwind eschews that relationship. In this mode, the individual references do not directly inform the narrative: the presence of each is seemingly just as arbitrary as their selection is.

The sheer abundance and velocity of such references hints that they are to be considered as an accumulation (rather than individually). As an indiscriminate barrage, unconcerned with genre, the collection of references accentuates the way *Detention* pushes against subgeneric categorisation. *Detention* borrows liberally from other sub/genres and cycles, including the teen high school movie and science fiction (via its time-travel and alien invasion themes). To offer a more detailed illustration, the body swap between Sloan and Ione unmistakeably refers to *Freaky Friday* (1976), as underscored by an intertitle referring to the swap as a 'freaky flip flop'.[13] Yet, detailed knowledge of *Freaky Friday* is not needed to understand the characters' situation. *Freaky Friday* represents a niche of body swap

---

[13] *Freaky* (2020) is a more recent slasher-adjacent film that also utilises body swapping: in this case, an ageing serial killer (The Blissfield Butcher) swaps bodies with a high-schooler who would customarily be the film's Final Girl (Millie). The title draws on *Freaky Friday* to underline *Freaky*'s high-concept blend of horror and comedy.

comedies, including *Like Father Like Son* (1987), *Vice Versa*, *18 Again!* and *Big* (all 1988). Simultaneously, *Freaky Friday* has been remade multiple times (in 1995, 2003, 2018) meaning it is a heterochronic property, which is likely to be recognised by viewers of different generations.

Each non-slasher sub/genre referred to comes with its own tropes, and these add to *Detention*'s abundance. That is, the hypercoded style marries these disparate elements together into a cohesive whole. Principally, *Detention* subsumes these other sub/genres into its slasher film structure, and just as the structure's robustness means it sustains despite the removal of seemingly key elements (see Chapter 5), it also survives abundant additions. *Detention*'s excessive inclusion of other sub/genres amplifies a strategy found elsewhere in the slasher subgenre. Many preceding slasher properties sought to refresh their premises by drawing on other genres. For example, both the *Friday the 13th* and the *Leprechaun* series illustrate what Bordwell calls an attempt to innovate by 'genre-blending' (2006, 53). The tenth and fourth entries into these respective series (*Jason X* [2001] and *Leprechaun 4: In Space* [1996]) relocated their action into space to reinvigorate their standard plotlines. Doing so allowed both properties to layer sci-fi tropes on top of the undergirding horror action.[14] Such hybrids are particularly common during the postmodern slasher phase. As Cherry observes, 'horror filmmakers frequently push against the boundaries of the genre . . . taking elements from other genres and thus creating genre hybrids' (2009, 34), and 'generic hybridity' is 'one of the key features of postmodern cinema' (2009, 19; see also Handwerk 2008, 225; Moine 2008, 122). More specifically, Collins (1993, 242–3) contends that 'two divergent types of genre film' can be found in the period, the first relying on 'ironic hybridization of pure classical genres', providing 'eclectic juxtapositions of elements that very obviously don't belong together', and the second being unironically 'obsessed with recovering some sort of missing harmony, where everything works in unison'. Whereas the postmodern slasher falls into the first camp, *Detention* brings together both of Collins's types, containing eclectic juxtapositions that are unified under the hypercoded style.

As with its amplified style, the variety of juxtapositions included in *Detention* stresses that the film is a construction, persistently calling attention to the absurdity that viewers can become immersed in and enjoy

---

[14] Much as *Leprechaun 4: In Space* and *Jason X* augment their horror by drawing on sci-fi, other slashers incorporate norms and tropes from other genres. For example, *Deep Murder* (2018)'s slasher story is set within a softcore porn narrative setup; *Stage Fright* (2014) is a slasher musical; *Bring It On: Cheer or Die* (2022) is a high school dance movie in which a slasher picks off members of the central cheer squad and so forth.

such fictions. While Berliner avers that 'genre bending often affects us precisely because it works below the level of our conscious understanding, exploiting our accustomed responses to coded stimuli without letting us know we have been so manipulated' (2001a, 32), hypercoding works differently, bringing coding itself to the surface precisely so that it becomes conspicuous. Moreover, the blend of sub/genres underlines that such categories are themselves constructed, and that even though categorisation seemingly entails the exclusion of other sub/genres and their unique tropes, such categories are regularly subject to interruption and amalgamation.

Detention's hypercoding accommodates semiotic excessiveness, harmonising these seemingly separate elements. That integration is indicative of metamodern inclusivity, while the resultant juxtapositions convey a desire to adopt idiosyncratic perspectives and create new insights about the subgenre and its operations. For instance, slasher narratives are usually based in restricted locations, and feature young people who are culled in their prime. The locations' boundedness matches the subgenre's core thematic concern: life's finitude. Although it is mainly set around a high school, *Detention*'s time-travel theme expands its temporal boundaries, problematising the idea that the would-be teen victims' lives are precariously finite. This is just one way *Detention*'s hypercoded genre-blending illuminates and complicates the subgenre's normative operations.

Wreaking Havoc: Substance in Stylistic Excess

Hypercoded texts such as *Dude Bro* and *Detention* follow the subgenre's normative structure: both portray teenagers being picked off by killers in defined locations, and both narratives progress towards a resolution in which the killer is defeated. That structure provides an undergirding stability. When the causal chains that connect one incident to the next are examined however, these hypercoded texts seem precarious because individual incidents – such as the revelation that Officer Sminkle's partner is a bag of oranges in *Dude Bro* – are nonsensical. That these texts still seem to make cohesive sense, assimilating these absurdities and challenges, attests to how robust the slasher's conventions and structure are. Furthermore, these hypercoded texts demonstrate that no matter how many seemingly disparate and disruptive elements are brought into juxtaposition – be they narratological or formal – cohesion can be engendered by harmonising stylistics, characterisation and thematics.

This chapter's case studies distil forms of amplification in a conspicuous fashion, and although hypercoding illustrates a metamodern sensibility, not all metamodern slashers are hypercoded. That said, many of the metamodern slashers probed in previous chapters also use stylistics to convey information about characterisation and thematics. For example, *Shrooms* (2007) hypostatises its characters' drug-influenced hallucinations in its form via its visual effects and unreliable subjective perspectives, while *Behind the Mask: The Rise of Leslie Vernon* (2006) employs distinct register shifts to convey its cogitations on conventions. Other case studies also utilise intensification strategies without foregrounding that tack. For instance, the protagonists in *KillerKiller* (2007), *Shrooms* and *Triangle* (2009) occupy augmented positions, combining killer and Final Girl into one entity, and the compression exhibited by *Murder Loves Killers Too* (2009) also exemplifies a form of distillation that intensifies its opening act. As the latter example evinces, augmentation coexists with subtraction in a kind of superposition: both techniques intensify the narrative or the experience of engaging with the narrative. Moreover, subsequent chapters will return to these ideas when discussing (1) the ways contemporary slasher films exaggerate cultural and aesthetic markers to signify 'pastness' in the wake of augmented access to earlier slasher texts (Chapter 7), and (2) the ways contemporary slasher requels exaggerate the tendency to retcon canonical events across a chain of sequels (which themselves routinely seek to outdo their predecessors in various ways: see Chapter 8).

For the moment, it is notable that hypercoding offers opportunities to innovate within the subgenre. As Chapters 4 and 5 proposed, such innovation can be risky if it entails diverging from established expectations.[15] The potential for disruption addressed in this chapter is based in stylistics more than tropes or structures. Stylistics might initially seem somewhat unimportant as a subgeneric identifier, but as Hanich notes, 'the renewal of a genre depends on its variability and openness towards the integration of new contents, stylistic as well as aesthetic devices that strive to grant certain pleasures' (Hanich 2010, 255). The hypercoded slasher's perspicuous stylistic play demands attention, raising questions about the significance of the subgenre's aesthetics. Hypercoding undercuts Liao's adjudication that aesthetic pleasure is derived from 'appropriate genre expectations' (2016, 11), demonstrating that adjusting aesthetic and stylistic norms can reshape subgeneric expectations in powerful ways. Similarly, Warshow argues that once a mode – in this case, a subgenre – is founded, it becomes the 'accepted vehicle[e] of . . . a particular aesthetic effect' (1974, 129). By

---

[15] Incorporating other sub/generic elements is risky because the resultant film might not meet audience expectations. For example, some critics attribute *Happy Death Day 2U*'s (2019) disappointing box-office performance compared with its predecessor to its over-incorporation of sci-fi (to illustrate, see Kennedy 2019).

emphasising and overtly playing with stylistics, the hypercoded slasher challenges entrenched expectations.

This disruption of expectations is especially striking in the case of the slasher, precisely because the subgenre's stylistics are commonly overlooked; as Bettinson contends, 'attempts to appreciate the slasher genre [sic] on primarily aesthetic grounds – for example, by tracing historical patterns of schema-and-revision, artistic replication and renewal, reigning norms and shifting dominants – have been comparatively scarce' (Bettinson 2015, 138). This oversight might stem from a general critical disregard for the subgenre, or more specifically a supposition that slasher filmmakers pay little heed to their craft. Alternatively, scholars might postulate that the slasher's development is already sufficiently explained by existing paradigms within film studies. Hypercoding might initially appear to concretise Schatz's contention that as a generic 'form is varied and refined, it is bound to become more stylized' (1981, 116), for instance. However, even though hypercoded slashers certainly embellish, and accent those embellishments, these stylisations are not 'the "substance" or "content" of the work'. The stylisation is foregrounded, amplified and shapes how the film is enciphered, but the film is not 'about' the stylisation. In the hypercoded slasher, stylisation conveys the thematic meaning, resting on an alignment between form and narrative.

The hypercoded film's relationship to the metamodern zeitgeist is evinced in its marriage of narrative, stylistics, characterisation and thematics. Like other iterations of the metamodern sensibility, hypercoding reflects a surrounding sociocultural tenor. For example, hypercoding echoes Stoev's contention that 'we are living in a reality that seems increasingly unreal and illogical', which 'has a simultaneously apocalyptic and absurd flavour' (2022, 95). Smythe raises similar concerns over the contemporary moment, which he suggests is 'notable for its intensification of mobility . . . a state of perpetual motion', in which 'stability and groundedness are hard to come by' (2015, 368). This state is further amplified in the chaotic worlds of *Dude Bro* and *Detention*. The protagonists in these films are swept up in fast-moving sequences of incongruous incidents. Although that state of 'perpetual motion' might sound too disorienting to be productive, the absurdist comedy of *Dude Bro* and the optimistic milieu of *Detention* limn the situation as liberating. Constant renewal means new possibilities are abundant. A multiplicity of idiosyncratic perspectives is precipitated when disparate elements are continually brought together in unexpected combinations. That flux helps to push the subgenre away from the postmodern slasher's stagnant fatalism.

CHAPTER 7

Nostalgia

Chapters 4–6 concentrated on conventionality to evidence how metamodern slasher films innovate within the subgenre. Chapters 7–9 represent the book's next structural block, converging on approaches to temporality. This chapter will begin by contemplating how nostalgia operates in the metamodern slasher, forging bridges from the present to both the past and the future.

The metamodern slasher's take on temporality is contextualised by relationships between the subgenre's evolution and parallel developments in technology. The slasher was born into a technocultural moment when, 'for the first time . . . as a result of technologies that allow large-scale storage, access and reproduction of records of the past, the past appear[ed] to be included in the present' (Connor 2015, 42). For this book's purposes, the most significant of these technologies was VHS. Indeed, the analogue context of video collecting and rewatching, which flourished in the 1980 and 1990s, inadvertently shaped the insular stance on subgenericity adopted in postmodern slasher films. As Collins remarks, the 'omnipresence' of 'recirculated' texts – 'the fact that once-forgotten popular texts' could 'be "accessed" almost at will' because of advances in home-viewing technologies such as VHS – altered 'the cultural function of genre films past' (1993, 246), leading to 'an even more sophisticated hyperconsciousness concerning not just narrative formulae, but the conditions of their own circulation and reception in the present' (1993, 248; see also Scahill 2016, 321; Verevis 2005, 23). That hyperconsciousness manifested in the postmodern slasher's self-reflexivity, which spoke to a 'new and distinct demographic' of 'media obsessed and, hence, pop culture literate, extremely self-aware, and cynical' 1990s teenagers (Wee 2006, 54; see also Muir 2011, 472). These teens were represented onscreen by characters such as *Scream* (1996)'s resident film-buff Randy. However, this target demographic's media savviness is also implied by the ways intertextuality is used within these films. As Chapter 5 laid out, detailed subgenre knowledge was required to decode many of the subgeneric 'in-jokes' that litter such films. Chiming with this ploy, contemporaneous film collection culture fostered divisions 'between "us" (the fans/collectors) and "them" (the subcultural layman or "inauthentic" horror fan)' (Egan 2007, 113). In the still-analogue era of the 1990s, participating in collection culture required dedication and effort. Accessing content entailed travelling to video stores, finding out about new releases via specialist publications such as *Fangoria*, or even trading tapes on the 'video black market' (see Walker 2016, 141).

Thus, to understand these and consequent shifts, it is necessary to consider not only film content, but the broader filmic context surrounding the postmodern slasher. As Lewis observes, 'the movies turned 100 years old in the mid-1990s. And the studios predictably viewed the centenary as an occasion for nostalgia and self-congratulation' (Lewis 2012, 2138). This moment of 'self-congratulation' arguably informed the postmodern slasher's tone, particularly its smug in-joking. Yet, the moment was distinctive because a new home-viewing technology – DVD – was beginning its ascent to prominence. Lewis continues by proposing that studios began exploiting the 'cultural value of their inventory . . . using DVD releases to showcase quasi-historical data, "making of" documentaries, and director and star commentaries, fostering a film culture among even the most casual movie fans' (Lewis 2012, 2138). DVD special features commonly afford 'an extensive source of information pertaining to production and the historical milieu of a film' (Rombes 2010, 195). That is, information that previously required a fan's effort to acquire was routinely packaged alongside the film itself on DVD.

The move to an online, digital era amplified access to such information. Resources such as IMDb grant free, immediate access to searchable databases, meaning users can easily learn about a writer's, director's or actor's other work. Blogs and social media sites such as Reddit bring horror fans into asynchronous interactions. As noted in Chapter 5, the Internet allows non-fans to easily decode intertextual allusions. Review aggregators such as Rotten Tomatoes and Metacritic contain snippet summaries of numerous critical opinions, circumventing the need to seek and read individual sources. Past genre films have been made available for home-viewing via boutique Blu-ray labels such as Arrow Video and specialist streaming services such as Shudder. Private torrent trackers such as Cinemageddon and specialist streaming services offered by distributors such as Massacre Video, Troma and Unearthed Films provide access to what would otherwise remain obscure genre films. The ability to stream video on one's smartphone also makes film more readily consumable and accessible in a wider variety of contexts than television or

VHS could. In sum, individuals now have greater and more convenient access to a wider variety of films and information about films, reducing the barriers to entry and effort required to participate in knowledgeability about a subgenre.

In this technocultural moment of digital abundance, ownership is tacitly discouraged in favour of fluid, cloud-based, transient engagements with films (see Hilderbrand 2010, 27–8; Stamm 2013, 71). Individualised algorithmic curation and mass accessibility leads to idiosyncratic user experiences and unique juxtapositions (see Beer 2009; Cong 2020; Helles and Flyverbom 2019). The ability to download and/or stream audio-visual media has also somewhat deemphasised the normative dominance of synchronous live film consumption. The conveniences of asynchronous viewing were instigated by VHS, which allowed viewers to record and rewatch broadcasted programmes at one's leisure, then TiVo, which helped users to effortlessly schedule recordings of television broadcasts. Services such as Netflix and 'catch up' platforms such as BBC iPlayer (for instance) further deemphasise scheduling, affording greater scope for freer forms of asynchronous consumption.[1]

This technocultural situation informs the metamodern sensibility. Where *Scream* was reputedly made by and for cineliterate individuals who had developed a sophisticated understanding of film by rewatching classics on television and VHS, metamodern films are made by and for individuals who have unprecedented access to film and film cultures. If, as Collins proposed, 'the ever-expanding number of texts and technologies' in the 1990s was 'both a reflection of and a significant contribution to the "array"—the perpetual circulation and recirculation of signs that forms the fabric of postmodern cultural life' (1993, 246), the amplified array of digital culture instead forms the fabric of metamodern cultural life and informs metamodern approaches to genres and conventions. Augmented access to a wider selection of films, intensified media saturation and the idiosyncratic user experiences encouraged by algorithmic curation have fragmented the subgeneric landscape. The sheer volume of available films distracts from the subgeneric 'canon', and filmmakers cannot reliably presume a majority of audience members will have the same precise points of reference. Therefore, it is unsurprising to find that metamodern slashers are characterised by broad gestures as opposed to niche intertextual references, which would rely on viewers having more specialised shared knowledge.

---

[1] For a detailed discussion of these technological developments and the complexities of viewer control, scheduling and so forth, see Jenner (2018).

Access to information has increased exponentially since Collins was writing, but it is worth heeding his warning about a pervasive 'assumption that the increasing sophistication of the media produces a sensory overload in which individual viewers are overstimulated into numbness' (Collins 1993, 253). That suspicion of technology and the 'numbness' it might cause was contemporaneously echoed via characters' callous cynicism in postmodern slashers such as *Scream* and *Cherry Falls* (2000). Nevertheless, the same pervasive beliefs about media overload persist (see, for example, Alter 2017; Elgin 2008, 43; Levitin 2014; Shirky 2010), and so these claims need to be revisited in light of the turn towards a metamodern sensibility.

The present technocultural situation might be understood as a continuation of postmodernism's solipsistic pluralism. Jeffries, for instance, posits that 'customised culture' – 'tailoring cultural supply to your tastes' – might lead 'each of us' to become 'isolated intellectually in our own informational spheres' (2021, 272). However, this conclusion seems to mistake symptom for cause. Chapter 2 proffered that one's knowledge claims are tied to one's individual experiential sphere, given that each person yields their worldview out of a unique combination of information. The technology does not generate individualised subjectivity then, it simply caters to our pre-existing individualised perspectives in new ways. As Mittell contends, digital technology has enabled individuals 'to embrace a "collective intelligence" for information, interpretations, and discussions of complex narratives that invite participatory engagement' (2006, 31; see also Leadbeater 2010). That is, the technocultural situation facilitates novel potentials for collaboration and new abilities to communicate about our idiosyncratic experiences. Furthermore, rather than resulting in apathy, greater access to information is commonly perceived as empowering, providing opportunities to distribute digital information, to affect change by wielding data, and to mobilise inventive forms of protest and awareness-raising through information technologies (on this, see Castells 2015; Daly, Devitt and Mann 2019; Earl and Kimport 2011). This is perhaps because abundant access to information is so ubiquitous that it has become normalised: it is the foundation on which culture is now built.

Many of the metamodern slasher films addressed thus far evoke these technocultural changes. For example, *I Didn't Come Here to Die* (2010), *Dude Bro Party Massacre III* (2015) and *You Might Be the Killer* (2018) draw on the aesthetics of disused technologies (chiefly, VHS). Where captions are imposed in *You Might Be the Killer*, a digital filter is also applied to mimic celluloid film grain and impairments that befall aged film, including stains, dust and black vertical lines. The same kind of filter is applied in the opening and ending moments of *I Didn't Come Here to Die*. These aesthetic properties symbolically stand in for a host of meanings regarding the subgenre's cultural status. Such blemishes are associated with slasher films of the late-1970s and early-1980s, which were contemporaneously perceived as transient, disposable, trashy commercial products. Prints were not necessarily handled with preservation in mind since these films were not considered valuable cultural artifacts. For the same reasons, transfers of such films onto VHS and then early DVD were also not necessarily handled with great care or attention.[2] Among some fans, celluloid defects became an associated part of the subgenre's aesthetic. Exaggerated fetishisation of these aesthetic markers thereby elicits nostalgic fondness for the boom-period, even though the juxtaposition of high-definition digital footage and analogue flaws underscores how removed we are from the earlier period.[3] Neither *You Might Be the Killer* nor *I Didn't Come Here to Die* are set in the past. In both films, characters own smartphones, for instance. Pastness is imparted by replicating analogue defects, but this does not convey information about the fictional world. Rather, it signals that the present slasher film should be understood in relation to its technocultural predecessors.

Another way of pointing towards technocultural change is offered in *Detention* (2011). As Chapter 6 delineated, a mother and daughter swap places via time-travel, leading to mistranslation of cultural references. This strategy implies that a previously dominant mode of intertextual referencing (emblematised by *Scream*) has been undercut by a generational transference. Moreover, another of *Detention*'s intertextual devices entails capricious selection of reference points, suggesting that the generational shift is epitomised by idiosyncratic cultural interactions, which replace detailed knowledge of agreed cultural canons. Similarly, the penultimate scene of *Happy Death Day* (2017) also gestures towards generational and technocultural succession. Carter tells Tree that her situation reminds him of the lucrative hit time-loop film *Groundhog Day* (1993), but Tree responds that she has not heard of the film or its star Bill Murray. An older audience might baulk at her cultural 'ignorance' given the contemporaneous cultural prominence of both the film and Murray, but 1993 was long before Tree was born. A substantial portion of *Happy Death Day*'s viewership might share Tree's position.

---

[2] To illustrate, the 2004 Region 2 Vipco DVD release of the slasher film *Death Screams* (1982) was transferred with reels out of order, exposing how little care was taken over the transfer.

[3] For a more detailed dissection of these issues, see Jones (2018).

Although metamodern slashers conjure relations between past and present, that does not imply modern and postmodern artists ignored such issues. As Hutcheon argues, modernism and postmodernism 'share . . . reliance, however ironic, on tradition' (2002, 27). Metamodernism inherits that reliance. Indeed, given metamodernism's championing of inclusivity and its interest in bridging from past to present, it would be perverse if metamodernism repudiated modernism and postmodernism. As Chapter 1 established, metamodernism incorporates modernism and postmodernism, envisaging postmodernism as growing out of the modernist tradition and outlook. To use a technological analogy, metamodernism is 'backwards compatible' with both postmodernism and modernism. The distinction between metamodern and postmodern approaches to the past arise from divergences in sensibility, manifesting in differing tones. Postmodernists view knowledge of the past with scepticism. In this view, the past was experienced as 'confused, plural, and unstructured' by those who lived it, and we only 'come to know the past' though organised narratives and representations (Hutcheon 2002, 71 and 92). More bluntly, as I have proposed elsewhere, postmodernists usually associate time with 'collapse' and 'crisis' (see Chapter 5). Furthermore, as Booker asserts, the postmodern retreat into the past is coloured by a 'cynical, ahistorical, and emotionally flat worldview' (2007, 29). So, a postmodern outlook on the past is presented in postmodern slashers via the characters' 'emotionally flat' responses and superficial evocation of the subgenre's past through hollow intertextual references.

Metamodern filmmakers are much more at ease with reviving the past. One explanation for that ease is that despite recalling the past, metamodern films accentuate the present. In metamodern slasher films such as *Detention*, *Happy Death Day* and *Triangle* (2009), temporal chronologies are explicitly played with, but emphasis is placed on the lead protagonists' subjective experiences in the present. As evinced by Chapter 4's reflections on conventionality, metamodern films tie together present concerns the characters face – the urgencies of imperilment in the moment – to evaluations of the subgenre's present. In doing so, these films confidently incorporate the past in their vision of the present, demonstrating that the apparent 'chaos' of a heterogeneous media landscape – where past and present coexist in abundance – can quite readily be brought into harmony. The emphasis on characters' experiential reality underlines this cohesion. Even if an abundant heterogeneity of information is available, each individual only encounters a limited slice of that abundance. That information becomes a cohesive whole because one person experiences that unique combination.

This understanding of the present as a temporal bridging point and the site of our experiential reality allows the metamodern slasher to sidestep its postmodern antecedents' defeatist presentism, which is coloured by 'postmodernism's theoretical commitment to destroying History' (Guynn 2006, 12). In the postmodern slasher, the past is (mis)represented as passé, confirming Crane's hypothesis that 'the past' seems to 'be easily sloughed off' when it is treated ironically (2004, 154). Postmodern art's 'parodic reprise of the past' is reduced to 'presentist spectacle', and as such, it 'is not nostalgic' (Hutcheon 2002, 93; see also Booker 2007, 51). The metamodern slasher's presentism is distinct from the postmodern slasher's precisely because metamodern art adopts productive forms of nostalgia.

As Lowenthal proclaims, 'nostalgia expresses longings for times that are safely, rather than sadly, beyond recall' (1989, 28). I will unpack this dense phrase later in the chapter. For the time being, note that although the past is no longer accessible as it was, it is also not dismissed or rejected. The past's continued pertinence is evinced by the yearning that underpins nostalgia (the 'longings' Lowenthal refers to). Lowenthal's explanation for the past's continued relevance ties into the technocultural circumstances outlined above. First, he suggests film technology instigates nostalgia because of the medium's ability to render images of the past 'with compelling vitality' (Lowenthal 1989, 30). Second, he argues that 'nostalgic yearning' is commonly thought to arise out of 'the search for a simple and stable past as a refuge from the turbulent and chaotic present' (Lowenthal 1989, 21). Thus, because the present technocultural situation is perceived as amplifying such 'chaos', the compulsion to nostalgia also ought to intensify. It is unsurprising then that while DVD afforded studios opportunities to recirculate and valorise their libraries in a new format, streaming platforms such as Netflix augment those opportunities, delivering old and new products alongside one another without overtly (derogatorily) marking older programming as 'repeats'/'re-runs'. Netflix's own original productions corroborate that outlook by frequently arousing fondness for the past (see Pallister 2019, 3). More broadly, Cook understands the 'substantial increase' in the production of 'nostalgic memory films' as an intensification of 'the desire to find some form of authenticity' as the digital era has unfolded (2005, 4).

Even so, metamodern art does not evade the past by attending to the present. Even though the past is not accessible first-hand, metamodernism does not share postmodernism's predominant wariness of the past. As established in Chapter 3, metamodern slasher films embrace subjective experience despite its inherent limitations, and our subjective experiences are located in the present. Taking for granted that our access to reality is necessarily limited, 'metamodernism attempts to think of "the past, present and future as a meaningful whole" knowing that such an enterprise will always, in one way or another, be incomplete' (Sandbacka 2017, 4). Most overtly, nostalgic metamodern slashers utilise what knowledge we do have about the past – understood via the present's limited lens – as the basis for subgeneric intervention.

The future potential of action in the present is also implicated in the metamodern slasher's approach to innovation. Postmodern slashers largely disregard the future, being informed by a postmodernist preoccupation with 'the difficulty, if not impossibility, of continuous novelty, [or] innovation', and the consequent idea that 'originality' is pretence, entailing merely the 'repetition, recycling and recontextualising of past forms' (Currie 2007, 10; see also King 2002, 120). This postmodern presentism is a form of inward-facing discontinuity that contrasts with the metamodern slasher's outward-facing continuity. In the metamodern view, our subjective perspectives mean that the future remains beyond our understanding. However, that means the future is suspended in superposition, encompassing a range of possibilities. *Dude Bro Party Massacre III* exemplifies one way of accentuating that potential, offering absurdist events that do not causally follow from preceding events: in this hypercoded example, the future is abundantly open. That same mindset emerges in less extreme ways in other case study examples. Each metamodern slasher film inspected thus far innovates or casts the subgenre in a fresh light, thereby saying something new about the slasher. Both *Happy Death Day*'s Tree and *Detention*'s Riley articulate this yearning by observing their distance from 1990s film culture (Riley denouncing *Scream* and Tree admitting her unfamiliarity with *Groundhog Day*), thereby signalling a generational turn away from the postmodern slasher's fatalism. These films illustrate Gibbons's proposal that 'temporal potentialities are . . . re-opened in metamodernist fiction through characters' felt sense of possible futures and the heterochronic present' (2021, 143). From this perspective, one can only act in the present, and those actions will shape the future. The metamodern slasher's presentism is concerned with bridging from the past to the future, and that stance is particularly apparent where nostalgia is elicited. Metamodern slasher films therefore 'harness a critical and productive nostalgia' (Brunton 2018, 74) that is mindful of 'the cultural work that nostalgia performs in the present' (Loock 2016, 292), which was overlooked by postmodernists.

These temporal matters will be explored via this chapter's case studies. The chapter's second half concentrates on a central case study – *Getting Schooled* (2017) – which is set in 1983. *Getting Schooled* revives character types that were popularised by 1980s films such as *The Breakfast Club* (1985), situating those (now) archetypal figures in a slasher context. This technique allows *Getting Schooled* to rewrite the boom-period slasher according to a metamodern sensibility. Most notably, instead of just being 'types', here characters move beyond those roles, growing and grieving in sincere ways. That main case study (and the extended discussion of temporality in Chapters 8 and 9) will first be contextualised by outlining other approaches to temporal continuity found in contemporary slasher films. The following section will thus contemplate numerous 'throwback' slashers that implicitly or candidly bridge between the subgenre's past and present.

No Time Like the Present: Slasher Throwbacks and Replication

At first glance, 'throwback' slashers appear to manifest a kind of 'retro' culture that has been broadly associated with postmodernism's 'cynicism or detachment', 'empty stylistic gestures . . . cultural amnesia' and 'loss of faith in the future' (Guffey 2006, 20–2). However, contemporary slashers have a more complicated relationship with the retro sensibility, hinting towards Guffey's reclamation of retro culture as 'implicitly invok[ing] what is yet to come, as well as what has passed' (2006, 23); that is, 'looking backwards in order to go forwards' (2006, 8).

Contemporary slashers conjure the subgenre's past in conjunction with the present in three main ways. The first is the most subtle: many low-budget, independent slasher films are modelled after 'classic' 1980s slashers, even though the narratives are set in the present. Movies such as *Halloween Night* (2006), *Trackman* (2007), *Girl House* (2014) and *Crazy Lake* (2016) are nostalgic 'throwbacks' to the boom-period. Within the films themselves, the connections to the boom-period are mainly implied, materialising in the straightforward evocation of tropes and the replication of stock situations. These throwbacks eschew the dialogic references to slasher predecessors found in postmodern slasher films, which plainly invite surface comparisons between past and present. Contextualised by their pervasive cynical, duplicitous tone, the postmodern slasher's comparisons to the past imply that boom-period slashers are hokey or clichéd. Contemporary throwback slashers also customarily eschew the humour that became more prominent in the subgenre from the mid-1980s onwards, given that an unmistakably comedic tone could be misconstrued as postmodern flippancy, or failure to pay due respect to boom-period slashers. Instead, contemporary throwbacks present conventions unselfconsciously, replicating the prevailing tone of slasher films that were made before the subgenre's formula had solidified (so before there were conventional norms to be self-conscious about). This mode intimates fondness for the boom-period, and that affection is confirmed in the attitudes expressed by film-making personnel. So, for example, cast members Blaze Hall and Caulin Donaldson gushingly refer to *Crazy Lake* as '70s/80s slasher horror' and 'old school' respectively in publicity interviews.[4]

These throwbacks do not merely mimic the past, however. Emphasis is placed on the present via their stylistics, as these throwbacks conform to the formal standards of independent horror filmmaking in the 2000s. This combination of past (narrative approach) and present (stylistics) carries three connotations. First, contemporary slashers are part of a subgenre continuum with boom-period slashers. Second, even in its classic form, the subgenre has continued relevance in the present for contemporary audiences. Third, throwback slashers furnish contemporary audiences with an approximation of what it was like to experience original boom-period slashers. Unlike *Dude Bro Party Massacre III*, which uses amplified stylistics to convey this experiential quality (see Chapter 6), throwback films distil the subgenre's formula. Stripping 'back to basics', these throwbacks are more akin to the subtractive examples addressed in Chapter 5. By retaining contemporary stylistics, these throwbacks stress that their experiential replication of the boom-period principally speaks to the present.

Contemporary throwbacks do not directly innovate in terms of questioning or overhauling the subgenre's norms, but they do present the past as a foundation on which to build new stories. Although they are only implicitly redolent of the subgenre's past, and the extent to which they are designed to ameliorate the subgenre is ambiguous, these throwback slashers express a metamodern sensibility in several ways. These films submit it is possible to create new sincere iterations of the established formula. They are earnest in tone, seeking to capture the subgenre's essence (as it was initially conceived). They are inclusive, granting newcomers ways into the subgenre: no prior subgeneric knowledge is required to engage with any of its pleasurable elements, and the stylistics are acclimated to contemporary norms.

The second way contemporary slashers revive the subgenre's past in conjunction with the present is more overt. As proposed in Chapter 6, slasher films are marked as belonging to a particular era because the

---

[4] These videos were published on the film's Facebook page on 14 March 2015 (https://www.facebook.com/CrazyLake/videos/1813056998919438/).

subgenre's centralisation of teens means they typically showcase contemporaneous youth-oriented cultural markers such as fashion, hairstyles and music. These cultural markers can cause older slasher films to look dated, especially to younger audiences. Some contemporary slasher films bypass that problem by intentionally embracing anachronistic cultural markers. This route is illustrated by *Bikini Girls on Ice* (2009), another throwback film set in the present that replicates the boom-period slasher formula. In comparison to *Trackman* or *Crazy Lake*, *Bikini Girls on Ice* attempts to forge more direct cultural bridges to the 1980s boom-period. *Bikini Girls on Ice* features songs by the band Crazy Lixx both during the closing credits and during an early sequence in which the eponymous 'Bikini Girls' wash a car. Crazy Lixx describe themselves as a 'Hair Metal band', who elicit 'the pure nostalgia of 80's arena hard rock' via stylistic pastiche.[5] Their prominent inclusion on *Bikini Girls on Ice*'s soundtrack recalls the 1980s, thereby underlining the film's replication of the boom-period's narrative norms. Simultaneously, Crazy Lixx are a contemporary band, and so *Bikini Girls on Ice* prompts nostalgia for the 1980s without disrupting its contemporary narrative setting and stylistics. Just as *Bikini Girls on Ice* is made with digital technology that was not available to slasher filmmakers in the 1980s, Crazy Lixx's music equally utilises digital production techniques. Both Crazy Lixx's contemporary nostalgia-inspired rock and *Bikini Girls on Ice*'s evocation of the boom-period slasher are indicative of a more expansive popular interest in 'retro' culture. Loock refers to such inclusions as a commoditised 'pastness' that stimulates 'feelings of generational belonging', while also advancing 'something new, a variation in narrative, style, setting, and cast that clearly locates them in the present (as timely contributions to the film cycle)'. Loock thereby argues that such texts are caught in 'dialectics between repetition and innovation' (2016, 294). Loock's observation

---

[5] This biographical description is offered on the band's official website (https://www.crazylixx.com/pages/biography). Other contemporary bands such as Airbourne and Reckless Love operate in the same vein. Another band, Steel Panther, offers an equivalent of Spinal Tap, exaggerating hair metal's ubiquitous sexism for comic effect. That approach foregrounds parodic, mocking detachment from the period, and the anachronistic musical style is principally a means to convey the joke.

Another throwback film using a similar technique is *Pool Party Massacre* (2017). Although set in the present, the opening credit sequence depicts the film's murders in a style mimicking the 8bit graphics that were the standard for 1980s home videogaming. The credit sequence is accompanied by the song 'Cutsman' by HORSE the Band, who utilise chiptune synthesiser sounds to replicate the music produced by 8bit videogame consoles.

aptly underscores that, as with other throwbacks, films like *Bikini Girls on Ice* replicate the boom-period formula, but do not explicitly innovate by challenging or modifying subgeneric norms.

The third way contemporary slashers recall the subgenre's past in conjunction with the present is to (at least partially) set the narrative in the early-1980s. For instance, *Die Die Delta Pi*'s (2013) prologue is staged in 1986, and the main portion of the narrative is set in the present. The distinction between time periods is marked by displaying assorted cultural markers to signify the 1980s. These include teen slang associated with the era ('bodacious', 'fuckin-a', 'grody' and so forth), as well as visual cues that bring together technological artefacts (a boombox), fashion (neon earrings) and sundry cultural items (a Rubik's cube) (see Figure 7.1). These cultural markers are surface-level symbols of the 1980s, and they are restricted to the prologue section. *Die Die Delta Pi* mainly foregrounds the present, and that emphasis informs its articulation of the past. For example, *Die Die Delta Pi* includes full-frontal nudity in its '1986' prologue. Although some nudity is commonplace in 1980s slasher films, full nudity is exceedingly rare in the period.

Die Die Delta Pi cannot authentically recreate the 1980s. However, its employment of cultural markers stresses that fashions and aesthetic standards mutate over time, and that these amendments are symptomatic of changing values and concerns. These broader relationships between past and present are advanced by *Die Die Delta Pi*'s narrative. The prologue

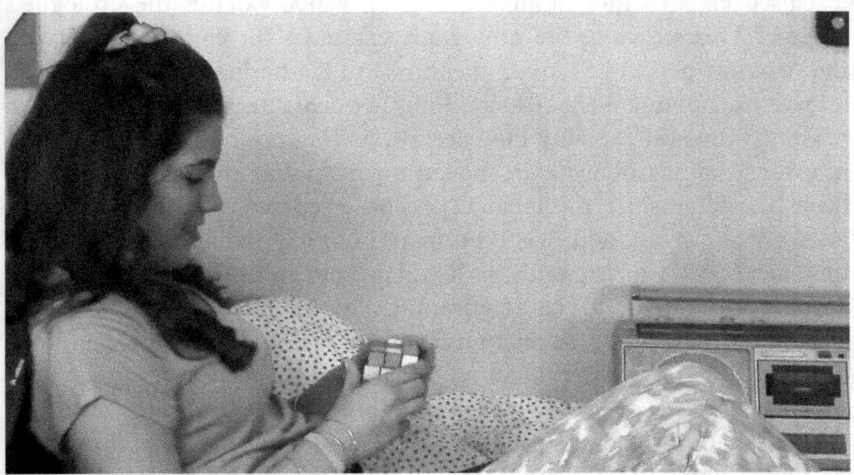

Figure 7.1 The 1980s is encapsulated by various cultural markers such as a Rubik's cube, boombox and fashion items in *Die Die Delta Pi* (2013)

provides index events that shape the narrative present. In 1986, a sorority initiation prank goes awry and one sorority sister (Marissa) is ostensibly burned to death. Meanwhile, the sorority house mother (Katherine) kills sorority and fraternity members. In the present, the Delta Pi house reopens and the murders begin again. The index events suggest the two sets of homicides are connected. That implication is anchored by links made between past and present throughout the film. The new occupants of Delta Pi house broadly replicate the former group's activities (because they follow sorority 'traditions'). Most significantly, a parallel present-day sorority initiation sequence is set at the same beach location where Marissa was burned. Here, one sorority sister (Josie) recounts the events of 1986 and flashbacks perspicuously bring the past footage into a continuum with the present for the viewer. Two of the present-day sisters (Josie and Diana) are daughters of former Delta Pi members who were present when Marissa was set alight. Several of the 1986 sorority sisters, including Diana's mother (Donna), are adults in the present-day footage. Indeed, Donna features more prominently than her daughter.

Die Die Delta Pi's temporal continuity plays out in two ways. First, the present-day massacre is a continuation of the prologue's events. In both periods, Katherine is the masked killer and is abetted by Marissa (who is revealed to be alive). One might reasonably expect the present-day slaughter to be triggered by the prank that disfigured Marissa, but the film's closing moments elucidate that Katherine was executing sorority sisters (with Marissa's help) prior to the prank. That information is disclosed via a further flashback to 1986, which extends the prologue's footage. This return to the prologue accentuates the continuity between the two time periods. Second, in contrast to Katherine's continued quest to exterminate members of Delta Pi, other characters from the prologue personify renewal. Notably, Donna expresses her profound regret over the prank, crying 'it's all my fault' and surmising, 'I don't think any of us have been [the same since the incident]'. Those repercussions are reified by Katey, who, we are told, has been in and out of 'psychiatric care' facilities since 1989. Consequently, past and present are connected via *Die Die Delta Pi*'s narrative and characterisation. Those connections take the form of continuity with and distinction from the past: as both Donna and one of the new sorority sisters (Cindy) proclaim at separate junctures, 'times have changed'. *Die Die Delta Pi* might not expressly innovate within the subgenre, but its characters allegorise tensions induced by the throwback slasher's combination of subgeneric reiteration and rejuvenation.

The Sleeper (2012) employs a different tactic, setting its prologue in 1979 and the main narrative action in 1981. Ergo, the entire narrative is set within the boom-period. As with *Crazy Lake*, *The Sleeper* is a throwback in that it offers a 'back to basics' narrative. Unlike *Die Die Delta Pi*, *The Sleeper* attempts to marry its simulation of the era with its aesthetic, including exaggerated film grain and visual 'noise' to gesture that *The Sleeper* itself is from the boom-period.[6] This nostalgic strategy is presentist insofar as the aesthetic is produced via digital filters in postproduction: the film mimics audio-visual cues associated with analogue 1980s films but, as with the production of Crazy Lixx's music, *The Sleeper*'s technological underpinnings inescapably underline the present.[7] Moreover, these postproduction effects are deployed inconsistently. Most of the footage is digitally shot and is presented without the filters that mimic celluloid damage. This inconsistency is double-edged. *The Sleeper* cannot stimulate nostalgia via its aesthetics alone given that it does not deliver an unwavering experiential replication of watching boom-period slashers. Simultaneously, *The Sleeper* brings these divergent styles into tension, creating discordance that calls attention to its approach. Despite mimicking the look and feel of boom-period slashers, the film does not attempt to pass itself off as an authentic 1980s cultural object. *The Sleeper*'s stylistic irregularity underscores that it was not made in the past, and its title card carries a copyright line that plainly states its production year in Roman numerals. The film's openness about its operations is coupled with ambiguity about the purposes and ends of its stylistic pastiche. Although not entirely nostalgic then, *The Sleeper* generates potentially productive tensions that invite deliberation on the subgenre's turn towards throwbacks.

Even greater inconsistency is sported by *LA Slasher* (2015), which acts as a counterexample insofar as its evocations of the past are so superficial and inconsistent that it cannot impart a sustained or coherent message about the connections between past and present. First, *LA Slasher* begins by employing the same aesthetic techniques as *The Sleeper* to recall the filmic past. Its opening shot – a text graphic, reading 'our feature presentation' – is accompanied by artificial digital film grain, suggesting that the film belongs to an analogue era. That aesthetic is then abandoned even more swiftly than it was in *The Sleeper*: following that graphic, the rest of the film is presented in pristine digital high-definition video.

Second, cultural markers are used to gesture to the past. The opening sequence is accompanied by ABC's 1982 hit song 'The Look of Love',

---

[6] Other contemporary slasher films such as *Lost After Dark* (2015) use the same approach, even including a 'missing reel' gag.

[7] For a more detailed discussion of the temporal implications of these techniques, see Jones (2018).

hinting that the subsequent film will be set in the 1980s. The film's masked killer is also first seen playing an arcade machine in a laundrette, implying that the film could be set in the 1980s (the heyday of the arcade machine). Where 1980s culture is drawn upon, it is associated with the killer. For instance, the killer dances to Lynn Jarrell's 'Save Your Love for Me' (1989) in a club, and he is also seen multiple times watching CRT televisions. Nevertheless, it quickly becomes apparent that the setting is contemporary. The protagonists use social media: 'the Socialite' refers to her 'Twitter followers'; 'the Stripper' takes selfies with her smartphone;[8] and the characters' social media posts (including the killer's) are presented via onscreen graphics. Furthermore, the killer's voiceover bemoans that 'reality TV' (which is anachronous to the 1980s) is 'the birthplace of the moron'. As 'the Actress' affirms, the technocultural present is integral to the killer's motive, which is a 'social statement': 'he's trying to get rid of anybody who just wants to be famous for five minutes', because the killer takes this ambition to represent 'everything that's wrong with the world'. Thus, film principally focuses on the present, regardless of its 1980s allusions.

Although presentism certainly does not preclude a film from forging bridges between past and present, *LA Slasher* falters because its allusions are both too superficial and overly 'loose'. To illustrate, the killer's climactic escape is accompanied by Go West's song 'King of Wishful Thinking' (1990), which is then superseded during the closing credits by Profound and Blaze's 'Wannabe Famous' (2014). A similar superseding of present over past is evident in the soundtrack's inclusion of Ellen and the Escapades's 2014 cover of Chesney Hawkes's 1991 hit 'The One and Only'. In both cases, the past yields to the present. Even so, the benchmark of pastness is blurry: in the opening, 1980s iconography is utilised, but in these instances, 1990s culture is drawn upon. The other examples inspected in this section take the 1980s (especially the early-1980s) as 'the' past. Since these are throwback slashers, the setting carries pertinent connotations: the early-1980s was the subgenre's boom-period. As Chapter 6 demonstrated, *Detention*'s vision of the past is anchored in the 1990s, thereby building distinct connections to the postmodern slasher phase. That rooting in a specific past undergirds *Detention*'s hypercoding, meaning the film remains coherent. Therefore, while *Detention* includes passing references from other periods as part of its hypercoded abundance, 'the' past (the 1990s) provides a bedrock that stabilises the text. By alluding to the 1980s and 1990s indiscriminately, *LA Slasher*'s vision of 'the past' becomes hazy,

---

[8] The protagonists are credited according to these typed titles rather than names.

and subsequently it is not obvious what function the past serves.⁹ Where cultural and aesthetic touchpoints are haphazardly juxtaposed, they are not married via a consistent stylistic approach.

Tellingly, although *LA Slasher* gestures towards a host of anachronistic cultural and aesthetic markers, it is not a throwback slasher insofar as it does not replicate the subgenre's core formula. Aside from its masked killer referring to himself as a 'slasher', the film lacks the conventional markers associated with the subgenre. *LA Slasher* instead expends more time aligning the content with the contemporary moment. One possibility is that *LA Slasher* includes hollow nods to the 1980s and 1990s to fit in alongside contemporary slasher films such as *Detention* and *Dude Bro Party Massacre III*, rather than passing substantial comment on the subgenre's lineage. More overtly, however, despite using the term 'slasher' in its title, *LA Slasher* owes more to torture porn in practice. The protagonists are abducted and held in an industrial warehouse location, bathed in the same sickly primary-hued light that became synonymous with the *Saw* films' aesthetic (see Jones 2019, 89). The cast includes Misha Barton (who starred in torture porn films *Walled In* [2009] and *Hope Lost* [2015]), as well as Barbara Nedeljakova (who starred in *Hostel* [2005]) and Ashlynn Yennie (who starred in the first two *The Human Centipede* films [2009, 2011]). *LA Slasher* was even rebranded as *Abducted* for its release in some territories, and that renaming chimes with one of torture porn's key themes. Most charitably, one might argue that *LA Slasher* conjures different eras to span between horror subgenres. Such linking would illuminate ways torture porn builds on the slasher's traits: torture porn films are ordinarily set in defined locations, often feature masked or unseen killers, and usually entail a cast of protagonists being eviscerated in succession in gory set-piece sequences (see Jones 2013, 18–19).¹⁰ Even if this were the intention, *LA Slasher* does not cohere its array of elements. It fails to commit to either torture porn or the slasher, and its temporal confusion stifles the film's ability to unequivocally connect these subgenres.

LA Slasher is a pertinent counterexample because it highlights that the other throwbacks probed in this section are closer to capturing a

---

⁹ Being charitable, one might argue that *LA Slasher* recalls the period encompassing 1982–1991 as the subgenre's heyday, but that does not fit with the slasher's primary period of cultural prominence: that is, if it is intended to refer to the subgenre's boom-period, those connotations are unlikely to be widely recognised.

¹⁰ This connection is explored in a more sustained way in *Bitch Ass* (2022), which is built on the concept of a masked killer subjecting victims to lethal iterations of children's games – including Rock, Paper, Scissors and Connect 4 – within a closed location (his home).

metamodern sensibility. *LA Slasher* offers no direct attempt to innovate, its tone is glib and sarcastic, and its temporal ambiguities are indicative of noncommittal apathy. All throwback slashers are to some degree underpinned by irony, since they only perform their pastness. This kind of irony is distinct from *LA Slasher*'s snarky ambivalence because it conveys a sincere message: the other throwbacks addressed in this section earnestly exude 'old school' slasher thrills, thereby expressing nostalgic fondness for a clearly delineated past (the slasher's boom-period).

Ahead of its Time: *Getting Schooled* and Revision

Having outlined several ways past and present are brought into conjunction in the period, a detailed case study will advance a more intricate articulation of metamodern nostalgia. *Getting Schooled* exemplifies how nostalgia can be implemented productively. The film connects the subgenre's boom-period to its present. *Getting Schooled* also illustrates that the past is not a fatalistic trap that limits the slasher film's potential for future development. An opening onscreen caption asserts that *Getting Schooled* is set in 1983. The film's protagonists – a group of teens in Saturday detention – are endangered by a teacher (Mr Roker). Roker is an ex-'Black Ops' Vietnam veteran who suffers severe delusional flashbacks after accidentally hitting himself in the head with a roll-up projector screen. His trauma is signalled by his delusional imaginings, such as hearing machine gun fire and helicopters. After dispatching the School Principal and Janitor, Roker picks off the teens until he is eventually bested by sole survivor, Julie.

Although set in 1983, *Getting Schooled* is unmistakably shot in digital HD, and does not endeavour to emulate a contemporaneous VHS aesthetic. As with *Die Die Delta Pi*, *Getting Schooled* draws on cultural markers that signify the past to build its narrative setting. The film's opening-credit graphics are redolent of the 1980s, evoking Memphis design by employing garish clashing colour combinations, geometric shapes and fonts filled by leopard print, polka dot and sprinkle patterns. The film's extradiegetic music consists of simulated synth and drum-machine sounds. The teens' fashion is stereotypical of the 1980s; for instance, Hillary is garbed in hot pink fishnet gloves and matching leg warmers, a pale denim jacket and heavy eyeshadow, while Rusty dons fingerless leather gloves, a leather jacket, a sleeveless plaid shirt, a 'Flock of Seagulls' haircut, and dark shades (even though he is indoors). The teens also utter slang terms associated with the period, such as 'bogus', 'barf me out', 'dweeb' and so forth.

Rather than being purely superficial or decorative, these cultural markers are embedded into *Getting Schooled* in two ways. First, unlike *LA Slasher*, these cultural markers relate to a definitively bounded period. Moreover, they are deployed consistently across the whole film because, unlike *Die Die Delta Pi*, *Getting Schooled* is entirely set in one era. Second, these symbols are undergirded by a deeper set of cultural and subgeneric evocations. *Getting Schooled*'s plot is informed by its 1980s context, distilling other narrative premises that were prevalent in popular cinema of the period. The slasher itself peaked in popularity in the 1980s, but *Getting Schooled* also unequivocally draws on the teen archetypes that 1980s comedy-dramas helped to anchor in the popular imagination. Given their shared Saturday detention setting, the paradigmatic 1985 hit *The Breakfast Club* is an obvious point of comparison, chiefly in bringing together distinct teen types: 'a brain, a beauty, a jock, a rebel and a recluse' as *The Breakfast Club*'s tagline has it.[11] *Getting Schooled* institutes the same types, but within a slasher context. That choice works quite naturally given that so many boom-period slasher films – including *Prom Night* (1980), *Graduation Day* and *Happy Birthday to Me* (both 1981) – are based around high schools, and so include similar (if not as neatly demarcated) teen archetypes. *Getting Schooled* also draws on the Vietnam film via its traumatised ex-military killer, Mr Roker. Following in the footsteps of late-1970s films such as *The Deer Hunter* (1978) and *Apocalypse Now* (1979), the Vietnam film resurged in the mid-to-late 1980s (perhaps thanks to the box-office success of *First Blood* [1982]), manifesting in films such as *Platoon* (1986), *Full Metal Jacket* (1987), *Good Morning, Vietnam* (1987) and *Jacknife* (1989), for example. Again, *Getting Schooled*'s combination of Vietnam film and slasher film is naturalised by the subgenre's past. For instance, slasher-adjacent films made in the 1970s and 1980s such as *Scum of the Earth* (1974) and *Don't Answer the Phone!* (1980) include traumatised Vietnam veterans as killers, while *The Final Terror* (1983) bridges between *Friday the 13th* (1980)'s version of 'survival in the forest' and *First Blood*'s post-Vietnam rendition of that theme. Some critics also propose that the boom-period slasher film arose in response to the horrors of the Vietnam war (see Muir 2007a, 18; Petridis 2019, 53). *Getting Schooled* does not just incorporate various elements of fashion and music to conjure the 1980s, then. Narrative and thematic threads are also amalgamated to create a sense of the era.

This era-specific cultural context – particularly the implicit filmic connections – highlights instances where *Getting Schooled* recalls subgeneric norms that were prevalent in the 1980s. Once those conventions are

---

[11] Other contemporary horror films employ similar themes and situations, including *Famine* (2011), *Bad Kids Go to Hell* (2012), *Deadly Detention* (2017), *Detention* (albeit in a more limited way) and the unrelated 2010 film *Detention*.

unveiled, they are then denaturalised. For example, Roker quips after he slays, following a trend in the subgenre most famously associated with Freddy Krueger and his immediate descendants in the late-1980s to early-1990s. So, for instance, when Roker disembowels Mike, Roker yells 'No guts, no glory!'. However, when Roker later cuts off the Principal's hand with a paper guillotine, he declares 'Principals don't belong here on Saturdays!'. Since it punctuates an execution, the line resembles the witticisms accompanying other murders. Nonetheless, the content of the line does not operate as a joke: it does not translate the method of violence into a verbal pun or draw on a widely recognised idiom. The timing and delivery emulate the shell of a convention, but by stripping out the content (the joke), the operations of that convention are exposed. The errant version is illuminated and its denaturalisation of convention is accentuated by regular and successful implementation of the convention elsewhere in the film.

The same approach is taken to characterisation. Discernible types are sketched out – jock, rebel, nerd, cheerleader, outcast – and these are recognisable as stock high school figures thanks especially to the success of *The Breakfast Club* (and other high school films that followed in its footsteps). Once set up in *Getting Schooled*, these types are then enriched. The moral of *The Breakfast Club* is that the teens find similarities that help them to bond despite their differences. Consequently, the characters do not themselves fundamentally change: they still epitomise the same core types at the end of *The Breakfast Club*. *Getting Schooled* administers an alternative trajectory: as the narrative progresses, information is revealed that undercuts the type-category each character initially represents. For example, unlike her equivalent in *The Breakfast Club* – Claire, whose 'hidden talent' is the ability to apply lipstick without her hands – Hillary discloses that she holds 'a blackbelt in taekwondo'. This revelation is presented as divergence from type because it undercuts other characters' expectations of Hillary. Julie submits they 'all have skills' that could help the group survive: she identifies that Shelly is 'smart' and Rusty is 'strong', but then pauses and stutters when trying to identify Hillary's skill. Julie's hesitation suggests that, like *The Breakfast Club*'s Claire, Hillary will have no hidden talents of practical use. Hillary's martial arts training undercuts that typing. Elsewhere, Rusty (the rebel) similarly surprises the other teens by divulging that he achieved a higher SAT test score than Shelly (the nerd). As with Hillary's proficiency in taekwondo, Rusty's intelligence is a 'hidden' talent because it is obscured by his outward adherence to the 'rebel' type. By setting up and then contravening these types, *Getting Schooled* articulates a yearning to transcend limited conventions.

Getting Schooled's metamodern sensibility is elucidated by three conjoined aspects of this repudiation of character typing. First, in contrast to the postmodern slashers' eye-rolling at boom-period clichés, here the boom-period is revived without irony. The revelation of Rusty's intelligence adds a new dimension to his character and questions the 'rebel' stereotype's assumed limitations, but it does not mock other instances of the type. Indeed, Rusty's characterisation potentially enhances the type by motioning that other seemingly stereotypical rebels might also carry hidden capacities that enrich those characters. Second, the reveals are symptomatic of *Getting Schooled*'s investment in characterisation. Third, the characterisation is a springboard for playing with expectations about the subgenre.

This conjunction of elements is plainly evinced when the teens express genuine care for each other's wellbeing and mourn for the lost. For instance, when Hillary dies, 'bad boy' Rusty cries and hugs her corpse (see Figure 7.2). A sentimental synth-string score confirms the moment's emotional gravity. Furthermore, after both Mike and Hillary's deaths, the teens regroup and candidly contemplate their losses in the detention room. These spotlighted moments offer insights into *Getting Schooled*'s critique of character typing. To illustrate, following Hillary's demise, Julie mournfully ruminates on her initial assessment of Hillary as a superficial 'princess' type: 'I thought "how typical" . . . Why do we have these misconceived ideas of one another? If this wouldn't [sic] have happened then we wouldn't be talking like this.' Here, Julie mourns not only for Hillary, but also for the potential friendship that did not flourish because of their segregation into ostensibly incompatible types. The latter is especially pronounced because Julie's 'type' is the 'outcast', so disconnection

Figure 7.2 Rusty mourns for Hillary in *Getting Schooled* (2017)

from others is her defining typological trait. Julie continues her speech by declaring 'I don't want to be like that anymore', indicating her conscious decision to both evolve beyond her type-category and to denounce the very idea of typing and the separation it causes. The narrative verifies her chosen path. After the others are eradicated, Julie is left alone and vulnerable, but the memory of her previous resolution (which replays in voiceover) spurs her into action. Julie confronts and defeats Roker not because of her survival instinct or just because she 'fits' into the Final Girl mould. Instead, she endures because she refuses her initial categorisation as an 'outcast'.

So, *Getting Schooled*'s character investment is the basis for its reflection on subgeneric conventions, and that investment is stressed via the teens' bonding. As is convention, the teens are assassinated when they are isolated. Rusty tries to prevent Mike from pursuing Roker alone and, when Mike is slain, Rusty warns the others to take note of 'what rushing away from the group gets us'. Julie later puts it in even starker terms: 'We have to stick together or we're dead.' While the structure ultimately separates them – they are picked off one-by-one, as is the subgenre's nature – the narrative affirms how important their bonding is by allowing the teens to express their concerns for one another.

Such reactions and ruminations are unusual in slasher films because they stall the action, but the absence of such moments feeds critical complaints that boom-period slasher victims are homogeneous fodder, that murders are akin to splattery 'money shots' in these films, and that slasher audiences are encouraged to take pleasure in 'faceless' victims' gruesome deaths. For example, Crane (1994, 148) disparagingly alleges that slasher fans' attitudes towards onscreen victims can be summated with three questions: 'How did they live? Who cares? . . . How did they die?' (see also Coffeen 2020, 39; Welt 1996, 79).[12] The attitude Crane describes manifests in the postmodern slasher via sardonic characters who joke about their peers' deaths, leaving only the lead protagonist(s) to take the losses seriously. As Muir avers, many postmodern slasher teen characters are 'callous and cynical' or 'heartless' (2011, 470 and 500). Newman similarly limns *Scream*'s teens as 'post-ironically unfeeling', treating 'real tragedy' as 'trivial' (2011, 390–1). *Getting Schooled*'s direction is markedly different, containing protracted shots of characters grieving and presenting that emotional response as the norm among its character base, then indicating

---

[12] Pascale advances a pertinent counter to such claims, noting the possibility that 'viewers are not just watching to see who dies, but also exhibit a simultaneous hopeful curiosity to see who lives' (2019, 153).

that their bonding is the basis for their growth and their survival. *Getting Schooled* rejects the postmodern slasher's sardonic cynicism by writing explicit portrayals of bonding and bereavement into its slasher scenario. *Getting Schooled*'s investment in character and emotional experience offers substance, countering the idea that the subgenre's characters are one-dimensional fodder.

Moreover, this approach rebuts Crane's vision of victims who are differentiated only by their death sequences. Crane's position implies that even the types are so superficial that such characters are interchangeable. In this view, the implication that characters are essentially indistinguishable from one another is reified when they are extinguished, because they are reduced to bloodied piles of flesh. In contrast, *Getting Schooled*'s mourning sequences ensure that the dead are recalled as individuals, resisting both their reduction to their mode of death or to a type. Rather than connoting their indistinguishability then, *Getting Schooled*'s corpses hypostatise the destruction of 'typed' moulds that these characters seemed to epitomise. Creating space for the characters' humanity serves a larger function then, casting subgeneric norms in a new light. Although the subgenre is named after the killer, it typically focuses on young people who strive to endure. *Getting Schooled* stresses that the subgenre's horror principally derives from the protagonists' future potentialities being extinguished. Since at least one teen usually survives the onslaught, slasher films carry a kernel of tragic optimism. *Getting Schooled*'s mechanisms accentuate that potentiality, not least by ensuring that its survivor perseveres, living on behalf of her fallen friends. The film closes with an unbroken minute-long shot of Julie smiling and dancing at her prom, with no indication that the killer could return. That is, her future seems secure in spite of the prior events.

Although the same basic premise could have played out without setting the film in 1983, the text's temporal setting is essential to conveying its meanings. 1983 was both the peak of the slasher's boom-period and the apex of its critical derision. By that point, the subgenre had been roundly criticised for being 'repulsive' in its 'unadulterated sadism' (Kroll 1981), 'exist[ing] for no other purpose than to shock . . . [with] horrors . . . of the sado-masochist kind' (Corry 1981), and displaying 'dumb kids being lopped, chopped and perforated' as 'spectacle' (Maslin 1982). The slasher film's characters were reputed to just occupy 'the limited role of the bloody victim' or contributor to the 'body count' (Groen 1981), remaining 'lifeless' throughout – 'even before the characters are murdered' – because 'the murders . . . are the point of such a movie' (Canby 1981).

Getting Schooled returns to that period to intervene in two ways. First, it addresses those criticisms by underlining the humanity and characterisation that was present in those texts all along. Boom-period characters were critically derided as one-dimensional victims-in-waiting at the time, but they have since been reclaimed retrospectively. For instance, *Friday the 13th Part III*'s (1982) resident prankster Shelly admits that he behaves like a 'jerk', proclaiming that the alternative is being exposed as 'a nothing'. Despite this negative self-assessment, and even though he is culled two-thirds of the way through the film, Shelly has been lauded as a fan favourite (see Dick 2019) and is even considered the series' best character by some (see Felci 2014).[13] For many fans, characters such as Shelly were more than the blank types critics took them to be. Indeed, the fan perspective on such characters has helped these texts to sustain over time. *Getting Schooled*'s characters are more developed and surprising than their archetypal boom-period equivalents, but that amplification of the characters' humanity captures how boom-period characters are perceived by those fans for whom repeat watching has fostered affection for even the boom-period's most formulaic characters. Much like *Dude Bro Party Massacre III*, the past is reclaimed by providing experiential access to a fan's fondness for the subgenre.

Second, *Getting Schooled*'s amplified humanity and emotional bonding revises the past. Rather than evading critical derision by diverting into the supernatural (as many slasher filmmakers did after the success of *A Nightmare on Elm Street* [1984]), *Getting Schooled* imagines an alternative timeline in which slashers doubled down on the human bonds that undergird the subgenre. The desire to rewrite history is evident in the particular choice of time setting. *Getting Schooled* is set on 20 April 1983, and that date is offered apropos of nothing in an onscreen caption. It is important that the viewer understands that the film is set in the 1980s to naturalise *Getting Schooled*'s fashion and idioms, but otherwise the date is unnecessarily specific. However, the date invites another comparison to *Getting Schooled*'s comedy-drama equivalent, *The Breakfast Club*. *The Breakfast Club* is set on 24 March 1984. When contextualised alongside *The Breakfast Club* – and *Getting Schooled*'s multiple allusions to that text invite such a comparison – the date makes an implicit claim: *Getting Schooled* precedes that famous representation. While *Getting Schooled*'s

---

[13] That reputation led to Shelly's digital resurrection as a playable character in the 2017 *Friday the 13th* videogame. Fan reclamation of supposed 'fodder' offers a parallel to the subgenre's idiosyncratic unexpected moments (see Chapter 6): both cases indicate that the subgenre's appeal is not simply based in seeing 'obnoxious' teens being murdered.

characters draw from types *The Breakfast Club* (and its subsequent imitators) helped to concretise in culture, *Getting Schooled*'s 1983 setting playfully amends history by suggesting that its enhanced characters are authentic progenitors of these types.

One need not have detailed knowledge of *The Breakfast Club* to understand *Getting Schooled*'s revisionism. Set in 1983 but made in 2017, *Getting Schooled* is inherently (and overtly) retrospective. The notion that boom-period characters adhere to stock types is amplified by a retrospective viewpoint. The subgenre's conventions were founded in its boom-period, and that includes establishing character types as part of the subgenre's conventional apparatus. Consequently, it stands to reason that many boom-period films would exhibit those very types, but not that those characters would have been perceived as 'stock' types during the boom-period. In the mid-1980s, *The Breakfast Club* helped to solidify these types in the cultural imagination, but the slasher's boom-period peaked earlier in the decade. *Getting Schooled*'s re-contextualisation of the high school coming-of-age film as a slasher movie indicates that the boom-period's characters are less 'stock' than they appear in retrospect, because retrospection deemphasises contemporaneous understanding. Furthermore, *Getting Schooled*'s revisionism highlights the contributions boom-period slashers made to founding these conventional characters, both in the slasher subgenre and in 'teen film' more generally.

Thus, *Getting Schooled*'s temporal setting draws attention to a history of representations that instilled and sustained these types (the grain against which *Getting Schooled*'s characterisation rubs). Just as the characters are treated sincerely, *Getting Schooled* does not mock or erase the past, however. Although it remodels the past in its narrative, that playful rewriting is contingent on an extant extratextual reality: the subgenre's past. *Getting Schooled* embodies a metamodern outlook in the sense that it 'extend[s], reanimate[s] and repudiate[s] twentieth-century' equivalents, and as such, demands that we pay 'attention to the textures of narrative form and . . . to the contingencies of historical reception' (James and Seshagiri 2014, 89). In this sense, *Getting Schooled* recasts the past according to a contemporary metamodern sensibility.

Time and Time Again: Looking Back, Moving Forward

This chapter has illustrated two related ways contemporary slashers engage with the past: via replication (throwbacks) and revision (*Getting Schooled*). Where contemporary slashers strip the subgenre 'back to basics', they exemplify Lowenthal's model of nostalgia as 'yearning . . . for a simple and stable past' (1989, 21). Instead of deriding or dismissing the past as passé (as postmodern slashers usually do), these throwback slashers replicate the boom-period's pleasures. Stripping 'back to basics' implies that the postmodern slasher's self-consciousness was less a marker of sophistication, and more an overcomplication that hinders the slasher's effectiveness by distracting from the core formula.

The extent to which throwbacks are metamodern is a more complicated question, not least because they operate in several different ways. Where throwbacks draw on 1980s film aesthetics or fashion, that replication could be considered insincere (insofar as it is inherently inauthentic) or naïve (inasmuch as they do not expressly acknowledge that the past cannot be recaptured). These qualities are precisely what make throwback slashers nostalgic. At this stage it is worth returning to Lowenthal's observation that 'nostalgia expresses longings for times that are safely, rather than sadly, beyond recall' (1989, 28). The past is 'safely . . . beyond recall' in the sense that it is no longer available for first-hand experiential access. That might not seem to apply to the slasher subgenre, given that the 1980s are within living memory for many and boom-period slasher films are still abundantly available in various formats.[14] However, although these films can still be experienced and some viewers will be able to remember their experiences of watching slasher films in the 1980s, one can no longer (re-)experience boom-period slashers as they were experienced at the time. Even if one were to watch a boom-period slasher such as *Night School* (1981) for the first time today, one's experience would be informed by the present cultural landscape, being shaped by one's knowledge about or experiences of horror or slasher films made after *Night School*, as well as one's distance from prevalent cultural mores and prominent aesthetic choices that would have felt natural when *Night School* was released in 1981, but which have since fallen out of fashion.

These experiences 'are *safely*, rather than *sadly*, beyond recall' (Lowenthal 1989, 28, emphasis added) because if one were able to (re-)experience the period first-hand, the experience would fail to elicit nostalgic pleasure. First, retrospective fondness is inspired by aspects of the past that were once prevalent, but which are now absent from contemporary slasher films. For example, one might be nostalgic about the 1980s fashion displayed in boom-period slashers. If it were possible to re-experience a 1980s slasher film as it was experienced at the time, the fashion would not necessarily be a notable presence. At the time, 1980s fashion was prevalent and normalised

---

[14] On issues relating to the digital restoration of such films, memory and 'authentic' experience, see Jones (2018).

by context. In the 1980s, viewers would have been garbed in 1980s fashion themselves. Where the fashion presented onscreen was overstated – being unrepresentative of garments everyday people might wear – contemporaneous viewers might have felt fondness for the fashion, but that fondness would still not be nostalgic (it would instead be more akin to aspirational desire, for example). It is only in its contextual absence, in its unfashionability, that 1980s fashion becomes the object of nostalgic yearning. Second, contemporary throwbacks do not replicate the past as it was. Instead, their articulations are condensed and exaggerated, thereby compensating for an inability to provide first-hand experiential access to the past. To illustrate, contemplate nostalgia for 1980s fashion again. It would be disappointing to re-experience the past as it was experienced at the time because most of the fashion represented onscreen might come across as mundane. Even when viewed retrospectively, nostalgia for 1980s fashion fixates on aspects that are most unlike our present dominant styles, while those akin to present fashion norms are likely to remain unnoticed or are unlikely to inspire much excitement. When employing cultural markers to signify the 1980s then, throwbacks include exaggerated versions of those markers, or augment by combining a multitude of markers. The result is a heuristic creation that is more archetypically '1980s' than any actual individual film from the period. If the throwback's amplified or amalgamated representations were presented in the 1980s context, they would come across as outlandish to contemporaneous audiences. Although throwbacks are redolent of boom-period slashers, the aim is not to replicate the past exactly but to elicit nostalgic fondness. This is why nostalgic replications also exaggerate by removing or downplaying flaws that hampered the original experience (which would hinder one's nostalgic pleasure) or converting those flaws into positive markers (as encapsulated by the digital reproduction of visual imperfections such as celluloid damage).[15] Indeed, the digital replication of analogue imperfections underscores the distance between throwbacks such as *The Sleeper* and the boom-period slashers they emulate.

In this regard, nostalgic throwbacks chime with the metamodern sensibility, even though they do not expressly renew the subgenre with notable innovations. Nostalgia is rooted in a form of presentism that is intertwined with the metamodern emphases on augmentation and subjective experiential access addressed in previous chapters. Here, those elements take on a specific character because of the nostalgic slasher's temporal connotations. *Getting Schooled* illuminates those aspects via its revisionist tactics.

---

[15] Note that nostalgic enjoyment of intentionally created 'flaws' is different from cynically laughing at a past film's unintentional shortcomings.

Working from the premise that we have no direct experiential access to the past, *Getting Schooled* intervenes by recasting the subgenre's past. Conventional character types and relations – established in the subgenre's earliest films – are recollected, then amended and amplified, thereby rewriting the subgenre's past in a way that redresses prevailing criticisms surrounding those conventions. By taking the time to invest in its characters' emotional responses, *Getting Schooled* remodels the past after a metamodern outlook. *Getting Schooled*'s temporal setting highlights how much the subgenre and the surrounding culture have transformed from the boom-period to the present. Throwbacks also implicitly acknowledge that the subgenre has mutated, given that a desire to return 'back to basics' points towards dissatisfaction with the subgenre's direction of development.

Whether by replicating or revising, nostalgic metamodern slashers incorporate the past to facilitate meaningful development in the subgenre's present. Nostalgic metamodern slashers acknowledge that fashions and aesthetic standards transform over time and that these shifts reflect changing values and concerns within the zeitgeist. Such values, concerns, and their stylistic manifestations are accepted on their own terms, as opposed to being cynically dismissed as passé. As Gibbons proposes, 'the postmodernist preoccupation with senses of ending, entropic disintegration, and apocalyptic visions of the world's destruction resulted in reductive presentism' (2021, 138). 'Metamodern fictions', in contrast, reject the notion that the past is a fatalistic trap because the future is 'absent', instead 'resurrect[ing] historicity and resuscitat[ing] the future as a field of possibilities' (Gibbons 2021, 147). In the metamodern slasher then, nostalgia does not mean mournfully attempting to capture the past as it was (which is futile) or being trapped by the past. On the contrary, metamodern slashers recognise that if the subgenre's past can be distinguished from its present, some change must have occurred. Since the subgenre has altered in the past, it can also continue to adapt in the future.

In this respect, the metamodern slasher's inherent cogitation on the subgenre separates it from the kind of 'conservative renderings' Rosewarne refers to, in which 'a key component of nostalgia is the rewriting of the past to make it something worth pining for', something 'better and worth glorifying' (2020, 80). Metamodern slashers do not take the past's relative inaccessibility as an opportunity to purely idealise the past, or to express an impossible desire to return to (a romanticised version of) the past. Rather, these films bring the past into confluence with the present, indicating that past and present are intertwined. They also express a longing to turn towards the future. Revivifying the boom-period slasher is a way of signalling that ambition: in contrast to the postmodern slasher's fatalistic view of the subgenre, subgeneric development was still possible during the boom-period. That possibility is resurrected in the metamodern slasher film by implicating subgeneric development in its representations. Therefore, the metamodern slasher eschews the vision of nostalgia as 'a reactionary, regressive condition imbued with sentimentality', in favour of the understanding that nostalgia grants 'a way of coming to terms with the past' so that we 'can move on' (Cook 2005, 3).

This chapter has posited core issues surrounding temporality, providing a foundation for the next two chapters. Nostalgic metamodern slashers deliver a counter to Kirby's (2006) fear that the era after postmodernism (which Kirby calls the 'pseudomodern' period) will be defined by digital media's impermanence and mutability, resulting in an 'amnesiac' culture of 'triteness . . . shallowness'. As an alternative, nostalgic metamodern slashers bring the past into conjunction with the present in ways that enliven understandings of both the subgenre's past and its present. The next chapter will address a particular type of contemporary slasher film that might seem to exemplify Kirby's anxieties even more directly: sequel-remake-reboots (or requels). Such films have certainly stood accused of being 'shallow', and the propensity for requels to ignore previous attributes, ideas or entire entries in an established series certainly sounds as if it could be symptomatic of an 'amnesiac' culture. However, as I will demonstrate, the two approaches deliberated in this chapter – replication and revision – offer a more nuanced understanding of the requel's take on temporality.

CHAPTER 8

Remake, Sequel, Reboot, Requel

As Chapter 7 proffered, postmodernists customarily cast the past as a fatalistic trap. In the postmodern slasher film, that idea is hypostatised where, for instance, conventions are treated as passé but are reiterated regardless. The metamodern slasher takes a different stance. A recurring theme of the analyses so far – especially evident in *Triangle* (2009), *Detention* (2011), *Dude Bro Party Massacre III* (2015), *Getting Schooled* (2017) and *Happy Death Day* (2017) – is that revisiting the past affords opportunities to instigate change. In the metamodern slasher film, the present acts as a temporal bridge between past and future, with the implication that the future is undetermined. Consequently, characters can bring about future change within the narrative and filmmakers affect the subgenre's future via their present contributions. To develop these ideas, this chapter will attend to slasher film series as chains of continuity.

This focus on slasher series arises out of the subgenre's entrenched association with sequels. Indeed, some have argued that 'the genre most identified with the sequel is the Slasher [sic]' (Varndell 2014, 75; see also Berliner 2001b, 108). That association is unsurprising for two reasons. First, the slasher's home genre is itself amenable to sequelisation; as Mee argues, 'horror cinema has long relied on seriality and familiarity as much as it has on change and development' (2017, 197). Second, as Loock posits, 'sequelisation emerged as one of Hollywood's major production trends during the 1970s and 1980s' (2017, 93); that is, in tandem to the slasher's boom-period. The subgenre's synonymy with sequelisation is a product of surrounding industrial practices. Therefore, it is unsurprising that the subgenre's 1980s heyday was defined by the box-office prominence of sequel-heavy series such as *Friday the 13th*, *Halloween* and *A Nightmare on Elm Street*.

The association was also potentially fortified by corresponding negative connotations surrounding both slashers and sequels. Critics commonly allege that the subgenre is derivative, and slasher sequels compound that reputation. Sequels too are broadly condemned for repeating an original property's premise, themes, central character arcs and/or operations. Sequels are thus broadly perceived as exercises in 'narrative regurgitation' (Jess-Cooke 2009, vi), such that even the term 'sequel' has become synonymous with the idea of being 'imitative, derivative, appropriational' (Jess-Cooke and Verevis 2010, 5). As Budra and Schellenberg remark, this negative characterisation of the sequel as an 'exploitative device, a cynical ploy to sell an inevitably inferior new text on the basis of an earlier work's success' charts back to at least 1719 (1998, 4). Purportedly then, sequels have nothing to add or say, and so they are subordinate to original works (including the film on which a sequel is based).[1] Two implications follow from this stance. First, the longer the chain of sequels, the more diluted the original idea becomes. Later sequels are perceived as increasingly inferior given that each allegedly 'feed[s] off the life force of the last big hit' (Muir 2007a, 15; see also Tudor 2002, 106). Second, sequels are perceived as money-grubbing exercises, attempting to milk cash from audiences who enjoyed the original. More bluntly, sequels are frequently envisaged as 'watered-down drivel, mass-produced with the basest of profit motives in mind' (Goggin 2010, 106; see also Bernard 2020, 89; Klein and

---

[1] *The Third Saturday in October Part V* (2022) reifies this notion. As with *Dude Bro Party Massacre III*, *The Third Saturday in October Part V* is a contrived throwback sequel to a nonextant series. Its pre-credit sequence caption states that *The Third Saturday in October* 'predated *Friday the 13th*, but was made as a cheap cash-in following the success of *Halloween*', and is now 'a lost relic of a bygone era'. *Part V* is presented as if it was made in 1994 and the film is dull, being hampered by amateur acting, thin plotting and poor pacing. Presumably, however, these detrimental elements are intentional, seeking to pastiche low-budget direct-to-video sequels. A contrived original (*The Third Saturday in October*) was also released alongside *Part V*, and the 'first' film does not suffer from the same weaknesses *Part V* exhibits. Skipping over the imagined intervening films (*Part II*, *Part III* and *Part IV*) exposes how much better the 'first' film is compared with its sequel (despite its framing as a mere 'cash-in' on *Halloween* [1978]). When double-billed at festivals such as Popcorn Frights and Chattanooga Film Festival in 2022, the films convey that sequel chains lead to declining quality. Additionally, these double-bills schedule *Part V* prior to the 'first' film. That heterochronic 'nonsequential' scheduling also echoes the experiential approach utilised by *Dude Bro Party Massacre III* (see Chapter 6). *Part V* opens with a director's statement that the film is meant to speak to anyone who recollects 'renting the *Friday the 13th* and *Halloween* movies over and over from your local mom and pop video store'. Watching *Part V* prior to *The Third Saturday in October* captures an experience of renting sequels out of order, based on their availability.

Palmer 2016, 12).² For both reasons, sequels are often not taken seriously as objects of study.

These negative associations and connotations continue to haunt the slasher subgenre, and they have been amplified by a subsequent industrial trend. If the 1980s was the era of the sequel, the 2000s – the period following sequel saturation – is the epoch of the remake or reboot. As with sequels, the slasher subgenre followed this broader industrial turn. The 2000s slasher has thus become synonymous with remakes, chiefly remakes of boom-period slasher properties. Remakes evoke the same kinds of negative appraisals that surround sequels. Remaking is commonly condemned as a 'parasitical', money-grubbing mode (Forrest and Koos 2002, 3; see also Eberwein 1998, 18; Rosewarne 2020, 39).³ Remakes are also reputed to be derivative, since they are plainly based on prior works (see Horton and McDougal 1998, 6; Loock 2012, 124; Mee 2022, 18). In both of these respects, remakes are indicative of Hollywood's modus operandi, combining 'cinema's more general ability to repeat and replay the same film over and again through reissue and redistribution' with the expectation that studio films will 'deliver reliability (repetition) and novelty (innovation) in the same production package' (Verevis 2005, 1 and 4). Resultantly, however, remakes are commonly written off by critics as 'unoriginal, uninspired, unnecessary' (Rosewarne 2019, 8), just as sequels are. This is markedly the case for slasher remakes. As Mee contends, 'horror remakes are especially susceptible to critical contempt' because they belong 'to an already derided genre' (2017, 193), and slashers are commonly perceived as particularly 'formulaic and derivative examples of the genre' (2022, 18). Due to these ingrained views of remakes, the horror genre and the slasher subgenre, it is almost inevitable that slasher remakes attract negative critical assessment. Roche (2014, 7) and Hantke (2007, 191) suggest

---

[2] This reputation is not helped by horror sequels such as *Hellraiser: Revelations* and *Children of the Corn: Genesis* (both 2011), which were reportedly rushed into production so that Dimension Films could retain the rights to these series (see https://bloody-disgusting.com/movie/3383469/children-corn-secretly-shooting/). These incidents affirm the notion that when it comes to horror sequels, textual content is secondary to business imperatives. However, the view that sequels are designed purely for profit can be framed more charitably. Sequels are 'a relatively safe investment' (Loock 2017, 96). For example, advertising original films entails setting up a narrative premise while also targeting specific audiences. For the sequel, that work has already been done. Rather than supplying 'evidence of Hollywood's moneygrubbing impulses and creative exhaustion' (Loock 2017, 106), sequels evince efficiency in this respect.

[3] Again, we might frame this more generously by noting that, like sequels, remakes are relatively safe investments, offering studios 'a fighting chance to make money in a notoriously difficult industry' (Rosewarne 2020, 13).

that horror fans share that dissatisfaction, and their broad claims are confirmed with greater precision by Mee (2017, 198).[4] That fan attitude is also articulated in the 2006 slasher film *The Remake*, in which a horror fan goes on a killing spree to halt the production of a remake, declaring that there should be 'no more fucking remakes!'.

Although remakes have tended 'to be differentiated rhetorically, if not conceptually, from sequels' (Nowell 2012, 71–2), the boundaries between these categories have become increasingly blurry in recent years. For a host of contemporary slasher films, it is difficult to distinguish whether the text is distinctly a reboot, a sequel or a remake. As Mee observes, such films are 'reimaginings, reversions, revisions, rebirths', resulting in films that are 'revamped ... reduxed and reinvented' versions of an established property (Mee 2022, 37). Such texts – commonly termed 'requels' – conflate and ambiguate these categories.[5] Within the slasher subgenre, these trends manifest in two crucial ways. First, there are numerous ostensible slasher remakes such as *April Fool's Day* (2008), *My Bloody Valentine* (2009)

---

[4] Loock (2017, 101) and Rosewarne (2020, 71) both contend that broader publics continue to engage with remakes despite the negative critical discourse surrounding the form. Nonetheless, it is worth noting that fans are (by definition) more invested in the sub/genre than the average cinemagoer, and so fans might express dissatisfaction with the way 'classic' horror texts are re-envisaged, while broader audiences might not notice or share those dissatisfactions. Loock and Rosewarne refer to continued box-office revenue as evidence of satisfaction. However, while audiences might be willing to watch remakes, engagement does not guarantee enjoyment. If a cinemagoer seeks a horror film, and slasher remakes are prevalent at that time, the cinemagoer might frequent such a screening. Indeed, Roche (2014, 17) considers this a substantial demographic for remakes. Yet, the fact of an individual attending a screening does not itself reveal much about what horror film content might have satisfied them more, had alternatives been available.

[5] Ochonicky (2020) provides separate definitions of reboot, sequel and remake. However, non-academic parties such as filmmakers, marketers, distributors, critics and audience members might be less inclined to delimit these categories.

Although requel production has escalated recently, this is not a uniquely contemporary phenomenon. Indeed, *Wes Craven's New Nightmare* (1994) might be considered a requel. It follows directly from the *A Nightmare on Elm Street* series' core premises, draws on an established killer's identity and motivations and incorporates returning characters, who are played by the series' regular cast members (including Robert Englund, Heather Langenkamp and John Saxon). As such, it plays as a sequel. However, *New Nightmare* is also a remake of sorts, reimagining the original's core 'Nancy versus Freddy' conflict and directly replicating scenes from the original film (such as Nancy talking to her father before her final showdown with Freddy). The film is equally a reboot, inasmuch as it seeks to instigate a *New Nightmare* following the series' previously proclaimed endpoint (*Freddy's Dead: The Final Nightmare* [1991]). Freddy's dramatic makeup redesign and the film's metafictional narrative approaches overtly express its 'newness' (that is, its departure and separation from the preceding film series).

and *Prom Night* (2008) that have varying relationships to their origin texts. So, for instance, *Black Christmas* (2006) is based on the earlier proto-slasher of the same name, but adds in substantial backstory about its killer Billy, making it something of a prequel as well as a remake.[6] Roche captures this tenuous relationship between the original and the new story by referring to such films as 'non-remakes' (2014, 14). Some such texts – including *Halloween* (2018), *Candyman* (2021) and *Scream* (2022) – are titled as if they are remakes of originals, but these narratives continue the original's story. For example, Anthony, the protagonist in *Candyman* (2021), is revealed to be the baby who was saved from being burned to death in the original's climax. Second, several slasher franchises including *Scream* and *I Know What You Did Last Summer* have been translated into television series.[7] For instance, helmed by its creator Don Mancini, the TV series *Chucky* (2021–) continues from narrative situations established in the most recent films in his *Child's Play* series (*Curse of Chucky* [2013] and *Cult of Chucky* [2017]).[8]

This situation illustrates another way metamodern slashers build on foundations laid by their postmodern predecessors. Taken superficially, the context of remaking and rebooting corroborates postmodern notions that originality is not possible. Yet, these new 'requel' iterations do not merely confirm the slasher's reputation as a repetitive, money-grubbing subgenre, flagrantly recycling material for capital gain. As Loock remarks, these properties are 'revived to be sold to both the original generation of viewers and a new one' (2016, 291), and it is worth noting a nuance in Loock's position: the aim is to target a new generation and the older generation as they are now. That is, the outputs must be aligned with the present sociocultural situation in order to speak to contemporary audiences. This relationship between the cultural moment and audience expectations is paramount. In 1993, Collins asserted that 'technological and cultural changes' such as the recirculation of genre texts via home

---

[6] Rob Zombie employs a similar tactic in the remake *Halloween* (2007).
[7] This move is contextualised by other recent slasher-based television series such as *Scream Queens* (2015–2016) and *Slasher* (2016–), and other translations of horror series into television series, including *Hannibal* (2013–2015), *Bates Motel* (2013–2017), *The Exorcist* (2016–2018) and *Ash versus the Evil Dead* (2015–2018). On these industrial trends, see Gaynor 2022.
[8] Mancini has retained a surprising amount of creative control over the series. Unlike most other major horror series, which are contributed to by various writers who reinvent the characters, Don Mancini created the original story, has remained a core writer on all parts of the canon series and has directed three of the film series' entries. The exception is the remake *Child's Play* (2019), which Mancini was not involved in.

video technologies and television instigated the redefinition of 'genericity' and its functions (1993, 47). Consequently, Collins avers, 'contemporary genre films must somehow make sense of or map' the continually mutating 'cultural terrain' they enter into (1993, 47). As noted in Chapter 7, digital technologies have amplified the propensity for cultural recirculation and, following Collins, genre texts respond to the technocultural contexts that situate them.[9] So, as Hernández-Santaolalla and Raya argue, despite 'a sensation of continuity between the originals and . . . new versions' of slasher properties, there are empirical, statistically demonstrable divergences between texts that belong to different eras (2021, 20). These disparities reflect transformations in audience predispositions, prevailing sociocultural norms and so forth. Moreover, many of these new iterations make significant narrative modifications to the materials on which they are based. Even the most direct film remakes of recognised properties regularly boast acute differences from their originals: for example, the remakes *My Bloody Valentine* (2009) and *Terror Train* (2022) entirely reimagine the killers' identities. Elsewhere, *When a Stranger Calls* (2005) takes an augmentative approach to its source material. The first fifteen minutes of the 1979 original replicate the short film (*The Sitter* [1977]) that was the basis for the feature, and beyond that, the subsequent story follows the same babysitter lead protagonist in new situations. The remake of *When a Stranger Calls* instead stretches *The Sitter*'s events into a full feature. In doing so, it draws attention to the fact that *When a Stranger Calls* is not precisely the 'original' version of the story, and stresses that its opening is the movie's most notable and memorable part. Where slasher films have been adapted to television series, that also entails augmenting the storyline in substantial ways to expand the narrative; although loosely based on the same basic plotline from Lois Duncan's novel, the television series *I Know What You Did Last Summer* (2021) is over four hours longer than the famous 100-minute film version. In an even more extreme example, aside from its title and college campus setting, *Black Christmas* (2019) has almost nothing in common with either the 1974 or 2005 films of the same name. Far from concretising postmodern fatalism then, requels confirm that change is not only possible, but also discernible.

---

[9] This insight helps to naturalise the pivot from slasher film sequels to television series. As several scholars have observed, the 1980s sequel-boom potentially resulted from audiences becoming accustomed to television's seriality, repetitiveness and episodicity (see Kornfield 2016, 206; Loock 2017, 100; Verevis 2005, 41). The turn back to television is thus perhaps a response to subsequent technocultural shifts such as the rise of on-demand video streaming and binge-watching.

Time After Time: Retconning, Retrocausality and Revis[it]ing the Past

At minimum, this line of thought invites re-evaluation of remakes, reboots and sequels, rather than dismissing them out of hand as lazy copies of the originals (as is commonplace). Indeed, in contrast to the notion that films in these categories are inferior replications, the categories can offer filmmakers greater freedoms to remodel and introduce new elements. For instance, sequels work forward from an origin story and frequently include recurring characters. Those elements provide familiar ground, meaning audiences are equipped to tolerate some degree of deviation or experimentation elsewhere.[10] Arguably, the more familiar audiences are with a series' premise, the greater liberties filmmakers can take with the narrative, themes and aesthetics. Note that this stance reverses the notion that sequels necessarily become weaker the longer a sequel chain becomes. In this view, the longer the chain becomes, the better established the core premises are, the less risk there is in terms of the sequel finding an audience (see Loock 2016, 281), and the more room filmmakers have to experiment with new ideas, trajectories or aesthetic modifications. Such experimentation is encouraged by the inherent need to differentiate the sequel from the original, if only in minor ways.

As I have argued elsewhere, that experimentation commonly materialises in filmmakers playing with expected spatial and temporal premises (see Jones 2010 and 2022). To illustrate, the *Child's Play* series' underlying possession theme allows its filmmakers to introduce forms of spatial variation. The original *Child's Play* (1988) presents a human killer (Charles Lee Ray, aka Chucky) evading death, using black magic to relocate his soul into a toy (a 'Good Guy' doll). When the doll starts becoming flesh, Chucky finds out he must transfer his soul into 'the first human being [he] revealed [his] true self to': a six-year-old called Andy. As the series progresses, this stipulation concerning the spatial relocation of Chucky's soul becomes looser. By the third film, *Child's Play 3* (1991), the Chucky doll is rebuilt. Chucky concludes that this reconstruction (somehow) resets the curse: he announces, 'wait a minute, I got a new body and I ain't told anyone about my little secret yet'. Chucky shifts focus from a now sixteen-year-old Andy to a younger boy (Tyler). The next film, *Bride of Chucky* (1998), introduces

---

[10] The same is true of genre conventions, which, as metamodern slasher films demonstrate, provide audiences with sufficient grounding to tolerate experimentation. As Chapters 4–6 evinced, audiences rely on those structures to decode films, just as filmmakers rely on audiences' familiarity with those structures in order to innovate.

an amulet that allows Chucky to take residency in any human body. By the sixth film, *Curse of Chucky*, the amulet is gone but Chucky retains his supernatural ability to relocate his soul into any body. The seventh film, *Cult of Chucky*, then discloses he discovered a 'groovy new spell on voodoofordummies.com' that allows him to displace his soul into 'anyone or *anything*' (emphasis added). Furthermore, the spell allows him to inhabit multiple vessels simultaneously. Consequently, as the story continues across multiple iterations, the makers take greater liberties with the essential 'soul transference' premise, relying on familiarity with the core idea to introduce new variations. These amendments emerge as an increasingly relaxed spatial approach, meaning Chucky can exist in dozens of places at once. The variety and number of vessels he can inhabit increases in tandem with the number of entries in the series. So, in the television series *Chucky*, Chucky forms an army by simultaneously possessing seventy-two dolls (plus Nica, the human protagonist of *Curse of Chucky* and *Cult of Chucky*).

It might initially appear that requels are too restrictive to allow for this kind of variation. For example, one way of viewing the requel is that it is hopelessly caught between needing to replay the original's plot (given that it is part-remake), continuing a story and themes set up across the preceding films (since it is part-sequel), and advancing reasonably significant departures from the preceding series (because it is part-reboot). The requel thus occupies a superposition, being concurrently pulled in several seemingly incompatible directions. However, just as long chains of sequels grant filmmakers greater freedom to introduce variance, the requel's competing demands can be leveraged if they are seen as precipitating liberating 'looseness' instead of restrictions. That looseness is most evident in the ways requels utilise temporal variations to distinguish themselves from preceding films in the respective series.

Scrutinising requels' temporal aspects illuminates striking differences between postmodern and metamodern conceptions of past-present-future relations. As was illustrated via the examples of replication and rewriting in Chapters 6 and 7, metamodern slashers counter postmodern fatalism by playing with the past. For instance, *Dude Bro Party Massacre III* – a 'sequel' to a non-existent original – creates its own legacy to work forward from. The film pretends to be in continuity with preceding films, but the makers are not limited by that past because the 'history' is generated only for its utility in the present. *Dude Bro*'s strategy thereby undercuts the notion that the past fatally constrains the subgenre's present renditions. Elsewhere, *Getting Schooled* playfully revises history so that its iteration of the past accords to present values, but also frees its protagonists (and the subgenre) from the limitations of stock subgeneric character typing. *Getting Schooled* recognises the past but yields possibilities for future growth within the subgenre by bringing the past into concert with the present.

These techniques are pertinent to this chapter because metamodern requels also work forward from a seemingly fixed past. Although a series' narrative past is an important anchor for orienting its requel, that past is not strictly fixed. The requel's 'remake' function implies that aspects of the canonical history established by the series' previous entries might be subject to re-evaluation or renovation. This vision of the past amplifies a tendency found in chained sequels. To push a story forward, sequels routinely adopt retroactive continuity: that is, revisiting and modifying story elements 'to create new narrative potential in the present (and thus in the future)' (Friedenthal 2017, 6). 'Retconning' is certainly not a new phenomenon, nor is it new to the slasher subgenre. Indeed, *Friday the 13th Part 2* (1981) famously retcons the series' initial premise: that Jason drowned because his summer camp 'counsellors weren't paying any attention', and so his mother massacres new counsellors to prevent the camp from reopening. In *Part 2*, it is proclaimed that Jason's 'body was never recovered from the lake after he drowned . . . he's still out there'. Initially, this is presented as a campfire legend (of dubious veracity), but the film soon confirms Jason's existence, and the series then follows him as the new central killer.

To develop on the established story as a chain of sequels progresses and develops, filmmakers introduce narrative variations. Commonly, new writers and directors contribute to such series, and each ordinarily takes the series in new directions by adding to its lore. In light of those additions, some degree of retroactive continuity is usually required to maintain the main story's coherence (see Proctor 2017, 232). Continuity can be decidedly tricky for slasher sequels because the antagonist is usually (temporarily) eradicated at the end of each film. Typically, writers of one instalment need not worry about how the killer can be brought back from the dead, leaving the next team of filmmakers to achieve that end. The challenge is perhaps best exemplified by the makers of *Friday the 13th: The Final Chapter* (1984) exterminating Jason Voorhees, the writers of the fifth instalment (*Friday the 13th: A New Beginning* [1985]) omitting Jason entirely (replacing him with an impostor) and the scribe of *Friday the 13th Part VI: Jason Lives* (1986) employing a lightning bolt to resurrect Jason as one of the undead,[11] which then leads to supernatural shenanigans in the seventh and ninth films (*Friday the 13th Part VII: The New Blood* [1988] and *Jason Goes to Hell: The Final Friday* [1993]).

---

[11] This is not meant as a disparagement: *Jason Lives*'s opening sequence is awesome.

New writers might also add to the series' lore because they are tasked with 'reinvigorating' a series by studios that are keen to sustain audience interest. This situation poses challenges in terms of maintaining a series' narrative continuity, but some writers successfully negotiate such complications. For example, *Friday the 13th* generally has strong continuity across the series. The first three sequels pick up where the previous one ended. Continuity is provided across parts four to six by the continued presence of protagonist Tommy Jarvis. The sixth film begins with Jason in the grave (carrying on from his demise at the close of the fourth film) and ends with Jason chained at the bottom of Crystal Lake. The seventh film cannily begins and ends with Jason chained at the bottom of Crystal Lake, meaning viewers who missed that instalment could enter directly into the eighth entry (*Friday the 13th Part VIII: Jason Takes Manhattan* [1989]) without issue. It is not until the ninth film (*Jason Goes to Hell: The Final Friday*) that direct continuity is broken: Jason is simply present without explanation of how he returned. The tenth entry (*Jason X* [2001]) eschews continuity issues by being set primarily in a distant future. The remaining 'Jason' films (*Freddy vs. Jason* [2003] and the 2009 reboot) are not canonically indebted to the main series but even so, they do not overly disturb the continuity developed across the first ten films; they could be classed as sequels without seriously troubling the ongoing storyline.

The metamodern slasher's approach to retroactive continuity elucidates its divergence from the postmodern slasher's implicit vision of the past as a trap. Metamodern slasher requels engender productive continuities by selectively retaining, reforming or removing a series' familiar facets. This technique parallels the productive nostalgia outlined in Chapter 7. Where nostalgia is usually associated with melancholic longing for an irretrievably lost past, the metamodern slasher's articulation of nostalgia is conditioned by a belief that the present is intertwined with the past. The metamodern slasher does not reinvent nostalgia itself, it just places emphasis differently, conceiving of nostalgia as a present-regarding phenomenon. Nostalgia's generative potentialities are pertinent to the current discussion because, as Ochonicky posits, 'retroactive continuity . . . is an inherently nostalgic practice', in which 'a temporal relationship is established between the older text(s) and the new text, as the latter revises some aspect of the former' (2020, 334–5). Those revisions can entail 'undoing or correcting developments that appear in supposedly inferior instalments' (Ochonicky 2020, 336). Rather than seeing the past as a trap that fatally constrains authors in the present, the past can be revamped to regenerate a series' narrative. This type of retconning shapes the present text by altering the past, ensuring the series' future sustainability.

Since retconning even occurs in high-profile blockbuster sequels,[12] the strategy is so familiar that it potentially seems mundane. When set against the postmodern vision of the past as a fatalistic trap however, retconning's profound implications are highlighted, and those implications illuminate the metamodern slasher's principal concerns. To explain, contemplate some common intuitions about time.[13] First, time flows in one direction, from past to present to future (see Savitt 1995, 7; Sklar 1974, 354–5). Second, time's passing is observable because change occurs, and change is constituted by cause-effect sequences (see Jaques 1982, 41; Mellor 1981, 7; Prior 1993). Third then, time's monodirectional flow implies that causes precede effects (see Hume 2007, 56; Poincare 2000, 31). These premises lead to the intuition that when we act in the present, the effects of those acts will occur in the future (even if that future is only seconds away). Note here that there seems to be an asymmetry in time. Effects and outcomes occur in the future. From the present, we might not be able to predict those effects and, moreover, someone or something might intervene, halting an effect before it occurs. The past, in contrast, is where events have already occurred. The past seems to be 'fixed' and closed in comparison to the future, which seems more open to change. This is a possibilist vision of time.[14]

The postmodern slasher is instead oriented by a deterministic model of time. In the strong version of this model, the future is just as closed and fixed as the past, meaning future events are fated to unfold in a particular way. As Sartorio has it, 'if determinism is true . . . our acts are the inevitable result of events over which we have no control' (2016, 1). We can put this in a more charitable way by observing that what appear to be possibilities in the present are contingent on preceding conditions (on this, see

---

[12] For example, retconning is evident in the enormously lucrative *Fast & Furious* film series. A post-credits scene in *Fast & Furious 6* (2013) retroactively integrates the series' least financially successful entry – *The Fast and the Furious: Tokyo Drift* (2006), which previously appeared to be a standalone spinoff film – into the series' ongoing main storyline.

[13] The following claims are controversial in the philosophical literature surrounding time, but I take it that most readers will find these premises reasonable. Also, these claims are simplified versions of the positions; the nuances of these debates are not important for my purposes. I have supplied citations for anyone wishing to engage with these arguments in greater detail.

[14] As a matter of terminological clarity, my use of 'presentism' refers to emphasis placed on the here-and-now within slasher films. That usage is distinct from the way 'presentism' is used in the philosophy of time, where there is a concern over the ontological status of present events in comparison to past and future events.

Skow 2012). That is, it is not that one can do anything at all in the present: the range of possibilities is constrained by one's present circumstances and surrounding environment, for instance. A set of causes and effects have led to the present state's constraints, and further causes and effects preceded those. Theoretically, that chain could be traced backwards to the beginning of time. In this view, one's choices in the present are limited by factors that preceded one's existence. The hard determinist makes a further claim, however: any decision one makes in the present is essentially an effect caused by those preceding factors. We need not linger on the details of hard determinism here. It is enough to notice the kinship between this position and the ways postmodern slasher films evoke the subgenre's past as a set of fatally limiting constraints. Preceding chapters have demonstrated that postmodern slashers conceive of the subgenre's future as closed, affording no possibility for significant alteration or innovation. Complaints surrounding remakes as 'regurgitating' unoriginal ideas seem to naturally follow from that view. As I have also averred, metamodern slashers are innovative, submitting that the subgenre's future is instead open to rejuvenation.

So far, the metamodern slasher might seem to embody a possibilist vision of time, accepting that even though the future is mutable, the past is still fixed. Nonetheless, retconning illuminates the metamodern slasher's affinity with a more audacious conception of time. Retroactive continuity involves reshaping the narrative past in the narrative present. As Kelleter posits, 'remakes and series . . . are oriented backwards as much as forwards; they provide continuity by changing their own past' (2012, 26). Even if (for example) a sequel presents new information via a flashback to the past, the sequel's content entails in-narrative re-evaluation of contingent events in preceding films. This can be understood as a form of retrocausality or backwards causation.[15] To be clear, I am not concerned with the feasibility of backwards causation either as a metaphysical or an empirical phenomenon.[16] For my purposes, retrocausality usefully exposes the liberatory potential of metamodern requelling. In this view, metamodern

---

[15] One of the first articles to seriously consider backwards causation is Dummett (in Dummett and Flew 1954), but others such as Forrest (1985) and Oddie (1990) have also offered rigorous defences of the model. It is interesting to observe that 'cinema emerged as physics was coming to understand that, at least in theory, no reason exists why time unfolds in a sequential, one-way direction' (Rombes 2010, 196). Film narratives, which play with time and continuity in essential ways via editing, seem to embody these principles.

[16] The latter has gained some traction via quantum theory and the properties of tachyons (for example, see Dowe 1996).

slasher films not only speak to the subgenre's future but can also figuratively reshape the subgenre's past.

Retrocausation is most palpably illustrated in this chapter by the *Halloween* series, and its requel *Halloween* (2018). The *Halloween* series is remarkably cavalier about its canonical story. *Halloween*'s various sequels openly ignore previous entries, rather than seeking to maintain retroactive continuity. *Halloween* (2018) could be seen as the severest sweep of all given that it revises the past by ignoring all prior films in the timeline bar the original. However, by addressing the film's direct engagement with Victor Frankl's thought, it becomes apparent that *Halloween* (2018) approaches the series' past in the spirit of renewal and a desire to innovate, not destroy. To highlight and contextualise *Halloween* (2018)'s metamodern potentialities, another requel – *Scream* (2022) – will first be briefly inspected as a counterexample. The *Scream* series' continued adherence to postmodernism stifles its potential to renew or innovate. The archetypal postmodern slasher *Scream* was already 'rebooted' once during the metamodern period via *Scream 4* (2011), and despite the remodelling and innovation declared in its tagline ('New decade. New rules'), *Scream 4* clings to the postmodern slasher's ethos and tone. Despite overtly discussing its own status as a requel, *Scream* (2022) remains constrained by the past, thereby reifying the *Scream* series' commitment to a deterministic postmodern stance. As always, I am not only concerned with narrative content, but also with what the content articulates about the subgenre. *Scream* (2022) insinuates that the subgenre's future is just as limited as it was in 1996 when the original *Scream* was released. *Halloween* (2018), in contrast, suggests that by purposefully re-envisaging established narrative history to open new possibilities, the subgenre can be renewed.

I raise retrocausation to underscore how metamodern requels rewrite the past from the present, thereby unearthing productive possibilities for the subgenre's future. The chapter's final case study section encapsulates that mindset by more literally recasting an aspect of the subgenre's past from the perspective of the (metamodern) present. Here, I present a pre-metamodern (indeed, pre-*Scream*) slasher sequel as a forerunner of the metamodern requel: *Freddy's Dead: The Final Nightmare* (1991). *Freddy's Dead* epitomises the complaints surrounding sequels' diminishing returns,[17] being widely considered the series' weakest entry (perhaps except for the 2010 remake of *A Nightmare on Elm Street*). *Freddy's Dead* was envisaged as *The Final Nightmare*, and the tagline boasted that New

---

[17] For example, see Doles (2016, 93); Loock (2017, 98); Rosewarne (2020, 53).

Line Cinema had supposedly 'saved the best for last'. Yet, the film's critical and relative box-office failures ensured the series had to end. From the perspective of the present, I recast this sequel's past negative reputation by proposing that *Freddy's Dead* is designed to be the *Final Nightmare* proclaimed by its title. In a narrative manoeuvre akin to *Halloween* (2018), *Freddy's Dead* trashes the *Elm Street* series' lore (including its antagonist's core motivation) and transforms its villain into a fully-fledged caricature of his former self. This flippant self-destruction is a precursor of the postmodern slasher's cynical attitude. Yet, *Freddy's Dead* is also prototypically metamodern. Freddy's cartoonish absurdity is certainly exaggerated, but it is also a sincere admittance of what the series and its pop culture icon villain had become by that point. *Freddy's Dead* is nihilistic in that it actively seeks to eradicate the series (both in cultural and narrative terms), but it also honestly and openly lays out why the series had to end, using hypercoding to underline that case.

Dead Ringer: *Scream* (and *Scream* Again)

Recent sequels to long-running slasher series face challenges in having to move with the times (to attract new audiences), while also not alienating the series' core audience by altering too much. The *Scream* sequels exhibit a firm commitment to the latter, adhering closely to the principles and tone the original *Scream* trilogy helped to make synonymous with the postmodern slasher period. Attempts to reboot the *Scream* series are impeded from instituting substantial changes precisely because the series is synonymous with postmodern scepticism about innovation.

The first bid to reboot the series came eleven years after the original trilogy had ended in the guise of *Scream 4*, which, as Mee contends, acts as 'both sequel and remake' (2022, 34). The crossroads *Scream 4* finds itself at is symbolised by the first appearance of returning character Gale. Gale watches lead protagonist Sidney being interviewed online. Sidney declares that 'if I was a victim too long, it was up to me to reinvent myself'. This assertion (much like *Scream 4*'s tagline) gestures towards a desire to adapt. Gale closes the video stream and also seeks to 'reinvent' herself as a 'fiction' writer. Within seconds of endeavouring to start her new venture, Gale types 'I HAVE NO FUCKING IDEA WHAT TO WRITE'. That is, Gale has no sense of how to transcend her ingrained persona, which inhibits her ability to create something new. When the Ghostface murders begin again in Woodsboro, the pretence of innovation falls away for both characters. The immediate media reports surrounding these homicides drag Gale and Sidney back into their established roles. Gale is pulled back to type by another reporter's description of the incident as 'something right out of a Gale Weathers bestseller'. Five minutes of runtime after insisting she had reinvented herself, reporters relabel Sidney a 'local celebrity victim'. Furthermore, after the second murder sequence, Sidney's agent (Rebecca) consolidates Sidney's state: 'Accept your situation, you're a victim for life, so embrace it.' Gale and Sidney both conform to these assessments, reverting to familiar trajectories.

These key characters personify the situation *Scream 4* is in as a reboot-sequel: any pretence of renewal quickly dissolves because of external expectations about what *Scream* is and does. In *Scream 4*, the characters are aware of and comment on the 'postmodern meta shit' that *Scream* became famous for. In a seemingly inadvertent amplification of the series' self-consciousness, *Scream 4* seems embarrassed about the series' postmodern fatalism, but simultaneously reinforces it. The reason for that self-consciousness arises from a mismatch between the postmodern attitude and the zeitgeist in 2011. Contemporaneous reviews commonly referred to *Scream 4*'s 'peculiarly retrograde . . . style' (No Author 2011). For instance, Groen (2011) noted that *Scream 4*'s 'awfully dated' postmodernism meant that 'not even [*Scream*'s] smug irony endures' because 'it's hard to congratulate yourself for being in on a stale joke'. Even more telling is Dutt's (2011) proposal that *Scream 4* takes an 'old school approach', drawing on 'the cheesy tactics of "scream and slash" cinema'. The latter phrasing conflates *Scream*'s title with a synonym for 'slasher' that was commonplace in the boom-period: the 'stalk and slash' film. Dutt's wording (perhaps accidentally) indicates that by 2011, *Scream* was akin to its antecedents: 1980s and 1990s slashers are both equally 'old school'.

A more apt step for the lore of *Scream* was followed by *Scream* fan filmmakers in the wake of *Scream 4*. These fan filmmakers firmly embraced the series' self-referential fatalism. For example, Jack Stanis's fan film *Slash* (2013) is based in a fictional world where the protagonists are familiar with the *Scream* films.[18] Indeed, *Scream 4* is shown on a television in the opening sequence. After receiving menacing phone calls, the protagonists are slain by someone wearing *Scream*'s iconic Ghostface costume. The killer employs a voice-changer (as *Scream*'s killers do) and appropriates dialogue from *Scream* (such as the line 'scary night, isn't it? With the murders and all, it is like right out of a horror movie'). One victim (Jessica) even points out that the latter is a line 'from the first *Scream* film'. Other lines are pilfered without explicit citation.

---

[18] Since 2013, Stanis has made two more *Slash* fan movies, and a fourth is currently in production.

Slash's murderers (Jeremy and Olivia) execute their friends in a manner that parallels Stu and Billy's ploy in *Scream*, including their attempt to frame another party for the murders, and their plan to stab one another to make themselves look like survivors. Unfortunately for Jeremy (who concentrates on the original *Scream*), this situation also parallels the plot of *Scream 4*. Just as Jill turns on Charlie in the denouement of *Scream 4*, Olivia too swerves from her plans with Jeremy, stabbing him in the heart so that she can be the 'sole survivor'. Had Jeremy paid more attention to the later sequel, he may have been equipped to defend himself against this eventuality. Instead, all he can do is repeat dialogue uttered by Charlie as he expires in *Scream 4*: 'The heart! That's not the way we rehearsed it.' *Slash* thereby takes *Scream*'s metatextual dissection to its next step: rather than having killers who are (or claim to be) influenced by horror films *a la* Billy and Stu, *Slash*'s killers are influenced by *Scream* itself.

Perhaps even more pertinent is another fan film: Jared Vollman's *Scream: Generations* (2012). *Scream: Generations*'s trajectory is almost identical to *Slash*'s in that the killer copies *Scream*'s voice-changer phone calls, replicates action and dialogue from the original *Scream* and so forth. However, here, the killer (Ian) is a *Scream* superfan, who even owns a signed *Scream* script. His motive is that *Scream 4* was a box-office failure, meaning that the makers 'are just giving up' on the series. Literalising his proclamation that he would 'kill to see a *Scream 5*', Ian intends that his homicidal re-enactment of *Scream*'s content will reignite interest in the *Scream* series.

When Ian's wish came true a decade later and the fifth *Scream* film was finally made, its killers duplicated his motive from *Scream: Generations*.[19] *Scream* (2022) is more transparently self-conscious than *Scream 4* about its relationship to the past, but it again is inhibited by the series' defining postmodern sensibility. Being released more than a quarter of a century after the original, *Scream* (2022) had to acknowledge that the 1990s are now a distant past to many. The passage of time is marked on the ageing bodies of its returning stars, who once again reprise their legacy roles. Notably, David Arquette's Dewey makes an early appearance to the young teen cast dressed in a tan corded jacket and a denim blue shirt, with a holstered revolver on his hip; he is presented like a Sheriff from a Western, implying that he belongs to an antiquated, fabled cinematic past that is out of sync with the present.

---

[19] This replication does not appear to be an intentional meta-level joke since Vollman is not credited in *Scream* (2022).

The young protagonists also underline how long ago the late-twentieth century is from their perspective. The *Scream* series utilises a surrogate for *Scream* in the form of *Stab*, and here several teen characters signal that *Stab* – and therefore *Scream* – is outdated. When Richie, one of the killers in *Scream* (2022), remarks he has not seen the original *Stab*, he conflates it with another classic twentieth-century film; 'I've never seen *Gone with the Wind* either.' This comparison flags that 1939 (when *Gone with the Wind* was released) is commensurate with 1996 from his perspective: both are purely 'old'. Moreover, Richie disparages *Stab*, first by stating 'I don't consider [not having seen *Stab*] a huge hole in my cinematic education', and second by noting that *Stab* 'sounds a lot like *Halloween*'. Thus, *Scream*, it is implied, is redundant and unoriginal. As with everything else in the *Scream* universe, these assertions are duplicitous. Richie is later outed as such an avid *Stab* fan that he is willing to murder for the series. Nevertheless, Richie's initial comments echo Tara's attitude towards *Stab* in the film's opening scene: Tara describes the film as 'super 90s . . . over-lit, and everyone had weird hair'. Tara's assessment draws attention to how 'underlit' *Scream* (2022) is compared with the parallel opening scene of *Scream*, suggesting that aesthetic standards have altered significantly in the intervening years. Her assessment of hairstyles also points out that fashions have mutated (along with audience expectations) since the 1990s. Via this opening declaration – coming less than four minutes into the film – *Scream* (2022) tries to accentuate its difference from the original, hinting that these shifts are rationales for rebooting the series.

This sequence also sets up that even though *Scream* is passé, *Scream* (2022) prioritises its progenitor as a defining emblem for the past. As many scholars have noted, both sequels and remakes are intertextual by definition, because they refer to origin texts (Budra and Schellenberg 1998, 11; Loock 2017, 102; Mee 2017, 194). *Scream* (2022) amplifies that agenda by taking *Scream* as the point of reference par excellence. Where the original *Scream* films deployed intertextuality by referring to classic 'scary movies', here *Scream* itself replaces all other horror films combined. So, for instance, where *Scream* opens with the killer quizzing Casey on 'scary movies', in *Scream* (2022) the killer tests Tara on the *Stab* movies, replacing the 'trick' question about the killer in *Friday the 13th* (1980) with a similar question about the dual killers in *Stab* (and thus *Scream*). That is, *Scream* is now the classic that is only semi-remembered by a new generation. Furthermore, where Randy insists that there are 'certain rules' for surviving 'a horror movie' in *Scream*, in *Scream* (2022) Dewey outlines 'certain rules to surviving a *Stab* movie'. The original *Scream* is 'the past' in its entirety.

Consequently, the film's updates remain superficial. For example, writer Guy Busick refers to the detail of having the series' staple voice-changer built into the Ghostface mask (instead of being handheld) as if it is a magnitudinous deviation. Co-writer James Vanderbilt also proclaims that Billy Loomis's ghostly presence is a notable shift for the series,[20] despite merely bringing back a character from an earlier film (much as Randy reappeared posthumously on video in *Scream 3* [2000]). *Scream* (2022) mainly repeats sequences and redeploys spaces from the original. For instance, in *Scream*, Randy watches *Halloween* in Stu's house, talking to the television and imploring Jamie Lee Curtis's character to 'turn around' because the killer is behind her. Randy does not realise that Ghostface is behind him at that very moment. In *Scream* (2022), the same sequence is replicated in the same location: Randy's niece and spiritual surrogate Mindy watches the scene from *Stab* in which Randy watches *Halloween*, and Ghostface approaches Mindy as she implores *Stab*'s fictional version of her uncle to 'turn around'. Writer Guy Busick refers to this scene as 'a snake eating its own tail', although it perhaps more aptly illustrates another of his admissions: that their approach to 'meta reference' sometimes meant 'we had our heads too far up our own asses'.[21]

Furthermore, the connection to this past is advanced for its own sake rather than because it is meaningful. The climax takes place in Stu's house just because Amber's parents happened to buy the property. Similarly, the mild retcon of introducing Sam as the daughter of Billy Loomis (*Scream*'s killer) is not particularly meaningful. It allows Richie and Amber to frame Sam for the slaughter, but as the teens note, everyone in the friendship group 'is a suspect', so any of them could have been framed. Sam's connection to the series' past is just as superficial (and arbitrary, in narrative terms) as Amber's access to Stu's house. Articulating director Matt Bettinelli-Olpin's contention that the *Scream* series 'has to continually change in order to be good',[22] early in the film, Mindy argues that requels must 'build something new'. Nevertheless, *Scream* (2022) fundamentally fails to do so. It is also telling that Mindy's vision of 'build[ing] something new' is extremely narrow, consisting of introducing 'new main characters'. *Scream* (2022) follows that limited vision, just as it is committed to the series' postmodern ethos: as Mindy also affirms, 'real *Stab* movies are metaslasher whodunits. Full stop.'

---

[20] In the audio commentary accompanying the 2022 Region B Paramount Home Entertainment Blu-ray release of *Scream* (2022).
[21] Ibid.
[22] Ibid.

Perhaps because Vanderbilt did not want to follow *Halloween* (2018)'s disruption of its series' canon,[23] *Scream* (2022) does not strive to remodel its past. When Dewey posits that 'the killer's motive is *always* connected to something in the past' (emphasis added), his assessment admits that the narrative will repeat the same trajectory as its predecessors and will not attempt to deviate from that past. The characters then express their dissatisfaction with that replication of the past, and given the *Scream* series' self-conscious reflexivity, it is hard not to read these comments as self-criticism. In the climax, the series' returning lead protagonist Sidney declares to the killer, 'I've seen this movie . . . you really need some new material . . . you might actually be the most derivative one of all . . . I'm bored.' Her statement reads as criticism of continued sequelisation, and the unoriginality of this reboot. Similarly, Sam posits that 'every decade or so, some idiot gets the bright idea to put on the mask, assassinate his friends, and get famous . . . Last time it happened was in 2011.' Given that the preceding film (*Scream 4*) was released in 2011, Sam's statement conveys a complaint about the very film she inhabits. As a requel then, *Scream* (2022) is committed to rebooting the series but offers good reasons not to do so. Richie avers that 'someone has to save the franchise' because the previous film in the *Stab* series 'sucked balls' and 'Hollywood's totally fucking out of ideas.' Although these self-denigrating comments might be duplicitously ironic, *Scream* (2022) proves his point. Although Sidney aims to close the series – 'after tonight, no more books, no more movies, no more fucking Ghostface' – *Scream* seems fated to continue repeating, concentrating on the subgenre's past as opposed to looking towards its future. That destiny is entirely in keeping with the series' postmodern fatalism.[24]

Scream (2022) does not produce new possibilities by revising or erasing parts of the series' recognised history, or even hypercoding its expected elements. Instead, it rehashes the past in a manner that insinuates the subgenre is stuck. If the point of *Scream* (2022) is to meditate on the value of requels as sequel-reboot-remakes, it also replicates the original *Scream*'s attitude towards the subgenre's past. *Scream* presented boom-period slashers as clichéd relics of limited relevance to its present. It then repeated the slasher's conventions and tactics regardless (albeit with a knowing eye-roll). *Scream* (2022) does the same with the requel by

---

[23] Ibid.
[24] At the time of writing, *Scream VI* is in production, even though Neve Campbell is not returning. Whether the film's relocation to New York instead of Woodsboro and turn away from Sidney's storyline will result in tonal rejuvenation remains to be seen.

belittling and yet repeating the series' own past. Its vision connotes that the subgenre is just as seriously limited now as it was in 1996.

Return to Form: Laurie's Search for Meaning in *Halloween* (2018)

In contrast to *Scream*, the *Halloween* series is barely constrained by its past. Pace Muir's proposal that '*Halloween* is a film franchise with . . . a sense of continuity' (Muir 2007b, 658), *Halloween* is compelling precisely because of the series makers' insouciant attitudes to continuity. The complete *Halloween* series does not hold together as a single story. The original *Halloween* and *Halloween II* (1981) work together in the way the early *Friday the 13th* films do; the sequel picks up directly after the preceding film. *Halloween III: Season of the Witch* (1982) famously provides a standalone story that has no relation to the preceding films, other than being set around Halloween night. *Halloween 4: The Return of Michael Myers* (1988) brings killer Michael Myers and his psychiatrist Dr Loomis back to the series, but reveals that lead protagonist Laurie has died. The fourth, fifth and sixth films instead follow Laurie's daughter Jamie (who dies in the sixth film, *Halloween: The Curse of Michael Myers* [1995]). The seventh film – *Halloween H20: 20 Years Later* (1998) – brings Laurie back from the grave, with a hazy backstory about having faked her own death. However, here Laurie has a son (John) of roughly Jamie's age. Consequently, it is unclear whether Laurie abandoned Jamie (leaving Haddonfield, then almost immediately conceiving John), or whether this is an alternate timeline in which Jamie did not exist. In any case, Michael unambiguously kills Laurie in the eighth film, *Halloween: Resurrection* (2002). A remake and sequel were then produced, in which Michael and Laurie are reimagined as new characters. Then, in 2018, a *Halloween* reboot brought the original Laurie back, this time with a different child (Karen), and no mention of Jamie or John. That story continues in *Halloween Kills* (2021) and *Halloween Ends* (2022).[25]

In short, the *Halloween* 'series' has a far looser sense of continuity than other major slasher series, omitting and replacing significant chunks of its timeline without explanation rather than attempting to sustain a coherent continuing narrative. The series' unusual approach to continuity is not the product of organised long-term decision-making about the series'

---

[25] Since this chapter deals with requels and their operations, I will not attend to these latter sequels in any detail.

direction, but neither is it the result of pure carelessness, nor lazily bypassing the complexities required to maintain continuity. For example, *Halloween H20*'s director Steve Miner states that his intention was to 'ignore' the intervening sequels, remarking that they lacked 'suspense' and had 'devolved' into 'gorefests'.[26] Miner decided to disavow aspects of the series' past in order to cultivate new (and 'better') opportunities. Read sympathetically then, Miner's methods are aligned with the subtractive mode delineated in Chapter 5. Unconstrained by previous entries, *Halloween H20* revises the series' past to intervene in the present.

Halloween (2018) takes this idea even further. Not only does Laurie return after being dispatched in *Halloween: Resurrection*, but other killings are also erased. In *Halloween* (2018), Laurie states that Michael has slaughtered five people (presumably, the original film's five victims). Consequently, more than fifty other homicides Michael commits in the second through to the eighth films are expunged. Moreover, a core part of the lore is debunked. In *Halloween II*, it is established that Laurie and Michael are siblings. That fact is reiterated across subsequent sequels, and even Rob Zombie's 2007 remake. In *Halloween* (2018), Laurie's granddaughter Allyson asserts that the rumour of a familial connection between Michael and Laurie is 'just a bit [of the story] that some people made up'. The line seems to be directed towards audience members who are aware of the series' past, specifically stressing this film's divergence from canonical lore.

This dismissal is more important than it may initially appear to be. In most of the *Halloween* films, Michael is motivated by the desire to annihilate his blood relatives (particularly his sister and her children). His familicidal drive is reasonably intelligible across the series,[27] even if the reasons why Michael is intent on slaying his relatives remains a mystery. Even in the producer's cut of *Halloween: The Curse of Michael Myers*, in which it is posited that Michael is under a cult's control, Michael is still compelled to murder his family every 31 October. His essential drive endures, even though it is induced by ill-defined extrinsic factors (the cult's rituals) rather than ambiguous intrinsic factors (Michael's

---

[26] Miner, in the Audio Commentary accompanying the 2014 Region A Anchor Bay Entertainment Blu-ray release of *Halloween H20: 20 Years Later*.

[27] One exception is *Halloween: Resurrection*, where Myers's motives are muddy. It is not clear why he revisits his childhood home to execute teens unless he suddenly becomes territorial. Even so, how he knows about the reality show being shot in the house is not explained. Myers is presented as territorial in *Halloween Kills*, but that follows the requel trilogy's express rescinding of his familicidal motivation.

inaccessible psychological state). By renouncing the familial relationship altogether, *Halloween* (2018) removes one of the only handles viewers had for grasping Michael. When Allyson debunks the familial connection, her friend Vicky proposes that it 'is scary to have a bunch of your friends get butchered by some random crazy person'. That supplanting assessment acknowledges that the familial relationship between Laurie and Michael had explanatory force, and so the removal of that factor means Michael has no tangible motivation at all. More than setting out *Halloween* (2018)'s stall, this move acts as an implicit metacommentary on the series as a whole. Just as the relationship between siblings is jettisoned along with the narrative explanation it provided, the relationships between 'sibling' films in the series is abandoned, along with the narrative explanations those sequels supplied.

Despite *Halloween* (2018)'s negation of numerous *Halloween* sequels, *Halloween* remains a stable origin point (as it does for all the *Halloween* sequels), offering anchoring foundations. Each continuity line attempts to vivify a story that began with *Halloween*. *Halloween* (2018) authentically builds from the first film, setting up a new direction via which to continue the characters' stories. This view of *Halloween* (2018) as innovating and progressing might appear to be undercut precisely by the return of Laurie, who initially comes across as a mouthpiece for postmodern fatalism. In her first scene in *Halloween* (2018), she takes $3,000 dollars from investigative journalists for little more than dismissing their bid to 're-examine' the events of 1978, declaring flatly that 'no new insights or discoveries' are available. Her attitude seemingly articulates the postmodern sentiment that we are doomed only to repeat. As an opening sentiment, Laurie's statement suggests that *Halloween* (2018) will rerun a conflict between Laurie and Michael that has played out several times before (in *Halloween*, *Halloween II*, *Halloween H20*, *Halloween: Resurrection*, the remake and its sequel). In another respect, this opening position assures long-time series fans that *Halloween* (2018) will return to 'old school' form.

However, Laurie is next seen outside of Allyson's school. The sequence parallels a moment from *Halloween* in which Laurie sees Myers stood across the street from the school, seemingly looking directly at her (see Figure 8.1). Although this echo again assures long-term fans that *Halloween* (2018) is connected to the original *Halloween*, it also highlights that acute changes have occurred in the forty-year interregnum. The parallel shots underline that Laurie's status as recurring Final Girl is not as straightforward as it seems: her 'resurrection' in the series means she occupies a generic position more akin to a supernatural killer. Slasher series are typified by the killer's return from the dead in each sequel. Laurie's

Figure 8.1 Parallel shots of Michael in *Halloween* (1978) and Laurie in *Halloween* (2018)

appearance outside Allyson's school accentuates the unusual move that follows from rewriting the series' continuity: across the series, Final Girl Laurie is resurrected from the dead multiple times.[28] By repeating a moment from the first film but making a notable substitution (replacing Michael with Laurie), *Halloween* (2018) stresses that the film series has taken convention-defying routes to reinvigorate the series, implying that *Halloween* (2018) will do the same. What appears to be a minor (perhaps trivial) detail exposes *Halloween* (2018)'s metamodern sensibility.

Another seemingly minor detail contained in the scene underscores just how crucial the sequence is. Allyson's class is concerned with Viktor Frankl's work, and the teacher quotes from Frankl as Allyson looks out at

---

[28] As I argued in Chapter 3, *Happy Death Day* also points towards this norm via its time-loop structure. *Halloween* (2018)'s version directs attention towards the series as a structure of meaning, because unlike Tree, Laurie is unaware of her resurrection.

Laurie.²⁹ Understanding of Frankl's thought offers another key to unlocking *Halloween* (2018)'s agenda and interpreting Laurie's seemingly fatalistic initial assertions. Frankl's work (particularly *Man's Search for Meaning* [1959]) is based on his experiences as a Holocaust survivor, and his ability to find hope even within the bleakest of situations. If taken too literally, the inclusion of this fleeting reference point invites a potentially offensive comparison between the Holocaust and the 'genocide' of slasher protagonists. Regardless, Frankl's work was not merely about his experiences in the concentration camps: to make such a direct parallel would be to misinterpret Frankl's use of that situation as the inspiration for and illustration of his larger agenda. As Frankl has it in the preface to the 1992 edition of *Man's Search for Meaning*, his 'autobiographical account' of the Holocaust 'serves as the existential validation of [his] theories' (1992, 11–12): of 'logotherapy' and 'tragic optimism' (1992, 137). This emphasis on finding optimism and coherent meaning in the face of horror is salient in the metamodern context, mirroring sentiments delineated in Chapters 2 and 3. Frankl's theoretical models illuminate *Halloween* (2018)'s themes and its interplay with its own past.

Laurie initially seems to be unremittingly beleaguered by the events of 1978. According to her daughter Karen, Laurie's obsession with Michael – her inability to 'put the past behind' her – poisoned Laurie's worldview. Karen thus avers that Laurie sees the world as a 'dark and evil place'. As such, Laurie appears to embody the person who (in Frankl's words) 'let [her]self decline because [she] could not see any future goal [and therefore] found [her]self occupied with retrospective thoughts' that drain life of meaning (1992, 80). That is certainly how others around Laurie perceive her stance. Allyson confronts Laurie with the view that her endless 'preparation' for Michael's reappearance 'was for nothing', positing that Laurie should 'get over it'. However, Laurie does not fit this model. Frankl notes that such a person 'prefer[s] to close their eyes and to live in the past' so as 'to help make the present, with all its horrors, less real' (1992, 80). In contrast, *Halloween* (2018) proves that Laurie was wise to remain vigilant. As the narrative progresses, Karen comes to realise that Laurie was not suspended in a state of futile retrospection but was instead poised in a state of potentiality: ready to take action in the present

---

²⁹ The parallel moment in *Halloween* entails the offscreen teacher talking about Samuels on 'fate'. There are echoes of that idea in *Halloween* (2018)'s focus on Frankl's vision of 'fate'. However, Samuels is a fictional invention (see Leeder 2014, 94n64). Not least because of Frankl's experiences as a genuine survivor, the deployment of Frankl's work has greater resonance and impact.

in order to ensure her (and her family's) continuation in the future. That is why Laurie 'prepared [her daughter] for the horrors of this world', using Karen's childhood to teach her 'how to fight'. Laurie's fixation on the past makes her acutely aware of the potential for horror to erupt in the present. Being prepared to overcome such horror indicates that Laurie has hope for a continued future. The connection between past, present and future is signified in the film's climax where three generations (Laurie, Karen and Allyson) work together to defeat Michael. Consequently, the film is based on a metamodern sensibility of bridging from the past to the present towards a productive future.[30]

The series' revisionism – especially its unusual tactic of resurrecting its Final Girl – is essential to its temporal bridging. In *Halloween* (2018), Laurie seems to be motivated by the credo that Frankl envisages as logotherapy's 'categorical imperative . . . "Live as if you were living already for the second time and as if you had acted the first time as wrongly as you are about to act now"' (Frankl 1992, 114). Laurie's 'rebirth' reinvigorates the series, but it also affords Laurie a 'do-over': a chance to live again and to prepare better in this timeline than the Laurie of *Halloween H20* and *Halloween: Resurrection* did. In this light, Laurie's insistence that

---

[30] Another contemporary remake – *Slumber Party Massacre* (2021) – also draws on intergenerational interactions, bridging between past and present. As the survivor of an attack by drill-wielding slasher Russ Thorn in 1993 (depicted in the film's prologue), Trish is left agoraphobic. In the present, her daughter Dana and her friends plan to avenge the dead and give Trish 'her life back' (thereby pointing towards a productive future). The teens return to the site of the original slaughter, replicating the events of 1993 as faithfully as possible, but this time, they are armed. After slaying Thorn, Thorn's mother (Kay) attacks Dana and her friends. The intergenerational divide is bridged when Trish arrives and rescues Dana by executing Kay. Dana's plan – replicating the past, but with distinct changes that facilitate a more productive future – resonates because this is a remake. The film mimics *The Slumber Party Massacre* in several ways, duplicating Thorn's key dialogue ('you know you want it'), for instance. Yet such replications are subject to modification. For example, a shower scene in the 1982 film needlessly pans down to take in the original Trish's posterior while she talks. In the remake, the sequence is reproduced, instead concentrating on a young man's body. The gender swap draws attention to the original's investigation of women's bodies in stages of undress. Famously, the 1982 version was intended as a feminist subversion of the slasher, but that approach was side-lined when it went into production. Incidents such as the shower sequence are the result of that misalignment between outlooks. The remake does not simply repeat the original's gratuity, however: when the camera pans down, Matt's buttocks are obscured by steam. That is, the remake subverts both the original's gendered bias and its uses of nudity per se. The remake is contextualised by the original, and the original's initial intention to reflect on the subgenre is brought to fruition in the remake.

'there are no new insights or discoveries' is born of her preparedness for Michael's return. From the character's perspective within a narrative universe consisting of *Halloween* and *Halloween* (2018), Laurie is correct that she already has the knowledge she requires to survive. From the perspective of the series as a whole, the situation looks different: new insights are possible because 'no situation repeats itself, and each situation calls for a different response' (Frankl 1992, 85). The generic circumstances may be familiar, but there is space for renewal within those boundaries. Furthermore, although all entries in the series since 1978 are erased in *Halloween* (2018)'s fictional world, this iteration of Laurie seems to have learned from mistakes made by her counterparts in the *Halloween* 'multiverse', which led to Laurie's demise in *Halloween: Resurrection*. *Halloween* (2018) therefore encapsulates Frankl's observation that 'in the past, nothing is irretrievably lost but everything irrevocably stored' (1992, 124).

This move is significant in redressing a power imbalance between Final Girl and slasher that *Halloween* helped to embed as a subgeneric norm. As Rieser (2001, 377) has it, 'the heroine's "success" is severely limited: she rarely wins anything, most of the time only barely surviving her ordeals . . . she does not gain valuable experience (unless we count the "knowledge" of constant potential endangerment as such)'. In *Halloween* (2018), the latter is precisely the foundation for Laurie's flourishing. By transforming Laurie into a survivor who convincingly confronts Michael, *Halloween* (2018) recasts the meaning of Laurie's survival in 1978. *Halloween H20* presented Laurie as someone capable, but who ultimately runs from her past: she changes her name, relocates, hides her history from those around her, drinks heavily to drown out her trauma and so forth. *Halloween H20*'s version of Laurie upholds Rieser's dismissal of '"knowledge" of constant potential endangerment': such knowledge ultimately hinders Laurie more than it helps her. When Michael reappears, she reacts and survives, but she is not prepared. In *Halloween: Resurrection*, Laurie is institutionalised and dies at Michael's hands. That trajectory imparts that Laurie was essentially broken by the events of 1978. In *Halloween* (2018), Laurie may be hardened by the events of 1978, but she has developed far beyond the cowering babysitter she once was. Rather than running, she stands her ground. Instead of hiding her past, Allyson notes that the events of 1978 are 'pretty much all she talks about. It defines her life'. Thus, Laurie's chance to live again is also a remodelling of the subgenre's norm that the Final Girl must eventually succumb to the killer because the killer must always return.

These cogitations on the subgenre and its transformations are embedded in the text via Laurie. That is, *Halloween* (2018) is metamodern both in its parallel between narrative and subgeneric concerns, and also in its sincere investment in the characters' experiential viewpoints. By erasing the sibling connection between Michael and Laurie, Michael has no reason to target her.[31] Even so, that does not invalidate her feeling of fear and the preparedness it instigates. Laurie's understanding of her situation is perfectly in consonance with the subgenre's norms and patterns. The subgeneric context validates Laurie's vigilance, then. Yet, those around her (such as Karen) view Laurie as subject to 'paranoia and neuroses', and it is apparent why Laurie's fears are not taken seriously.[32] The text is sincere in both respects, taking Karen's and Laurie's perspectives on the situation seriously. Sufficient insight is provided into Karen's mindset – notably her desire to prevent Laurie's obsession from consuming Allyson's life – such that Karen does not come across as foolish for not believing Laurie.

This said, one might reasonably criticise the *Halloween* series, and particularly *Halloween* (2018)'s strategy of reenvisaging the past, in order to generate new productive opportunities. For some critics, *Halloween* (2018) had a retrocausal effect, recasting the series as 'a confusing mess of retcons, remakes, and spinoffs' (Salemme 2018).[33] An alternative view is that *Halloween* (2018) illuminates the series' metamodern approach to temporality, granting new opportunities for engagement (rather than being confusing or alienating). The series' incongruities allow viewers to invest in the series by creating their own idiosyncratic canon. Fans frequently respond to film series in this way, producing their own edits of films in

---

[31] Laurie's significance to Michael was delineated in several sequels and the 2007 remake, each of which are eschewed by *Halloween* (2018). In *Halloween* (2018), the two only collide because Dr Sartain takes Michael to Laurie's compound. David Gordon Green's sequels to *Halloween* (2018) also negotiate this disconnection. Michael does not encounter Laurie (who is hospitalised) in *Halloween Kills*, and Michael is led to Laurie's home as he tracks down another intermediary character (Corey) in *Halloween Ends*. The trilogy thereby undercuts the idea of a particularised conflict between Laurie and Michael.

[32] Indeed, from the viewer's perspective, Laurie's supposed paranoia is justified because Myers has proven to be a credible recurring threat across the (herein absent) sequels. Moreover, her assertions about Michael echo Loomis's unheeded warnings in *Halloween* (1978). When Dr Wynn chides Loomis – 'if you knew that the precautions weren't strong enough [to prevent Michael escaping], you should have told somebody' – Loomis proclaims 'I told everybody! Nobody listened!'. Loomis's proclamation is then corroborated by the conversations he has with law enforcers. Over the phone, we hear him pleading to be believed ('You've got to believe me officer, he is coming to Haddonfield . . . Because I know him! I'm his doctor!') and when he warns Sheriff Brackett, his apprehensions are dismissed as 'fancy talk'.

[33] The supposed confusion is not helped by three films bearing the title *Halloween* (five including television and director's cuts).

order to 'fix' plot holes or to erase what they perceive to be unsatisfactory developments.[34] *Halloween* encourages precisely that mode via its bold adjustments to continuity. It is in this sense that *Halloween* is the 'Choose Your Own Adventure' of horror series (Mendelson 2018; see also Leeder 2022, 68; Ochonicky 2020, 337). As such, the *Halloween* requel is reflective of the contemporary technocultural situation, the metamodern prizing of individualised experience and the metamodern slasher's commitment to viewers as collaborators in meaning-making.

The Point of No Return: *Freddy's Dead* as Proto-Metamodern Requel

As I argued earlier in this chapter, the notion that metamodern requels re-envisage the past from the present naturally leads towards deliberation on how the subgenre's past sequels might be reinterpreted from the present perspective; that is, in light of both metamodernism and the requel trend. *Freddy's Dead: The Final Nightmare* might seem like an unusual choice to exemplify a proto-metamodern requel for several reasons. First, *Freddy's Dead* emanated out of what was reputedly the series' nadir. The critical consensus of the period was that the series had exhibited a 'steady decline in quality of both storyline and chill factor', and thus it was 'time to bury this ugly phenomenon' (Menell 1991). Shone (1992) compared Freddy to a 'crepuscular old ham' who had taken too many 'curtain calls', while Hutchinson (1992) flatly greeted the promise of the film's title with 'good riddance'. Even *Freddy's Dead*'s director (Rachel Talalay) admitted that it was 'probably time to wrap up the series' (in Schoell and Spencer 1992, 148). Secondly, its title expressly proffers that it is the end of a chain – *The Final Nightmare* – rather than a reboot (as its successor, *New Nightmare*, suggests). Nonetheless, the title also conveys that *Freddy's Dead: The Final Nightmare* is not merely another sequel: it does not follow the series' naming convention, and so is not '*A Nightmare on Elm Street 6: Freddy's Dead*'. Instead, the title gestures that *Freddy's Dead* sits outside of the series, deliberating on what the series is. By concluding the extant chain of sequels, it also liberates the series, inviting the possibility of new films unconstrained by the established continuity.

---

[34] For example, *Friday the 13th Part V: The Killer is Jason Edition* seeks to write Jason Voorhees back into *Friday the 13th: A New Beginning* (https://originaltrilogy.com/topic/Friday-the-13th-Part-V-The-Killer-Is-Jason-Edition-Released/id/11089). Many such fan edits exist for the *Halloween* series (see https://ifdb.fanedit.org/fanedit-search/tag/franchise/halloween/).

The declared intent was to halt the series, and New Line even staged a funeral for its antagonist as part of the film's publicity campaign. However, Freddy was always already dead in the *Elm Street* series, having been immolated prior to the first film's events. He was 'killed off' multiple times during the sequels; as Freddy puts it in *Freddy's Dead*, 'they tried burning me, then they tried burying me . . . they even tried holy water, but I just keep on ticking'. The statement '*Freddy's Dead*' hardly means that he would not return, but rather that the series had reached a point of departure. As I will argue, *Freddy's Dead* signals this in three ways. First, it admits why the series had to end by administering a hypercoded version of an *Elm Street* film. Second, this hypercoded version essentially detonates the series as it stood. Third, *Freddy's Dead* makes striking retroactive amendments to the canon to ensure that the series could not resume as it was.

On the face of it, *Freddy's Dead* comes across as the product of its moment, reproducing the postmodern zeitgeist via its inclusion of empty pop cultural references. A clunky cameo from contemporaneously popular comedian Roseanne Barr and her then-husband Tom Arnold is symptomatic of that technique, being inconsequential to the plot. That one teen (Spencer) consequently compares Springwood to 'Twin Peaks' confirms that the encounter with the couple bridges between *Freddy's Dead* and the popular cultural moment that situated the film on its release. A similar attitude is evident in the film's opening. Following a pattern that started in *A Nightmare on Elm Street 3: Dream Warriors* (1987) (which opens with an Edgar Allan Poe quotation) and *A Nightmare on Elm Street 4: The Dream Master* (1988) (which opens with a quote from the Book of Job), *Freddy's Dead* begins by quoting Nietzsche, then abruptly replaces that quote with a line of Freddy's dialogue from *A Nightmare on Elm Street 3: Dream Warriors*. While the prior quotations are all concerned with sleep and add gravitas to the proceedings via their literary origins, Freddy's line – 'Welcome to Prime Time, bitch' – is selected almost arbitrarily, especially given that it bears no obvious direct relation to the preceding epigraph from *Thus Spake Zarathustra*. One interpretation of this inclusion is that, like the *Scream* films that would follow it, *Freddy's Dead* is trapped within itself, holding little reverence for the cultural past, and being mainly focused on its own (arbitrary) cultural presence. In this view, the self-referential quotation underlines the film's navel-gazing insularity. Still, the juxtaposition between Nietzsche and Freddy quotations also sets out *Freddy's Dead*'s stall. However superficially, the preceding *Elm Street* films employed epigraphs to elevate those texts. *Freddy's Dead* disparages that mechanism by aimlessly selecting one of Freddy's crass puns.

Both aspects – vulgar quipping and irreverence for the series' past – are of importance and relevance to *Freddy's Dead*'s agenda.

This same irreverence is also evident where *Freddy's Dead* attends to short-term narrative goals with little regard for future consequences. That outlook is a product of the preceding series' struggles with sustaining continuity, which were exacerbated by tight production schedules. As Nutman affirms, the 'increased frequency of the sequels' release dates and . . . condensed production periods' did not help the filmmakers to maintain quality (1989, 53). Key personnel – writers and directors – were replaced for each of the sequels up to and including *Freddy's Dead*, and each added new elements as they retroactively developed the ongoing story. A flippancy about continuity emerged within the series as it evolved, and original creator Wes Craven posited that this was a consequence of rushing to develop and sell new material, claiming that individuals were hired 'to knock out a script' rather than bringing a 'distinctive vision' to the series (in Shapiro 1994, 35). The flippant approach to continuity is embraced most candidly in *A Nightmare on Elm Street 4: The Dream Master*, in which the surviving protagonists from the preceding instalment – who had therein been heralded as 'the last of the Elm Street children' – are unceremoniously dispatched before the film's midpoint.

Freddy's Dead imparts an amplified version of that same attitude. As the supposed *Final Nightmare*, the writers were entirely liberated from considering how their choices might limit future attempts to revive the character or continue the story. Accordingly, *Freddy's Dead* includes bold revisions to the series' lore and characterisation. Freddy's past is depicted, revealing that he had a daughter and murdered his wife. As Taylor observes, 'Talalay's retcon imagines him as a perversion of the quintessential family man' (2020, 71) and, as such, the film reinvents his identity. In one of these sequences, it is also uncovered that Freddy's iconic bladed glove is among an array of similar weapons at his disposal. Freddy's standard glove is deeply interwoven into the character, not least since the sound of his blades screeching against metal frequently stands in for his presence across the series, and because the series' protagonists frequently refer to his 'finger knives' when initially describing Krueger. The revelation that he wielded other weapons therefore undercuts a core aspect of his character design.

Most significantly, Freddy's central motive is reoriented because of these inclusions. In the series' backstory, Freddy culled many of Springwood's children. The town's parents then formed a vigilante mob to assassinate him and he returned from the grave to massacre their remaining children. In prior entries, the characters assert their belief that Freddy is punishing the parents who burnt him alive, although there is some ambiguity over this assumption. It cannot be the case that Freddy's assassination by aggrieved parents causes him to kill per se, because Freddy also murdered children while he was alive. His immolation interrupts and (at most) spurs on his murder spree. Whatever originally motivated Freddy to eradicate Springwood's children likely continues to drive him when he slays teens in their sleep. In *Freddy's Dead*, Freddy states his motive for the first time, declaring 'they took [my daughter] away from me, but I made them pay. I took all their children away from them.' His proclamation indicates why he dispatched teens both before and after his demise, evincing that being burned to death was not his impetus (as characters insist throughout the series). This revelation rewrites Freddy's motivation, inviting reconsideration of his intentions across all preceding films.

These modifications to Freddy's motivation are accompanied by alterations that amplify his supernatural abilities. Here, Freddy can 'erase' people from history. After slaughtering John, Carlos and Spencer, only the surviving protagonists remember them ('it's like they never existed', notes Tracy). His supernatural ability is also rationalised by the introduction of 'ancient dream demons' who imbue Freddy with the promise of existing 'forever' (which is obviously at odds with the film's title). Moreover, in this iteration, Freddy is no longer limited by the confines of Springwood or his relationship with Elm Street's parents. Again, contrary to the notion of *Freddy's Dead* being *The Final Nightmare*, Freddy proposes that it is 'time to start all over again' and expand his reach. When he posits that 'every town has an Elm Street', a crooked Elm Street sign erupts out of the ground. Consequently, *Freddy's Dead* seeks to push the series beyond its familiar parameters by detonating its foundations. This iteration not only re-envisages Freddy's motive, but also abandons the location that defines the series (which, until this point, was contained in its titles).

From here, other foundational aspects of the series are subject to exaggerated reimagining, making *Freddy's Dead* more akin to a nihilistic reboot than a sequel. As Freddy sets his sights on America beyond Elm Street, Springwood itself is reinvented as a bizarre childless dystopia populated by delusional adults. The township and the populace's shared history, which were the series' bedrock until this point, are replaced by a hypercoded version that exaggerates the parental denial and neglect that pervade the series. For instance, instead of facing up to the evidence of Freddy's threat, Elaine sections her daughter Kristen in *A Nightmare on Elm Street 3: Dream Warriors*, then actively drugs her with sleeping pills, thereby exposing Kristen to Freddy's lethal ire in *A Nightmare on Elm Street 4: The Dream Master* (leading Kristen to exclaim 'Mother, you just murdered me!'). *Freddy's*

Dead transmutes the Elm Street parents' misguided 'rationalist' denialism into a caricatured township of delirious paranoiacs who have lost touch with their surrounding reality. While Loock contends that 'follow-ups are always driven by a logic of one-upmanship . . . an intensification-oriented principle . . . in order to retell a familiar story in an enhanced and therefore potentially new way' (Loock 2017, 99), *Freddy's Dead*'s exaggerations step too far to just 'retell' the story: they transform the story.

This ambitious overhaul of the series' core facets is tied into *Freddy's Dead*'s rumination on and remodelling of the series' tone. In the earlier films (markedly the first) Freddy is seen relatively fleetingly and is back-lit to obscure his visage. By the fifth film (*A Nightmare on Elm Street: The Dream Child* [1989]), he has a well-lit, dominant screen presence. The film series and its associated merchandise led to the character becoming a pop-cultural icon. Toys, a Nintendo videogame, comic-books and even children's pyjamas bridged between the adult horror film that gave birth to Freddy and a younger audience's fascination with the character (on this, see Conrich 2000, 223). Freddy's jibes during murder sequences became a character trademark, especially following the spinoff television series (*Freddy's Nightmares* [1988–1990]) and Freddy's spot hosting MTV in 1988. Both situations called on Freddy to play the wisecracking host. These isolated incidents were retrospectively interpreted as a trajectory, in which Freddy drifts from a legitimately scary villain to a joker or a 'vaudeville comedian' (Muir 2011, 158; see also Shary 2002, 159; Whitehead 2003, 38). However, this reputation is only fully realised in *Freddy's Dead*.

Freddy's Dead does more than embrace those aspects of Freddy's identity: the film revels in its hypercoded exaggeration of Freddy. Muir criticises *Freddy's Dead* for being 'tongue-in-cheek and over-the-top . . . ridiculous and unbelievable', 'slip-shod', lacking in 'authenticity or resonance' and suffering from 'terrible lapses of tone' (Muir 2011, 159–61). I instead agree with Taylor (2020) that these same traits evidence the film's cohesive camp sensibility. Additionally, *Freddy's Dead*'s absurdist register also elucidates the series' latent cartoonishness. As Englund admits, 'we intentionally made a decision' to make *Freddy's Dead* like 'a Warner Bros cartoon', and the film's death sequences convey that tone. For example, Freddy offers a finger-to-the-lips 'shhhh' motion to camera before dancing around behind the hearing-impaired character Carlos; Freddy mimics Bugs Bunny,[35] gurning to camera as he wheels a bed of spikes into shot for

---

[35] In the documentary *Never Sleep Again: The Elm Street Legacy* (2010), Englund explicitly states he had the comparison to Bugs Bunny in mind during that sequence.

Figure 8.2 Freddy gurns to camera *a la* Bugs Bunny in *Freddy's Dead: The Final Nightmare* (1991)

John to land on (see Figure 8.2); Spencer is made to bounce around the room to commonplace cartoon sound effects such as ludicrous 'boings!' and the rapid, pitch-shifted bongo beats used by cartoon foley artists to signal running. As Freddy flies into shot dressed as a witch on a broomstick, declaring 'I'll get you, my pretty' (*a la The Wizard of Oz* [1939]), set against Mussorgsky's 'Night on Bald Mountain',[36] the film skirts ever-closer to a Looney Tunes short rather than the tale of a grim child killer.

These moves demonstrate awareness of *Elm Street*'s reputation at that point in time, and *Freddy's Dead* self-critiques by exaggerating those qualities. Its inclusion of influences from outside the slasher film are used to augment and affirm *Elm Street*'s growing reputation as a 'cartoonish' or 'lite' version of its former self. This is pertinent because the series' first

---

[36] 'Night on Bald Mountain' is used in Disney's *Fantasia* (1940), where demon-summoned spectres ride through the sky on broomsticks and phantom steeds. I point to Bugs Bunny here because classical pieces by Liszt, Rossini, Beethoven and so forth are also littered throughout the Looney Tunes catalogue, and Freddy's guise as the witch is also reminiscent of Bugs Bunny's penchant for suddenly and unexpectedly appearing in costume. Specifically, the sequence is redolent of *What's Opera, Doc?* (1957), which incorporates various pieces of Wagner, features Bugs dressed as a maiden, and recalls *Fantasia*'s 'Night on Bald Mountain' sequence in its opening moments (when Elmer Fudd's demonic-looking shadow appears to summon lightning). While *Freddy's Dead* does not refer to these cultural touchstones directly, that cultural baggage adds to the film's cartoonish tone.

entry concluded with Nancy declaring her victory over Freddy by stating 'I know you too well now . . . I take back every bit of energy I gave you [by being afraid].' The premise of Freddy's power and his ability to arouse fear is his mystery (which was conveyed via his fleeting onscreen appearances). As he became more familiar, knowable and visible as a pop-culture icon, his ability to inspire fear diminished for audiences, just as it did for Nancy. Although Freddy returned in each sequel, he did so as a less terrifying version. *Freddy's Dead* amplifies that arc, confessing that *Elm Street* had become less frightening. The film not only insists that this version of Freddy is dead, but also reifies the reasons why the series had to end.

Freddy's Dead's cartoonishness is the clear endpoint of a pathway, but by exaggerating these elements, the film ensured the façade could not continue forward without becoming a more literal child-friendly cartoon.[37] Nevertheless, this self-critique is not only related to the series' inability to satisfy adult horror viewers who were initially attracted to *A Nightmare on Elm Street*'s dark portrayal of a 'filthy child murderer'. Parents' groups had long decried the series' cultural prevalence and perceived appeal to children; indeed, in the late-1980s, 'the National Coalition on TV violence found . . . that sixty percent of children ages [sic] 10–13 recognized Freddy Krueger; compared to only 33 percent who recognized Abraham Lincoln' (Muir 2007a, 15; see also Conrich 2000, 231). Accordingly, the series' popularity led to increasing calls to protect child viewers from exposure to the *Elm Street* films.[38] These complaints also speak to Freddy's rise as a pop-culture icon and the erosion of his scariness, signalling that Freddy had ostensibly mutated from child murderer into child entertainer.

Freddy's Dead captures this problem via its childish vision of the *Elm Street* universe. Talalay posited that 'I personally have worked to turn Freddy into a sort of combination of the Freddy we had before with a few elements of Bart Simpson added into it'; that is, Freddy is conceived not only as a cartoon, but also specifically an 'evil child' (Talalay in *The Making of Freddy's Dead* [1991]). *Freddy's Dead* itself is impetuously immature insofar as narrative liberties are taken without regard for future consequences. Protagonists are also culled in 'childish' ways. Carlos dies after being tormented by Freddy scratching his claws on a chalkboard

---

[37] Note also that Innovation Publishing contemporaneously released a comic-book adaptation of the film. Even though it came with the warning 'not intended for children' on its cover, younger readers were not thereby prohibited from purchasing the comic.
[38] *New Nightmare* comments on this reputation directly via the character Dr Heffner, who expresses concern that Heather may have exposed her son to the series, resulting in his 'instability'.

(evoking the school classrooms seen elsewhere in the film), while Spencer is executed in a videogame. Even though the protagonists are teens, they are infantilised. Tracy, Spencer, Carlos and Maggie were all abused by their parents, and in their nightmares they each regress to childlike subservience when faced with nightmare versions of their parents. In flashback, Maggie is limned as a child, sporting ribboned pigtails and a pink floral dress; the scene then transitions and Maggie is shown in the same outfit as an adult. These depictions echo the series' tonal and thematic past. Parental abuse – particularly the implied sexual abuse of Tracy by her father – is subsumed within *Freddy's Dead*'s overarching goofy absurdity. This is a complex manoeuvre, gesturing towards the kind of grim content parents' groups were anxious about, suggesting that parental control might itself endanger young people while also dispelling Freddy's threat by rendering him as a caricature. *Freddy's Dead* therefore does not just recover the slasher from criticism by toning down its violence and amping up its cartoonishness. Its tone undercuts critics' concerns over the slasher subgenre's supposed negative influence on young people. That is, its hypercoding might make *Freddy's Dead* seem silly, but the tone is essential to conveying sincere messages about the series' and the subgenre's statuses. Posed as *The Final Nightmare*, the film also seeks to have the last word on these subjects.

Finally, *Freddy's Dead* enacts a form of narrative retrocausation. As I have observed, *Freddy's Dead* was trashed by critics on its release. However, when retrospectively read via the current context of metamodern requelisation, *Freddy's Dead* takes on a different set of implications. The interpretation above exemplifies a productive form of presentism, in which the past is constantly reinvented. From the perspective of the present, *Freddy's Dead* is a playful yet cutting commentary on the *Elm Street* series' development. Furthermore, the film invites retroactive reinterpretation of the series' preceding entries, and not only because of its remodelling of Freddy's motivations. Being far more cartoonish than the series' previous sequels, *Freddy's Dead* retroactively redeems those prior entries from similar accusations. For instance, in comparison to *Freddy's Dead*, even Freddy's turn as a musclebound comic-book superhero ('Super Freddy!') in *A Nightmare on Elm Street: The Dream Child* seems less silly than it did prior to *The Final Nightmare*'s release. A sequel's retrocausal potentials might be overlooked because of biases built into standard assumptions about time: that cause precedes effect, that the past is fixed and so forth. Films such as *Freddy's Dead* afford productive ways to re-envisage the bridges between past and present, such that texts which have been dismissed as being indicative of 'the sequel's' faults can be recouped as yielding salient meanings.

Come Again?: The Metamodern Requel

Requels represent an important aspect of the movement from postmodernism to metamodernism. Sequels themselves paved the way for the postmodern slasher, given that sequels began 'to show a high degree of self-awareness in the 1980s, often drawing attention to [their] own status as sequel[s] and commenting on the process of sequelisation' including 'self-referential cinematic moments' that 'reward audience memory and intertextual knowledge' (Loock 2017, 105). That is, sequels exhibited the 'kind of postmodern self-awareness' (Loock 2017, 106) that would later become synonymous with *Scream* and its brethren. Remakes have been conceived as part of this same trajectory; for example, Roche remarks that 'remakes . . . belong to the post-*Scream* (1996) era of in-your-face metafiction' (2014, 119). This association between remakes and postmodernism is rooted in their apparent shared admittance that originality is no longer possible: that 'in postmodern aesthetics . . . endless remakes' mean 'the original and unique work of art has been replaced by a tarnished and overwritten work of culture' (Roth 2002, 225). Of course, 'critics have been lamenting about the sequel's dismal impact on originality since cinema began' (Jess-Cooke and Verevis 2010, 2), but that problem is amplified by the postmodern stance that the 'original' basis for a sequel or remake is itself unoriginal.

The metamodern requel, however, poses a challenge to this conception, corroborating Mee's contention that remakes and sequels display 'variety, creativity and innovation' (Mee 2022, 18). Metamodern slasher requels redeem both the sequel (as a cultural form) and the subgenre that has become synonymous with sequels. So, through their divergent approaches to rewriting the past, *Halloween* (2018) and *Freddy's Dead* both eschew the pure repetition and continuity that series customarily rely on to facilitate continued audience engagement across a cohesive unfolding narrative timeline. These requels draw on similarities to preceding entries, but frequently those points of comparison stress differences between the requel and other entries in the series. Because *Scream* (2022) remains too closely committed to the original's postmodern stance, it reminds viewers of 'the charismatic original',[39] while also accentuating the original's 'absence' or the fact that one is not engaging with the original (see Berliner 2001b, 109).

This attitude is contiguous with the nostalgic impulse examined in Chapter 7. Numerous scholars have posited that remaking is designed to

---

[39] Given *Scream*'s postmodern sentiments, perhaps 'the charismatic unoriginal' would be more apt.

tap into nostalgia, seeking to 'rekindl[e] emotions associated with a past that is no longer properly accessible to us' (Rosewarne 2020, 82; see also Braudy 1998, 333; Ochonicky 2020, 336).[40] Such a 'futile, nostalgic desire to reexperience the original' (Berliner 2001b, 109) is disrupted in *Halloween* (2018), which resists repeating the original's plot (as a remake usually would), disunifies the series' continuity (which a sequel would usually rely on), and fleshes out an alternative arc, meaning the story can continue in accordance with the present prevailing sensibility (as opposed to reiterating the original's tone and values). The problem Berliner outlines is tackled head-on in *Freddy's Dead*, which utilises the original's absence – the intervening sequels' erosion of the original as it was – as an organising principle for its themes and stylistic amplifications.

As this chapter has argued, metamodern slasher requels play with the very notion of retroactive continuity that is fundamental to sequel series, abandoning or modifying lore just as other metamodern slashers manipulate seemingly essential subgeneric conventions. Metamodern slasher requels are freed to innovate via an underlying confidence in the series' recognised codes, themes, narrative patterns or characters, as well as the robustness of subgeneric conventions. The metamodern slasher requel amplifies what Zeitlin terms a 'postmodern' manoeuvre, in which sequels 'incorporate and transform their precursor texts' (1998, 161). Zeitlin's proposal that the postmodern sequel 'can work a transformative effect upon its precursor, which thereby becomes derivative, secondary, subsequent' (1998, 162) is perhaps overblown, but the metamodern requel's retrocausal retconning more plainly shows how antecedent films can be recast – in narrative or even cultural terms – by later films.

The metamodern requel's temporal approaches defy complaints that sequels are 'lesser' works simply because they succeed an 'original'. As Hutcheon argues, 'to be second is not to be secondary or inferior; likewise, to be first is not to be originary or authoritative' (Hutcheon 2013, xv).[41] Metamodern requels refute that supposed inferiority by not allowing antecedents to constrain subsequent iterations. Both *Freddy's Dead* and *Halloween* (2018) denounce the idea that multiple predecessors can limit their stories. *Halloween* (2018) seeks to tell an alternative tale of Laurie's struggle against Michael, liberating Laurie from her previous deaths.

---

[40] However, nostalgia for the originals can also feed negative assessment of a remake (see, for example, Roche 2014, 8).

[41] *Shrooms* (2007) plays with this same principle: Tara's visions offer multiple renditions of the same events, and their placement in the text's chronology does not itself reveal whether one set of visions is more reliable than another (see Chapter 2).

Freddy's Dead casts off *Elm Street*'s constraints by razing the series. In both cases, the past is taken to task in the present to instil creative, productive approaches that face towards the series' and subgenre's futures.

Scream (2022)'s perpetuation of postmodernism again illuminates the metamodern requel's strategies through contradistinction. As Sandbacka avers (following Jameson), 'in postmodernism, temporality is reduced to the present' (2017, 3). That reduction is illustrated by the fatalistic presentism of *Scream* (2022) and its predecessors. *Scream* (2022)'s cogitations on requels are limited by its ensnaring postmodern presentism, meaning requelling is cast as bestowing no real opportunities for originality, innovation or enrichment. This view is rooted in apathy: existing in the present means being surrounded and shaped by predetermined circumstances beyond one's control or understanding. In contrast, metamodern presentism entails perceiving the present as a moment in a chain, leading from past to future. The present is subject to special emphasis because it is the site of one's experiential reality, meaning the present is pertinent to each of us in a fundamental way. Moreover, given that one cannot act in the past or the future, the present is also emphasised because it is the only temporal situation that affords opportunities to affect change.

The metamodern requel's combination of experiential presentism and rebuilding of a series' history might appear to overwrite '"objective" history' with 'memory', the latter being 'coloured by the vagaries of subjective response and amnesia' (Cook 2005, 2). This sounds somewhat akin to a postmodern understanding of history, wherein 'reconstructions of the past produce replacement memories that simulate first-hand experience' (Cook 2005, 2). Yet, unpacking an analogy to historical documents invalidates the concern. Historical documents are interpreted according to the decoder's experiences and knowledge. Those same documents can be subsequently reinterpreted in light of new experiences or knowledge, even though the document's content goes unmodified. Despite prevalent discursive complaints that requels somehow 'overwrite' and damage original texts (see Mee 2022, 52), metamodern requels do not literally erase and replace the past. The requel's antecedents remain accessible – indeed, the technocultural situation has amplified our ability to readily access earlier slasher texts (see Chapter 7) – and those antecedents are unchanged (at least in a literal sense) by any subsequent films. *Halloween* (2018) omits swathes of its lore, but one can return to the antecedent sequels and engage with those plot threads unimpeded. *Halloween* (2018) just uncovers new options for viewers to find their own favoured route through the series. *Freddy's Dead* contains an alternative to the accepted understanding of Freddy's motivations. In doing so, it encourages re-viewing and reassessment of preceding films in a new light, just as other retcons do.[42] This does not mean those prior films are literally altered, just that *Freddy's Dead* makes new perspectives on those events available. Thus, these metamodern requels do not adhere to a postmodern understanding of history. Rather, they are akin to Cook's model of nostalgic cinema, which does not 'claim to educate us about the past itself, imposing narrative order on chaotic reality', but instead raises questions about 'our relationship to the past, about the connections between past and present, and our affective responses' (Cook 2005, 2).

Remakes, sequels, reboots and requels grant interesting ways to explore their predecessors' narrative premises and offer potential for innovation. As I have suggested, these forms provide opportunities to explore temporal relations. Even so, that potential is commonly overlooked because of the deeply entrenched negative connotations surrounding these forms: discursive associations with unoriginality seem to obfuscate the innovations and experimentation contained within these films. This is decidedly true of the slasher film because the subgenre itself is typically derided as a crude, one-dimensional form. Those associations are especially evident where critical engagement with sequels is reduced to passing gestures towards surface-level symbols. For instance, Arnzen observes that in horror film sequels, 'the icons associated with the film (Jason's mask, Freddy's glove, the repetitive titles) replace the creative text as event' (1994, 180). To expand on the ideas raised within this chapter then, the next chapter will examine exactly that iconography. While Chapters 7 and 8 have proffered that the slasher film's past can be evoked to enrich the subgenre, Chapter 9 will delineate another version of that approach, illustrated by what I will call 'new icon' films: movies introducing slasher villains that could launch new series.

---

[42] *Behind the Mask: The Rise of Leslie Vernon* (2006) employs a similar strategy, inviting reassessment of assumptions about subgeneric conventions based on Leslie's explanations (see Chapter 4).

CHAPTER 9

The New Icons

The preceding chapters have outlined assorted reasons slasher films are received negatively. First, slasher films were largely perceived as being mainly (perhaps only) a conduit for gory slayings. For example, Sconce notes that the *A Nightmare on Elm Street* series was reputed to be 'a highly formulaic and thus uninteresting group of films, thin on plot and heavy on special effects' (1993, 105), based around 'increasingly elaborate' and 'ingeniously staged kill sequences' (1993, 113). Sconce's observation captures a second negative connotation: that slasher films are one-dimensional, being based around stock characters and situations. Ergo, Di Muzio proposes that in 'slasher films . . . character development is kept to a minimum and the storyline is straightforward' (2006, 281), and this complaint is utilised to condemn the slasher film as immoral (because the form supposedly offers nothing but murder without substance). Third, the supposed one-dimensionality of slasher films is exacerbated by the subgenre's alleged over-repetition of conventional tropes. Fourth, the initial boom-period of slasher production augmented the sense that these attributes were being repeated, and that impression only intensified with the rise of chained sequels in the 1980s. Given these connotations, motives for making and watching slasher films are also criticised. The subgenre's fans are condemned for wanting to see gory fictional murders (see Di Muzio 2006; Dika 1990, 88; Welt 1996, 80), while filmmakers are derided for exploiting that demand (see Nowell 2011, 60). These factors compound each other. For instance, during the boom-period, market saturation led some filmmakers to employ increasingly spectacular death scenes to distinguish their creations.[1]

Much as the subgenre's development was shaped by a broader industrial turn towards sequelisation in the 1980s, the slasher was equally

---

[1] This trait was aided by the development of practical and makeup effects in the 1980s, although arguably the art also improved because productions were investing in special effects, since they were a major selling point for these films (see Mathijs 2010, 153).

influenced by an adjacent trend in Hollywood filmmaking: the rise of 'high-concept' filmmaking, which also became prominent in the 1980s (Verevis 2005, 118; Wyatt 1994, 15). In his founding text on the subject, Wyatt contends that the 'high-concept' model was particularly successfully deployed in 'strict genre films' such as horror, and 'sequel or series films' in the period (Wyatt 1994, 170–171).[2] Consequently, the slasher subgenre contains pertinent examples of high-concept filmmaking thanks to its synonymy with chained sequels: many have observed that the *Friday the 13th*, *Halloween* and *A Nightmare on Elm Street* series utilised high-concept strategies (see Abbott 2010, 28; Bernard 2020, 21–22; Nowell 2011, 99; Rockoff 2002, 172). It is unclear whether the slasher's reputation for formulaic, one-dimensional storytelling and visual spectacle derives from its association with high-concept filmmaking, or whether the association highlighted those elements as being especially notable. Either way, high-concept films are 'undemanding, spectacle-heavy . . . genre films' (Nowell 2012, 82), that place distinct 'emphasis on style' (Wyatt 1994, 18), 'generic iconography', and an '"economical" means of transmitting information' (Wyatt 1994, 55). These traits are the basis of the subgenre's negative critical reputation.

Of note to this chapter is the high-concept strategy's emphasis on 'reducibility' (Feasey 2003, 167). Famous chain-sequel slashers – Freddy Krueger, Michael Myers and Jason Voorhees – were dubbed horror 'icons' in the 1980s (Cherry 2009, 25; Lennard 2014, 136), and these figures epitomised the high-concept ethos of reducibility. Each is instantly recognisable because of their distinctive visual facets, including their weapons of choice (Jason's machete, Michael's butcher's knife) and modes of dress (Jason's hockey mask, Michael's blue boiler suit and white mask) (see Koven 2006, 100; Nowell 2011, 203; Shimabukuro 2015, 54). Thus, for example, Welt proposes that Jason's hockey mask is 'one of the most persistent and notorious metonymic devices in movieland . . . an object lesson in semiotics' and might be 'responsible for the character's success as a cult figure' (1996, 81–2). That is, the character and the series' success is essentially reducible to this one symbol, in Welt's view. Freddy is even more perspicuously high-concept in design, being identifiable by his burned visage, his striking red and green sweater, his idiosyncratic fedora and his unique weapon (a bladed glove) (on this see Conrich 2000, 224). Arguably *Child's Play*'s Chucky's consistent presence as a red-haired, dungaree-wearing killer

---

[2] On the latter, see also Jess-Cooke (2009, 41)

doll is equally striking because of the mismatch between the ostensible innocence of his cherubic face and his diminutive stature on the one hand, and his gruff heartlessness and violent behaviour on the other.

Postmodern slashers sport a more complicated relationship with this kind of reducibility. Although *Valentine* (2001)'s killer sports a cupid mask and *Cry Wolf* (2005)'s dons a bright orange ski-mask, neither were sufficiently exceptional to launch a new icon. *I Know What You Did Last Summer* (1997) offers a heavily slickered fisherman (Ben Willis), but his hook weapon is derived from an urban legend and his galoshes are quite unmemorable, especially compared with a preceding hook-handed slasher – Candyman – who is garbed in a striking fur coat with exaggerated collar and cuffs. The *Scream* series' Ghostface wears a unique mask and cowl, but that disguise is donned by multiple characters rather than belonging to one icon per se.[3] Other postmodern slashers such as *Urban Legend* (1998) and *Cherry Falls* (2000) opt for a distinctive conceit 'hook' instead of a singular killer. Furthermore, where 1980s icons return in the postmodern period – in *Jason X* (2001) and *Halloween H20: 20 Years Later* (1998), for instance – those films are distinguished from prior entries via their adoption of the postmodern tone rather than by their killers' familiar visual coding. Most overtly, Chucky's resurrection in *Bride of Chucky* (1998) is influenced by the 'snarky . . . wink-wink' humour of the period (Leydon 2004, 8). Series writer Don Mancini affirms that with *Bride of Chucky*, he wanted to play with Chucky's status as a recognisable 'pop culture icon'. Mancini also observes that this direction was necessitated by the film being greenlit in a 'post-*Scream* era', meaning 'a degree of self-referentiality' was expected. Therefore, 'Chucky . . . talks about himself with full knowledge of the urban legend he has become'.[4] *Bride of Chucky* magnifies Chucky's sarcastic callousness, but the film's overarching flippant tone means its commentary also duplicitously undermines Chucky's iconic status. The series' absurd premise is acknowledged via various disparaging comments about Chucky's stature, including Tiffany's insistence that she is 'not into short guys', Damien's assertion that Chucky 'ain't big enough to take care of a woman like' Tiffany, and Jade's offensive description of Chucky as a 'fucking midget'. Whereas the original trilogy relied on a contrast between Chucky's stature and the credibility of the threat

---

[3] *Friday the 13th: A New Beginning* (1985) attempted this move in the height of the high-concept period, replacing Jason while retaining the iconic hockey mask. The manoeuvre resulted in box-office failure, fan disgruntlement and Jason's return in the next sequel.

[4] Mancini, in the Audio Commentary accompanying the 2003 Region 2 Prism Leisure Corporation DVD release of *Bride of Chucky*.

he poses, *Bride of Chucky*'s derision of its returning antagonist raises the possibility that the series ought not to be valorised or revived at all. Unlike *Freddy's Dead: The Final Nightmare* (1991), which uses a similar tactic to close the initial *Elm Street* series, *Bride of Chucky* is a reboot, reopening and setting the series' course.

This complicated relationship with slasher icons provides the foundation on which metamodern films build. This chapter will first argue that bids to create new slasher icons nostalgically capture the magic of the slasher's 1980s heyday and concurrently carry the subgenre forward. Metamodern new icon films such as *The Orphan Killer* (2011) and *Terrifier* (2016) indicate that the subgenre can attract new audiences who have not 'seen it all before' and who can authentically enjoy new iterations. More generally, these metamodern new icon slashers do not rely on intertextual references to subgenre 'classics' but rather authentically articulate the qualities and strategies that made the major icons 'classic' in the first instance.

Of particular note is the chapter's central case study, the four-part *Hatchet* series, which has to date spawned more sequels than other comparable attempts to manufacture a new icon. Contemplating how *Hatchet*'s creator Adam Green characterises his intentions with the property, the case study section will outline complexities that arise from building a new icon in light of the subgenre's past and present: *Hatchet* aims to be fresh and forward-facing, but it is simultaneously a throwback that recalls the subgenre's heyday; it seeks to appeal to an older generation of slasher fans while also attracting a younger generation; it strives to eschew the postmodern slasher, but also has to work around elements such as metafictional in-joking that became associated with the subgenre thanks to *Scream* (1996) and its successors. *Hatchet* reveals that new icons offer a complicated combination of valorising the subgenre's past, being attuned to the contemporaneous metamodern sensibility and also contributing to the subgenre's continuance by innovating. As such, *Hatchet* combines seemingly incompatible facets of the subgenre into a cohesive property. The chapter closes with a final case study that explicitly evaluates the state of the subgenre and its icons. *Axe Murdering with Hackley* (2016) is set in an office context, presenting its killers as white-collar workers and portraying its eponymous slasher as an 'old school' figure who is struggling to fit into the contemporary slasher landscape. Its twist on the formula affords opportunities to comment on the slasher subgenre's development from the boom-period to the present, and the film posits that innovation is required to maintain the subgenre's cultural relevance.

Death by Design: Creating New Icons

Although this chapter is concerned with 'new slasher icons', the idea of generating potential slasher icons is not itself new. Whether or not they were intended purely as solo outings, *Shocker* (1989), *Dr. Giggles* (1992) and *Funnyman* (1994) all could have become sustained slasher series if there had been sufficient interest in the lead killers to precipitate sequels. Notably, these films were all made after the initial slasher boom-period, and so followed in the wake of the chained sequels that transformed characters such as Chucky, Freddy Krueger, Michael Myers and Jason Voorhees from memorable killers into iconic slashers.[5] These 'antihero' antagonists anchor their respective franchises, being the main (sometimes only) recurring presence providing continuity across each series (on the latter, see Budra 1998, 195; Sconce 1993, 104; Walderzak 2019, 54). Perhaps in a bid to leverage or manufacture icon status, *Dr. Giggles*, *Funnyman* and *Shocker* centralise the killer in their film titles, being bolder than the *Friday the 13th*, *Halloween* and *A Nightmare on Elm Street* series in this respect.[6] Numerous contemporary slashers follow suit: killers are foregrounded in titles such as *Wrestlemaniac* (2006), *Trackman* (2007), *Mask Maker* (2011) and *Lumberjack Man* (2015). Any of these properties has potential for further narrative development by following their respective killers. Even so, none of these have yet spawned further sequels to date.

Elsewhere in the contemporary slasher landscape, filmmakers build slasher series in other ways. One intriguing example is MJ Dixon's *Slasher House* (2012), which focuses on an amnesiac protagonist (Red) who wakes in a cell in an abandoned industrial location. Following instructions

---

[5] Paradoxically, chained sequels also lead each of these killers to drift from their roots, displeasing some fans. On this, see Ochonicky (2020, 336), and Chapter 8's discussion of *Freddy's Dead*.

[6] The naming conventions of each series means that the minority of films bear their killers' names. There are exceptions, including *A Nightmare on Elm Street Part 2: Freddy's Revenge* (1985), *Friday the 13th Part VI: Jason Lives* (1986) and *Halloween 4: The Return of Michael Myers* (1988). These subtitles reveal the importance of the killer to each series, but these titles are not as bold as simply naming the whole property after the killer. *Freddy vs. Jason* (2003) latterly took that step, selling the film on its crossover battle between two icons. The *Child's Play* series also took a definitive turn in its postmodern phase: the initial trilogy of *Child's Play* films was followed by *Bride of Chucky*, and the killer's name has since featured in every title bar the 2019 remake. Notably, this chapter's core case studies – the *Hatchet* series, *Laid to Rest* (2009), *See No Evil 2* (2014) and *Terrifier* – follow the earlier convention of not directly naming the film series after the killer, except in some sequel titles (*Chromeskull: Laid to Rest 2* [2011]; *Victor Crowley* [2017]). That move replicates a formulaic attribute that worked for 1980s icons.

painted on the walls, she confronts and overcomes a variety of other individuals who are similarly trapped in the location. It is eventually disclosed that the environment is controlled by an unseen individual who intends that the abductees should harm one another. This setup owes more to *Saw* (2004) than *Halloween* (1978) until it is explained that each of the protagonists is a slasher killer. Instead of being a Final Girl, Red hunts and executes slashers. Unlike *KillerKiller* (2007)'s supernatural every-victim, Red is an organised, living, human assassin. Each of her opponents is introduced with an onscreen caption and a very brief flashback to confirm that they have committed murders in the past. These flashback sequences have an additional purpose, however; *Slasher House* is the origin point for a tree of prequel films based on those characters and their crimes. For example, two of the killers – Cleaver and Thorn – have to date received two spinoff films apiece, and each of those series has a further film in production. *Slasher House* is a self-contained narrative, but it presents a variety of killers that could each be the basis of a film series. The follow-ups – *Slasher House 2* (2016) and the announced *Slasher House 3* – build on that potential. Although *Slasher House* represents an inventive way of bringing new slasher characters to the marketplace, Dixon's films are more clearly invested in cultivating a cohesive overarching storyworld (the 'Mycho Universe') than generating the next slasher icon per se. Despite converging on a trilogy with 'slasher' in the title – *Slasher House* – the Mycho Universe is not singularly rooted in the subgenre. For instance, *The Haunting of Molly Bannister* (2019) is a supernatural chiller based around a possessed doll who was initially seen in *Slasher House 2*.

Other slasher filmmakers more unequivocally articulate that they aim to manufacture a new icon, or that their character has potential to become a new icon. Filmmakers such as Robert Hall (creator of *Laid to Rest*'s Chromeskull) makes comparisons between his creation and familiar iconic slashers, stating that his 'inspirations were obviously a little bit of Jason, a little bit of Michael Myers' (Hall in Yapp 2008).[7] Similarly, Jen Soska (co-director of *See No Evil 2*) submits that 'there's no reason' *See No Evil*'s (2006) slasher 'Jacob Goodnight can't become another Michael Myers . . . or another Freddy' (Soska in Wixson 2014). Such comparisons imply that these slashers might grow into the next set of icons, hinting at that aspiration.

The same is true of *Terrifier*'s killer Art the Clown, who creator Damien Leone presents as a composite of major icons: 'I . . . took personality traits

---

[7] The series' potential for further growth has likely been quashed because Hall sadly died in May 2021.

from my favorite slashers and attributed them to Art . . . Art is essentially the silent stalker *a la* Jason Voorhees and Michael Myers but with Freddy Krueger's sense of humor' (Leone in Downey 2018). Arguably, the latter is the most apt point of comparison. As with Freddy (and unlike Jason Voorhees), Art is physically slight and his ability to intimidate emanates from his creepiness and palpable cruelty. Art implements the balance of dark comedy and sadism that made Freddy such an effective villain in the original *A Nightmare on Elm Street* (1984). Art's playfulness is motioned by his mimed proposal to protagonist Tara in a takeaway pizza restaurant, for example, but any such whimsy is undercut by the extraordinary violence he later commits, especially when he cuts Dawn in two with a hacksaw, from crotch to neck. When Art smiles, it is with a grimace that is redolent of a chimp's grin: bearing clenched teeth to intimidate others. That tone is underscored when he smiles and finger waves to 'Cat Lady' (the character's credited name), which would seem impish if Art were not splattered with blood, having just shot Tara in the face multiple times at point-blank range. Art's buffoonery is symptomatic of his wilful disregard for others, mocking others' suffering. When he silently laughs as he causes harm, Art conveys defiance: his self-assurance that no-one can hinder him. In that context, Art's clown costume – with its oversized shoes and jaunty hat, offset by his blackened teeth, witch's hook nose, bony protruding cheeks and angular face – is built on a mismatch between cutesy and horrific. As with Freddy Krueger's red-green sweater, a combination designed to induce ocular discomfort (see Craven in Hutson 2014, 98), Art's very presence onscreen stimulates tension.

Art's design draws on principles that helped to establish Freddy as an icon, then. Indeed, Leone identifies that 'a classic killer needs either a signature weapon, or a signature look' (Leone in Forever Midnight 2013). This principle stresses the need to set the character apart from other slashers: the look needs to be 'signature' so that it is distinctive.[8] Thus, *Terrifier*'s Art the Clown is modelled after a monochrome Pierrot clown, with billowing white sleeves and black eye makeup/lipstick. That costume distinguishes Art from the more commonplace colourful Bozo clown type found in slasher films such as *Camp Blood* (2000), *Killjoy* (2000), *Cleaver: Rise of the Killer Clown* (2015), *Klown Kamp Massacre* (2010), *Stitches* (2012) and so forth, not to mention the shadowy, mundane killers of *Final Exam* (1981) and *He Knows You're Alone* (1980). One reason Art's design works so well is that he is discordant within the everyday

---

[8] *Panman* (2011)'s killer – a demonic chef who dons a large stockpot instead of a mask – offers an exaggerated, comedic rendition of this attribute.

Figure 9.1 A design based in incongruities – Art the Clown grimaces in a pizzeria in *Terrifier* (2016)

environment he inhabits. As noted above, his costuming engenders tension by mixing cutesy and horrific, but that capacity is amplified by his incongruous presence in (for instance) an urban fast-food restaurant early in *Terrifier* (see Figure 9.1). Here, the clown costume signals Art's brazen impunity. It does not matter to him that he will be easily identifiable. Art is memorable because he stands out, both within the narrative and within the subgenre. That match between narrative content and subgeneric purpose is in keeping with the metamodern sensibility, but here it underlines Art's potential to become an iconic slasher.

Although an antagonist must be recognisable to gain traction, distinctiveness alone is not sufficient to ensure a character will become iconic. Elsewhere, Leone hints that *Terrifier* could become a long-running series, stating that Art 'has a ton of potential' and would require 'at least a couple of films to tell his full story' (Leone in Whittington 2017).[9] Starring in multiple films aids a character's reach in the marketplace, but recurrence is also itself insufficient to guarantee that a slasher will become an icon. For example, the eponymous pig-masked killer of Eamon Hardiman's *Porkchop* series is unlikely to be recognised by a vast number of

---

[9] *Terrifier 2* was released in 2022. Notably, one trailer for the sequel consists of YouTube reviewers hyping the film (https://www.youtube.com/watch?v=jVmmQmlLKCE) and begins with Wink from ScreamCheez proposing that 'Art the Clown is like a new horror icon' and Jamie Powell declaring that Art 'is an iconic horror character'.

horror fans.[10] As with the *Camp Blood* or *Axegrinder* series,[11] one factor inhibiting *Porkchop*'s killer from attaining the recognition required for icon status is its microbudget and limited distribution compared with theatrical releases such as the *Halloween* films. Even so, a character must capture audiences' imagination in the right way to develop from a presence in the marketplace to an 'icon'. Arguably, a slasher icon is akin to a meme that 'goes viral'; the figure's ability to chime with consumers is a key ingredient that is out of the creator's control. Leone recognises this in the case of *Terrifier*, stating that 'it would be a dream come true if Art became a horror icon . . . unfortunately, it's not up to me' (Leone in *Forever Midnight* 2013).[12]

The Orphan Killer is especially worth scrutinising in this light. *The Orphan Killer*'s antagonist (Marcus Miller) is designed to bring recognised slasher icons to mind. Miller sports a full facemask *a la* Michael Myers or Jason Voorhees. As with Art the Clown, there is a clear attempt to also distinguish Miller from those icons. Miller speaks, in contrast to Voorhees and Myers (who are mute). Creator Matt Farnsworth submits that this 'simple trick . . . has taken [*The Orphan Killer*] to icon status' (Farnsworth in Terror Weekend 2012; see also Farnsworth in Danna 2011). Farnsworth's phrasing here is not incidental. *The Orphan Killer* was patently and consistently marketed as 'a new horror icon': that phrase was used in the film's trailer.[13] Writer-director Farnsworth is unabashed about his 'intention to create something [he] could franchise' (Terror Weekend 2012), heavily hyping the film to achieve that end. For instance, in one interview, he describes *The Orphan Killer* as an 'icon' five times, as well as avowing 'it's a hit' and asserting that fans refer to the film as both their 'new favourite slasher' and 'an instant classic' (Unsworth 2012; see also Danna 2011). Farnsworth insists that *The Orphan Killer* is iconic in the hopes of convincing others, willing that status into being via repeated assertion to that effect. However, the strategy does not seem to have worked. The film was followed by a sequel – *Bound x Blood: The Orphan Killer 2* (2019) – that

---

[10] The *Porkchop* series encompasses three films – *Porkchop* (2010), *Porkchop II: Rise of the Rind* (2011), *Porkchop 3D* (2012) – and a spinoff, *Pig Girl* (2014).

[11] At the time of writing, there are eight *Camp Blood* films (2000–2020) and five *Axegrinder* films (2006–2022).

[12] The actor who portrays Art (David Howard Thornton) is less measured, suggesting that Art 'is an iconic character' (Thornton in Moguel 2018) and that *Terrifier* showcases 'the iconic horror villain' (Thornton in Boiselle 2018b).

[13] *The Orphan Killer*'s trailer explicitly proclaims that its narrative origin event 'created a new horror icon' (https://www.youtube.com/watch?v=0yUnOzDPapY&ab_channel=TheOrphanKiller).

had an extremely limited release and (at the time of writing) is no longer available to stream on-demand. Much of the promotional material for the sequel has now been removed from Farnsworth's personal social media accounts.[14] As this case illustrates, manufacturing a new slasher icon is tricky, because although one can thoughtfully design a character with the intent of creating a new icon, one cannot manufacture audience response to the design. Thoughtful design is at best a matter of minimising risk of rejection. Even so, that design entails a delicate balance of old and new facets, drawing on design principles exhibited by established icons while also being unique enough to stand out. The new icons thereby reify a tension that underpins the metamodern slasher: being in sufficient concert with norms so that the film identifiably belongs to the subgenre, while also offering distinctive new elements to push the subgenre forward.

Old School, New Context: *Hatchet*

As one of the most successful attempts to produce a new slasher icon (resulting in four films to date), Adam Green's *Hatchet* is illustrative of the need to balance old and new subgeneric facets. The *Hatchet* series is based around a central antagonist, Victor Crowley, who displays similarities to various established slashers. For example, Crowley exterminates anyone who strays into his territory (Honey Island Swamp) and so is akin to Jason Voorhees, who presides over similar terrain (Camp Crystal Lake and its surrounding woodlands). Crowley's backstory involves a group of boys aiming to scare Victor by throwing firecrackers into his home, causing a fire that ultimately transforms Crowley into a supernatural slasher. This backstory mirrors another woodland slasher – *The Burning* (1981) – in which a group of boys plays a prank on summer camp caretaker Cropsy, resulting in a fire that severely disfigures him. The incident mutates Cropsy into a homicidal maniac and the stuff of campfire legend. Crowley's backstory echoes such influences, but it is also distinguished from them. For instance, unlike Cropsy, Crowley was born with facial disfigurements and Crowley's father accidentally slays his son with a

---

[14] Indeed, Farnsworth appears to be distancing himself from the project, and is currently focusing on his new venture as a fitness coach. In 2020, he posted that 'I used to work in showbusiness' (past tense), suggesting that he is no longer a filmmaker (https://twitter.com/MattFarnsworth/status/1258169999669129216 7 May 2020). One catalyst for this shift might be a near-fatal incident: on 23 January 2020, he posted an image of himself injured and hospitalised with the caption 'this was me 4 1/2 years ago . . . I died that night and had to be revived . . . #soberlife' (https://twitter.com/MattFarnsworth/status/1220402783980965888).

hatchet while trying to save him from the fire. In contrast to Cropsy (who survives the titular immolation), Crowley is undead. Crowley thus has supernatural abilities that distinguish him from his forbears, such as exorbitant strength and the capacity to regenerate. Crowley's physical design is also reminiscent of extant woodland slashers, most notably the longhaired, axe-wielding, overall-wearing antagonist of *Madman* (1981). Crowley is superficially distinguished from this influence by his darker hair, his muscularity (exposed via his shirtless torso) and adoption of a hatchet (as opposed to an axe). More pertinently, elements of Crowley's design are tied into his backstory: his favoured weapon is redolent of his demise, and he bears his fatal hatchet head wound in his undead form. Consequently, Crowley does not directly mimic any single preceding slasher, but rather echoes these influences, combining them into a cohesive independent entity that is suggestive of influential boom-period slashers.

Instead of dwelling on Crowley as a figure however, this section will address the *Hatchet* series as a property that is situated by its relationship to the subgenre's past, present and future. That is, even though Crowley symbolises the property, the *Hatchet* series produces the conditions for Crowley's potential standing as a slasher icon via its engagements with the subgeneric context. Of particular interest is how *Hatchet*'s creator – Adam Green – conceives *Hatchet* as an attempt to cultivate a new iconic slasher property. When Zaius (2018) proposes that Green has 'created a true horror icon in Victor Crowley', Green carefully responds that Crowley is 'still not at the level of a Jason, Michael Myers, or Freddy', and that he 'was always pretty resistant to that word [icon] until' the fourth *Hatchet* film was released. Green then flags that the term was imposed on the series by 'critics and people saying, "this is the next icon of horror"', or marketers who dubbed the film 'The Holy Grail of Slasher Films'. This contention allows Green to implicitly self-promote by articulating others' praise for the property. He then deferentially acknowledges *Hatchet*'s place in the subgenre's hierarchy: 'I'm like dude, come on, *Halloween* is the Holy Grail of slasher films' (Green in Zaius 2018). Elsewhere, Green also admits the 'loyal' *Hatchet* fanbase is 'not quite as big as' the following for *Halloween*.[15] Despite his deference then, Green's comments nevertheless situate *Hatchet* in a continuum with iconic slasher properties (primarily *Halloween*), minimally implying that they are comparable to some extent.

---

[15] Green in Audio Commentary accompanying the 2011 Region 2 Arrow Films DVD release of *Hatchet II* (2010). Any further reference to this commentary track will be cited as '*Hatchet II* commentary' and will refer to this release.

The intent to intervene in the subgenre is marked out much more overtly early within the series' lifespan. At the end of *Hatchet II*'s credits, a branding logo is displayed, which reads '*Hatchet* Army . . . Here to Save Horror'. Although unstated, it seems reasonable to assume that the 'army' is constituted by the series' filmmakers, its fans or perhaps both. In any case, this cohesive 'army' has a stated shared intention: 'to Save Horror'. The logo not only boldly casts *Hatchet* as a pivotal property, but also critiques the genre's state. The shape of that criticism is implied by *Hatchet*'s content; that is, how it is distinguished from other horror films of the period. Given this chapter's central theme, the most immediately apparent distinguishing factor is its introduction of Crowley as a potential icon. Retrospectively, Green proposes that 'there really aren't any [other new icons]' (Green in Zaius 2018), intimating that the subgenre needs new slashers akin to famous villains such as Candyman and Chucky, and that the *Hatchet* films fill that subgeneric void. Since a lack of new slasher icons might be symptomatic of the icon era being 'over', the *Hatchet* films could be interpreted as past-regarding throwbacks, nostalgically harking back to a prior era in which Freddy Krueger, Michael Myers and Jason Voorhees became highly marketable figures. Still, such an interpretation overlooks the ways in which *Hatchet*'s tone and approach is informed by the contemporaneous generic landscape.

Notably, the *Hatchet* films react against an association between the slasher subgenre and teen horror that was a legacy of the *Scream* era. Key postmodern slasher films cast actors who played prominent roles in teen television drama,[16] and following those box-office successes, 'teen' horror films rose to prominence more broadly. If *Hatchet* arrived 'to Save Horror' in 2006, it partially sought to rescue the genre from the likes of *The Cave*, *Cry Wolf*, *The Exorcism of Emily Rose* or *The Skeleton Key*, all of which were prominent releases in 2005, and all of which were rated PG-13. Moreover, many of the other properties that epitomised the American horror landscape in 2005 were remakes (even if only in name), such as *The Boogeyman*, *Dark Water*, *The Fog* and the remake of *When a Stranger Calls*, and again, each was rated PG-13. *Hatchet* interjected in this landscape by delivering an incontrovertibly R-rated, original property.[17]

---

[16] For example, Neve Campbell and Jennifer Love Hewitt both starred in the series *Party of Five* prior to taking respective lead roles in *Scream* and *I Know What You Did Last Summer*, while Michelle Williams (*Halloween H20*) and Joshua Jackson (*Urban Legend*, *Scream 2* [1997]) were both known for their roles in the series *Dawson's Creek*.

[17] To this end, the UK DVD box art for *Hatchet* also carried the tagline 'it's not a remake, it's not a sequel, and it's not based on a Japanese one'.

The horror landscape contextualising *Hatchet*'s inception did not solely consist of PG-13 horror, however. Other horror filmmakers had already expressed similar dissatisfaction with PG-13 teen fare, leading to the grim, bleak tone of so-called torture porn films such as *The Texas Chainsaw Massacre* (2003), *Saw* and *Hostel* (2005). In their adoption of a serious tone, these torture porn films react against the ironic humour that was perceived as diverting the genre following *Scream* (on this, see Jones 2013, 19–21). *Hatchet* again responds to this contemporaneous climate. Although *Hatchet*'s gore is a retort to 'bloodless' PG-13 horror, *Hatchet* does not forsake comedy. If, as reputed, films such as *Hostel* and *Saw* provide mean-spirited, humourless horror experiences, *Hatchet* leans into comedy as an alternative.

The *Hatchet* series' comedy demands attention because it illustrates the series' concentration on and attempt to negotiate the conflict between post-*Scream* teen horror and torture porn, a fissure in the generic landscape that birthed *Hatchet*. On first glance, the early *Hatchet* films might appear to be akin to the postmodern slashers, particularly in their employment of comedy. For example, *Hatchet II* includes express dialogic intertextual in-joking: a hunter (Chad) asks who Crowley is, inquiring whether he is 'like a Jason Voorhees or something?', for instance. That intertextual reference not only connotes that Crowley might be an equivalent to an iconic slasher, but also hints at the extra-narrative understanding that Crowley is played by Kane Hodder, who has portrayed Voorhees more than any other actor to date (four times). However, while the audience may be aware of such connections, there is a notable difference between *Hatchet* and *Scream* here. For *Scream*'s characters, Jason Voorhees is a movie character. Extant horror films are mentioned with metafictional intent in *Scream*, reminding viewers that *Scream* itself is a fictional construct. In contrast, Jason is part of *Hatchet*'s in-world reality rather than a cinematic entity: he is an equivalent to Crowley, being another 'local boogeyman story' used 'to keep kids away from the swamp'. Therefore, it is implied that Voorhees is just as real to *Hatchet*'s characters as he is to *Friday the 13th*'s teens, who also treat Jason as a scary campfire tale until they encounter him.

Part of *Hatchet*'s bid to 'Save Horror' entails intertwining comedy and horror, recognising and building away from the postmodern slasher's snarky metafictional in-joking while also pushing against torture porn's reputed grim seriousness. So, Green has it that the series' spirit is 'all in good fun', which is 'something that horror could use again' in the era of *Saw*.[18]

---

[18] Green in 'The Making of *Hatchet*' featurette, 2008 Region 2 Universal Pictures International DVD Release. Any further reference to this featurette will be cited as 'Making of *Hatchet*'.

Horror and comedy are difficult to balance (see Carroll 1999; Paul 1994). If a horror film leans too far into comedy the characters can become caricatures, or violence can become slapstick. The latter can dilute the horror by undermining the consequences – pain and perishing – that lend narrative weight to the violence. Green seeks to avoid those pitfalls by 'keep[ing] the comedy out of [*Hatchet*'s] horror'.[19] Nevertheless, it is not accurate to say that the horror elements are entirely separate from *Hatchet*'s comedy. Seeking to avoid a PG-13 rating, *Hatchet*'s horror is over-the-top. The series avoids lapsing into spoof by ensuring that the characters treat violent incidents with gravity.[20] This internal commitment to 'playing it straight' helps to present Crowley as a credible threat. As such, the extravagant violence raises the stakes for the characters facing that threat. So, when Ainsley's body is torn in half in *Hatchet*'s opening sequence, he screams 'Oh God! Help me!'. Instead of cracking a joke – as is common among comical slasher films, including *The Gingerdead Man* (2005), *Jack Frost* (1997) and *Leprechaun Back 2 Tha Hood* (2003) – Victor responds by snarling.

Hatchet's comedy mainly arises from the more everyday conversations protagonists have before and between moments of imperilment. So, for instance, when Tony Todd stars in the first film as Reverend Zombie, he tells Ben that he does not 'do night tours [of the swamp] anymore . . . after what happened'. One might expect his rationale for halting the tours to be related to Crowley, especially given Todd's patently stagey performance and the story's establishing context: 'last Halloween . . . in the mist of night . . . [a passenger] saw two eyes staring at him from the woods. Chilled him to his very marrow.' The story then turns sharply for comic effect: 'he slipped . . . and sued me for negligence, that cocksucker!'. Such overtly comedic dialogue endeavours to keep viewers amused between the action scenes. As such, the series redresses one of the boom-period slasher's reputed flaws: namely, that much of the runtime is expended on sequences that stall the action, following protagonists as they engage in mundane activities (see Clasen and Platts 2019, 25). Even when character-building, critics complained that the dialogue and characters remained inane – especially if the acting and/or writing is

---

[19] Green, 'Making of Hatchet'.
[20] *Terrifier 2* (2022) offers a similar balance, juxtaposing the protagonists' terror, Art the Clown's contrasting sadistic delight, and over-the-top deaths. The violence is naturalised by the sequel's leaning towards hypercoding: for example, the film's 138-minute runtime is formally excessive, providing an immoderate terrain for its abundant gore sequences, including blowtorch immolation, penile mutilation, heart biting, limb snapping, eye gouging and multiple decapitations.

stilted – or inconsequential inasmuch as most characters are eradicated, so the future ambitions and desires they refer to are destined to be thwarted (see Conrich 2010, 174; Crane 1994, 145). The most entertaining aspects of such dialogue are memorable incongruities, such as *Friday the 13th: A New Beginning*'s Demon and Anita singing 'ooh baby, hey baby' to each other as Demon defecates in an outhouse. As with the incongruities discussed in Chapter 6, such moments can amuse slasher film viewers, yet they are notable because they are isolated, unusual incidents, and it is not clear that they are intentionally written as comedy. *Hatchet* consistently and purposefully deploys comedy to increase the series' overall entertainment quota. In this respect, the *Hatchet* films are more akin to *Friday the 13th Part VI: Jason Lives*, which makes regular use of intentionally humorous dialogue to keep the narrative moving.

Another related element that shapes *Hatchet*'s tone is investment in its characters. Formal techniques are employed to encourage such connections. For example, as Marybeth swims to escape from Crowley in the opening of *Hatchet II*, the camera dips below water regularly, mimicking her experience by near-muting the environmental sound whenever the camera is submerged. Such techniques convey Marybeth's first-person sensory experience, inviting empathy for her position. Furthermore, the series invests in Crowley's backstory from the outset, fleshing out his history via flashbacks. Green suggests that the backstory is 'very dark and kind of sad' (Green in Hanley 2013), and its counterpoint to the 'funny moments' is intended to develop 'some shred of sympathy from the audience' (Green in Champ 2010). *Hatchet*'s sincere investment in character development, motivation and the characters' emotional realities balance its exaggerated gore and comedic dialogue.

This balance marks *Hatchet* as metamodern, not least since it additionally speaks to contemporaneous tensions within horror filmmaking. Green argues that the fan audience is split in this regard, observing that 'a good portion of the audience . . . really want some story, they want some characters . . . another portion of the audience who loves these films equally . . . don't want story and they don't care about performances', instead wanting to see action.[21] Arguably, *Hatchet*'s comedy is an inclusive compromise, entertaining the latter contingent while also fostering emotional connection to the characters. This equilibrium reflects the complexities of inventing a new icon while also accounting for the wider subgeneric context.

---

[21] *Hatchet II* commentary.

Moreover, Green makes a claim for the series' sincerity by situating *Hatchet* as a genuine contribution to the subgenre rather than a product, the success of which can be measured in profit. Such claims to artistic integrity respond to negative connotations surrounding the subgenre. As posited in Chapter 8, the slasher film has been associated with money-grubbing opportunism because of its initial production boom and the proliferation of sequels as the 1980s progressed. Indeed, Green contends that the legacies of that period fundamentally shape slasher filmmakers' ambitions: he observes that 'after the 80s . . . it wasn't about creativity and originality anymore', because 'buyers at [festival] screenings . . . just want to know . . . "How do we market it to make it like that movie that made a lot of money?"' (Green in Hanley 2013).[22] Green not only distances himself from that commercial imperative, but also rationalises his divergent viewpoint by referring to subgeneric allegiance: he explains that buyers hold such attitudes because 'they're not fans' so 'they don't know' what makes a 'really good' slasher film (Green in Hanley 2013). Green thereby implies that as a fan, he understands what slasher aficionados want and what the subgenre needs.

Nevertheless, Green's position illustrates that new icon filmmakers are caught between a desire to create a substantial property that can be iterated across a chain of films, and the subgenre's reputed legacy of 'diluting' such properties in order to maintain profitability. One way of overcoming the latter implication is to affirm the role fans play in supporting the property: gaining and retaining the interest of a core returning audience is required to develop and sustain a series. Green adopts this stance, asserting that *Hatchet*'s distributors (Dark Sky) allow him to 'make the movie that the fans want to see', without pressuring him to 'reach a broader audience' (Green in Hanley 2013). The series' inclusion of gory murders – which precludes *Hatchet* from obtaining a PG-13 certificate and thus wider audience reach – evidences Green's claim to artistic freedom.

Yet this prioritisation of fan interests exposes further tensions. As Green acknowledges in his comments about diverging outlooks on story

---

[22] Other new icon filmmakers corroborate these concerns. For example, Robert Hall avers that 'no one [involved in the making of *Laid to Rest*] is here to get any money out of the deal' (Hall in Benardello 2011), implying that the film was unlikely to be particularly profitable compared with Hollywood studio filmmaking. Damien Leone frames the approach to *Terrifier* in slightly different terms, noting that if Art becomes 'a horror icon . . . it would be downright disrespectful to the character and to the fans to not produce' further sequels. The caveat to this proposal is that it is necessary to 'maintain some integrity and never jump the shark' (Leone in Whittington 2017), meaning that sequels ought to prioritise characters, story and artistic merit, not profit-generation.

and action, slasher fans are not a unified, homogenous group. Because the subgenre has endured over time, fans are also divided along generational lines. Green stresses his desire to 'show respect' to both an older audience who have 'grown up with this stuff' and also a younger demographic for whom *Hatchet* is 'their slasher movie'.[23] Again, this potential split between past and present informs *Hatchet*'s development. Green's remarks about the fourth *Hatchet* film's inception speak to this concern.[24] Green discloses that the fourth film (*Victor Crowley*) was inspired by two incidents involving key horror directors of an older generation. First, Green relates that at Wes Craven's memorial, a common thread in 'conversations . . . between my generation of genre filmmakers' was the question 'have we contributed anything [to the genre] that matters?'. Therefore, Green imparts that Craven's passing and legacy triggered younger filmmakers to consider their own creations as having potential to shape the genre. Given that the story is intended to explain why a fourth *Hatchet* film was made, it is implied that the *Hatchet* series is Green's attempt to make a serious, lasting contribution to the genre. Second, and more directly, Green observes that shortly before his demise, another significant horror director – George Romero – explicitly encouraged Green to make 'another Crowley picture'. Green states that a fan caught his intimate exchange with Romero in a photograph, which Green now cherishes.[25] This detail bridges between Green as a fan of Romero (who Green refers to as a 'legend'), the photographer's fandom of both filmmakers and Green's appreciation of his own fans. The unnamed photographer and the treasured photograph symbolise the importance of fan-filmmaker interactions. The photographer-fan becomes a pivotal part of the dialogue between filmmakers (here, Romero and Green), but there is also a levelling of Green and the photographer,

---

[23] *Hatchet II* commentary.

[24] The following quotations relating to Craven's memorial and Green's encounter with George Romero are taken from interviews with Green in the featurette 'Raising the Dead . . . Again' from the 2017 Region 2 Warner Home Video DVD Release of *Victor Crowley*.

[25] Green also notes that he faced several personal crises (including the end of his marriage and the death of his friend, Dave Brockie) prior to making *Victor Crowley*. Again, those incidents are presented as an explanation for how and why *Victor Crowley* came into being, adding to the narrative that the film was personal (rather than motivated by profit). Other new icon filmmakers similarly affirm their subgenre fandom to similar ends. For example, Matt Farnsworth insists that 'I've always been a blood and guts slasher fan' (in Unsworth 2012); Robert Hall indicates that 'I wear my influences on my sleeve . . . One of my favourite films is *Halloween*' (Hall in Yapp 2008; see also Hall in The Arrow 2009); Damien Leone asserts 'I'm a diehard slasher fan so I like to think I know what slasher fans enjoy most' (Leone in Boiselle 2018a) and so forth.

insofar as both are genre fans. As opposed to being 'just' consumers then, such fans take on a collaborative, productive role; here, taking the photograph, but also spurring *Victor Crowley*'s production.[26]

In these twin stories, Romero and Craven represent an older generation of filmmakers (differentiated from what Green refers to as 'my generation'), but the fact that both subsequently died means that *Victor Crowley* is framed as a 'passing of the torch', not least because of Romero's encouragement (his 'blessing'). In light of this bridging between generations, it is worth returning to Kane Hodder's casting as Crowley. Stunt casting is commonplace across the series: Robert Englund (who played Freddy Krueger), Tyler Mane (who played Michael Myers) and Tony Todd (who played Candyman) all take roles as Crowley's victims. These casting decisions stimulate intertextual meaning, suggesting that Crowley – the new killer on the block – dispatches and replaces these former slasher legends. This is not to say that *Hatchet* disparages the past since Crowley is played by Kane Hodder, whose fame is equally contingent on the subgenre's 1980s heyday. These connotations are illuminated by the veritable who's-who of horror filmmakers who cameo in *Hatchet II*, including John Carl Buechler, Marcus Dunstan, Tom Holland, Lloyd Kaufman, Joe Lynch and Dave Parker. Notably, these figures are primarily associated with either the 1980s or horror of the early-to-mid 2000s. That is, there is a notable dearth of cameos from horror filmmakers or actors who are synonymous with the postmodern slasher. Given this eschewal of the postmodern phase, the stunt casting does not come across as merely providing in-joke references for knowing fans (even though it certainly can function in that way). Rather, the cameos bridge between pre-*Scream* slashers and the subgenre's present, signalling that a new iconic slasher can be created in the latter context.[27]

Hatchet's careful balancing of past and present permeates the series. The first film's tagline declares that *Hatchet* is 'old school, American horror',

---

[26] One might recall Chapter 5's dissection of intertextuality here, because the postmodern slasher's in-jokes also entail levelling fan and filmmaker; the in-joke mechanism relies on fans having sufficient subgeneric knowledge to share in the filmmaker's allusions. The mechanism also instils division in that the laughter such 'jokes' inspire is essentially directed at a casual viewer's lack of knowledge (and thus their exclusion from 'getting' the joke). Green's anecdote about the fan photographer is strikingly different because there is no 'in-joke': it is presented as an earnest expression of unity.

[27] Some other new icon films follow suit. Danielle Harris – who is most famous within the subgenre for her lead roles in *Halloween 4* and *Halloween 5: The Revenge of Michael Myers* (1989) – stars as lead protagonist in *Hatchet II* and *Hatchet III* (2013), and also stars in *See No Evil 2* and *Chromeskull: Laid to Rest 2*.

by which it is meant that the film seeks to be 'reminiscent of what slasher movies used to feel like in the 80s' (Green in Hanley 2013). That 'feeling' is partly captured by leaning towards practical FX work over CGI. Echoing the tagline, Green states that the effects were 'all done the *old school* American horror way' (emphasis added) because opting for 'a cartoon or an animation of blood splattering' is the product of 'sheer laziness'.[28] This attitude to FX evokes the period in which practical effects rose to dominance (the 1980s) while eschewing the subsequent period in which CGI gained traction as an alternative effects technology (the 1990s).[29] 'Old school' FX are a shorthand for Green's (nostalgic) understanding of what made pre-*Scream* slasher films authentic, why they appealed to fans, and why the subgenre has sustained over time. Utilising those techniques signals that *Hatchet* strives to bridge between that past and the subgenre's present. Instead of trying to purely revive a bygone era however, films such as *Hatchet* follow the metamodern desire to renew the subgenre by building on the past. Consequently, Green suggests that 'as a fan, I try to think of things I haven't seen before' (Green in Champ 2010); that is, he states that his intention is to utilise his knowledge of the subgenre (including its history) to yield something new.

This sensibility is hypostatised in credit-sequence music in the first two films. *Hatchet II*'s closing credits are accompanied by Overkill's song 'Old School'. Although the song was released in 2005, the band itself represents an earlier era, having formed in 1980, risen to popularity in the late-1980s and fallen out of fashion by the mid-1990s. The song title and

---

[28] Green, '*Hatchet II* commentary'. Other new icon filmmakers echo the same sentiments. Farnsworth posits that *The Orphan Killer* was inspired by 'a lack of good current slasher films', and a yearning to return to 'real blood flowing films. Old school style' (Farnsworth in Danna 2011). This approach signals Farnsworth's fondness for the subgenre's boom-period: '80's all the way' (Farnsworth in Terror Weekend 2012). Robert Hall employs a similar phrasing when asked about his influences, asserting 'I'm old school' (Hall in Yapp 2008). Jen Soska also cites her intention to make *See No Evil 2* with 'that classic 80s slasher feel to it' (Jen Soska in Pollard 2017), being 'very much inspired by the 1980s', and calling *See No Evil 2* 'a love letter to the slasher films of that decade' (Jen Soska in Benardello 2014). Farnsworth equally rejects CGI on the grounds that it is 'not visceral' (Farnsworth in Unsworth 2012). The writer-directors of *Laid to Rest* (Robert Hall) and *Terrifier* (Damien Leone) also both call for the return of practical FX in horror (Hall in The Arrow 2009; Leone in Forever Midnight 2013), and their statements come with the added clout that both have experience working as FX artists.

[29] Developments in CGI FX were advanced in the period thanks to successful and much-publicised (although moderate) deployment in 1990s blockbusters *Terminator 2: Judgment Day* (1991) and *Jurassic Park* (1993).

lyrics match Green's valorisation of the 1980s as 'the' past, proclaiming 'here's to the old school, didn't matter if you looked cool . . . they said that this would never last, we never gave a fuck'. The song epitomises the idea that keeping up with fads ('looking cool') is less important than having a good time and remaining true to one's vision, even if one's outlook appears outmoded. That Overkill are associated with the 1980s but were seeing renewed success around the time of *Hatchet II*'s release in 2010 makes the song an apt choice.[30] Balancing that tack is the first film's credit music, which delineates the intent to invent a new icon. The title/chorus refrain of Marilyn Manson's track 'This is the New Shit' (2003) sets up the idea that *Hatchet* offers fresh content, and using music of the moment connotes that *Hatchet* is in keeping with the contemporaneous cultural present. More tellingly, the end credit music is Goldfrapp's remix of 'This is the New Shit'. That choice articulates the desire to produce 'new shit' by recombining established elements in surprising ways. Together, these musical choices convey *Hatchet*'s metamodern mindset of looking to the past to move forward, illustrating the extent to which that outlook pervades the series.

In sum, *Hatchet* exemplifies numerous complexities entailed by creating a slasher property that has the potential to launch a new icon. The series finds a place within the subgenre by including enough comedy to differentiate itself from the then-popular grimness of torture porn, while also treating its horror seriously enough to distinguish it from the postmodern slasher's sardonic irony. The gore is outlandish enough to attain an R-rating – so that the series is distinct from post-*Scream* PG-13 teen horror – yet also carefully invests in its characters, thereby trying to appeal to divergent audience needs. Additionally, the ongoing series contends with criticism surrounding the subgenre, particularly its alleged propensity for generating money-grubbing sequels. This is achieved by demonstrating an awareness of the subgenre's history, accentuating Green's status as a genre fan, and framing the series as 'old school' in various ways. However, that impetus is balanced by two other demands: appealing to the next generation of horror fans and indicating that the series contributes to the subgenre's future development. *Hatchet* thereby elucidates that developing a new icon requires balancing seemingly incompatible elements. The series embodies a metamodern sensibility by suspending those disparate elements in superposition.

---

[30] Indeed, their 2014 album *White Devil Armory* gave Overkill their highest position on the Billboard album chart (see https://www.billboard.com/music/overkill/chart-history).

Old Dog, New Tricks: *Axe Murdering with Hackley*

My final case study volunteers a macroscopic view of the slasher subgenre and its icons. *Axe Murdering with Hackley* follows its eponymous slasher (loosely modelled after Jason Voorhees),[31] who works alongside fellow slashers for the company RKS. The film's conceit is that RKS is a corporate organisation and its killers are akin to white-collar office workers. Hackley is a 'veteran' slasher who complains that his ability to meet his kill quota is being stifled by 'mountains of red tape . . . status report after status report' and 'corporate bureaucracy', even though his nemesis – a younger killer named Rival – has no such issues (maintaining a consistent 'employee of the month' record). The film follows Hackley as he is put on a 'performance improvement plan' so that he can meet the business's needs. Those requirements are coded iterations of subgeneric demands; so, *Axe Murdering with Hackley* investigates similar tensions to those outlined in the previous section, but here they are examined from the icon's perspective, not the filmmaker's. As a fading icon struggling to negotiate the contemporary landscape, Hackley articulates ways innovation is constrained by the subgenre's history. Hackley's resistance to merely clinging to and replicating the past is the conduit for critical evaluation of the subgenre. *Axe Murdering with Hackley* uses the comic friction triggered by this offbeat premise to contemplate the subgenre's continuing relevance in the contemporary cultural climate.

Hackley is an anti-throwback figure. That quality is salient because Hackley's dissatisfaction with his job could initially be misread as merely romanticising the subgenre's golden age. For instance, Hackley mourns that slashers could previously slay with impunity, stating 'I remember the day when if you just wanted to kill somebody . . . you didn't even need a reason . . . they could have tripped and fallen, and you could have cut their head off.' Still, he also crucially acknowledges that 'it was a different time'. The latter is vital given that *Axe Murdering with Hackley* is not just a love letter to the slasher's boom-period. The film is equally willing to critique that era. For example, when their manager expresses that he is

---

[31] Hackley's mask is similar to Jason's. Hackley also notes that some of his nearly 200 murders were conducted by his mother, alluding to the contributions Jason's mother made to the *Friday the 13th* series' body count (during its first instalment). Moreover, Hackley's colleague Rancid observes that Hackley has battled with a psychic (as Jason did in *Friday the 13th Part VII: The New Blood* [1988]) and was sent to a space station (as Jason was in *Jason X*).

'disappointed' that Rival 'didn't kill the black guy first',[32] Hackley points out both that 'I'm black, you idiot!', and also that the convention is 'backwards and stupid'. Elsewhere, Rival taunts Hackley by playing the rap video Hackley partook in many years earlier. The video echoes the short-lived rap career of Freddy Krueger, which was symptomatic of the latter icon's broad marketisation and deterioration as a scary entity.[33] Hackley objects to Rival's office prank, qualifying his subsidiary musical career as an embarrassing necessity of the period: 'it was the 80s . . . you know they made me do that'. Therefore, the film does not idealise or take an uncritical view of the slasher boom-period. Rather, *Axe Murdering with Hackley* confronts elements of the subgenre's past that even Hackley is happy to leave behind. By recollecting the subgenre's history throughout, the film underlines that past and present are intertwined.

Most significantly from a metamodern perspective, Hackley is not interested in replicating his heyday successes, but with finding ways to move on from the past. For instance, he posits to his manager that instead of adhering to a routine of stalking the potential victim and finding a specific behavioural reason to justify the slaughter, 'we could just kill [the target]. Can you imagine how ballsy that would look? . . . Think about the headline . . . "anyone could be a victim"'. Hackley's manager swiftly dismisses Hackley's attempt to innovate, indicating that they are constrained by established norms: as he has it, 'we can't go off company handbook. We have [policies] for a reason.' Rather than poking fun at 'outdated' 1980s slasher films, the main target for *Axe Murdering with Hackley*'s humorous critique is the bureaucratisation of murder, which stands in for unquestioning adherence to subgeneric norms. Hackley thus complains that his boss has not 'been in the field for twenty years' and so cannot appreciate that their 'rules' not only 'don't work anymore', but also actively impede his ability to 'kill effectively'. Hackley's desire to innovate is also stifled by his position as an employee rather than a senior

---

[32] This scene refers to a reputed convention that black protagonists are killed early in slasher films. Both *Bloody Murder 2: Closing Camp* (2003) and *Crazy Lake* (2016) (for example) recognise this supposed convention, having black characters express that they are likely to be targeted early because of their skin colour. The veracity of that reputation has been refuted by content analysis (see Ménard, Weaver and Cabrera 2019, 635).

[33] In 1988, DJ Jazzy Jeff and the Fresh Prince released 'A Nightmare on My Street', which referred directly to Freddy Krueger throughout. In the same year, the Fat Boys' song 'Are You Ready for Freddy?' included a guest cameo by Robert Englund, who rapped in-character as Freddy. The previous year, The Elm Street Group released the musical album *Freddy's Greatest Hits*, which featured spoken (rather than rapped) interjections by Englund as Freddy.

executive at RKS. Despite Hackley's wealth of experience, his manager immediately rejects Hackley's proposals, quashing the possibility of reform at the root. Hackley remains stuck repeatedly 'going through the motions'. His inability to enjoy his work is articulated via the narrative's presentation of serial homicide as a mundane corporate enterprise. This setup implies that slasher films are no longer pleasurable because of the subgenre's slavish adherence to stagnant procedures.

The validity of Hackley's criticisms is underscored in the opening: *Axe Murdering with Hackley* begins with a (contrived) teaser trailer for '*Hackley XVII* . . . coming fall, 1985', before leaping to the present day. The voiceover states (of *Hackley XVII*'s plot) 'you thought it was over. You were wrong . . . Hackley's reign of terror will never end.' That declaration is almost immediately undercut by the switch to *Axe Murdering with Hackley*'s narrative present, in which Hackley slowly paces behind two potential victims. One walks backwards so she faces Hackley, pausing for a selfie with him before observing 'just don't take your eyes off of him and we'll be fine' (see Figure 9.2). In his vlog, Hackley notes that it took 'thirteen fucking hours' of stalking before he had the opportunity to exterminate them. Hackley is disarmed by the 'rule' that slashers cannot attack targets until their backs are turned. The arbitrary convention makes for an intolerably dull situation.

A further problem is unveiled via this incident: the teens are now all too aware of the rules slashers must follow. Here, *Axe Murdering with Hackley*

Figure 9.2 Corporate 'head-hunter' – teens use 'the rules' against the slasher in *Axe Murdering with Hackley* (2016)

implicitly points an accusatory finger at *Scream* as a catalyst for the subgenre's torpor. Throughout, corporate policies (slasher film conventions) are plainly referred to using the term 'rules', reproducing nomenclature that is synonymous with *Scream*, thanks to Randy's famous in-film lecture that 'there are certain rules that one must abide by in order to successfully survive a horror movie'. Furthermore, Hackley's nemesis – flavour or 'employee of the month', Rival – is a rendition of *Scream*'s Ghostface. Rival's cowl is redolent of Ghostface's costume, and posters for his in-film series *Yell* utilise the typeface used for *Scream*'s logo. Moreover, Rival's snarky belligerence captures *Scream*'s teens' callousness and willingness to mock their dead peers' misfortune; Rival is presented as 'a douche' who needlessly taunts Hackley about his precarious employment position.

Even so, *Axe Murdering with Hackley* does not purely map a schism between the boom-period and postmodern slasher films. *Scream* is implicated, but it is not solely blamed for Hackley's dissatisfaction, just as Rival is not the primary source of Hackley's complaints. When Hackley argues that the 'rules' were created by 'a bunch of suits . . . in some office somewhere', a further layer of the film's critique is uncovered. *Axe Murdering with Hackley*'s marriage of slashers and corporate bureaucracy implies that the subgenre fell victim to its own (relative) financial success. The boom-period demonstrated that the subgenre had potential to make decent returns on modest budgets. That potential is pertinently illustrated by the *A Nightmare on Elm Street* series, which transformed New Line Cinema from fledgling production company into a mini-major during the 1980s. That success was not achieved via the film series alone, but by the kinds of licensing, merchandising and extra-filmic production *Axe Murdering with Hackley* calls to mind during its rap video prank sequence: when Hackley complains 'they made me do that', 'they' refers to studio executives interested in maximising profit. That the rap video is used to mock Hackley evinces that such decisions are unwise, diluting or damaging an icon's long-term reputation. Hackley stands for a contrasting set of values, being committed to his craft and seeking to innovate.

The influence of contemporary corporate executive interference on the subgenre is directly criticised when 'upper management' bring in a 'reboot consultant' to help bring Hackley up-to-date. The consultant's name – Michael Harbor – indicates that the consultant is a surrogate for Michael Bay, who spearheaded several slasher remakes/reboots under the Platinum Dunes banner.[34] *Axe Murdering with Hackley* suggests that figures

---

[34] These remakes include *Friday the 13th* (2009) and *A Nightmare on Elm Street* (2010), as well as slasher-adjacent remakes such as *The Texas Chainsaw Massacre* and *The Hitcher* (2007).

such as Bay reboot 'classic' properties for monetary gain, having no real understanding of or interest in the subgenre. It is clear that Harbor knows very little about the icon he has been tasked with rebooting. For example, he recommends that they can 'keep the iconic parts . . . the mask and axe and stuff. The parts we can market', but they should replace Hackley himself with a young male model called LaMarc (see Figure 9.3). Harbor also asserts that they can align the new Hackley with the contemporary climate ('make it "today"') by replacing Hackley's 'backstory' ('nobody cared about it anyway') and showing off LaMarc's abs. In this view, superficiality reigns: image (LeMarc's abs, Hackley's mask) is everything, and content (Hackley's backstory) is erased. Hackley responds to the pitch by executing Harbor and unceremoniously disposing of his corpse in a dumpster. Being attuned to Hackley's attitude, the film rejects Harbor's prioritisation of image: the murder happens offscreen. Although Hackley acknowledges that he no longer fits into the contemporary subgeneric climate, *Axe Murdering with Hackley* stresses that rebooting does not resolve that mismatch. As such, the film implies that Hackley does not need to change. To move forward, the subgenre – at least the version embodied by RKS's corporate model – must accede to the kinds of norm-eschewing innovations Hackley proposes.

As with *Hatchet*, *Axe Murdering with Hackley* also takes aim at the broader genre surrounding slasher films, applying its critical lens to torture porn. Hackley's performance improvement plan entails him training

Figure 9.3 Michael Harbor presents 'Hackley 2.0' aka LaMarc in *Axe Murdering with Hackley* (2016)

up an intern (Mitresaw). Mitresaw is modelled after *Saw*'s Jigsaw killer, being a whitehaired man afflicted with cancer whose proclaimed modus operandi mimics Jigsaw's; as Mitresaw states, 'I want my victims to look upon me and see frailty . . . to make them realise how much they are wasting [their lives]'. The pairing of Hackley with Mitresaw leads the killers to cross-compare and critique each other's tactics. Hackley remarks that their job is to separate 'good guys' and 'bad guys', quickly dispatching people who fall into the latter camp.[35] Following Jigsaw's rhetoric in the *Saw* films, Mitresaw contends that Hackley's method is 'flawed' because the victims have 'no time to think, to grow' and 'the world doesn't exist solely in shades of black and white, good and evil . . . people live in varying shades of grey'. Hackley considers Mitresaw's strategies to be 'depressing and gross', but that does not invalidate Mitresaw's criticism that the classic slasher approach is an 'archaic system'. Hackley seems to agree with Mitresaw's assessment that Hackley needs a 'new vision', and Hackley concedes 'I do like where you're going with that *Fifty Shades of Grey* stuff'. These conversations recognise the relationship between torture porn and the slasher subgenre, signalling that torture porn narratives' ethical ambiguities were perhaps a response to the boom-period slasher's blunter ethical adjudications (see Jones 2013, 18–19). Their exchanges articulate that the slasher subgenre could perhaps be 'reborn' into the contemporary climate by embracing some of those ethical complexities (as indeed, metamodern slashers do; see Chapter 2).[36]

Ergo, it is not that *Axe Murdering with Hackley* merely valorises the past or makes a nostalgic case for 'back to basics' slasher throwbacks. Instead, the film submits that iconic slashers endure in the present, but, because the world has altered so much since the slasher's boom-period, the subgenre needs to innovate in order to remain culturally relevant. Furthermore, the film continually indicates that the slasher subgenre has that very potential to adapt and rebuild. *Axe Murdering with Hackley* identifies two major hindrances to subgeneric innovation. The first is strict adherence to formulaic elements at the expense of new modes. The second is interference from corporate executives who hinder creativity by encouraging repetition of the norms, and who have only a superficial understanding of the subgenre and its appeals.

---

[35] This stark adjudication is underlined by the abundance of Christmas-themed slasher films, which are routinely energised by killer Santas who bluntly separate individuals according to whether they have been 'naughty' or 'nice'.

[36] Simultaneously, Jigsaw's obsession with following 'the rules' perhaps admits that torture porn inherited a flaw from the postmodern slasher that hampers both subgenres.

Subgeneric Upcycling

Thanks to chained sequels produced in the slasher's boom-period, the subgenre has become synonymous with memorable killers. The examples inspected in this chapter confirm that iconic killers continue to be essential to the subgenre. Slasher icons attract sustained narrative attention across multiple sequels and, as such, they act as focal points for subgenre fans. Presumably casual subgenre viewers might also be more likely to engage with films that feature slasher icons; as personifications of recognisable 'brands', slasher icons draw attention in a crowded marketplace. Moreover, an icon's recurrence across multiple films implicitly reassures relatively unknowledgeable casual viewers that a slasher property is of sufficient interest to generate sustained demand. Microbudget filmmakers and distributors can leverage those associations by producing multiple sequels (as with the *Camp Blood* and *Porkchop* series), thereby suggesting such demand. As *The Orphan Killer* evinces, some ambitious filmmakers even transparently attempt to manufacture icon status.

However, inventing a new icon is an extremely difficult proposition. To become iconic, the killer has to be designed with care, encompassing familiar elements while also being distinctive. That tricky balance is captured by *Terrifier*'s creator Damien Leone, who states that 'it's important to give audiences a fresh spin even if on the surface it feels like something they've seen a million times' (Leone in Forever Midnight 2013; see also Leone in Whittington 2017). The films probed in this chapter thus encapsulate the metamodern commitment to future-facing innovation. More bluntly than Leone – although just as accurately – Chromeskull's creator Robert Hall has it that filmmakers need to 'be fuckin' creative for Christ sakes' (Hall in The Arrow 2009). Even though slasher films, sequels – and slasher sequels in particular – might be reputedly repetitious, launching a new character that can carry a film series necessitates bringing fresh ideas to the subgenre.

Cultivating novel perspectives also entails accounting for the subgenre's past. Unless one has a reasonable breadth of subgeneric knowledge, one risks producing an undistinctive and consequently forgettable slasher. Furthermore, as *Hatchet* illustrates, the property that situates the killer also needs to be attuned to the sub/generic context. In this respect, the new icon films are imbued with metamodern deliberation on the subgenre and its evolution. That ethos is exemplified by the Soska twins' approach to *See No Evil 2*, which aims to 'recreate [the series' killer] Jacob Goodnight' (Jen Soska in Hatfull 2014), not just by redesigning Goodnight himself but also by accounting for the property's relation to the subgeneric context. So, Sylvia Soska posits that they aimed to 'take on the stereotypes you normally see in slasher films and turn them on their head' (in Benardello 2014), 'playing with people's expectations' (in Pollard 2017) and avoiding the main pitfall that waylays 'modern slasher films': being 'formulaic' (in Collinson 2014).[37] This outlook helps to clarify Jen Soska's assertion that they 'wanted to do a throwback to movies when it wasn't a formula. Before you knew what a slasher was' (Jen Soska in Collinson 2014). This statement might initially seem puzzling, because it implies rejection of the subgeneric knowledge Sylvia Soska refers to. Returning to a pre-formula, naïve state ('before you knew what a slasher was') could result in a film riddled with precisely the stereotypes and clichés Sylvia Soska decries: insufficient knowledge of the subgenre might lead a filmmaker to believe they are creating original content because they are unaware of prior iterations of those same ideas. This is precisely the complaint that drives the postmodern slasher's knowingness and its implication that originality is impossible. Jen Soska's remarks are vital then, offering an antidote to this possibility. Her position implies that *See No Evil 2* aims to surprise by playing with norms, thereby allowing fans to recall the experience of being as excited and surprised as they were the first time they saw a slasher film (before encountering repeated conventional elements). Moreover, as with *Hatchet*, it is also implied that slasher films can attract new audiences who have not 'seen it all before' and who can authentically enjoy new iterations.

Combining seemingly dichotomous elements – past and present, old and new – and holding them in a superposition, new icon films generate a cohesive whole that encapsulates the metamodern sensibility. They merge past and present in a manner that is simultaneously future-facing (establishing a new set of horror icons) and retrospective (nostalgically replicating what made the past classics so memorable and enjoyable). Most pertinently, they speak to the complexity of innovation, given the subgenre's evolution to date. The postmodern phase markedly added a layer of complication by self-consciously charting subgeneric norms and conventions, packaged with an attitude that originality is precluded by the need to include those same norms and conventions. When accounting for the subgenre's past then, the metamodern slasher builds on that terrain while also forging a path forward towards the subgenre's future.

---

[37] Although the Soskas did not write the sequel's script, they affirm that they had significant creative input into the narrative. For example, Jen Soska indicates that 'WWE Studios . . . had the same vision' as them, and that the finished film has 'a lot of our sensibility . . . our humour, and . . . our characterisation' (Jen Soska in Hatfull 2014).

The new icon films' temporal bridging highlights one final attribute of the metamodern slasher: namely, the 'upcycling of past styles, conventions and techniques' (Van den Akker and Vermeulen 2017, 21). As Van den Akker and Vermeulen observe, upcycling entails reusing material, but doing so in a way that captures 'the original's style and substance while purportedly adding value', unlike recycling, which 'results in a product with less purity and use value than the original' (Van den Akker and Vermeulen 2017, 21). Their cultural analogy suggests that 'the postmoderns "recycled" popular culture' whereas 'metamodern artists' revive artefacts, 'allow[ing] them to resignify the present and reimagine a future' (Van den Akker and Vermeulen 2017, 21). The postmodern slasher 'recycles' by repeating elements from the subgenre's past without adding 'use value': the phase is characterised by its inward-focus and a cynical manner. The subgenre's normative facets are reproduced and self-scrutinised, without a forward-facing objective. Metamodern slashers instead draw from the past – evoking and staying true to the original's essence – while also productively transforming elements into something fresh. The slasher subgenre embodies this analogy in a pertinent way because of the subgenre's cultural status. Both recycling and upcycling involve reusing waste, and the slasher subgenre is roundly dismissed as cultural detritus. *Axe Murdering with Hackley* hypostatises these implications via its 'former icon', a character who is ostensibly destined for the scrapheap. In contrast to the postmodern slasher's fatalistic resignation, Hackley tries to upcycle himself, making a case for his continued relevance via his capacity to yield fresh insights. Hackley's story iterates the subgenre's evolution from the boom-period to the present, while his adaptability, resilience and forward-facing aspiration captures the potentials metamodern slasher films have in upcycling the subgenre itself.

Conclusion

Having covered a fair amount of conceptual ground, this conclusion aims to tie together the book's major contentions about metamodernism and the metamodern slasher. Given that the previous three chapters were concerned with time, it seems appropriate to begin with metamodernism's heterochrony. As Chapter 1 proffered, metamodernism is premised on the idea that sociocultural changes mean that postmodernism no longer captures the zeitgeist's prevailing sensibility. Thus, postmodernism now speaks to an outlook that was more clearly prevalent in the past. One of the difficulties with theorising these alterations is that our viewpoints are limited to the present moment (see Chapter 7). As McHale notes,

> every literary-historical moment is post some other moment, just as it is pre some other moment, though of course we are not in the position to say exactly what it is pre – what it precedes and prepares the way for – except retrospectively. (2004, 5)

McHale's observation accentuates several pertinent traits of temporal flow. First, when change occurs, emphasis is placed on the present. So, for instance, postmodernism's advent did not entail retrospectively substituting the term 'modernism' for 'pre-postmodernism'. Rather, new terms are coined to capture what is happening in the present. Second however, despite postmodernism's apparent disparagement of history, this approach to naming in the present accepts that the past has occurred: 'modernism' was, such that it could be succeeded by 'post'modernism. Third, by pinning down postmodernism as a sensibility that succeeds modernism, it is implied that a subsequent period or term will eventually come to replace postmodernism (regardless of postmodernism's disregard for the future). Arguably, postmodern theorists' tendency to play circular language games is a bid to avoid pinning down the term, thereby conveying that it cannot be finally known or replaced. Despite this insular presentism, postmodernism's reign has waned.

Metamodernism builds on and away from postmodernism in various ways, and its heterochrony is a key aspect of that orientation. A metamodern view of time emphasises the present, but also accepts that which postmodernism erroneously rejects: the possibility of meaningful relations between past, present and future. Metamodernism's status as a conceptual successor to postmodernism concretises that possibility, as does metamodernism's building on and away from both modernism and postmodernism. Metamodernism acknowledges that past and present are intertwined, and that the present is a temporal bridging point between past and future. This view of temporal continuity speaks to a metamodernist valuation of inclusivity and cohesion.

As argued in Chapter 8, this understanding of time is possibilist rather than determinist. Countering postmodernism's fatalism, a metamodern vision of time accepts that the future is as yet unwritten. Indeed, that possibility is evoked in many of the preceding chapters, including Chapter 2 and 3's analyses of time-loop narratives and Chapter 4's case studies, which explore conventionality but eschew the postmodern slasher's fatalist connotations. The possibilist view of time accords with metamodernism's emphasis on the present as the site of subjective experiential reality. From that limited epistemic position, the future is unknowable. That does not suggest that there is no future, but instead that the future is ambiguous because it is as yet undetermined. Accordingly, our actions in the present can affect the future. A further implication follows, however. From our limited perspectives in the present, the past is also ambiguous. Via memories, the past is cast according to our subjective present. Documents that record the past are also written from and interpreted via subjective positionalities. This is not to deny that past events objectively occurred, but to underline that the meanings and significances of such events are multiple and mutable. As indicated by the discussions about repeating and revising seemingly fixed events (*Shrooms* [2007], *Triangle* [2009], *Detention* [2011], *Happy Death Day* [2017]), nostalgic returns to the past (*Hatchet* [2006], *Dude Bro Party Massacre III* [2015], *Getting Schooled* [2017], throwback slashers), and retrocausality in requels (Chapter 8), the past is not simply inert: it is subject to renegotiation in the present, and that renegotiation shapes our understanding of the present. Furthermore, loosening the causal relationship between past and present undermines the hard determinist position that the future is causally dictated by an immutable preceding chain of events. The metamodern understanding of temporal relations stimulates the possibility of change, which I have illustrated via the metamodern slasher's subgeneric innovations.

Nevertheless, the ambiguity over past and future also generates precarity. That precarity manifests in the metamodern slasher via the loosening of presumed causal relations – for example, the moralistic causality of premarital sex (see Chapter 2) or 'unlikability' (see Chapters 5 and 7) leading to death in slasher films – or the instabilities that follow from modifying subgeneric conventions and structures (see Chapters 4, 5 and 6). This precarity is also central to the metamodern slasher in a broader sense. The subgenre evolved through several production peaks: an initial boom-period, a phase dominated by supernatural slashers and sequels, and a postmodern phase. Each peaked in popularity, then waned (especially in terms of theatrical profitability), leading critics to declare the subgenre moribund. As observed in Chapter 4, the postmodern slasher seems to internalise that critical stance via its rendition of the subgenre as being doomed to endlessly repeat passé structures and clichéd conventions. The metamodern slasher recoups the subgenre from this supposed decrepitude via its innovations, but that unveils further tensions. The subgenre's recognised norms must be accounted for so that the metamodern slasher can be identified as belonging to the subgenre, but distinctive new elements or outlooks must also be provided to push the subgenre forward. As illustrated in Chapters 4–9, creating fresh content entails accounting for the subgenre's past and future simultaneously, balancing the familiar with the divergent. Each metamodern slasher film exemplifies some attempt to bring these discordant elements into a cohesive whole. Moreover, as Chapter 2 contended, these slasher filmmakers are not a unified cabal with a shared agenda. The variances they offer impart that the subgenre can move forward. Yet bringing these films together as markers of that progress means accepting that the metamodern slasher's productive multiplicities potentially pull the subgenre in different directions, seemingly exacerbating the subgenre's instability.

By replacing Vermeulen and van den Akker's oscillation with superposition, my model of metamodernism underscores that this precarity is a particular strength. Superposition refers to multiple, equally plausible possibilities coexisting simultaneously, even if those possibilities are seemingly mutually exclusive. The superposition is thus a source of tension. This facet builds on and away from the postmodern slasher's ironic duplicity. Ironic duplicity elicits seemingly divergent possibilities, but these possibilities are equally invalidated by the postmodern slasher's noncommittal apathy. Meaning is under constant threat of revocation because the postmodern slasher's stances can always already be negated with a wink (or a shrug). In contrast, as Chapter 2 demonstrated, metamodern slashers commit to the equal validity and importance of each possibility raised.

Precarities are stabilised by the metamodern slasher's undergirding ethos of collaboration, which means accepting heterogeneity. Furthermore, where the postmodern slasher's duplicity is tied into its inert relativism and emphasis on aimless game-playing, the metamodern slasher is driven by clear attempts to innovate within the subgenre; that is, a commitment to taking action.

A further tension emerges out of the metamodern slasher's inclusivity and sincerity, which might appear to conflict with its frequent ambiguities and tacit meanings. Sometimes, metamodern slashers are reasonably overt: for instance, characters in Chapter 4's case studies expressly discuss subgeneric conventions; Chapter 6's hypercoded examples and several of Chapter 7's nostalgic slashers are conspicuous in their stylisation; *Happy Death Day*, *Murder Loves Killers Too* (2009) and *Triangle* plainly employ atypical narrative structures and so forth. Even in these cases however, the connections between those elements and meditations on the subgenre remain tacit. That ambiguous communication induces tension since one might reasonably expect the metamodern slasher's sincerity and inclusivity to equate to openness, and so explicitness or unequivocal communication. Even so, this tension is one of the metamodern slasher's strengths, not a flaw. As I have argued, metamodern slashers work from the background assumption that broad understandings of the subgenre's norms are commonplace. Accordingly, messages about the subgenre are pitched such that general background knowledge will be sufficient for noticing and comprehending the metamodern slasher's innovations. Where more detailed knowledge is required (as per Chapter 4's case studies), that information is transparently supplied in the text so that viewers can ascertain the implied meanings. This inclusivity is augmented by maintaining a tacit approach, given that viewers can readily derive pleasure from these films even without noticing their cogitations on the subgenre. It is acknowledged that viewers arrive at texts with their own idiosyncratic perspectives, resulting in varied interpretations. That variance is validated by the metamodern slasher's ambiguities, which invite viewers to collaborate by cultivating a multiplicity of potential meanings.

Tensions are transformed into productive strengths where metamodern slashers deliberate on the subgenre. That contemplation is integral to the metamodern slasher, arising out of the approaches taken to: (1) form and stylistics; (2) conventionality; (3) characterisation and character perspective; and (4) viewership. Throughout the book, I have demonstrated ways these elements are married together via my case study analyses. I will now briefly take each in turn to unpack some broader reflections on these elements.

Form and Stylistics

In contrast to the postmodern slasher's ludic, metafictional devices, which illuminate artificialities of narrative construction, narrative is usually the main source of pleasure in the metamodern slasher. Yet, that is not to suggest that metamodern slashers avoid any formal and stylistic experimentation that might draw attention to a film's construction. As time-loop slasher examples – *Happy Death Day* and *Triangle* – illustrate, narrative structure can elucidate characters' adaptations and test the extent to which those protagonists conform to an expected subgeneric type (the Final Girl). *Behind the Mask: The Rise of Leslie Vernon* (2006) employs formal shifts between two filmmaking registers (a 'cinematic' mode and a verité mode) to explore conventional narrative situations and coding. Chapter 5's case studies remove structural elements or compress normative pacing structures to rework the subgenre's expected operations. The discussion of requels in Chapter 8 ruminated on the chain of sequels as a formal structure, observing that various films remove or manipulate chunks of lore to experiment with the expectations serial narratives generate. Chapter 6 assessed how subgeneric norms are amended via unmistakable exaggerations of expected aesthetic or stylistic codes. In each case, these techniques are in concert with narrative content and aims, rather than being disruptive or being an end in themselves. Foregrounding of form and stylistics is in keeping with the metamodern slasher's sincere tone, being part of the earnestness that epitomises metamodernism. The same principles hold for each element addressed below.

Conventionality

Reflection on conventionality is naturalised in the metamodern slasher because the postmodern slasher helped to embed such deliberation in the subgenre: that is, contemplating subgeneric conventions is itself a conventional tactic within the subgenre. Conventions are particularly important insofar as a subgenre is at least partially defined by its conventions, and films belong to a subgenre inasmuch as they exhibit sufficient adherence to core conventions. Conventionality then provides some stability, helping to balance out the precarities found elsewhere in the metamodern slasher. Again, that is not to imply that metamodern slashers simply follow subgenre conventions. Chapter 3 illustrated that new insights can be precipitated by viewing conventional situations from idiosyncratic perspectives, while Chapter 5 evinced that fresh surprises can be yielded by tweaking conventions. Chapter 6 took a wider view on the relationships between subgeneric conventions, the expectations that follow from that conventionality and the extent to which norms can be deviated from. Most plainly, Chapter 4 proposed that conventions continue to develop, motioning towards the inevitability (not just the possibility) of future change within the subgenre. As such, the expectations arising from established conventions grant filmmakers opportunities to develop or innovate within the subgenre. Conventions bestow insight into the subgenre's operations or offer conduits for investigating normative expectations surrounding the slasher. Actively modifying conventions, however, opens possibilities for future rejuvenation: that is, altering the conventions themselves and/or amending the expectations that surround conventions.

Characterisation and Character Perspective

One clear way metamodern slasher films remodel conventions is by experimenting with character types. By adopting alternative perspectives on conventional situations or by experimenting with narrative structure, *Behind the Mask*, *Halloween* (2018), *Shrooms* and *Triangle* investigate the Final Girl as a character type. In each case, the narrative drives the protagonist into undertaking that conventional role, but the initial disjuncture between the protagonist and that conventional role itself encourages cogitation on the Final Girl as a type. Characterisation is intertwined with the narrative action in these films, meaning that the characters grow in response to narrative events as they develop. *KillerKiller* (2007), *Murder Loves Killers Too*, *Shrooms*, *Triangle* and *You Might Be the Killer* (2018) all explore expectations surrounding the lead protagonist, the Final Girl type, narrative trajectory (leading the Final Girl to eradicate the slasher) and the relationships between these elements. Simultaneously, *Axe Murdering with Hackley*, *Behind the Mask*, *Murder Loves Killers Too*, *Shrooms*, *Triangle* and *You Might Be the Killer* each contain the killer's perspective, and the insights they provide seriously complicate the moralistic separation of 'good versus evil' that might superficially seem to distinguish killer from Final Girl (or the other protagonists). This is especially the case in *KillerKiller* and *You Might Be the Killer* (and possibly *Shrooms*), where the lead protagonist is initially mistaken about their innocence. In this light, the focus on returning centralised killers in Chapters 8 and 9 further complicates the boundaries between 'hero' and 'villain', which are supposedly demarcated by character typing.

Other stock types are equally subject to appraisal in the metamodern slasher film. *I Didn't Come Here to Die* (2010) rationalises its protagonists' actions to eschew the sense that the subgenre's victims are one-dimensional 'types' or that typing alone explains their motivations. *Getting Schooled* draws on well-worn stock types, then enhances those types by individualising them. *KillerKiller* blurs the boundaries between killer and victim by depicting a supernatural 'every-victim' murdering slasher 'types'. *Detention* takes its teen's heightened emotional states seriously, reifying their experiential realities onscreen in title cards.

In each case, the metamodern slasher's sincere investment in the characters' perspectives impels its investigation of conventionalised characterisation. As Chapter 2 delineated, metamodern slasher films foreground emotional resonance and subjective experience, aligning narrative perspective with protagonists' viewpoints. This investment allows metamodern slasher films to flesh out their characters, limning them as flawed, but psychologically real, individualised beings. This path also naturally accentuates the precarity, uncertainty and ambiguity inherent to both the characters' situations and their limited viewpoints. In the postmodern slasher, the latter typically triggers paranoia among the characters. That paranoia is amplified where postmodern slashers withhold information from viewers as part of a ludic 'whodunit' structure. In the metamodern slasher, these facets are instead inclusive, offering access to the protagonists' emotional states. Moreover, the postmodern slasher's limited perspectives convey its restricted view of the subgenre's future, which is exacerbated by its insularity. That is, limited perspectives are symptomatic of the postmodern slasher's self-conscious inward turn, which stems from an assumption that innovation and originality are no longer possible. The metamodern slasher builds on and away from this stance, and its emphasis on subjective, experiential, individualised perspectives – coupled with its overt challenging of stock types – connotes that individual films and filmmakers can make acute, distinct contributions to the subgenre. Perspectival multiplicity produces variance, and that heterogeneity introduces new ideas and techniques to the subgenre. In this light, it is discernible why there is a marked emphasis on unusual stylistic choices within the metamodern slasher: idiosyncratic filmmaking voices and filmmaker perspectives on the subgenre are encouraged by the metamodern sensibility. Metamodern slasher filmmakers do not work towards a specific, unified goal, but the accretion of various attempts to innovate equates to collective progress. That understanding of progress accords with the metamodern emphasis on meaning-making being born of collaboration between individuals.

This stance also helps to explain an underlying tension in the metamodern slasher's take on characterisation. The tendency towards epistemic alignment with protagonists seems to valorise individualism. At the most extreme, in *Happy Death Day* and *Triangle*, a single protagonist's concerns reshape the structure of time itself, for example. Although that structuring is in consonance with a subjective, experiential understanding of time, the emphasis on a single individual perhaps does not seem to sit comfortably with metamodernism's inclusive, collaborative principles. Nonetheless, it is first important to note that the combination of individualism and collaboration brings together seemingly mutually exclusive elements; that is, it exemplifies another superposition. Second, even these apparently extreme examples of individualism narrate that superposition via their protagonist's concerns: so, for instance, *Happy Death Day*'s Tree becomes part of her surrounding community because of the time-loop (see Chapter 3). Third, and most crucially in this case, the accretion of metamodern slashers illuminates the strategies implemented. Taken individually, none of the films examined in this book make a transformative intervention in the subgenre. Their significance is evident when assembled as heterogeneous illustrations of the metamodern sensibility. This is why I have brought together detailed case studies of individual films in one book under the banner 'the metamodern slasher'.

Viewership

The metamodern slasher is consequently characterised by idiosyncratic perspectives: first, from within the film via the characters' subjective stances (with which the narrative is aligned), and second, via the filmmakers' perspectives on the subgenre (their unusual takes on familiar conventions and norms, which are frequently expressed via distinctive structural and stylistic choices). These conjoined investments in subjective perspectives provide a foundation for the metamodern slasher, balancing its precarities. Another set of idiosyncratic perspectives is equally crucial to the metamodern slasher, however: namely, the viewer's position. From Chapter 2 onwards, I have demonstrated that the metamodern slasher invites viewers to become collaborators in meaning-making. In its form, stylistics, themes and narrative content, the metamodern slasher prizes individualised, subjective perspectives, and these combined factors imply that viewers' idiosyncratic experiential perspectives are also valuable.

That position is encouraged by the metamodern slasher's mode of skewing subgeneric norms to deliver new insight, inviting viewers to take those insights into their engagements with other slasher films (see Chapter 4). Metamodern slashers also empower viewers to generate their own understandings by sustaining ambiguities (as in the case of *Shrooms*), or by creating their own idiosyncratic canon (as in the case of the

Halloween series), for example. The metamodern slasher also more broadly solicits collaboration in meaning-making by displaying confidence in the viewer's sophistication and interpretive ability. In contrast to the idea that metafictional techniques will disrupt viewers' ontological moorings (see Chapter 3), metamodern slashers proceed from the principle that viewers understand fiction is constructed and can invest in fiction regardless. Chapter 6's hypercoded examples illustrate that confidence, but so too do structurally playful examples such as Chapter 2 and 3's time-loop slasher films and Chapter 5's compressive case studies. Most broadly, these films ensure that viewers are not excluded from the meanings communicated. Where the postmodern slasher's in-joking is ordinarily conveyed via specific intertextual references (see Chapter 5), the metamodern slasher takes an inclusive stance, ensuring that viewers are furnished with enough information to remain 'in' on the joke. The metamodern slasher's evaluations of conventions require only a rudimentary familiarity with the subgenre. It is assumed that viewers will be pre-equipped with understandings of the subgenre's norms by default because of the attention drawn to form and convention in the subgenre's preceding phases and the translation of that knowledge into the surrounding culture (thanks to the crossover successes of *Scream* [1996] and its peers).

As argued in Chapter 7, heterogeneity of viewer perspectives has been fostered by the technocultural situation out of which the metamodern slasher arose, which favours asynchronous idiosyncratic cultural interactions over detailed knowledge of a shared cultural canon. More broadly, that technocultural context further stresses why the metamodern slasher is so invested in subjective perspectives. As McAdams remarks, 'a dominant cultural frame in American society is individualism' (2013, 273), and that individualism has taken on a particular character in the digital age. For instance, Bavel and Packer (2021, 96) note that social media is thought to have created 'echo chambers and filter bubbles' that split the American population in various ways (most notably along political lines). Bavel and Packer indicate that such 'division' is a symptom of our 'group-oriented psychology' (2021, 18). According to this view, social media caters to a deeply ingrained human desire to affiliate with others who share our anxieties about issues we consider salient. Two notable implications follow. First, that psychological model is itself based in a kind of superposition: 'our social identities provide a powerful basis for . . . division', but also, simultaneously 'for unity' (Bavel and Packer 2021, 18). Second, the technocultural situation brings people together around sociopolitical matters they genuinely care about, including health scares, economic crises, environmental damage and so forth.

The metamodern sensibility does not reflect these specific issues – which were arguably just as pertinent to sociopolitical discussion during the slasher's boom-period as they are now – but rather the tenor of the contemporary moment. Faced with crisis, one could respond with defeatist, fatalistic apathy, or by retreating inwards to escape those external pressures. Following the argument presented throughout this book, the postmodern slasher hypostatises such an attitude. In this light, the postmodern slasher might reproduce or even result from cynicism about the possibility of resolving macroscopic sociopolitical matters such as environmental crisis (for example). If so, the metamodern slasher evinces a turn in the zeitgeist, perhaps born of the realisation that cynicism, apathy and/or escapism only amplify those concerns: environmental crisis has deepened precisely because too little political action has been taken, for instance. Another potential motivator for such a shift is the 'confluence and interaction between ecological crisis, digital transformation, pandemics, and wars', meaning they become 'metacrises': Pipere and Martinsone posit that metamodernism captures the ways such metacrises 'require the active search for different ways of life . . . reassessing our mental and social life, values, and behavior' (2022, 458; see also Stoev 2022, 113).

Clearly, metamodern slasher fiction cannot present solutions to such problems, nor does it strive to. Still, the metamodern slasher speaks to a yearning for practical change in its formal innovations and narrative optimism. That this optimism is tinged with tragedy articulates the extent of the challenge – the potential that attempts to instigate change might fail – while also maintaining the essential yearning and drive to try, regardless of the outcome. In the metamodern slasher, the stakes could not be higher since these narratives are always based in struggles for survival. In its concentration on the present as a temporal bridging point, the metamodern slasher also reifies a sense of urgency and the need to learn from the past to move forward towards the future. The metamodern slasher's focus on emotional experience speaks to the sense that people sincerely care about the sociopolitical issues of the moment, understanding that these matters have direct ramifications not only on oneself, but also on others. The metamodern slasher's attention to individual characters is also indicative of the personalisation of ethical responsibility, then. Ethical responsibility connects the individual to others, suggesting that one's actions commonly have impacts on others, that one has duties towards others and so forth.

Many of the case study examples covered in this book – including *Axe Murdering with Hackley*, *Behind the Mask*, *Hatchet* and *You Might Be the Killer* – perspicuously lean into comedy. These films might not seem to be compatible with sincere sentiments about the contemporaneous sociopolitical context. That perhaps seems especially likely for absurdist hypercoded slashers such as *Dude Bro Party Massacre III*. However, it is notable that these films employ ironic humour to convey sincere messages (as proposed in Chapter 1). Furthermore, the very real and urgent concerns that shape our daily activities, occupying much of our lives and energy – working to earn money, supporting one's family and so forth – themselves seem absurd when contextualised against the enormity of, for example, the existential threat of environmental crisis. Most of us continue to care about our daily experiences even if it sometimes feels as if the world is crumbling around us, and the most exaggerated hypercoded examples concretise how absurd that incongruity is.

I am not claiming that contemporary slasher films can instigate significant sociopolitical interventions, but instead that the metamodern lens allows us to see how these popular films capture a mood that pervades the zeitgeist. These parting comments only briefly touch on these larger sociopolitical issues. I use these comparisons to: (1) underline that the metamodern sensibility manifests in tonal shifts, which distinguishes it from postmodernism; (2) draw out some of the technocultural circumstances that inform the metamodern mindset; and (3) connect those circumstances to themes such as collaboration, tragic optimism and the yearning for renewal that have arisen across the preceding chapters. Both in terms of content and message, the metamodern slasher demonstrates that Humphries was overly pessimistic when he proclaimed that 'the state of [the horror genre] is not conducive to optimism' back in 2002 (189).

The Metamodern Slasher Film has sought to account for a variety of contemporary American slasher films, thereby countering the prominent critical notions that in the twenty-first century, the subgenre is dominated by remakes and is (perhaps thus) creatively bankrupt. As the case study analyses evince, the subgenre is replete with interesting films and innovative ideas. Contrary to its reputation as a one-dimensional, derivative subgenre, the metamodern slasher confirms that the subgenre's robust structure, conventions and norms facilitate experimentation. Like much scholarship on horror film, this book seeks to counter the vilification and denigration that continues to surround the (sub)genre, most notably in the critical press. That impulse has also informed my case study selection in this book. Many of the independent movies examined here have been overlooked by higher-profile film outlets and reviewers. Drawing attention to these films and the richness of their offerings underscores that the critical press's coverage amounts to an unrepresentative, overly narrow view of the subgenre because that coverage almost exclusively concentrates on larger name studio features and theatrical releases.

CONCLUSION

The main thrust of this book has been to bring metamodernism into conjunction with the slasher film. The metamodern lens casts new light on the subgenre, and the subgenre's development from boom-period to postmodern slashers, then to contemporary slasher films. At the time of writing, *The Metamodern Slasher Film* is the first book to use metamodernism to analyse film in a sustained way, and the first academic work to employ metamodernism to dissect a specific aspect of popular culture (here, horror film). By bringing this paradigm into dialogue with film studies and horror studies literature, I hope to have proven that metamodernism is a fruitful model for both horror studies scholars, and for film studies scholars more broadly.

The book's sustained focus has allowed me to develop the model of metamodernism itself. Throughout, I have sought to underline why I believe the slasher film is a decidedly pertinent cultural form for elucidating the metamodern sensibility, but it is also important to acknowledge that the subgenre's films have shaped my approach to the theory. The apparent incompatibility of a reputedly repetitious subgenre that centralises death and a model that so palpably values innovation and optimism has enlivened the project of writing this book. The focal concepts that drive each chapter – epistemology, ontology, meaning-making, subtraction, augmentation, nostalgia, retrocausation and so forth – are informed by the subgenre's films perhaps more than the extant scholarship surrounding metamodernism, although these conceptual threads have been vital to developing a coherent, usable model of metamodernism.

Via the analysis of contemporary slasher films, I have connected numerous ideas that are raised in extant scholarly articles and chapters about metamodernism, such as heterochrony, the yearning for enrichment via renewal, combining irony and sincerity and so forth. Tying these threads together in this sustained way is vital for developing metamodernism. The monograph format has allowed me to account for a variety of metamodern scholarship, bringing disparate works into dialogue. My approach has also entailed drawing on other adjacent post-postmodern models to refine metamodernism. Most compellingly, working with metamodernism in a sustained way revealed that the extant scholarship pulls in different directions. One of the core underlying values of the metamodern sensibility is collective cohesion, so those unresolved tensions risk undermining the paradigm altogether. By engaging with various aspects of metamodern theory and by bringing metamodernism into conversation with other scholarship concerning time, innovation and subjectivity (for instance), I have developed a more tightly imbricated iteration of the model.

The metamodern turn is still in its preliminary stages, as is the scholarship seeking to grip the metamodern sensibility. However, metamodernism's focus on the potential for rejuvenation signals that just as postmodernism's capacity to capture the prevailing tenor of the moment diminished, metamodernism will also eventually metamorphose into something new. What will follow is as yet unknown. However, as a lifelong follower of the slasher subgenre, I look forward to seeing how the subgenre will develop in response to future changes in the zeitgeist. I have every faith that no matter how often the slasher appears to be 'killed off', the subgenre will continue to return and evolve.

Bibliography

Abbott, Stacey. 2010. 'High Concept Thrills and Chills: The Horror Blockbuster.' In *Horror Zone: The Cultural Experience of Contemporary Horror Cinema*, edited by Ian Conrich, 27–44. London: I. B. Tauris.

Abramson, Seth. 2017. 'What is Metamodernism?' *The Huffington Post*, 9 January 2017. https://www.huffpost.com/entry/what-is-metamodernism_b_586e7075e4b0a5e600a788cd.

Adair, Heather V. 2019. 'Updating Thought Theory: Emotion and the Non-Paradox of Fiction.' *Pacific Philosophical Quarterly* 100 (4): 1055–73. https://doi.org/10.1111/papq.12294.

Adam, Frane and Hans Westlund, eds. 2013. *Innovation in Socio-Cultural Context*. New York: Routledge.

Adams, Gabrielle S., Benjamin A. Converse, Andrew H. Hales and Leidy E. Klotz. 2021. 'People Systematically Overlook Subtractive Changes.' *Nature* 592 (7853): 258–61. https://doi.org/10.1038/s41586-021-03380-y.

Adler, Jonathan M., Joshua W. Wagner and Dan P. McAdams. 2007. 'Personality and the Coherence of Psychotherapy Narratives.' *Journal of Research in Personality* 41 (6): 1179–98. https://doi.org/10.1016/j.jrp.2007.02.006.

Adolf, Marian, Jason L. Mast and Nico Stehr. 2013. 'Culture and Cognition: The Foundations of Innovation in Modern Societies.' In *Innovation in Socio-Cultural Context*, edited by Frane Adam and Hans Westlund, 25–39. New York: Routledge.

Akker, Robin van den and Timotheus Vermeulen. 2017. 'Periodising the 2000s, or, the Emergence of Metamodernism.' In *Metamodernism: Historicity, Affect, and Depth After Postmodernism*, edited by Robin van den Akker, Alison Gibbons and Timotheus Vermeulen, 1–20. London: Rowman & Littlefield.

Alter, Adam. 2017. *Irresistible*. New York: Penguin.

Arnzen, Michael A. 1994. 'Who's Laughing Now? . . . The Postmodern Splatter Film.' *Journal of Popular Film & Television* 21 (4): 176–84. https://doi.org/10.1080/01956051.1994.9943985.

The Arrow. 2009. 'Interview: Robert Hall.' JoBlo. Last Modified 17 April 2009. https://www.joblo.com/horror-movies/news/interview-robert-hall-02.

Balanzategui, Jessica. 2015. 'Crises of Identification in the Supernatural Slasher: The Resurrection of the Supernatural Slasher Villain.' In *Style and Form in* the *Hollywood Slasher Film*, edited by Wickham Clayton, 161–79. Basingstoke: Palgrave-Macmillan.

Bargár, Pavol. 2020. 'The Modern, the Postmodern, and . . . the Metamodern? Reflections on a Transforming Sensibility from the Perspective of Theological Anthropology.' *Transformation: An International Journal of Holistic Mission Studies* 28 (1): 3–15. https://doi.org/10.1177/0265378820976944.

Bavel, Jay J. Van and Dominic J. Packer. 2021. *The Power of Us*. New York: Little, Brown Spark.

Beasley, Chris and Heather Brook. 2019. *The Cultural Politics of Contemporary Hollywood Film: Power, Culture, and Society*. Manchester: Manchester University Press.

Beer, David. 2009. 'Power Through the Algorithm? Participatory Web Cultures and the Technological Unconscious.' *New Media & Society* 11 (6): 985–1002. https://doi.org/10.1177/1461444809336551.

Belshaw, Christopher. 2021. *The Value and Meaning of Life*. New York: Routledge.

Benardello, Karen. 2011. 'Interview: Robert Hall Talks *ChromeSkull: Laid to Rest 2*.' Shock Ya. Last Modified 1 October 2011. https://www.shockya.com/news/2011/10/01/interview-robert-hall-talks-chromeskull-laid-to-rest-2.

—. 2014. 'Interview: Jen and Sylvia Soska Talk *See No Evil 2*.' Shock Ya. Last Modified 26 November 2014. https://www.shockya.com/news/2014/11/26/interview-jen-and-sylvia-soska-talk-see-no-evil-2-exclusive/.

Bentley, Nick. 2018. 'Trailing Postmodernism: David Mitchell's *Cloud Atlas*, Zadie Smith's *NW*, and the Metamodern.' *English Studies* 99 (7): 723–43. https://doi.org/10.1080/0013838X.2018.1510611.

Berkun, Scott. 2007. *The Myths of Innovation*. Cambridge: O'Reilly.

Berliner, Todd. 2001a. 'The Genre Film as Booby Trap: 1970s Genre Bending and *The French Connection*.' *Cinema Journal* 40 (3): 25–46. https://doi.org/10.1353/cj.2001.0006.

—. 2001b. 'The Pleasures of Disappointment: Sequels and *The Godfather Part II*.' *Journal of Film and Video* 53 (2/3): 107–23. https://www.jstor.org/stable/20688360.

Bernard, Mark. 2020. *Halloween: Youth Cinema and the Horrors of Growing Up*. New York: Routledge.

—. 2022. '*The Texas Chainsaw Massacre*: A "Peculiar, Erratic" Franchise.' In *Horror Franchise Cinema*, edited by Mark McKenna and William Proctor, 53–65. London: Routledge.

Bertens, Hans. 1995. *The Idea of the Postmodern: A History*. London: Routledge.

Bettinson, Gary. 2015. 'Resurrecting *Carrie*.' In *Style and Form in the Hollywood Slasher Film*, edited by Wickham Clayton, 131–45. Basingstoke: Palgrave-Macmillan.

Boiselle, Matt. 2018a. 'Interview: Director Damien Leone Discusses the Guts Behind *Terrifier*.' Dread Central. Last Modified 14 March 2018. https://www.dreadcentral.com/news/269238/interview-director-damien-leone-discusses-the-guts-behind-terrifier/.

—. 2018b. 'Interview: David Howard Thornton Steps into the Big Shoes of Art the Clown.' Dread Central. Last Modified 25 March 2018. https://www.dreadcentral.com/news/269479/interview-david-howard-thornton-steps-into-the-big-shoes-of-art-the-clown/.

Booker, M. Keith. 2007. *Postmodern Hollywood: What's New in Film and Why it Makes Us Feel So Strange*. Westport: Praeger.

Bordwell, David. 2006. *The Way Hollywood Tells it: Story and Style in Modern Movies*. Berkeley: University of California Press.

Bordwell, David and Janet Staiger. 2005. 'Since 1960: The Persistence of a Mode of Film Practice.' In *The Classical Hollywood Cinema: Film Style & Mode of Production to 1960*, edited by David Bordwell, Janet Staiger and Kristin Thompson, 607–18. London: Routledge.

Braudy, Leo. 1998. 'Rethinking Remakes.' In *Play It Again, Sam: Retakes on Remakes*, edited by Andrew Horton and Stuart Y. McDougal, 327–33. Berkeley: University of California Press.

Briefel, Aviva and Sam Miller. 2011. 'Introduction.' In *Horror After 9/11: World of Fear, Cinema of Terror*, edited by Aviva Briefel and Sam Miller, 1–10. Austin: University of Texas Press.

Brown, Tom. 2012. *Breaking the Fourth Wall: Direct Address in the Cinema*. Edinburgh: Edinburgh University Press.

Brun, Georg, Ulvi Doğuoğlu and Dominique Kuenzle, eds. 2008. *Epistemology and Emotions*. Aldershot: Ashgate.

Bruner, Jerome. 1986. *Actual Minds, Possible Worlds*. Harvard: Harvard University Press.

Brunton, James. 2018. 'Whose (Meta)modernism?: Metamodernism, Race, and the Politics of Failure.' *Journal of Modern Literature* 41 (3): 60–76. https://doi.org/10.2979/jmodelite.41.3.05.

Budra, Paul. 1998. 'Recurrent Monsters: Why Freddy, Michael and Jason Keep Coming Back.' In *Part Two: Reflections on the Sequel*, edited by Paul Budra and Betty A. Schellenberg, 189–99. Toronto: University of Toronto Press.

Budra, Paul, and Betty A. Schellenberg. 1998. 'Introduction.' In *Part Two: Reflections on the Sequel*, edited by Paul Budra and Betty A. Schellenberg, 3–18. Toronto: University of Toronto Press.

Burns, David J. 2015. 'What Comes After Postmodernism? Implications for Marketers.' *Journal of Global Scholars of Marketing Science* 25 (1): 59–74. https://doi.org/10.1080/21639159.2014.980035.

Buscombe, Edward. 2012. 'The Idea of Genre in the American Cinema.' In *Film Genre Reader IV*, edited by Barry Keith Grant, 12–26. Austin: University of Texas Press.

Canby, Vincent. 1981. '*Happy Birthday to Me*.' *The New York Times*, 15 May 1981.

Candiotto, Laura. 2019. 'From Philosophy of Emotion to Epistemology: Some Questions About the Epistemic Relevance of Emotions.' In *The Value of Emotions for Knowledge*, edited by Laura Candiotto, 3–24. Cham: Palgrave-MacMillan.

Carmona, Carlos Ruiz. 2017. 'The Role and Purpose of Film Narration.' *Journal of Science and Technology of the Arts* 9 (2): 7–16. https://doi.org/10.7559/citarj.v9i2.247.
Carroll, Noël. 1990. *The Philosophy of Horror, or, Paradoxes of the Heart*. London: Routledge.
—. 1999. 'Horror and Humor.' *The Journal of Aesthetics and Art Criticism* 57 (2): 145–160. https://doi.org/10.2307/432309.
Castells, Manuel. 2015. *Networks of Outrage and Hope: Social Movements in the Internet Age*. Cambridge: Polity.
Cesare, Adam. 2020. *Clown in a Cornfield*. New York: HarperTeen.
Champ, Christine. 2010. 'Interview: Director Adam Green Talks *Hatchet II*.' MTV. Last Modified 1 October 2010. http://www.mtv.com/news/2764640/interview-director-adam-green-talks-hatchet-ii/.
Cherry, Brigid. 2009. *Horror*. London: Routledge.
Church, David. 2006. 'Return of the Return of the Repressed: Notes on the American Horror Film (1991–2006).' *Offscreen* 10 (10). https://offscreen.com/view/return_of_the_repressed.
Clarke, Donald. 2016. 'Various Shockers and High-End Horrors.' *The Irish Times*, 28 October 2016.
Clasen, Mathias, Jens Kjeldgaard-Christiansen and John A. Johnson. 2020. 'Horror, Personality, and Threat Simulation: A Survey on the Psychology of Scary Media.' *Evolutionary Behavioral Sciences* 14 (3): 213–230. https://doi.org/10.1037/ebs0000152.
Clasen, Mathias and Todd K. Platts. 2019. 'Evolution and Slasher Films.' In *Evolution and Popular Narrative*, edited by Dirk Vanderbeke and Brett Cooke, 23–42. Leiden: Brill Rodopi.
Clayton, Wickham. 2020. *See! Hear! Cut! Kill! Experiencing* Friday the 13th. Mississippi: University Press of Mississippi.
Clover, Carol. 1993. *Men, Women and Chainsaws: Gender in the Modern Horror Film*. London: BFI.
Coffeen, Fraser. 2020. 'The Eyes Behind the Mask: How *Friday the 13th* Changed POV in Slasher Films.' In *Horror Homeroom:* Friday the 13th *at 40*, edited by Elizabeth Erwin and Dawn Keetley, 36–44. http://www.horrorhomeroom.com/special-issue-1/.
Cohn, Dorrit. 2012. 'Metalepsis and Mise en Abyme.' *Narrative* 20 (1): 105–14. https://doi.org/10.1353/nar.2012.0003.
Collins, Jim. 1993. 'Genericity in the Nineties: Eclectic Irony and the New Sincerity.' In *Film Theory Goes to the Movies*, edited by Jim Collins, Hillary Radner and Ava Collins, 242–63. New York: Routledge.
Collinson, Gary. 2014. 'Interview: Jen and Sylvia Soska Talk *See No Evil 2*.' Flickering Myth. Last Modified 30 August 2014. https://www.flickeringmyth.com/2014/08/interview-jen-sylvia-soska-talk-see-evil-2/.
Cong, Hongyan. 2020. 'Personalized Recommendation of Film and Television Culture Based on an Intelligent Classification Algorithm.' *Personal and*

Ubiquitous Computing 24 (2): 165–76. https://doi.org/10.1007/s00779-019-01271-8.

Connor, Steven. 2015. 'Postmodernism Grown Old.' In *Supplanting the Postmodern*, edited by David Rudrum and Nicholas Stavris, 31–48. New York: Bloomsbury.

Conrich, Ian. 2000. 'Seducing the Subject: Freddy Krueger, Popular Culture and the *Nightmare on Elm Street* Films.' In *Horror Film Reader*, edited by Alain Silver and James Ursini, 223–35. New York: Limelight Editions.

—. 2010. 'The *Friday the 13th* Films and the Cultural Function of a Modern Grand Guignol.' In *Horror Zone: The Cultural Experience of Contemporary Horror Cinema*, edited by Ian Conrich, 173–88. New York: I. B. Tauris.

—. 2015. 'Puzzles, Contraptions and the Highly Elaborate Moment: The Inevitability of Death in the Grand Slasher Narratives of the *Final Destination* and *Saw* Series of Films.' In *Style and Form in the Hollywood Slasher Film*, edited by Wickham Clayton, 106–17. Basingstoke: Palgrave-Macmillan.

Cook, Pam. 2005. *Screening the Past: Memory and Nostalgia in Cinema*. London: Routledge.

Corry, John. 1981. '*Friday the 13th Part II*.' *The New York Times*, 4 May 1981.

Cowan, Gloria and Margaret O'Brien. 1990. 'Gender and Survival vs. Death in Slasher Films: A Content Analysis.' *Sex Roles* 23 (3–4): 187–96. https://doi.org/10.1007/BF00289865.

Craig, Pamela and Martin Fradley. 2010. 'Teenage Traumata: Youth, Affective Politics, and the Contemporary American Horror Film.' In *American Horror Film: The Genre at the Turn of the Millennium*, edited by Steffen Hantke, 77–102. Jackson: University Press of Mississippi.

Crane, Jonathan Lake. 1994. *Terror and Everyday Life: Singular Moments in the History of the Horror Film*. London: Sage.

—. 2004. '"It was a dark and stormy night . . .": Horror Films and the Problem of Irony.' In *Horror Film and Psychoanalysis: Freud's Worst Nightmare*, edited by Stephen Jay Schneider, 142–56. Cambridge: Cambridge University Press.

Culler, Jonathan. 2002. *Structuralist Poetics: Structuralism, Linguistics and the Study of Literature*. London: Routledge.

Currie, Mark. 2007. *About Time: Narrative, Fiction and the Philosophy of Time*. Edinburgh: Edinburgh University Press.

—. 2011. *Postmodern Narrative Theory*. Second edition. Houndmills: Palgrave-Macmillan.

—. 2013. 'Introduction.' In *Metafiction*, edited by Mark Currie, 1–18. New York: Routledge.

Cutting, James E. 2016. 'The Evolution of Pace in Popular Movies.' *Cognitive Research: Principles and Implications* 1 (1): 1–21. https://doi.org/10.1186/s41235-016-0029-0.

Daly, Angela, S. Kate Devitt and Monique Mann, eds. 2019. *Good Data*. Amsterdam: Institute of Network Cultures.

Danna, Corey. 2011. 'Interview: Matt Farnsworth – Director (*The Orphan Killer*).' Horror News. Last Modified 8 September 2011. https://horrornews.net/54474/interview-matt-farnsworth-director-the-orphan-killer/.

Declercq, Dieter. 2020. 'Irony, Disruption and Moral Imperfection.' *Ethical Theory and Moral Practice* 23 (3–4): 545–59. https://doi.org/10.1007/s10677-020-10105-z.

Dember, Greg. 2018. 'After Postmodernism: Eleven Metamodern Methods in the Arts.' Medium. Last Modified 17 April 2018. https://medium.com/what-is-metamodern/after-postmodernism-eleven-metamodern-methods-in-the-arts-767f7b646cae.

Denham, Alison. 2020. 'Making Sorrow Sweet: Emotion and Empathy in the Experience of Fiction.' In *Affect and Literature*, edited by Alex Houen, 190–210. Cambridge: Cambridge University Press.

Di Muzio, Gianluca. 2006. 'The Immorality of Horror Films.' *International Journal of Applied Philosophy* 20 (2): 277–94. https://doi.org/10.5840/ijap200620222.

Dick, Jeremy. 2019. 'Shelly Lives: Remembering Horror's Greatest Prankster.' Horror Geek Life. Last Modified 29 September 2019. https://www.horrorgeeklife.com/2019/09/29/shelly-lives-friday-the-13th-part-3/.

Dika, Vera. 1990. *Games of Terror:* Halloween, Friday the 13th *and the Films of the Stalker Cycle*. London and Toronto: Associated University Presses.

Doles, Steven. 2016. 'Cycle Consciousness and the White Audience in Black Film Writing: The 1949–1950 "Race Problem" Cycle and the African American Press.' In *Cycles, Sequels, Spin-offs, Remakes, and Reboots: Multiplicities in Film and Television*, edited by Amanda Ann Klein and R. Barton Palmer, 80–95. Austin: University of Texas Press.

Dowe, Phil. 1996. 'Backwards Causation and the Direction of Causal Processes.' *Mind* 105 (418): 227–48. https://doi.org/10.2307/2254560.

Downey, Paul. 2018. 'Interview: Damien Leone talks *Terrifier*.' Bloody Flicks. Last Modified 7 March 2018. https://bloody-flicks.co.uk/2018/03/07/interview-damien-leone-talks-terrifier/.

Dudai, Yadin. 2008. 'Enslaving Central Executives: Toward a Brain Theory of Cinema.' *Projections* 2 (2): 21–42. https://doi.org/10:3167/proj.2008.020203.

Dulk, Allard den. 2020. 'New Sincerity and *Frances Ha* in Light of Sartre: A Proposal for an Existentialist Conceptual Framework.' *Film-Philosophy* 24 (2): 140–61. https://doi.org/10.3366/film.2020.0136.

Dummett, Michael and Anthony Flew. 1954. 'Can an Effect Precede its Cause?' *Aristotelian Society Proceedings Supplement* 28 (1): 27–62. https://doi.org/10.2307/4106593.

Duncan, Pansy. 2016. *The Emotional Life of Postmodern Film: Affect Theory's Other*. New York: Routledge.

Dutt, Apoorva. 2011. 'Nothing to *Scream* About . . . or is There?' *DNA*, April 17.

Earl, Jennifer and Katrina Kimport. 2011. *Digitally Enabled Social Change*. Cambridge: The MIT Press.

Eberwein, Robert. 1998. 'Remakes and Cultural Studies.' In *Play It Again, Sam: Retakes on Remakes*, edited by Andrew Horton and Stuart Y. McDougal, 15–28. Berkeley: University of California Press.

Egan, Kate. 2007. *Trash or Treasure?: Censorship and the Changing Meanings of the Video Nasties*. Manchester: Manchester University Press.

Eidelman, Scott and Christian S. Crandall. 2012. 'Bias in Favor of the Status Quo.' *Social and Personality Psychology Compass* 6 (3): 270–81. https://doi.org/10.1111/j.1751-9004.2012.00427.x.

Elgin, Catherine Z. 2008. 'Emotion and Understanding.' In *Epistemology and Emotions*, edited by Georg Brun, Ulvi Doğuoğlu and Dominique Kuenzle, 33–49. Aldershot: Ashgate.

Eshelman, Raoul. 2008. *Performatism, or the End of Postmodernism*. Aurora: Davies Group.

Fairservice, Don. 2001. *Film Editing: History, Theory and Practice*. Manchester: Manchester University Press.

Feasey, Rebecca. 2003. 'Sex, Controversy, Box-Office: From Blockbuster to Bonkbuster.' In *Movie Blockbusters*, edited by Julian Stringer, 167–77. London: Routledge.

Federman, Raymond. 1981. 'Surfiction: Four Propositions in the Form of an Introduction.' In *Surfiction: Fiction Now . . . and Tomorrow*, edited by Raymond Federman, 5–18. Chicago: Swallow Press.

Felci, Michael. 2014. '*Friday the 13th* Movies: Top 5 Characters.' Desert Sun, 13 June 2014. https://eu.desertsun.com/story/life/entertainment/2014/06/13/friday-thirteenth-movies-franchise-slasher-series/10499953/.

Fenton, Andrew. 2016. 'Movie became a Monster.' *The Daily Telegraph*, 17 December 2016.

Fjellestad, Danuta. 2021. 'The Ludic Impulse in Post-Postmodern Fiction.' In *Ludics: Play as Humanistic Inquiry*, edited by Vassiliki Rapti and Eric Gordon, 293–315. Singapore: Palgrave-Macmillan.

Fordy, Tom. 2018. 'You Can't Kill the Boogeyman.' *The Telegraph*, 18 October 2018.

Forever Midnight. 2013. 'Our Exclusive Interview with Damien Leone.' Forever Midnight. Last Modified 19 September 2013. https://forever-midnight.squarespace.com/news/2013/9/19/k86c228kldhhsto6plg9uuzlvrdob8.

Forrest, Jennifer and Leonard R. Koos. 2002. 'Reviewing Remakes: An Introduction.' In *Dead Ringers: The Remake in Theory and Practice*, edited by Jennifer Forrest and Leonard R. Koos, 1–36. Albany: State University of New York Press.

Forrest, Peter. 1985. 'Backward Causation in Defence of Free Will.' *Mind* 94 (374): 210–17. https://doi.org/10.2307/2254746.

Fortuna Jr, Grzegorz. 2018. 'Narrative Strategies in Contemporary Independent American Horror Movies.' *Panoptikum* 19 (1): 121–130. https://doi.org/10.26881/pan.2018.19.09.

Francese, Joseph. 1997. *Narrating Postmodern Time and Space*. Albany: State University of New York Press.

Francis, James. 2013. *Remaking Horror: Hollywood's New Reliance on Scares of Old.* Jefferson: McFarland.
Frankl, Viktor E. 1992. *Man's Search for Meaning.* Boston: Beacon Press.
Freeland, Cynthia A. 2000. *The Naked and the Undead: Evil and the Appeal of Horror.* Oxford: West View Press.
Friedenthal, Andrew J. 2017. *Retcon Game: Retroactive Continuity and the Hyperlinking of America.* Jackson: University Press of Mississippi.
Frow, John. 2006. *Genre.* London: Routledge.
Gallese, Vittorio and Michele Guerra. 2020. *The Empathic Screen.* Oxford: Oxford University Press.
Garcia, Chris. 1996. 'Monster Invasion.' *Fangoria* 158: 8.
—. 1997. 'Scream with Fear.' *Fangoria* 159: 20–5 and 71.
Gaynor, Stella Marie. 2022. *Rethinking Horror in the New Economies of Television.* Cham: Palgrave-Macmillan.
Genette, Gerard. 1980. *Narrative Discourse: An Essay in Method.* Translated by Jane E. Lewin. Ithaca: Cornell University Press.
Gibbons, Alison. 2015. '"Take that You Intellectuals!" and "kaPOW!": Adam Thirlwell and the Metamodernist Future of Style.' *Studia Neophilologica* 87 (1): 29–43. https://doi.org/10.1080/00393274.2014.981959.
—. 2017. 'Contemporary Autofiction and Metamodern Affect.' In *Metamodernism: Historicity, Affect, and Depth After Postmodernism*, edited by Robin van den Akker, Alison Gibbons and Timotheus Vermeulen, 117–30. London: Rowman & Littlefield.
—. 2021. 'Metamodernism, the Anthropocene, and the Resurgence of Historicity: Ben Lerner's *10:04* and "The Utopian Glimmer of Fiction".' *Critique: Studies in Contemporary Fiction* 62 (2): 137–51. https://doi.org/10.1080/00111619.2020.1784828.
Gibbons, Alison, Timotheus Vermeulen and Robin Van Den Akker. 2019. 'Reality Beckons: Metamodernist Depthiness Beyond Panfictionality.' *European Journal of English Studies* 23 (2): 172–89. https://doi.org/10.1080/13825577.2019.1640426.
Gill, Pat. 2002. 'The Monstrous Years: Teens, Slasher Films, and the Family.' *Journal of Film and Video* 54 (4): 16–30. http://www.jstor.org/stable/20688391.
Godin, Benoît. 2017. *Models of Innovation: The History of an Idea.* Cambridge: The MIT Press.
Goggin, Joyce. 2010. 'From Remake to Sequel: *Ocean's Eleven* and *Ocean's Twelve*.' In *Second Takes: Critical Approaches to the Film Sequel*, edited by Carolyn Jess-Cooke and Constantine Verevis, 105–20. New York: State University of New York Press.
Gracia, Jorge J. E. 1995. *A Theory of Textuality: The Logic and Epistemology.* New York: State University of New York Press.
Grant, Barry Keith. 2004. 'Introduction.' In *Planks of Reason: Essays on the Horror Film*, edited by Barry Keith Grant, ix–xv. London: Scarecrow Press.
—. 2007. *Film Genre: From Iconography to Ideology.* London: Wallflower.

Green, Melanie C., Timothy C. Brock and Geoff F. Kaufman. 2004. 'Understanding Media Enjoyment: The Role of Transportation into Narrative Worlds.' *Communication Theory* 14 (4): 311–27. https://doi.org/10.1111/j.1468-2885.2004.tb00317.x.

Griffin, Hollis. 2020. 'Living Through It: Anger, Laughter, and Internet Memes in Dark Times.' *International Journal of Cultural Studies* 24 (3): 381–97. https://doi.org/10.1177/1367877920965990.

Grindon, Leger. 2005. 'Genre Theory in Film Studies.' In *Routledge Encyclopedia of Narrative Theory*, edited by David Herman, Manfred Jahn and Marie-Laure Ryan, 200–1. Abingdon: Routledge.

Groen, Rick. 1981. '*Friday the 13th* Sequel: Once More with the Gore.' *The Globe and Mail*, 4 May 1981.

—. 2011. 'By Now, this Series is so Meta, it's not Funny.' *The Globe and Mail*, 15 April 2011.

Grove, David. 2005. *Making* Friday the 13th*: The Legend of Camp Blood*. Surrey: FAB Press.

Guffey, Elizabeth. 2006. *Retro: The Culture of Revival*. London: Reaktion.

Guynn, William. 2006. *Writing History in Film*. London: Routledge.

Habermas, Tilmann and Susan Bluck. 2000. 'Getting a Life: The Emergence of the Life Story in Adolescence.' *Psychological Bulletin* 126 (5): 748–69. https://doi.org/10.1037/0033-2909.126.5.748.

Handwerk, Gary. 2008. 'Romantic Irony.' In *The Cambridge History of Literary Criticism, Volume 5: Romanticism*, edited by Marshall Brown, 203–25. Cambridge: Cambridge University Press.

Hanich, Julian. 2010. *Cinematic Emotions in Horror Films and Thrillers: The Aesthetic Paradox of Pleasurable Fear*. New York: Routledge.

Hanley, Ken W. 2013. 'Interview: Adam Green on *Hatchet III*.' Diabolique. Last Modified 12 June 2013. https://diaboliquemagazine.com/interview-adam-green-on-hatchet-iii-holliston-and-the-mpaa/.

Hantke, Steffen. 2007. 'Academic Film Criticism, the Rhetoric of Crisis, and the Current State of American Horror Cinema: Thoughts on Canonicity and Academic Anxiety.' *College Literature* 34 (4): 191–202. https://doi.org/10.1353/lit.2007.0045.

Harries, Dan. 2000. *Film Parody*. London: BFI.

—. 2010. 'Introduction.' In *American Horror Film: The Genre at the Turn of the Millennium*, edited by Steffan Hantke, vii–xxxii. Jackson: University Press of Mississippi.

Hart, Adam Charles. 2018. 'Killer POV: First-Person Camera and Sympathetic Identification in Modern Horror.' *Imaginations* 9 (1): 69–86. https://doi.org/10.17742/IMAGE.p70s.9.1.6.

Harvey, David. 1989. *The Condition of Postmodernity: An Enquiry into the Origins of Cultural Change*. Oxford: Blackwell.

Hassan, Ihab. 2003. 'Beyond Postmodernism: Toward an Aesthetic of Trust.' In *Beyond Postmodernism: Reassessments in Literature, Theory, and Culture*, edited by Klaus Stierstorfer, 199–212. Berlin: Walter de Gruyter.

Hatfull, Jonathan. 2014. '*See No Evil 2* Soska Sisters: "Horror Movies are Cooler!".' Sci-fi Now. Last Modified 17 October 2014. https://www.scifinow.co.uk/interviews/see-no-evil-2-soska-sisters-horror-movies-are-cooler/.

Helles, Rasmus and Mikkel Flyverbom. 2019. 'Meshes of Surveillance, Prediction, and Infrastructure: On the Cultural and Commercial Consequences of Digital Platforms.' *Surveillance & Society* 17 (1/2): 34–9. https://doi.org/10.24908/ss.v17i1/2.13120.

Hendrix, Grady. 2021. *The Final Girl Support Group*. London: Titan Books.

Herman, David. 1997. 'Toward a Formal Description of Narrative Metalepsis.' *Journal of Literary Semantics* 26 (2): 132–52. https://doi.org/10.1515/jls-2021-2044.

Hernández-Santaolalla, Víctor and Irene Raya. 2021. 'Male Monsters Still Stalk, Yet More Violent: A Comparative Analysis of Original Slasher Films and Their Remakes.' *Sexuality & Culture* 26 (3): 1167–89. https://doi.org/10.1007/s12119-021-09937-3.

Hilderbrand, Lucas. 2010. 'The Art of Distribution: Video On-Demand.' *Film Quarterly* 64 (2): 24–8. https://doi.org/10.1525/fq.2010.64.2.24.

Hills, Matt. 2005. *The Pleasures of Horror*. New York: Continuum.

Hitcher, Waldo. 2006. *The Innovation Paradigm, Replaced*. New York: J. Wiley.

Holland, Mary K. 2013. *Succeeding Postmodernism: Language and Humanism in Contemporary American Literature*. New York: Bloomsbury.

Horton, Andrew and Stuart Y. McDougal. 1998. 'Introduction.' In *Play It Again, Sam: Retakes on Remakes*, edited by Andrew Horton and Stuart Y. McDougal, 1–10. Berkeley: University of California Press.

Hume, David. 2007. *An Enquiry Concerning Human Understanding*. London: Oxford University Press.

Humphries, Reynold. 2002. *The American Horror Film: An Introduction*. Edinburgh: Edinburgh University Press.

Hutcheon, Linda. 1980. *Narcissistic Narrative: The Metafictional Paradox*. Waterloo: Wilfrid Laurier University Press.

—. 2002. *The Politics of Postmodernism*. Second edition. London: Routledge.

—. 2013. *A Theory of Adaptation*. Second edition. London: Routledge.

Hutchings, Peter. 2004. *The Horror Film*. Harlow: Pearson.

Hutchinson, Tom. 1992. 'Pfeiffer goes Slumming for an Oscar.' *Mail on Sunday*, 19 January 1992.

Hutson, Thommy. 2014. *Never Sleep Again: The Elm Street Legacy*. Burbank: Red Rover.

Iser, Wolfgang. 1978. *The Act of Reading: A Theory of Aesthetic Response*. Baltimore: The Johns Hopkins University Press.

Jacobs, Dany. 2014. *The Cultural Side of Innovation: Adding Values*. New York: Routledge.

James, David and Urmila Seshagiri. 2014. 'Metamodernism: Narratives of Continuity and Revolution.' *PMLA* 129 (1): 87–100. https://doi.org/10.1632/pmla.2014.129.1.87.

Jameson, Fredric. 1991. *Postmodernism, or the Cultural Logic of Late Capitalism.* Durham: Duke University Press.
Jancovich, Mark. 1992. *Horror.* London: B. T. Batsford.
Jaques, Elliott. 1982. *The Form of Time.* New York: Crane Russak.
Jeffries, Stuart. 2021. *Everything, All the Time, Everywhere: How We Became Postmodern.* London: Verso Books.
Jenner, Mareike. 2018. *Netflix and the Re-invention of Television.* Cham: Palgrave-Macmillan.
Jess-Cooke, Carolyn. 2009. *Film Sequels: Theory and Practice from Hollywood to Bollywood.* Edinburgh: Edinburgh University Press.
Jess-Cooke, Carolyn and Constantine Verevis. 2010. 'Introduction.' In *Second Takes: Critical Approaches to the Film Sequel*, edited by Carolyn Jess-Cooke and Constantine Verevis, 1–10. New York: State University of New York Press.
Johnson, Kevin C. 2007. 'Dissecting Torture. *St. Louis Post-Dispatch*, 26 October 2007.
Jones, Stephen Graham. 2021. *My Heart is a Chainsaw.* London: Titan Books.
Jones, Steve. 2010. '"Time is Wasting": Con/sequence and S/pace in the *Saw* series.' *Journal of Horror Studies* 1 (2): 225–39. https://doi.org/10.1386/host.1.2.225_1.
—. 2013. *Torture Porn: Popular Horror After Saw.* Basingstoke: Palgrave-MacMillan.
—. 2018. 'Preserved for Posterity?: Present-Bias and the Status of Grindhouse Films in the "Home Cinema" Era.' *Journal of Film and Video* 70 (1): 3–16. https://doi.org/10.5406/jfilmvideo.70.1.0003.
—. 2019. 'Spierig Brothers' *Jigsaw* (2017): Torture Porn Rebooted?' In *Horror: A Companion*, edited by Simon Bacon, 85–92. Oxford: Peter Lang.
—. 2022. 'If Nancy Doesn't Wake Up Screaming: The *Elm Street* Series as Recurring Nightmare.' In *Horror Franchise Cinema*, edited by Mark McKenna and William Proctor, 81–93. London: Routledge.
Kahneman, Daniel, Olivier Sibony and Cass R. Sunstein. 2021. *Noise: A Flaw in Human Judgment.* New York: Little, Brown Spark.
Kaplan, E. Ann. 1988. 'Introduction.' In *Postmodernism and its Discontents: Theories, Practices*, edited by E. Ann Kaplan, 1–9. London: Verso.
Kelleter, Frank. 2012. '"Toto, I Think we're in Oz Again" (and Again and Again): Remakes and Popular Seriality.' In *Film Remakes, Adaptations and Fan Productions: Remake/Remodel*, edited by Kathleen Loock and Constantine Verevis, 19–44. New York: Palgrave-Macmillan.
Kennedy, Michael. 2019. '*Happy Death Day 2U*'s Sci-Fi Twist Hurts the Slasher Sequel.' Screen Rant. Last Modified 28 December 2019. https://screenrant.com/happy-death-day-2u-movie-sci-fi-twist-problem-bad/.
Kermode, Mark. 2001. 'I Was a Teenage Horror Fan.' In *Ill Effects: The Media/Violence Debate*, edited by Martin Barker and Julian Petley, 57–66. New York: Routledge.
Kerswell, J. A. 2010. *Teenage Wasteland: The Slasher Movie Uncut.* London: New Holland.
King, Geoff. 2002. *Film Comedy.* London: Wallflower Press.

Kirby, Alan. 2006. 'The Death of Postmodernism and Beyond.' *Philosophy Now* (58). https://philosophynow.org/issues/58/The_Death_of_Postmodernism_And_Beyond.
—. 2009. *Digimodernism: How New Technologies Dismantle the Postmodern and Reconfigure Our Culture.* New York: Continuum.
Klein, Amanda Ann and R. Barton Palmer. 2016. 'Introduction.' In *Cycles, Sequels, Spin-offs, Remakes, and Reboots: Multiplicities in Film and Television*, edited by Amanda Ann Klein and R. Barton Palmer, 1–21. Austin: University of Texas Press.
Kleinberg, Jon M., Robert D. Kleinberg and Sigal Oren. 2021. 'Optimal Stopping with Behaviorally Biased Agents: The Role of Loss Aversion and Changing Reference Points.' *Proceedings of the 22nd ACM Conference on Economics and Computation.* https://doi.org/10.48550/arxiv.2106.00604.
Konrad, Eva-Maria, Thomas Petraschka and Christiana Werner. 2018. 'The Paradox of Fiction: A Brief Introduction into Recent Developments, Open Questions, and Current Areas of Research, including a Comprehensive Bibliography from 1975 to 2018.' *Journal of Literary Theory* 12 (2): 193–203. https://doi.org/10.1515/jlt-2018-0011.
Konstantinou, Lee. 2017. 'Four Faces of Postirony.' In *Metamodernism: Historicity, Affect, and Depth After Postmodernism*, edited by Robin van den Akker, Alison Gibbons and Timotheus Vermeulen, 87–102. London: Rowman & Littlefield.
Kornfield, Sarah. 2016. 'Re-solving Crimes: A Cycle of TV Detective Partnerships.' In *Cycles, Sequels, Spin-offs, Remakes, and Reboots: Multiplicities in Film and Television*, edited by Amanda Ann Klein and R. Barton Palmer, 316–34. Austin: University of Texas Press.
Koven, Mikel. 2006. *La Dolce Morte: Vernacular Cinema and the Italian Giallo Film.* Lanham: The Scarecrow Press.
Kroll, Jack. 1981. 'The Beauty of Horror.' *Newsweek*, 9 March 1981.
Krzywinska, Tanya. 2002. 'Hands-On Horror.' In *ScreenPlay: Cinema/Videogames/Interfaces*, edited by Geoff King and Tanya Krzywinska, 206–23. London: Wallflower Press.
Laidler, Mark. 2005. 'Zapping Freddy Krueger: Children's Use of Disapproved Video Texts.' In *Wired Up: Young People and the Electronic Media*, edited by Sue Howard, 41–54. London: Taylor and Francis.
Lash, Dominic. 2020. *The Cinema of Disorientation: Inviting Confusions.* Edinburgh: Edinburgh University Press.
Leadbeater, Charles. 2010. *We-Think: Mass Innovation, Not Mass Production.* Second edition. London: Profile Books.
Leeder, Murray. 2014. *Halloween.* Leighton Buzzard: Auteur.
—. 2018. *Horror Film: A Critical Introduction.* New York: Bloomsbury.
—. 2022. 'If I Were a Carpenter: Prestige and Authorship in the *Halloween* Franchise.' In *Horror Franchise Cinema*, edited by Mark McKenna and William Proctor, 66–80. London: Routledge.

Lennard, Dominic. 2014. *Bad Seeds and Holy Terrors*. New York: State University of New York Press.
Levchenko, Natalia, Pecherskyh Lubov, Olena Varenikova and Nataliya Torkut. 2021. 'Communicative Model: Author, Hero, Text, Recipient in a Postmodern Novel.' *Postmodern Openings* 12 (3): 96–106. https://doi.org/10.18662/po/12.3/329.
Leverick, Fiona. 2006. *Killing in Self Defence*. Oxford: Oxford University Press.
Levitin, Daniel J. 2014. *The Organized Mind*. New York: Penguin.
Lewis, Jon. 2012. 'The End of Cinema (as We Know it).' In *The Wiley-Blackwell History of American Film*, edited by Cynthia Lucia, Roy Grundmann and Art Simon, 2138–57. London: Blackwell.
Leydon, Joe. 2004. '*Seed of Chucky*.' *Daily Variety*, 15 November 2004.
Liao, Shen-yi. 2016. 'Imaginative Resistance, Narrative Engagement, Genre.' *Res Philosophica* 93 (2): 461–82. https://doi.org/10.11612/resphil.2016.2.93.3.
Lipovetsky, Gilles. 2005. *Hypermodern Times*. Translated by Andrew Brown. Cambridge: Polity.
Lockwood, Dean. 2008. 'All Stripped Down: The Spectacle of "Torture Porn".' *Popular Communication* 7 (1): 40–8. https://doi.org/10.1080/15405700802587232.
Loock, Kathleen. 2012. 'The Return of the Pod People: Remaking Cultural Anxieties in *Invasion of the Body Snatchers*.' In *Film Remakes, Adaptations and Fan Productions: Remake/Remodel*, edited by Kathleen Loock and Constantine Verevis, 122–44. New York: Palgrave-Macmillan.
—. 2016. 'Retro-Remaking: The 1980s Film Cycle in Contemporary Hollywood Cinema.' In *Cycles, Sequels, Spin-offs, Remakes, and Reboots: Multiplicities in Film and Television*, edited by Amanda Ann Klein and R. Barton Palmer, 277–98. Austin: University of Texas Press.
—. 2017. 'The Sequel Paradox: Repetition, Innovation, and Hollywood's Hit Film Formula.' *Film Studies* 17 (1): 92–110. https://doi.org/10.7227/FS.17.0006.
Lowenthal, David. 1989. 'Nostalgia Tells it Like it Wasn't.' In *The Imagined Past: History and Nostalgia*, edited by Christopher Shaw and Malcolm Chase, 18–32. Manchester: Manchester University Press.
Lyotard, Jean-Francois. 1984. *The Postmodern Condition: A Report on Knowledge*. Translated by Geoff Bennington and Brian Massumi. Minneapolis: University of Minnesota Press.
MacDowell, James. 2017. 'The Metamodern, the Quirky and Film Criticism.' In *Metamodernism: Historicity, Affect, and Depth After Postmodernism*, edited by Robin van den Akker, Alison Gibbons and Timotheus Vermeulen, 25–40. London: Rowman & Littlefield.
Malina, Debra. 2002. *Breaking the Frame: Metalepsis and the Construction of the Subject*. Columbus: The Ohio State University Press.
Malpas, Simon. 2005. *The Postmodern*. London: Routledge.
Martin, Bob. 1981. 'The Postal Zone.' *Fangoria* 14: 5–7.

Maslin, Janet. 1982. '*Friday the 13th Part III*-in 3-D Opens.' *The New York Times*, 13 August 1982.
Mathijs, Ernest. 2010. 'They're Here!: Special Effects in Horror Cinema of the 1970s and 1980s.' In *Horror Zone: The Cultural Experience of Contemporary Horror Cinema*, edited by Ian Conrich, 153–171. New York: I. B. Tauris.
McAdams, Dan P. 1993. *The Stories We Live By: Personal Myths and the Making of the Self*. London: The Guilford Press.
—. 2013. *The Redemptive Self: Stories Americans Live By*. Second edition. Oxford: Oxford University Press.
McAdams, Dan P. and Kate C. McLean. 2013. 'Narrative Identity.' *Current Directions in Psychological Science* 22 (3): 233–8. https://doi.org/10.1177/0963721413475622.
McHale, Brian. 2004. *Postmodernist Fiction*. London: Routledge.
Mee, Laura. 2017. 'The Hollywood Remake Massacre: Adaptation, Reception and Value.' In *Adaptation, Awards Culture, and the Value of Prestige*, edited by Colleen Kennedy-Karpat and Eric Sandberg, 193–209. London: Palgrave-Macmillan.
—. 2022. *Reanimated: The Contemporary American Horror Remake*. Edinburgh: Edinburgh University Press.
Mellor, D. H. 1981. *Real Time*. Cambridge: Cambridge University Press.
Ménard, A. Dana, Angela Weaver and Christine Cabrera. 2019. '"There are Certain Rules that One Must Abide By": Predictors of Mortality in Slasher Films.' *Sexuality & Culture* 23 (2): 621–40. https://doi.org/10.1007/s12119-018-09583-2.
Mendelson, Scott. 2018. '*Halloween* is the "Choose Your Own Adventure" of Horror Movie Franchises.' Forbes. Last Modified 7 June 2018. https://www.forbes.com/sites/scottmendelson/2018/06/07/blumhouses-halloween-will-make-the-franchise-continuity-even-more-complicated/.
Menell, Jeff. 1991. '*Freddy's Dead*.' *The Hollywood Reporter*, 16 September 1991.
Meyvis, Tom and Heeyoung, Yoon. 2021. 'Adding is Favoured Over Subtracting in Problem Solving.' *Nature* 592 (7853): 189–90. https://doi.org/10.1038/d41586-021-00592-0.
Miller, Catriona. 2014. 'You Can't Escape: Inside and Outside the "Slasher" Movie.' *International Journal of Jungian Studies* 6 (2): 108–19. https://doi.org/10.1080/19409052.2014.907820.
Mittell, Jason. 2006. 'Narrative Complexity in Contemporary American Television.' *The Velvet Light Trap* 58 (1): 29–40. https://doi.org/10.1353/vlt.2006.0032.
Modleski, Tania. 1986. 'The Terror of Pleasure: The Contemporary Horror Film and Postmodern Theory.' In *Studies in Entertainment Critical Approaches to Mass Culture*, edited by Tania Modleski, 155–65. Bloomington: Indiana University Press.
Moguel, Jackie Rae. 2018. 'Interview with Art the Clown Himself, David Howard Thornton.' Pop Horror. Last Modified 19 May 2018. https://www.pophorror.com/interview-with-art-the-clown-himself-david-howard-thornton/.

Moine, Raphaëlle. 2008. *Cinema Genre*. Translated by Alistair Fox and Hilary Radner. Malden: Blackwell.

Moraru, Christian. 2011. *Cosmodernism: American Narrative, Late Globalization, and the New Cultural Imaginary*. Ann Arbor: University of Michigan Press.

Morreall, John S. 1985. 'Enjoying Negative Emotions in Fictions.' *Philosophy and Literature* 9 (1): 95–103. 10.1353/phl.1985.0118.

Moshinsky, Avital and Maya Bar-Hillel. 2010. 'Loss Aversion and Status Quo Label Bias.' *Social Cognition* 28 (2): 191–204. https://doi.org/10.1521/soco.2010.28.2.191.

Muir, John Kenneth. 2007a. *Horror Films of the 1980s*. Volume 1. Jefferson: McFarland.

—. 2007b. *Horror Films of the 1980s*. Volume 2. Jefferson: McFarland.

—. 2011. *Horror Films of the 1990s*. Jefferson: McFarland.

Murray, Gabrielle. 2008. '*Hostel II*: Representations of the Body in Pain and the Cinema Experience in Torture Porn.' *Jump Cut* 50 (1). https://www.ejumpcut.org/archive/jc50.2008/TortureHostel2/index.htm.

Neale, Steve. 2000. *Genre and Hollywood*. London: Routledge.

Nealon, Jeffrey T. 2012. *Post-Postmodernism: Or, The Cultural Logic of Just-in-Time Capitalism*. Stanford: Stanford University Press.

Nelson, Andrew Patrick. 2015. 'Franchise Legacy and Neo-Slasher Conventions in *Halloween H20*.' In *Style and Form in the Hollywood Slasher Film*, edited by Wickham Clayton, 81–91. Basingstoke: Palgrave-Macmillan.

Newman, Kim. 2011. *Nightmare Movies: Horror on Screen since the 1960s*. Second edition. London: Bloomsbury.

No Author. 2011. 'Lots of Bark and Very Little Bite.' *The Observer*, 21 August 2011.

Nowell, Richard. 2011. *Blood Money: A History of the First Teen Slasher Film Cycle*. London: Continuum.

—. 2012. '"Between Dreams and Reality": Genre Personae, Brand *Elm Street*, and Repackaging the American Teen Slasher Film.' *Iluminace* 24 (3): 69–100. https://bit.ly/3HStrkf.

Nutman, Philip. 1989. 'Fathering *The Dream Child*: Part One.' *Fangoria* 87: 52–6 and 67.

Ochonicky, Adam. 2020. 'Nostalgia and Retcons: The Many Returns, Homecomings, and Revisions of the *Halloween* Franchise (1978–2018).' *Adaptation* 13 (3): 334–57. https://doi.org/10.1093/adaptation/apaa006.

Oddie, Graham. 1990. 'Backwards Causation and the Permanence of the Past.' *Synthese* 85 (1): 71–93. https://doi.org/10.2307/20116833.

Pagel, James F. 2014. *Dream Science: Exploring the Forms of Consciousness*. London: Academic Press.

Pallister, Kathryn. 2019. 'Introduction.' In *Netflix Nostalgia: Streaming the Past on Demand*, edited by Kathryn Pallister, 1–8. Lanham: Lexington Books.

Pantaleo, Sylvia. 2010. 'Mutinous Fiction: Narrative and Illustrative Metalepsis in Three Postmodern Picturebooks.' *Children's Literature in Education* 41 (1): 12–27. https://doi.org/10.1007/s10583-009-9096-x.

Pascale, Marius A. 2019. 'Art Horror, Reactive Attitudes, and Compassionate Slashers.' *International Journal of Applied Philosophy* 33 (1): 141–59. https://doi.org/10.5840/ijap201981116.

Paul, William. 1994. *Laughing Screaming: Modern Hollywood Horror Comedy*. New York: Columbia University Press.

Perkins, Claire. 2012. 'The *Scre4m* Trilogy.' In *Film Trilogies: New Critical Approaches*, edited by Claire Perkins and Constantine Verevis, 88–108. New York: Palgrave-Macmillan.

Perren, Alisa. 2012. *Indie, Inc.: Miramax and the Transformation of Hollywood in the 1990s*. Austin: University of Texas Press.

Petridis, Sotiris. 2014. 'A Historical Approach to the Slasher Film.' *Film International* 12 (1): 76–84. https://doi.org/10.1386/fiin.12.1.76_1.

—. 2019. *Anatomy of the Slasher Film: A Theoretical Analysis*. Jefferson: McFarland.

Phillips, Kendall R. 2012. *Dark Directions: Romero, Craven, Carpenter, and the Modern Horror Film*. Carbondale: Southern Illinois University Press.

Pinedo, Isabel. 1996. 'Recreational Terror: Postmodern Elements of the Contemporary Horror Film.' *Journal of Film and Video* 48 (1/2): 17–31. https://www.jstor.org/stable/20688091.

Pipere, Anita and Kristıne Martinsone. 2022. 'Metamodernism and Social Sciences: Scoping the Future.' *Social Sciences* 11 (10): 457–76. https://doi.org/10.3390/socsci11100457.

Platts, Todd K. 2020. '"It's Worth Recognising Only as an Artefact of Our Culture": Critics and the *Friday the 13th* Franchise (1980–2001).' In *Horror Homeroom: Friday the 13th at 40*, edited by Elizabeth Erwin and Dawn Keetley, 16–25. http://www.horrorhomeroom.com/special-issue-1/.

Poincare, Henri 2000. 'The Measure of Time.' In *Time and the Instant: Essays in the Physics and Philosophy of Time*, edited by Robin Durie, 25–35. Manchester: Clinamen Press.

Pollard, Andrew. 2017. 'The Soska Sisters: *See No Evil 2*.' Starburst. Last Modified 25 April 2017. https://www.starburstmagazine.com/features/the-soska-sisters-see-no-evil-2.

Pratt, Andy C. and Paul Jeffcutt. 2009. 'Conclusion.' In *Creativity, Innovation and the Cultural Economy*, edited by Andy C. Pratt and Paul Jeffcutt, 265–76. London: Routledge.

Prince, Gerald. 2013. 'Metanarrative Signs.' In *Metafiction*, edited by Mark Currie, 55–68. New York: Routledge.

Prince, Stephen. 2009. *Firestorm: American Film in the Age of Terrorism*. New York: Columbia University Press.

Prior, Arthur. 1993. 'Changes in Events and Changes in Things.' In *The Philosophy of Time*, edited by Robin Le Poidevin and Murray MacBeath, 35–46. Oxford: Oxford University Press.

Proctor, William. 2017. 'Reboots and Retroactive Continuity.' In *The Routledge Companion to Imaginary Worlds*, edited by Mark J. P. Wolf, 224–35. New York: Routledge.

Rafter, Nicole Hahn. 2006. *Shots in the Mirror: Crime Films and Society*. Oxford: Oxford University Press.
Rieser, Klaus. 2001. 'Masculinity and Monstrosity: Characterization and Identification in the Slasher Film.' *Men and Masculinities* 3 (4): 370–92. https://doi.org/10.1177/1097184X01003004002.
Roche, David. 2014. *Making and Remaking Horror in the 1970s and 2000s: Why Don't They Do It Like They Used to?* Jackson: University Press of Mississippi.
—. 2015. '(In)Stability of Point of View in *When a Stranger Calls* and *Eyes of a Stranger*.' In *Style and Form in the Hollywood Slasher Film*, edited by Wickham Clayton, 17–36. Basingstoke: Palgrave-Macmillan.
Rockoff, Adam. 2002. *Going to Pieces: The Rise and Fall of the Slasher Film, 1978–1986*. Jefferson: McFarland.
Rombes, Nicholas. 2010. 'Before and After and Right Now: Sequels in the Digital Era.' In *Second Takes: Critical Approaches to the Film Sequel*, edited by Carolyn Jess-Cooke and Constantine Verevis, 191–204. New York: State University of New York Press.
Rosewarne, Lauren. 2019. *Sex and Sexuality in Modern Screen Remakes*. Cham: Palgrave-Macmillan.
—. 2020. *Why We Remake: The Politics, Economics and Emotions of Film and TV Remakes*. London: Routledge.
Roth, Marty. 2002. 'Twice Two: *The Fly* and *Invasion of the Body Snatchers*.' In *Dead Ringers: The Remake in Theory and Practice*, edited by Jennifer Forrest and Leonard R. Koos, 225–42. Albany: State University of New York Press.
Rowe, Michael. 1998. 'Here Comes the *Bride of Chucky*.' *Fangoria* 177: 21–4 and 81.
Rudrum, David. 2015. 'Note on the Supplanting of "Post-".' In *Supplanting the Postmodern*, edited by David Rudrum and Nicholas Stavris, 333–48. New York: Bloomsbury.
Rudrum, David and Nicholas Stavris. 2015a. 'Introduction.' In *Supplanting the Postmodern*, edited by David Rudrum and Nicholas Stavris, xi–xxix. New York: Bloomsbury.
—. 2015b. 'Remodernism.' In *Supplanting the Postmodern*, edited by David Rudrum and Nicholas Stavris, 101–4. New York: Bloomsbury.
—. 2015c. 'Metamodernism.' In *Supplanting the Postmodern*, edited by David Rudrum and Nicholas Stavris, 305–9. New York: Bloomsbury.
Russo, John. 1992. *Scare Tactics: The Art, Craft, and Trade Secrets of Writing, Producing, and Directing Chillers and Thrillers*. New York: Dell.
Rust, Stephen A. 2014. 'Comfortably Numb: Material Ecocriticism and the Postmodern Horror Film.' *Interdisciplinary Studies in Literature and Environment* 21 (3): 550–61. https://doi.org/10.1093/isle/isu083.
Salemme, Danny. 2018. '*Halloween*'s 5 Timelines Explained (and which Movies You MUST See).' Screen Rant. Last Modified 18 October 2018. https://screenrant.com/halloween-movie-timelines-continuity/.

Samuels, Robert. 2008. 'Auto-Modernity after Postmodernism: Autonomy and Automation in Culture, Technology, and Education.' In *Digital Youth, Innovation, and the Unexpected*, edited by Tara McPherson, 219–40. Cambridge, MA: MIT Press.

Sandbacka, Kasimir. 2017. 'Metamodernism in Liksom's *Compartment No. 6*.' *CLCWeb: Comparative Literature and Culture* 19 (1): 1–9. https://doi.org/10.7771/1481-4374.2891.

Sapolsky, Barry S., Fred Molitor and Sarah Luque. 2003. 'Sex and Violence in Slasher Films: Re-examining the Assumptions.' *Journalism & Mass Communication Quarterly* 80 (1): 28–38. https://doi.org/10.1177/107769900308000103.

Sartorio, Carolina. 2016. *Causation and Free Will*. Oxford: Oxford University Press.

Savitt, Steven F. 1995. 'Introduction.' In *Time's Arrows Today: Recent Physical and Philosophical Work on the Direction of Time*, edited by Steven F. Savitt, 1–19. Cambridge: Cambridge University Press.

Scahill, Andrew. 2016. 'Serialized Killers: Prebooting Horror in *Bates Motel* and *Hannibal*.' In *Cycles, Sequels, Spin-offs, Remakes, and Reboots: Multiplicities in Film and Television*, edited by Amanda Ann Klein and R. Barton Palmer, 316–34. Austin: University of Texas Press.

Schatz, Thomas. 1981. *Hollywood Genres*. New York: Random House.

Schechtman, Marya. 1996. *The Constitution of Selves*. Ithaca: Cornell University Press.

Schneider, Steven Jay. 2000. 'Kevin Williamson and the Rise of the Neo-Stalker.' *Post-Script: Essays in Film and the Humanities* 19 (2): 73–87. https://www.proquest.com/docview/2142182/fulltext/682853C21A134270PQ.

Schoell, William and James Spencer. 1992. *The Nightmare Never Ends*. New York: Citadel Press.

Scholes, Robert. 2013. 'Metafiction.' In *Metafiction*, edited by Mark Currie, 21–38. New York: Routledge.

Sconce, Jeffrey. 1993. 'Spectacles of Death: Identification, Reflexivity, and Contemporary Horror.' In *Film Theory Goes to the Movies*, edited by Jim Collins, Hillary Radner and Ava Collins, 103–19. New York: Routledge.

Scrutchin, Michael B. 1997. 'Postal Zone: *Scream* for Joy.' *Fangoria* 162: 6.

Shapiro, Marc. 1994. 'Wes Craven's Psycho Analysis.' *Fangoria* 138: 32–36.

Shary, Timothy. 2002. *Generation Multiplex: The Image of Youth in Contemporary American Cinema*. Austin: University of Texas Press.

Shaw, Kristian and Sara Upstone. 2021. 'The Transglossic: Contemporary Fiction and the Limitations of the Modern.' *English Studies* 102 (5): 573–600. https://doi.org/10.1080/0013838x.2021.1943894.

Shimabukuro, Karra. 2015. 'I Framed Freddy: Functional Aesthetics in the *A Nightmare on Elm Street* Series.' In *Style and Form in the Hollywood Slasher Film*, edited by Wickham Clayton, 51–66. Basingstoke: Palgrave-Macmillan.

Shirky, Clay. 2010. *Cognitive Surplus: Creativity and Generosity in a Connected Age*. New York: Penguin.

Shone, Tom. 1992. 'Freddy's Final Cut.' *The Sunday Times*, 19 January 1992.

Sklar, Lawrence. 1974. *Space, Time, and Spacetime*. Berkeley: University of California Press.
Skow, Bradford. 2012. 'Why Does Time Pass?' *Nous* 46 (2): 223–42. https://doi.org/10.1111/j.1468-0068.2010.00784.x.
Smethurst, Paul. 2000. *The Postmodern Chronotope: Reading Space and Time in Contemporary Fiction*. Amsterdam: Rodopi.
Smith, Andy W. 2007. '"These Children that You Spit On": Horror and Generic Hybridity.' In *Monstrous Adaptations: Generic and Thematic Mutations in Horror Film*, edited by Richard J. Hand and Jay McRoy, 82–94. Manchester: Manchester University Press.
Smythe, Luke. 2015. 'Modernism Post-Postmodernism: Art in the Era of Light Modernity.' *Modernism/Modernity* 22 (2): 365–79. https://doi.org/10.1353/mod.2015.0033.
Stamm, Matthew D. C. 2013. 'A Disc-Less Future: The Rise and Fall of Physical Media.' *Film Matters* 4 (3): 71–3. https://doi.org/10.1386/fm.4.3.71_1.
Steinhoff, Uwe. 2017. 'Proportionality in Self-Defense.' *The Journal of Ethics* 21 (3): 263–89. https://doi.org/10.1007/s10892-017-9244-2.
Stewart, Susan. 1982. 'The Epistemology of the Horror Story.' *The Journal of American Folklore* 95 (375): 33–50. https://doi.org/10.2307/540021.
Stoev, Dina. 2022. 'Metamodernism or Metamodernity.' *Arts* 11 (5): 91–116. https://doi.org/10.3390/arts11050091.
Storm, Jason Ānanda Josephson. 2021. *Metamodernism: The Future of Theory*. Chicago: University of Chicago Press.
Storr, Will. 2017. *Selfie: How We Became So Self-Obsessed and What It's Doing to Us*. London: Picador.
Strohl, Matthew. 2012. 'Horror and Hedonic Ambivalence.' *The Journal of Aesthetics and Art Criticism* 70 (2): 203–12. https://doi.org/10.1111/j.1540-6245.2012.01512.x.
Syder, Andrew. 2002. 'Knowing the Rules: Postmodernism and the Horror Film.' *Spectator* 22 (2): 78–88. https://www.proquest.com/magazines/knowing-rules-postmodernism-horror-film/docview/1491294624/se-2.
Tamborini, Ron, James Stiff and Carl Heidel. 1990. 'Reacting to Graphic Horror: A Model of Empathy and Emotional Behavior.' *Communication Research* 17 (5): 616–40. https://doi.org/10.1177/009365090017005003.
Tan, Eduard Sioe-Hao and Valentijn Visch. 2018. 'Co-Imagination of Fictional Worlds in Film Viewing.' *Review of General Psychology* 22 (2): 230–44. https://doi.org/10.1037/gpr0000153.
Taylor, Tosha R. 2020. 'Self-Reflexivity and Feminist Camp in *Freddy's Dead: The Final Nightmare*.' In *Women Make Horror*, edited by Alison Peirse, 69–80. New Brunswick: Rutgers University Press.
Terror Weekend. 2012. 'Interview with Matt Farnsworth, *The Orphan Killer*'s Director.' Terror Weekend. Last Modified 28 February 2012. https://www.terrorweekend.com/2012/02/interview-with-matt-farnsworth-orphan.html.

Toth, Josh. 2010. *The Passing of Postmodernism: A Spectroanalysis of the Contemporary*. Albany: State University of New York Press.

Toth, Josh and Neil Brooks. 2007. 'Introduction: A Wake and Renewed?' In *The Mourning After: Attending the Wake of Postmodernism*, edited by Neil Brooks and Josh Toth, 1–9. Amsterdam: Rodopi.

Tudor, Andrew. 2002. 'From Paranoia to Postmodernism? The Horror Movie in Late Modern Society.' In *Genre and Contemporary Hollywood*, edited by Steve Neale, 105–16. London: BFI Publishing.

Tullmann, Katherine and Wesley Buckwalter. 2014. 'Does the Paradox of Fiction Exist?' *Erkenntnis* 79 (4): 779–796. https://doi.org/10.1007/s10670-013-9563-z.

Turner, Luke. 2015. 'Metamodernism: A Brief Introduction.' Metamodernism. Last Modified 12 January 2015. http://www.metamodernism.com/2015/01/12/metamodernism-a-brief-introduction/.

Unsworth, Martin. 2012. 'Interview: Matt Farnsworth, Director of *The Orphan Killer*.' Starburst. Last Modified 20 December 2012. https://www.starburstmagazine.com/features/interview-matt-farnsworth-director-of-the-orphan-killer.

Varndell, Daniel. 2014. *Hollywood Remakes, Deleuze and the Grandfather Paradox*. Houndmills: Palgrave-Macmillan.

Verevis, Constantine. 2005. *Film Remakes*. Edinburgh: Edinburgh University Press.

Vermeulen, Timotheus and Robin van den Akker. 2010. 'Notes on Metamodernism.' *Journal of Aesthetics & Culture* 2 (1): 56–77. https://doi.org/10.3402/jac.v2i0.5677.

—. 2015. 'Misunderstandings and Clarifications: Notes on "Notes on Metamodernism".' Metamodernism. Last Modified 3 June 2015. http://www.metamodernism.com/2015/06/03/misunderstandings-and-clarifications/.

Walderzak, Joseph. 2019. 'The Horror of Consumerism through Mise-en-Scène: A Class Analysis of a Failed Horror Remake Cycle, 2004–2010.' *Mise-en-Scène: The Journal of Film & Visual Narration* 4 (2): 48–57. https://issuu.com/mesjournal/docs/issuu-msj4-2_winter2019.

Walker, Johnny. 2016. 'Traces of Snuff: Black Markets, Fan Subcultures and Underground Horror in the 90s.' In *Snuff: Real Death and Screen Media*, edited by Neil Jackson, Shaun Kimber, Johnny Walker and Thomas Joseph Watson, 137–52. New York: Bloomsbury.

Walton, Kendall L. 1970. 'Categories of Art.' *The Philosophical Review* 79 (3): 334. https://doi.org/10.2307/2183933.

Warshow, Robert. 1974. *The Immediate Experience*. New York: Atheneum.

Waugh, Patricia. 1984. *Metafiction: The Theory and Practice of Self-Conscious Fiction*. London: Routledge.

Weaver III, James B. 1991. 'Are "Slasher" Horror Films Sexually Violent?: A Content Analysis.' *Journal of Broadcasting & Electronic Media* 35 (3): 385–92. https://doi.org/10.1080/08838159109364133.

Wee, Valerie. 2006. 'Resurrecting and Updating the Teen Slasher: The Case of *Scream.*' *Journal of Popular Film and Television* 34 (2): 50–61. https://doi.org/10.3200/jpft.34.2.50-61.

Welt, Bernard. 1996. *Mythomania: Fantasies, Fables, and Sheer Lies in Contemporary American Popular Art*. Los Angeles: Art Issues Press.

West, Alexandra. 2018. *The 1990s Teen Horror Cycle: Final Girls and a New Hollywood Formula*. Jefferson: McFarland.

West, Steven. 2019. *Scream*. Leighton Buzzard: Auteur.

Whitehead, Mark. 2003. *Slasher Movies*. Harpenden: Pocket Essentials.

Whittington, James. 2017. 'Interview with Damien Leone Director of *Terrifier*.' Horror Channel. Last Modified 28 October 2017. https://www.horrorchannel.co.uk/articles.php?feature=interview+with+damien+leone+director+of+terrifier&category=interviews.

Wixson, Heather. 2014. 'Exclusive Interview: The Soska Sisters & WWE's Kane Talk *See No Evil 2*.' Daily Dead. Last Modified 6 August 2014. https://dailydead.com/exclusive-interview-soska-sisters-wwes-kane-talk-see-evil-2/.

Wood, Robin. 2003. *Hollywood from Vietnam to Reagan . . . and Beyond*. New York: Columbia University Press.

Wyatt, Justin. 1994. *High Concept: Movies and Marketing in Hollywood*. Austin: University of Texas Press.

Yapp, Nate. 2008. 'Rob Hall and Bobbi Sue Luther (*Laid to Rest*) Interview.' Classic Horror. Last Modified 10 August 2008. http://classic-horror.com/newsreel/rob_hall_and_bobbi_sue_luther_laid_to_rest_interview.html.

Zaius, Dr. 2018. 'Interview: *Victor Crowley* Filmmaker Adam Green.' Geeks of Doom. Last Modified 8 February 2018. https://geeksofdoom.com/2018/02/08/interview-adam-green-victor-crowley.

Zavarzadeh, Mas'ud. 1975. 'The Apocalyptic Fact and the Eclipse of Fiction in Recent American Prose Narratives.' *Journal of American Studies* 9 (1): 69–83. https://www.jstor.org/stable/27553153.

Zeitlin, Michael. 1998. 'Donald Barthelme and the Postmodern Sequel.' In *Part Two: Reflections on the Sequel*, edited by Paul Budra and Betty A. Schellenberg, 160–73. Toronto: University of Toronto Press.

Filmography

18 Again! (1988, USA, Dir. Paul Flaherty).
All the Boys Love Mandy Lane (2006, USA, Dir. Jonathan Levine).
Apocalypse Now (1979, USA, Dir. Francis Ford Coppola).
April Fool's Day (1986, USA/Canada, Dir. Fred Walton).
April Fool's Day (2008, USA, Dirs. Mitchell Altieri and Phil Flores).
Ash versus the Evil Dead (2015–2018, USA, Crtrs. Ivan Raimi, Sam Raimi and Tom Spezialy).
Axe Murdering with Hackley (2016, USA, Dir. Tim Sanders).
Axegrinder (2006, USA, Dir. David Palmieri).
Bad Kids Go to Hell (2012, USA, Dir. Matthew Spradlin).
Bates Motel (2013–2017, USA, Crtrs. Anthony Cipriano, Carlton Cuse and Kerry Ehrin).
Behind the Mask: The Rise of Leslie Vernon (2006, USA, Dir. Scott Glosserman).
Big (1988, USA, Dir. Penny Marshall).
Bikini Girls on Ice (2009, Canada, Dir. Geoff Klein).
Bitch Ass (2022, USA, Dir. Bill Posley).
Black Christmas (1974, Canada, Dir. Bob Clark).
Black Christmas (2006, Canada/USA, Dir. Glen Morgan).
Black Christmas (2019, USA, Dir. Sophia Takal).
The Blair Witch Project (1999, USA, Dirs. Daniel Myrick and Eduardo Sánchez).
Blood Punch (2014, USA, Dir. Madellaine Paxson).
Blood Theater (1984, USA, Dir. Rick Sloane).
Bloody Murder (2000, USA, Dir. Ralph E. Portillo).
Bloody Murder 2: Closing Camp (2003, USA, Dir. Rob Spera).
Bloody New Year (1987, UK, Dir. Norman J. Warren).
Bodies Bodies Bodies (2022, USA, Dir. Halina Reijn).
The Boogeyman (2005, USA/New Zealand/Germany, Dir. Stephen Kay).
Bound x Blood: The Orphan Killer 2 (2019, USA, Dir. Matt Farnsworth).
The Breakfast Club (1985, USA, Dir. John Hughes).
Bride of Chucky (1998, USA/Canada, Dir. Ronny Yu).
Bring It On: Cheer or Die (2022, USA, Dir. Karen Lam).
The Burning (1981, USA, Dir. Tony Maylam).
Camp Blood (2000, USA, Dir. Brad Sykes).

Camp Death III in 2D (2018, Canada, Dir. Matt Frame).
Candyman (2021, Canada/USA, Dir. Nia DaCosta).
Cannibal Holocaust (1980, Italy, Dir. Ruggero Deodato).
Carrie (1976, USA, Dir. Brian De Palma).
The Cave (2005, USA, Germany, Dir. Bruce Hunt).
Cherry Falls (2000, USA, Dir. Geoffrey Wright).
Child's Play (1988, USA, Dir. Tom Holland).
Child's Play (2019, Canada/USA, Dir. Lars Klevberg).
Child's Play 2 (1990, USA, Dir. John Lafia).
Child's Play 3 (1991, USA, Dir. Jack Bender).
Children of the Corn: Genesis (2011, USA, Dir. Joel Soisson).
Chromeskull: Laid to Rest 2 (2011, USA, Dir. Robert Hall).
Chucky (2021–present, USA, Crtr. Don Mancini).
Cleaver: Rise of the Killer Clown (2015, UK, Dir. MJ Dixon).
The Clown at Midnight (1998, Canada, Dir. Jean Pellerin).
Crazy Lake (2016, USA, Dirs. Jason Henne and Christopher Leto).
Cry Wolf (2005, USA, Dir. Jeff Wadlow).
Cult of Chucky (2017, USA/Canada, Dir. Don Mancini).
Curse of Chucky (2013, USA/Canada, Dir. Don Mancini).
Dark Water (2005, USA, Dir. Walter Salles).
Dawson's Creek (1998–2003, USA, Crtr. Kevin Williamson).
Deadly Detention (2017, USA, Dir. Blair Hayes).
Death Screams (1982, USA, Dir. David Nelson).
Deathblood 4: Revenge of the Killer Nano-Robotic Blood Virus (2019, USA, Dir. Chris DePretis).
Deep Murder (2018, USA, Dir. Nick Corirossi).
The Deer Hunter (1978, USA/UK, Dir. Michael Cimino).
Detention (2010, USA, Dir. James D. R. Hickox).
Detention (2011, USA, Dir. Joseph Kahn).
Die Die Delta Pi (2013, USA, Dirs. Sean Donohue and Christopher Leto).
Don't Go in the House (1979, USA, Dir. Joseph Ellison).
Don't Open till Christmas (1984, UK, Dir. Edmund Purdom).
Don't Answer the Phone! (1980, USA, Dir. Robert Hammer).
Dr. Giggles (1992, USA/Japan, Dir. Manny Coto).
Dude Bro Party Massacre III (2015, USA, Dirs. Tomm Jacobsen, Michael Rousselet and Jon Salmon).
Edge of the Axe (1988, Spain, Dir. José Ramón Larraz).
The Exorcism of Emily Rose (2005, USA, Dir. Scott Derrickson).
The Exorcist (2016–2018, USA, Crtr. Jeremy Slater).
The Eyes of Laura Mars (1978, USA, Dir. Irvin Kershner).
Famine (2011, Canada, Dir. Ryan Nicholson).
Fantasia (1940, USA, Dirs. Samuel Armstrong, James Algar, Bill Roberts, Paul Satterfield, Ben Sharpsteen, David D. Hand, Hamilton Luske, Jim Handley, Ford Beebe, T. Hee, Norman Ferguson and Wilfred Jackson).

Fast & Furious 6 (2013, USA/Japan/Spain/UK, Dir. Justin Lin).
The Fast and the Furious: Tokyo Drift (2006, USA/Japan/Germany, Dir. Justin Lin).
Final Exam (1981, USA, Dir. Jimmy Huston).
Final Stab (2001, USA/Mexico, Dir. David DeCoteau).
The Final Terror (1983, USA, Dir. Andrew Davis).
First Blood (1982, USA, Dir. Ted Kotcheff).
The Fog (2005, USA/Canada, Dir. Rupert Wainwright).
Fraternity Massacre at Hell Island (2007, USA, Dir. Mark Jones).
Freaky (2020, USA, Dir. Chistopher Landon).
Freaky Friday (1976, USA, Dir. Gary Nelson).
Freaky Friday (1995, USA, Dir. Melanie Mayron).
Freaky Friday (2003, USA, Dir. Mark Waters).
Freaky Friday (2018, USA, Dir. Steve Carr).
Freddy vs. Jason (2003, USA, Dir. Ronny Yu).
Freddy's Dead: The Final Nightmare (1991, USA, Dir. Rachel Talalay).
Freddy's Nightmares (1988–1990, USA, Crtr. Jeff Freilich).
Freejack (1992, USA, Dir. Geoff Murphy).
Friday the 13th (1980, USA, Dir. Sean S. Cunningham).
Friday the 13th (2009, USA, Dir. Marcus Nispel).
Friday the 13th Part 2 (1981, USA, Dir. Steve Miner).
Friday the 13th Part III (1982, USA, Dir. Steve Miner).
Friday the 13th Part VI: Jason Lives (1986, USA, Dir. Tom McLoughlin).
Friday the 13th Part VII: The New Blood (1988, USA, Dir. John Carl Buechler).
Friday the 13th Part VIII: Jason Takes Manhattan (1989, Canada/USA, Dir. Rob Hedden).
Friday the 13th: A New Beginning (1985, USA, Dir. Danny Steinmann).
Friday the 13th: The Final Chapter (1984, USA, Dir. Joseph Zito).
Full Metal Jacket (1987, UK/USA, Dir. Stanley Kubrick).
Funnyman (1994, UK, Dir. Simon Sprackling).
Getting Schooled (2017, USA, Dir. Chuck Norfolk).
Ghostwatch (1992, UK, Dir. Lesley Manning).
The Gingerdead Man (2005, USA, Dir. Charles Band).
Girl House (2014, Canada, Dirs. Jon Knautz and Trevor Matthews).
Good Morning, Vietnam (1987, USA, Dir. Barry Levinson).
Graduation Day (1981, USA, Dir. Herb Freed).
Groundhog Day (1993, USA, Dir. Harold Ramis).
Gruesome (2006, USA, Dirs. Jeff Crook and Josh Crook).
Gutterballs (2008, Canada, Dir. Ryan Nicholson).
Halloween (1978, USA, Dir. John Carpenter).
Halloween (2007, USA, Dir. Rob Zombie).
Halloween (2018, USA, Dir. David Gordon Green).
Halloween II (1981, USA, Dir. Rick Rosenthal).
Halloween III: Season of the Witch (1982, USA, Dir. Tommy Lee Wallace).
Halloween 4: The Return of Michael Myers (1988, USA, Dir. Dwight H. Little).

Halloween 5: The Revenge of Michael Myers (1989, USA, Dir. Dominique Othenin-Girard).
Halloween Camp 2: Scream If You Wanna Die Faster (2004, USA, Dir. Andrew Van Slee).
Halloween Ends (2022, USA/UK, Dir. David Gordon Green).
Halloween H20: 20 Years Later (1998, USA, Dir. Steve Miner).
Halloween Kills (2021, USA, Dir. David Gordon Green).
Halloween Night (2006, USA, Dir. Mark Atkins).
Halloween: Resurrection (2002, USA, Dir. Rick Rosenthal).
Halloween: The Curse of Michael Myers (1995, USA, Dir. Joe Chapelle).
Hannibal (2013–2015, USA, Crtr. Bryan Fuller).
Happy Birthday to Me (1981, Canada, Dir. J. Lee Thompson).
Happy Death Day (2017, USA, Dir. Christopher Landon).
Happy Death Day 2U (2019, USA/Japan, Dir. Christopher Landon).
Hatchet (2006, USA, Dir. Adam Green).
Hatchet II (2010, USA, Dir. Adam Green).
Hatchet III (2013, USA, Dir. B. J. McDonnell).
Haunter (2013, Canada/France, Dir. Vincenzo Natali).
The Haunting of Molly Bannister (2019, UK, Dir. MJ Dixon).
He Knows You're Alone (1980, USA, Dir. Armand Mastroianni).
Hellraiser: Revelations (2011, USA, Dir. Víctor Garcia).
The Hitcher (2007, USA, Dir. Dave Meyers).
Home Sweet Home (1981, USA, Dir. Nettie Peña).
Hope Lost (2015, Italy, Dir. David Petrucci).
Hospital Massacre (1981, USA, Dir. Boaz Davidson).
Hostel (2005, USA/Czech Republic, Dir. Eli Roth).
The House at the End of Time (2013, Venezuela, Dir. Alejandro Hidalgo).
The House on Sorority Row (1982, USA, Dir. Mark Rosman).
The Human Centipede (First Sequence) (2009, Netherlands, Dir. Tom Six).
The Human Centipede 2 (Full Sequence) (2011, USA/Netherlands, Dir. Tom Six).
I Didn't Come Here to Die (2010, USA, Dir. Bradley Scott Sullivan).
I Know What You Did Last Summer (1997, USA, Dir. Jim Gillespie).
I Know What You Did Last Summer (2021, USA, Crtr. Sara Goodman).
Intruders (2015, USA, Dir. Adam Schindler).
Iron Man (2008, USA/Canada, Dir. Jon Favreau).
Jack Frost (1997, USA/UK, Dir. Michael Cooney).
Jacknife (1989, USA/Canada, Dir. David Hugh Jones).
Jason Goes to Hell: The Final Friday (1993, USA, Dir. Adam Marcus).
Jason X (2001, USA/Canada, Dir. James Isaac).
Jurassic Park (1993, USA, Dir. Steven Spielberg).
Killer Party (1986, Canada, Dir. William Fruet).
KillerKiller (2007, USA/UK, Dir. Pat Higgins).
Killjoy (2000, USA, Dir. Craig Ross Jr).
Klown Kamp Massacre (2010, USA, Dirs. Philip Gunn and David Valdez).

LA Slasher (2015, USA/UK, Dir. Martin Owen).
Laid to Rest (2009, USA, Dir. Robert Hall).
Lake Nowhere (2014, USA, Dirs. Christopher Phelps and Maxim Van Scoy).
The Last Horror Film (1982, USA, Dir. David Winters).
Leprechaun 4: In Space (1996, USA, Dir. Brian Trenchard-Smith).
Leprechaun Back 2 Tha Hood (2003, USA, Dir. Steven Ayromlooi).
Like Father Like Son (1987, USA, Dir. Rod Daniel).
Lost After Dark (2015, Canada, Dir. Ian Kessner).
Lover's Lane (1999, USA, Dir. Jon Steven Ward).
Lucky (2020, USA, Dir. Natasha Kermani).
Lumberjack Man (2015, USA, Dir. Josh Bear).
Madman (1981, USA, Dir. Joe Giannone).
The Making of Freddy's Dead: The Final Nightmare (1991, USA, Dir. Gene Rosow).
Maniac (1980, USA, Dir. William Lustig).
Maniac Cop (1988, USA, Dir. William Lustig).
Mask Maker (2011, USA, Dir. Griff Furst).
Midnight Movie (2008, USA, Dir. Jack Messitt).
Mother's Day (1980, USA, Dir. Charles Kaufman).
Murder Loves Killers Too (2009, USA, Dir. Drew Barnhardt).
My Bloody Valentine (1981, Canada, Dir. George Mihalka).
My Bloody Valentine (2009, USA/Canada, Dir. Patrick Lussier).
My So-Called Life (1994–1995, USA, Crtr. Winnie Holzman).
Never Sleep Again: The Elm Street Legacy (2010, USA, Dirs. Daniel Farrands and Andrew Kasch).
New Year's Evil (1980, USA, Dir. Emmett Alston).
Night School (1981, USA, Dir. Ken Hughes).
Nightmare Beach (1989, Italy, Dirs. James Justice and Umberto Lenzi).
A Nightmare on Elm Street (1984, USA, Dir. Wes Craven).
A Nightmare on Elm Street (2010, USA, Dir. Samuel Bayer).
A Nightmare on Elm Street Part 2: Freddy's Revenge (1985, USA, Dir. Jack Shoulder).
A Nightmare on Elm Street 3: Dream Warriors (1987, USA, Dir. Chuck Russell).
A Nightmare on Elm Street 4: The Dream Master (1988, USA, Dir. Renny Harlin).
A Nightmare on Elm Street: The Dream Child (1989, USA, Dir. Stephen Hopkins).
The Orphan Killer (2011, USA, Dir. Matt Farnsworth).
Pandemonium (1982, USA, Dir. Alfred Sole).
Panman (2011, USA, Dirs. Tim Pilleri and Jim Zaguroli).
Party of Five (1994–2000, USA, Crtrs. Christopher Keyser and Amy Lippman).
Perfect Strangers (1986–1993, USA, Crtr. Dale McRaven).
Pet (2016, Spain/USA, Dir. Carles Torrens).
Pieces (1982, Spain, Dir. Juan Piquer Simón).
Pig Girl (2014, USA, Dir. Eamon Hardiman).
Platoon (1986, USA/UK, Dir. Oliver Stone).
Pool Party Massacre (2017, USA, Dir. Drew Marvick).
Porkchop (2010, USA, Dir. Eamon Hardiman).

Porkchop II: Rise of the Rind (2011, USA, Dir. Eamon Hardiman).
Porkchop 3D (2012, USA, Dir. Eamon Hardiman).
Prom Night (1980, Canada, Dir. Paul Lynch).
Prom Night (2008, USA/Canada, Dir. Nelson McCormick).
Psycho (1960, USA, Dir. Alfred Hitchcock).
The Remake (2006, USA, Dir. Tommy Brunswick).
Return to Horror High (1987, USA, Dir. Bill Froehlich).
Ripper (2001, Canada/UK, Dir. John Eyres).
Saw (2004, USA, Dir. James Wan).
Scary Movie (2000, USA, Dir. Keenen Ivory Wayans).
Scream (1996, USA, Dir. Wes Craven).
Scream (2015–2019, USA, Crtrs. Jay Beattie, Jill E. Blotevogel, and Dan Dworkin).
Scream (2022, USA, Dirs. Matt Bettinelli-Olpin and Tyler Gillett).
Scream 2 (1997, USA, Dir. Wes Craven).
Scream 3 (2000, USA, Dir. Wes Craven).
Scream 4 (2011, USA, Dir. Wes Craven).
Scream Bloody Murder (2003, USA, Dir. Jon Hoffman).
Scream: Generations (2012, USA, Dir. Jared Vollman).
Scream Queens (2015–2016, USA, Crtrs. Ian Brennan, Brad Falchuk and Ryan Murphy).
Scum of the Earth (1974, USA, Dir. S. F. Brownrigg).
See No Evil (2006, USA/Australia, Dir. Gregory Dark).
See No Evil 2 (2014, USA/Canada, Dirs. Jen Soska and Sylvia Soska).
Shocker (1989, USA, Dir. Wes Craven).
Shrooms (2007, Ireland/UK/Denmark, Dir. Paddy Breathnach).
Silent Night, Bloody Night (1972, USA, Dir. Theodore Gershuny).
The Sitter (1977, USA, Dir. Fred Walton).
The Skeleton Key (2005, USA/Germany, Dir. Iain Softley).
Slash (2013, USA, Dir. Jack Stanis).
Slasher (2016–present, Canada, Crtr. Aaron Martin).
Slasher House (2012, UK, Dir. MJ Dixon).
Slasher House 2 (2016, UK, Dir. MJ Dixon).
Slasher House 3 (2023, UK, Dir. MJ Dixon).
Slasher Squad (2022, Australia, Dirs. Stuart Campbell and Nathan Stone).
Sleepaway Camp (1983, USA, Dir. Robert Hiltzik).
The Sleeper (2012, USA, Dir. Justin Russell).
Slumber Party Massacre (2021, South Africa, Dir. Danishka Esterhazy).
The Slumber Party Massacre (1982, USA, Dir. Amy Holden Jones).
Slumber Party Massacre II (1987, USA, Dir. Deborah Brock).
Snuff (1976, USA/Argentina, Dirs. Michael Findlay, Horacio Fredriksson and Simon Nuchtern).
Sorority House Massacre (1986, USA, Dir. Carol Frank).
Stage Fright (2014, Canada, Dir. Jerome Sable).
Stitches (2012, Ireland/Sweden/UK, Dir. Conor McMahon).

Student Bodies (1981, USA, Dir. Mickey Ross).
Terminator 2: Judgment Day (1991, USA, Dir. James Cameron).
Terrifier (2016, USA, Dir. Damien Leone).
Terrifier 2 (2022, USA, Dir. Damien Leone).
Terror Train (2022, Canada, Dir. Phillipe Gagnon).
The Texas Chain Saw Massacre (1974, USA, Dir. Tobe Hooper).
The Texas Chainsaw Massacre (2003, USA, Dir. Marcus Nispel).
The Third Saturday in October (2022, USA, Dir. Jay Burleson).
The Third Saturday in October Part V (2022, USA, Dir. Jay Burleson).
Timecrimes (2007, Spain, Dir. Nacho Vigalondo).
Torque (2004, USA, Dir. Joseph Kahn).
Trackman (2007, Russia, Dir. Igor Shavlak).
Triangle (2009, UK/Australia, Dir. Christopher Smith).
Tucker and Dale vs Evil (2010, Canada/USA, Dir. Eli Craig).
Unmasked Part 25 (1988, USA, Dir. Anders Palm).
Urban Legend (1998, Canada/USA, Dir. Jamie Blanks).
Urban Legends: Final Cut (2000, USA/Canada, Dir. John Ottman).
Valentine (2001, Canada/USA, Dir. Jamie Blanks).
Vice Versa (1988, USA, Dir. Brian Gilbert).
Victor Crowley (2017, USA, Dir. Adam Green).
Volcano (1997, USA, Dir. Mick Jackson).
Wacko (1982, USA, Dir. Greydon Clark).
Walled In (2009, USA/France/Canada, Dir. Gilles Paquet-Brenner).
Way of the Dragon (1972, Hong Kong, Dir. Bruce Lee).
Wes Craven's New Nightmare (1994, USA, Dir. Wes Craven).
What's Opera, Doc? (1957, USA, Dir. Chuck Jones).
When a Stranger Calls (1979, USA, Dir. Fred Walton).
When a Stranger Calls (2005, USA, Dir. Simon West).
The Wisher (2002, Canada, Dir. Gavin Wilding).
The Wizard of Oz (1939, USA, Dir. Victor Fleming).
WNUF Halloween Special (2013, USA, Dir. Chris LaMartina).
Wrestlemaniac (2006, USA, Dir. Jesse Baget).
Wrong Turn (2003, Germany/USA, Dir. Rob Schmidt).
You Might Be the Killer (2018, USA, Dir. Brett Simmons).

Index

Abramson, Seth, 35, 80
absurdity, 30, 40, 85, 115, 134, 135, 138, 140, 141, 150–1, 153, 161, 195, 213, 216, 223, 260
abundance, 98, 133, 135, 149–50, 153, 156, 157, 159, 161, 168, 234n; *see also* ambiguity
Adams et al. (2021), 106
Adler, Wagner and McAdams (2007), 76
Akker, Robin van den, 7, 21–2, 24, 33, 35, 37, 249, 252
alignment with characters *see* subjective perspectives
All the Boys Love Mandy Lane (2006), 45–6, 51
allusion *see* intertextuality
ambiguity, 3, 19, 22, 34–5, 36, 40, 41–2, 45, 46, 49, 50, 56, 58, 61, 62, 65n, 70, 86, 105–6, 122, 127n, 145, 167, 170, 182, 185, 246, 251, 252, 253, 256, 257; *see also* duplicity; language; superposition
analogue aesthetics, 69, 139–40, 157–8, 167, 179
apathy, 28, 29, 31, 36, 134, 170, 219, 252, 259
April Fool's Day (2008), 185
archetypes *see* character types
Arnzen, Michael A., 220
audience *see* fans; viewers
authority figures, 5, 16, 95, 136–8, 197, 208n, 211–13, 216
Axe Murdering with Hackley (2016), 224, 241–6, 249, 255, 259
Axegrinder (film series), 229

backwards causation *see* retrocausation
Balanzategui, Jessica, 44

Bargár, Pavol, 76–7
Bavel and Packer (2021), 258
Bay, Michael, 244
Beasley and Brook (2019), 106–7
Behind the Mask: The Rise of Leslie Vernon (2006), 85–94, 98, 99, 103, 112–13, 124, 152, 220n, 254, 255, 259
Belshaw, Christopher, 130
Bentley, Nick, 2, 67
Berliner, Todd, 151, 218
Bertens, Hans, 40
Bettinelli-Olpin, Matt, 199
Bettinson, Gary, 153
Bikini Girls on Ice (2009), 164–5
Bitch Ass (2022), 169n
Black Christmas (2006), 186
Black Christmas (2019), 187
Bloody Murder (2000), 25
Bloody Murder 2: Closing Camp (2003), 137n, 242n
Bodies Bodies Bodies (2022), 115n
body swap films, 145, 148–50
The Boogeyman (2005), 232
Booker, M. Keith, 59, 108, 159
boom-period slasher
  influence on subsequent slasher films, 44, 82, 163–5, 167–8, 171, 173, 175–6, 177, 180–1, 184, 224, 231, 234, 241–2, 244, 246, 247, 249, 261
  nostalgia for, 140–1, 158, 162, 164, 170, 178–9, 239n
  market saturation, 10, 15, 30, 84, 221
  rapid development of formula in, 10, 30, 38, 84, 101, 113, 177
  see also analogue aesthetics; throwback slasher films

Bordwell, David, 142, 150
The Breakfast Club (1985), 171, 172, 176–7
breaking the fourth wall, 62, 64–5, 68, 72, 80; *see also* metalepsis
Breathnach, Paddy, 49–50
Briefel and Miller (2011), 29, 82
Bring It On: Cheer or Die (2022), 150n
Brooks, Neil, 57
Bruner, Jerome, 77–8
Brunton, James, 161
Budra and Schellenberg (1998), 183
Buechler, John Carl, 238
Bugs Bunny, 213–14
The Burning (1981), 113, 230
Burns, David J., 23–4
Buscombe, Edward, 102
Busick, Guy, 199

Camp Blood (film series), 227, 229, 247
Campbell, Neve, 200n, 147, 232n
Canby, Vincent, 175
Candyman (2021), 186
Candyman (character), 223, 232, 238
captions, 96, 97, 121, 139, 141, 142–4, 146, 148–9, 157, 170, 176, 226, 247
The Cave (2005), 232
change within the slasher subgenre *see* innovation
character types, 5, 16–17, 34, 38–9, 39–40, 42–3, 45, 49, 58, 63, 77, 79, 80, 84n, 86, 98, 99, 103, 106–7, 108, 110, 113, 116, 117, 118, 122, 126, 128, 132, 136, 161–2, 171, 172–4, 175, 176, 177, 180, 189, 195–6, 221, 227, 254, 255–6; *see also* authority figures; Final Girl
Cherry Falls (2000), 19, 38, 157, 223
Cherry, Brigid, 3, 17, 29, 150
Child's Play (film series), 186, 188–9, 222–3, 225
  Bride of Chucky (1998), 18, 82n, 188–9, 223–4, 225n
  Child's Play (1988), 188
  Child's Play (2019), 186n, 225n
  Child's Play 3 (1991), 188
  Chucky (character), 188–9, 222–4, 225, 232
  Chucky (TV series), 186, 189
  Cult of Chucky (2017), 186, 189
  Curse of Chucky (2013), 186, 189
  see also Mancini, Don
Children of the Corn: Genesis (2011), 184n
Church, David, 26, 82
Clasen and Platts (2019), 17, 44
Clayton, Wickham, 38
Cleaver: Rise of the Killer Clown (2015), 227
Clover, Carol, 2, 5, 6n, 45
The Clown at Midnight (1998), 25
Clown in a Cornfield, 16
Cohn, Dorrit, 65
Collins, Jim, 150, 154, 156, 157, 186–7
comedy *see* humour
Connor, Steven, 52, 154
Conrich, Ian, 1, 44
continuity, 23, 161, 162, 166, 182, 187, 189, 190–1, 193, 201–2, 203–4, 209, 211, 217, 218, 225, 251; *see also* retroactive continuity
conventionality *see* subgeneric conventions
Cook, Pam, 160, 181, 219, 220
Corry, John, 175
Craig and Fradley (2010), 26
Crane, Jonathan Lake, 96, 108, 160, 174, 175
Craven, Wes, 67, 113n, 211, 237, 238
Crazy Lake (2016), 162, 163, 164, 167, 242n
crisis, 56, 119, 159, 160, 259, 260; *see also* precarity
criticisms of slasher subgenre, 1–2, 15, 25, 38, 55, 56, 78, 84, 96–7, 115–16, 124n, 126, 129, 130, 138–9, 147n, 153, 174–6, 180, 182–3, 184–5, 186, 193, 194, 216, 217, 218, 220, 221, 222, 234–5, 236, 240, 242n, 247, 252, 260
Cry Wolf (2005), 223, 232
Cunningham, Sean A., 38
Currie, Mark, 64, 108, 161
Cutting, James E., 120
cynicism, 2, 18, 20, 27, 29, 32, 35, 36, 76, 82, 83, 97, 100, 101, 109, 148, 154, 157, 159, 162, 174, 179n, 180, 183, 195, 249, 259

INDEX

Dark Water (2005), 232
Death Screams (1982), 136–7, 158n
Deep Murder (2018), 150n
Dember, Greg, 22, 24, 30
Detention (2011), 63, 68–70, 72, 135, 142–52, 153, 158, 159, 161, 168, 169, 171n, 182, 251, 256
determinism *see* fatalism
development within the slasher subgenre *see* innovation
Di Muzio, Gianluca, 116, 130, 221
Die Die Delta Pi (2013), 165–6, 167, 170, 171
Dika, Vera, 2, 4, 34
direct-to-video films *see* independent horror
Dixon, MJ, 225–6
Dr. Giggles (1992), 27n, 225
Don't Answer the Phone! (1980), 171
Don't Go in the House (1979), 52
Donaldson, Caulin, 163
Dude Bro Party Massacre III (2015), 135–42, 151, 157, 161, 163, 169, 176, 182, 183n, 189, 251, 260
Dulk, Allard den, 33
Dunstan, Marcus, 238
duplicity, 18, 19, 26, 28, 33–4, 36, 38, 44, 57n, 133–4, 162, 198, 200, 223, 252, 253; *see also* irony
Dutt, Apoorva, 196
DVD, 155, 158, 160

Edge of the Axe (1988), 45, 136–7
Egan, Kate, 155
Eidelman and Crandall (2012), 129
Elgin, Catherine Z., 60–1
Elliott, Pearse, 50
emotion
  detachment, 6, 27, 29, 31, 33, 98, 124, 157, 159, 174, 202–3, 244
  foregrounded in metamodern slashers, 2, 24, 31, 39, 40, 41, 42, 52, 72–3, 74, 77, 94, 119, 134, 143–4, 173, 174–5, 176, 180, 235, 256, 259
  viewers' emotional responses to fiction, 11, 30–2, 34, 40n, 65, 142, 135, 218, 248
  see also subjective perspectives

Englund, Robert, 66, 185n, 213, 238, 242n
Eshelman, Raoul, 21
The Exorcism of Emily Rose (2005), 232
experimentation *see* innovation
The Eyes of Laura Mars (1978), 52

Fangoria, 1, 155
fans
  cultural capital, 27, 30, 31, 36, 105, 108, 111, 112, 149, 154–5, 238
  experiential perspective adopted in films, 140–2, 163, 167, 176, 178–9, 183n, 185, 248
  fan edits of slasher films, 208–9
  fan film, 196–7
  fan filmmaker interactions, 67–8, 108, 237–8
  filmmakers as, 108, 236–8, 239, 240
  represented as characters, 27, 94, 95–6, 142, 154, 185, 197, 198
  versus other viewers, 27–8, 30, 88, 89, 105, 108, 111, 112, 113, 141, 154–5, 258
Fantasia (1940), 214n
Farnsworth, Matt, 229–30, 237n, 239n; *see also* *The Orphan Killer* (film series)
Fast & Furious (film series), 192n
fatalism, 16, 29, 31, 35, 54, 58, 83, 85, 86, 94, 96, 100, 105, 107, 109, 116–17, 122, 129, 134, 153, 162, 170, 180, 182, 187, 189, 192–3, 194, 196, 200, 203, 205, 219, 235, 249, 251, 252, 255
Federman, Raymond, 61
film distribution technologies *see* DVD; streaming video; VHS
Final Exam (1981), 5, 227
Final Girl, 5–6, 16, 34, 38, 45, 49, 53–4, 56, 58, 63, 77, 79, 90–1, 92, 94, 99–100, 103, 118, 120–1, 123–5, 126, 174, 206, 207, 226, 254, 255
  as killer, 34, 42, 45–6, 51, 52, 53–4, 78, 99–100, 107–8, 123–4, 124–5, 126, 130–1, 149n, 152, 203–4, 255
The Final Girl Support Group, 16
Final Stab (2001), 25
The Final Terror (1983), 171

Fjellestad, Danuta, 44, 58
The Fog (2005), 232
Fordy, Tom, 82
Fortuna Jr, Grzegorz, 129
frame breaks *see* breaking the fourth wall
Frankl, Viktor E., 204–7
Fraternity Massacre at Hell Island (2007), 44
Freaky (2020), 149n
Freddy vs. Jason (2003), 191, 225n
Friday the 13th (film series), 6, 26, 39–40, 89, 96, 112, 121, 125n, 150, 176, 182, 190, 191, 201, 222, 225, 233, 241n
   Friday the 13th (1980), 1n, 5, 16, 27, 38, 110, 113, 115, 125n, 171, 183n, 198, 241n
   Friday the 13th (2009), 191
   Friday the 13th: A New Beginning (1985), 190, 209n, 223n, 235
   Friday the 13th Part 2 (1981), 39, 121, 190
   Friday the 13th Part III (1982), 42–3, 176
   Friday the 13th Part VI: Jason Lives (1986), 26, 39, 190, 191, 225n, 235
   Friday the 13th Part VII: The New Blood (1988), 190, 191, 241n
   Friday the 13th Part VIII: Jason Takes Manhattan (1989), 191
   Friday the 13th: The Final Chapter (1984), 138, 190, 191
   Jason Goes to Hell: The Final Friday (1993), 128n, 190, 191
   Jason Voorhees (character), 39–40, 112, 125n, 190, 191, 209n, 220, 222, 223, 225, 226, 227, 229, 230, 231, 232, 233, 241
   Jason X (2001), 82, 150, 191, 223, 241n
   see also Freddy vs. Jason (2003)
Friedenthal, Andrew, J., 190
Frow, John, 84, 107
Funnyman (1994), 27n, 225
future, 8, 32, 35, 36, 47, 54, 63, 76, 117, 147, 148, 161, 170, 175, 180, 182, 189–90, 191, 193–4, 206, 219, 240, 247, 248–9, 251–2, 255, 259, 262; *see also* fatalism; optimism; time: past-present-future relations

genericity *see* subgeneric conventions
Getting Schooled (2017), 161–2, 170–7, 179–80, 182, 189–90, 251, 256
Gibbons, Alison, 7, 29, 144, 161, 180
The Gingerdead Man (2005), 234
Girl House (2014), 162
Goggin, Joyce, 183
Graduation Day (1981), 52, 171
Grant, Barry Keith, 78, 105
Green, Adam, 231, 232, 233–4, 235–8, 239, 240; *see also Hatchet* (film series)
Griffin, Hollis, 32–3
Grindon, Leger, 128
Groen, Rick, 175, 196
Groundhog Day (1993), 75n, 158, 161
Guffey, Elizabeth, 162
Gutterballs (2008), 4n
Guynn, William, 160

Hall, Blaze, 163
Hall, Robert, 226, 236n, 237n, 239n, 247; *see also Laid to Rest* (film series)
Halloween (film series), 6, 39n, 79n, 124, 182, 194, 201–4, 206–7, 208–9, 218, 219, 222, 225, 229, 231, 257–8
   Halloween (1978), 1n, 26, 31, 38, 110, 183n, 194, 198, 199, 201, 202, 203, 204, 205n, 207, 208n, 218, 226, 231, 237n, 257–8
   Halloween (2007), 186n, 201, 202, 203
   Halloween (2018), 16, 186, 194, 195, 200, 201–9, 217, 218–19, 255
   Halloween II (1981), 201, 202, 203
   Halloween III: Season of the Witch (1982), 201
   Halloween 4: The Return of Michael Myers (1988), 201, 225n, 238n
   Halloween 5: The Revenge of Michael Myers (1989), 137–8, 201, 238n
   Halloween Ends (2022), 201, 208n
   Halloween H20: 20 Years Later (1998), 79n, 82, 108, 201, 202, 203, 206, 207, 223
   Halloween Kills (2021), 201, 202n, 208n
   Halloween: Resurrection (2002), 79n, 201, 202, 203, 206, 207
   Halloween: The Curse of Michael Myers (1995), 201, 202

INDEX

Michael Myers (character), 2, 39n, 124, 201, 202–3, 204, 205, 206, 207, 208, 218, 222, 225, 226, 227, 229, 231, 232, 238
Halloween Camp 2: Scream If You Wanna Die Faster (2004), 25
Halloween Night (2006), 162
Hanich, Julian, 133n, 152
Hantke, Steffen, 28, 184–5
Happy Birthday to Me (1981), 171
Happy Death Day (2017), 63, 72–9, 80, 101, 158, 159, 161, 182, 204n, 251, 253, 254, 257
Happy Death Day 2U (2019), 152n
Harris, Danielle, 238n
Harvey, David, 12, 29, 119
Hassan, Ihab, 23
Hatchet (film series), 224, 225n, 230–40, 245, 247, 248, 259
  Hatchet (2006), 232n, 234, 238–9, 240, 251
  Hatchet II (2010), 232, 233, 235, 238, 239–40
  Hatchet III (2013), 238n
  Victor Crowley (2017), 225n, 231, 237–8
  see also Green, Adam
The Haunting of Molly Bannister (2019), 226
He Knows You're Alone (1980), 227
Hellraiser: Revelations (2011), 184n
Hernández-Santaolalla and Raya (2021), 187
heterochrony, 144–6, 148, 150, 161, 183n, 250, 251; *see also* time: past-present-future relations
heterogeneity, 135, 159, 253, 256, 257, 258; *see also* multiplicity
high-concept films, 222
Hills, Matt, 113n
Hitcher, Waldo, 106
Hodder, Kane, 112, 233, 238
Holland, Tom, 238
homage *see* intertextuality
hope *see* optimism
Hope Lost (2015), 169
Hostel (2005), 169, 233
The House on Sorority Row (1982), 5
The Human Centipede (film series), 169

humour, 26, 27n, 28, 32–3, 90, 94, 108, 137, 141–2, 153, 162, 171–2, 174, 179n, 213–14, 216, 223, 227, 233–5, 238n, 240, 259–60; *see also* in-jokes; irony; memes; play
Humphries, Reynold, 260
Hutcheon, Linda, 26, 35, 64, 83, 109, 159, 160, 218
Hutchings, Peter, 27n, 55
Hutchinson, Tom, 209
hybridity *see* multiplicity

I Didn't Come Here to Die (2010), 107, 113–19, 125, 157–8, 255–6
I Know What You Did Last Summer (1997), 25, 26, 30, 38, 52, 141, 186, 187, 223
I Know What You Did Last Summer (TV series), 186, 187
idiosyncrasy, 15, 59, 62, 81, 113, 123, 135, 140, 147, 151, 153, 156, 157, 158, 159, 208, 230, 253, 254, 256, 257–8; *see also* viewers: idiosyncratic perspectives
inclusivity, 36, 56, 59, 84, 88, 105, 107, 111, 134, 135, 151, 157, 159, 161, 163, 235, 251, 253, 256, 257, 258, 261; *see also* viewers: as collaborators in meaning generation
independent horror, 15, 25, 162, 163, 183n, 228–9, 247, 252, 260
indeterminacy *see* ambiguity
individualism *see* subjective perspectives
inevitability *see* fatalism
in-jokes, 27, 30, 105, 108, 112, 113n, 134, 154–5, 196, 224, 233, 238, 258; *see also* intertextuality
innovation, 2, 3, 6, 7, 15, 16–17, 20, 29–30, 31, 32, 35, 36, 54, 55, 58, 59, 63, 71, 72, 76–7, 81, 85, 94, 100, 101–2, 103–4, 105, 106, 107, 108, 109, 110, 111, 112, 113–14, 125, 128–31, 132, 133, 135, 148, 150, 151, 152, 153, 154, 157, 161, 163, 164–5, 166, 179, 180–1, 182, 184, 186, 187, 188, 190, 191, 193, 194, 195, 202, 203, 207–8, 213, 217, 218, 219, 220, 224, 225, 236, 239, 240, 241, 242, 244, 245, 246, 247, 248, 249, 251, 252, 253, 254, 255, 256, 257, 259, 260

instability *see* precarity
insularity, 20, 29, 36, 56–7, 102, 107, 116–17, 148, 154, 157, 161, 210, 249, 250, 256, 259
intertextuality, 3, 16, 26, 27, 36, 44, 105, 107, 108–11, 112, 113, 141, 148–9, 154–5, 156, 158, 159, 168–9, 176, 198, 217, 224, 233, 238, 241n, 258
intertitles *see* captions
Intruders (2015), 16
irony, 21, 22, 24, 27, 28, 29, 32–3, 36, 44, 62, 83, 90, 94, 96, 109, 127, 133–4, 148, 150, 159, 160, 170, 174, 196, 200, 233, 240, 252, 260

Jack Frost (1997), 234
James and Seshagiri, (2014), 35, 177
Jancovich, Mark, 17
Jeffries, Stuart, 29, 157
Jess-Cooke, Carolyn, 183, 217
Johnson, Kevin C., 84

Kahn, Joseph, 143–4
Kahneman, Sibony and Sunstei (2021), 58n
Kaufman, Lloyd, 238
Kelleter, Frank, 193
Kermode, Mark, 28
Killer Party (1986), 62n
KillerKiller (2007), 107, 125–8, 152, 226, 255, 256
Killjoy (2000), 227
King, Geoff, 83
Kirby, Alan, 181
Klown Kamp Massacre (2010), 227
Konstantinou, Lee, 33n
Kroll, Jack, 175
Krzywinska, Tanya, 66

LA Slasher (2015), 167–70
Laid to Rest (film series), 225n, 226, 236n, 238n; *see also* Hall, Robert
Laidler, Mark, 67
Langenkamp, Heather, 66, 185n
language, 30, 56, 61–2, 79, 250; *see also* ambiguity; duplicity; irony
The Last Horror Film (1982), 82
Lee Curtis, Jamie, 100

Leone, Damien, 226–7, 228, 229, 236n, 237n, 239n, 247; *see also Terrifier* (film series)
Leprechaun 4: In Space (1996), 150
Leprechaun Back 2 Tha Hood (2003), 234
Levchenko et al. (2021), 56, 57
Lewis, Jon, 155
Leydon, Joe, 223
Liao, Shen-yi, 152
Lipovetsky, Gilles, 23
Loock, Kathleen, 161, 164–5, 182, 184n, 185n, 186, 213, 217
Looney Tunes, 214
Lost After Dark (2015), 167n
Lover's Lane (1999), 25
Lowenthal, David, 160, 177–8
Lucky (2020), 137n
ludic *see* play
Lumberjack Man (2015), 225
Lynch, Joe, 238

McAdams, Dan P., 61, 76, 258
MacDowell, James, 19
McHale, Brian, 58–9, 250
McLean, Kate C., 76
Madman (1981), 5, 113, 121, 231
Malina, Debra, 65, 79
Mancini, Don, 186, 223; *see also Child's Play* (film series)
Mane, Tyler, 238
Maniac (1980), 52
Maniac Cop (1988), 95
Martin, Bob, 1
Mask Maker (2011), 225
Maslin, Janet, 175
Mee, Laura, 182, 184, 185, 195, 217
memes, 32–3, 111–12, 229
Menell, Jeff, 209
metafictional devices *see* breaking the fourth wall; metalepsis; pullback-reveal
metalepsis, 27, 64–5, 66–7, 70–1, 79–80, 109
metamodern sensibility, 2, 7, 9, 12, 16, 17–18, 19, 20, 22, 24, 34, 35–6, 52, 63, 68, 72, 78, 94, 101, 143, 151, 153, 156, 157, 159, 162, 163, 169–70, 173, 177, 179, 204, 206, 224, 228, 240, 248, 253, 256, 257, 259, 260, 261, 262

metamodernism
  alternatives to, 22–4
  origins of, 21
  relationship to modernism, 22, 23, 24, 29, 35, 63, 159, 250–1
  relationship to postmodernism, 2, 8, 12, 20–4, 30, 31–2, 33, 35, 37, 40, 41, 57, 62–3, 72, 79–80, 109, 159–61, 180, 219, 250–1, 262
  see also Akker, Robin van den; Gibbons, Alison; Vermeulen, Timotheus
microbudget horror films see independent horror
Midnight Movie (2008), 70–2
milieu see tone; zeitgeist
Miner, Steve, 202
Mittell, Jason, 157
Moine, Raphaëlle, 102, 105
moralism, 39–40, 130, 221, 252, 255
Moraru, Christian, 23
Muir, John Kenneth, 4, 39, 116, 174, 183, 201, 213, 215
multiplicity, 22, 33–4, 36, 58, 59, 150, 153, 157, 252, 253, 256; see also abundance; heterogeneity
Murder Loves Killers Too (2009), 107, 119–25, 126, 152, 253, 255
murder-mystery see whodunit
music, uses of, 75, 87, 144, 146, 147, 164, 168, 170, 171, 173, 239–40
My Bloody Valentine (2009), 186, 187
My Heart is a Chainsaw, 15–16
Mycho see Dixon, MJ

Neale, Steve, 84, 102–3
Nealon, Jeffrey T., 22, 23, 132n
Nelson, Andrew Patrick, 108
New Line Cinema, 66–7, 210, 244
Newman, Kim, 174
Night School (1981), 45, 51, 178
A Nightmare on Elm Street (film series), 66, 83n, 112, 182, 185n, 194–5, 209–16, 218, 219, 221, 222, 224, 225, 242n, 244
  Freddy Krueger (character), 2, 27n, 67, 95, 112, 113n, 138, 172, 185n, 195, 209, 210, 211–12, 213–14, 215, 216, 219, 220, 222, 225, 226, 227, 231, 232, 238, 242

Freddy's Dead: The Final Nightmare (1991), 185n, 194–5, 209–16, 217, 218–20, 224
Freddy's Nightmares (TV series), 213
A Nightmare on Elm Street (1984), 78–9, 112, 176, 185n, 210, 214–15, 227
A Nightmare on Elm Street (2010), 194
A Nightmare on Elm Street 3: Dream Warriors (1987), 210, 212
A Nightmare on Elm Street 4: The Dream Master (1988), 138, 210, 211, 212
A Nightmare on Elm Street Part 2: Freddy's Revenge (1985), 6, 225n
A Nightmare on Elm Street: The Dream Child (1989), 213, 216
Wes Craven's New Nightmare (1994), 62–3, 66–7, 83n, 185n, 209, 215n
  see also *Freddy vs. Jason* (2003)
Nowell, Richard, 7, 185, 222
Nutman, Philip, 211

Ochonicky, Adam, 191
optimism, 22, 32, 35, 36, 51, 54, 58, 63, 72, 76–7, 147, 153, 175, 205, 206, 259, 260, 261
originality see innovation
The Orphan Killer (film series), 224, 229–30, 239n, 247; see also Farnsworth, Matt
oscillation, 22, 33, 35, 37, 252

Pagel, James F., 107
Pandemonium (1982), 82
Panman (2011), 227n
Parker, Dave, 238
Pascale, Marius A., 174n
past
  films set in the, 63, 68–70, 72, 135–52, 153, 151, 157, 158, 159, 161–2, 163, 165–77, 179–80, 182, 183n, 189–90, 251, 256, 260
  as inaccessible, 31–2, 159–61, 178–9, 180, 191, 192, 217–18, 219, 250, 251
  as represented by cultural markers, 144–9, 152, 164–5, 167–9, 170–1, 178–9, 198, 210, 239–40, 242

past (*cont.*)
  as understood from present, 23, 26, 28, 31–2, 35, 45–7, 51–2, 76, 95, 97–8, 101, 108, 109, 110, 112, 115, 122, 126–7, 136, 141, 144–6, 147–8, 154, 155, 159–61, 162–81, 182, 189–90, 191, 192–5, 196, 197–8, 199, 200–1, 202, 205–6, 207–8, 209, 210–12, 216, 217, 218, 219–20, 224, 232, 237–40, 241–5, 246, 247–8, 249, 250, 251, 252
  see also analogue aesthetics; boom-period slasher; metamodernism: relationship to postmodernism; retroactive continuity; retrocausation; throwback slasher films; time: past-present-future relations
pastiche, 21, 59, 109, 110, 164, 167, 183n
Perkins, Claire, 38
Perren, Alisa, 25
Pet (2016), 16
Petridis, Sotiris, 86
Phillips, Kendall R., 27n
Pieces (1982), 138
Pipere and Martinsone (2022), 259
Platinum Dunes, 244
play
  in metamodern slashers, 30, 35, 55, 79, 99, 115, 122–3, 125, 126, 127, 128, 135, 152–3, 159, 173, 177, 188, 189, 216, 218, 227, 248, 258
  in postmodern slashers, 28–9, 44–5, 50, 57, 58, 61–2, 69n, 87, 91, 97, 98, 127, 223, 253, 254, 256
plurality *see* heterogeneity; multiplicity
point-of-view shots, 6, 43, 46, 47–8, 71, 73, 123
police *see* authority figures
Pool Party Massacre (2017), 164n
Porkchop (film series), 228–9, 247
postmodern slasher
  compared with metamodern slasher, 8, 18–19, 20–1, 22, 25, 30, 31–2, 34, 35, 36, 40, 57, 58, 62–3, 72, 73, 76, 79–81, 84–5, 86, 87, 88, 91, 94, 96, 97, 100, 101, 102–3, 105, 107, 108–10, 112–13, 117n, 119, 127, 129, 133–5, 138, 147–9, 150, 153, 154, 156–7, 159–61, 162, 168, 173, 174–5, 178, 180–1, 182, 186, 187, 189, 191, 192–3, 195, 203, 217, 218–19, 220, 223–4, 232–3, 238, 240, 243–4, 248, 249, 251, 252–3, 254, 256, 258, 259
  see also fatalism; in-jokes; intertextuality; pastiche; play: in postmodern slashers; *Scream* (film series); self-reflexivity; subgeneric conventions: postmodern slasher's stance on; tone: postmodern slasher's
Pratt and Jeffcut (2009), 129n
precarity, 39, 40, 42, 50, 56, 57, 58, 73, 79–80, 103, 107, 134, 140, 151, 153, 168, 244, 252, 253, 254, 256, 257, 258, 261; *see also* crisis
presentism, 12, 31–2, 117, 147, 160, 161, 167, 168, 179, 180, 192n, 216, 219, 250, 259
Prince, Gerald, 109
progress *see* innovation; future
Prom Night (1980), 1, 5, 27, 52, 171
Prom Night (2008), 186
Psycho (1960), 52, 78–9, 110
pullback-reveal, 64, 66, 68–70, 72, 87, 134

realism, 31, 43, 64, 85, 87, 89–90, 91, 103, 112, 119, 134–5, 138, 139
reboots, 1–2, 184, 185, 186, 188, 189, 195, 196, 198, 200, 212, 220, 224, 244–5
rejuvenation *see* innovation
The Remake (2006), 185
remakes, 1–2, 7, 15, 54, 184–7, 188, 189, 190, 193, 198, 206n, 217–18, 220, 232, 244, 260
requels, 152, 181, 185–6, 187, 189, 190, 191, 193–4, 199, 200–1, 209, 216, 217, 218, 219–20, 251, 254
retroactive continuity, 152, 190–2, 193, 194, 210, 211, 216, 218
retrocausation, 31, 146, 162, 176–7, 178–9, 180, 189, 193–4, 206, 208, 212, 216, 217, 218, 219, 251
Return to Horror High (1987), 26, 82, 136n
Rieser, Klaus, 207
Ripper (2001), 45
Roche, David, 184–5, 186, 217
Rockoff, Adam, 3, 25
Rombes, Nicholas, 155, 193n

INDEX

Romero, George A., 237–8
Rosewarne, Lauren, 180, 184, 185n, 218
Roth, Marty, 217
Rudrum, David, 21, 23, 24

Salemme, Danny, 208
Sandbacka, Kasimir, 161, 219
Sartorio, Carolina, 192
Saw (2004), 169, 226, 233, 246
Scary Movie (2000), 30, 137n, 141
Schatz, Thomas, 102–3, 153
Schneider, Steven Jay, 3, 108
Scholes, Robert, 109
Sconce, Jeffrey, 221
Scooby Doo, 44
Scream (film series), 4n, 16, 25–8, 30, 31, 36, 82, 83, 84, 85, 86, 88, 95, 96, 100, 103, 110, 125n, 138, 142, 147–8, 156, 157, 158, 161, 174, 194, 195–201, 210, 217, 223, 233, 243
  Scream (1996), 19, 25–6, 30, 43n, 52, 58, 78–9, 82, 83, 105, 113n, 125n, 127, 137, 141, 148, 154, 194, 196, 197, 198, 199, 200, 217, 224, 233, 243, 258
  Scream (2022), 186, 194, 197–201, 217, 219
  Scream (TV series), 186
  Scream 2 (1997), 28n, 82–3, 83–4, 108
  Scream 3 (2000), 28n, 199
  Scream 4 (2011), 69n, 194, 195–6, 197, 200
Scream Bloody Murder (2003), 44
Scream: Generations (2012), 197
Scum of the Earth (1974), 171
See No Evil 2 (2014), 79n, 225n, 226, 238, 239n, 247–8
self-reflexivity, 19, 25, 26–7, 29, 30–1, 38–9, 58, 62, 63, 68, 82, 84–5, 86, 94, 101, 102–3, 109, 112, 113, 129, 132, 148, 154, 174, 178, 196, 200, 248, 254, 256; *see also* breaking the fourth wall; in-jokes; intertextuality; metalepsis; pullback-reveal; subgeneric conventions
sensibility *see* metamodern sensibility; tone; zeitgeist
sequels, 6, 34, 54, 122, 126, 136n, 150, 182–4, 185, 187n, 188, 189, 190, 191, 192, 193, 195, 198, 209, 211, 216, 217–18, 220, 221–2, 225, 236, 247, 254
Shaw and Upstone (2021), 23, 24, 34n
Shaye, Robert, 66
Shocker (1989), 225
Shone, Tom, 209
Shrooms (2007), 41–50, 56–7, 58, 70, 98, 127n, 152, 218n, 251, 255, 257
sincerity, 18–19, 20–1, 24, 31, 32–3, 41, 70, 73, 77, 78, 79, 88, 94, 101, 116, 127, 134, 135, 144, 162, 163, 170, 177, 195, 207–8, 216, 235, 236, 253, 254, 256, 259–60
The Sitter (1977), 187
The Skeleton Key (2005), 232
Slash (2013), 196–7
Slasher House (film series), 225–6
Slasher Squad (2022), 128n
Sleepaway Camp (1983), 45, 110, 113
The Sleeper (2012), 166–7, 179
Slumber Party Massacre (1982), 206n
The Slumber Party Massacre (2021), 206n
Slumber Party Massacre II (1987), 138
Smythe, Luke, 153
Sorority House Massacre (1986), 5
Soska, Jen, 226, 239n, 247–8
Soska, Sylvia, 248
Stage Fright (2014), 150n
Stavris, Nicholas, 21, 23, 24
Stewart, Susan, 130
Stitches (2012), 227
stock characters *see* character types
Stoev, Dina, 58, 153
straight-to-video films *see* independent horror
streaming video, 15, 155–6, 160, 187n
Student Bodies (1981), 26
subgeneric conventions
  metamodern slasher's stance on, 16–17, 19, 21, 30, 34–5, 42, 45, 46, 49, 53–4, 55, 56, 58, 63, 71, 77, 78–9, 80, 81, 84–6, 88–90, 92, 94–7, 98–104, 105–8, 109, 110, 111, 112–15, 116, 117–28, 129, 130, 132, 134, 135–6, 138, 142, 150, 151, 152, 156, 159, 162–3, 166, 171–2, 174, 175, 177, 178, 180, 188, 189, 203–4, 207, 218, 230, 242, 243–9, 252, 253, 254–5, 256, 257, 258, 260

subgeneric conventions (*cont.*)
   postmodern slasher's stance on, 19, 25–7, 28–9, 30, 31, 38–9, 52, 79, 81, 82–4, 85, 88, 96, 100–1, 103, 108–9, 113, 129, 133–4, 137, 138, 150, 154, 178, 182, 200, 243–4, 252, 254
   as the slasher's defining features, 3–7, 29–30, 38
   see also character types; innovation
subjective perspectives
   as limited, 21, 31, 40, 41, 42, 46–7, 50, 55, 56, 57, 58, 60–1, 62, 97–8, 148, 157, 158, 159, 160–1, 193, 198, 250, 251, 256, 257, 262
   metamodern slashers' emphasis on, 16, 17, 21, 30–1, 39, 40–2, 43, 46, 49, 50, 52, 53, 54, 55–9, 60, 62, 63, 70, 73–3, 75, 76, 77–8, 80, 81, 88, 89, 92, 94, 97–9, 101, 103, 116–17, 119, 123–4, 125, 126, 134, 136, 140, 141–2, 144, 146, 153, 159, 160–1, 174–5, 179, 207, 208, 209, 219, 235, 240, 241, 251, 253, 255–6, 257, 258
   and self-conception, 41, 42, 52, 57, 60–1, 76, 77–8, 157, 251, 258
   as source of indeterminacy, 21, 40, 41–2, 43, 46–7, 50, 56, 57, 58, 61, 62, 70, 73, 97, 103, 136, 152, 159, 161, 219, 251, 256
   see also ambiguity; emotion; idiosyncrasy; point-of-view shots; viewers: idiosyncratic perspectives
superposition, 33–5, 39, 42, 46, 51, 52, 54, 56, 98, 152, 161, 189, 240, 248, 252, 257, 258
Syder, Andrew, 67, 108

Talalay, Rachel, 209, 211, 215
Tan and Visch, (2018) 28
Taylor, Tosha R., 211, 213
Terrifier (film series), 224, 225n, 226–8, 229, 234n, 236n, 247; *see also* Leone, Damien
Terror Train (2022), 187
The Texas Chain Saw Massacre (1974), 49
The Texas Chainsaw Massacre (2003), 233
The Third Saturday in October (film series), 183n

Thornton, David Howard, 229n
throwback slasher films, 162–70, 177–80, 183n, 196, 203, 224, 232, 238–9, 240, 241, 246, 248, 251
time
   past-present-future relations, 31, 32, 35, 122, 147, 154, 159, 160–1, 162, 166, 168, 182, 189, 191, 192–4, 206, 216, 219, 220, 231, 239–40, 248–9, 251–2, 259
   theories of, 192–3, 251
   see also continuity; fatalism; future; heterochrony; past; presentism; time-loop films
Timecrimes (2007), 41n
time-loop films, 41, 80, 101, 251, 254, 257, 258; *see also Happy Death Day* (2017); *Triangle* (2009)
Todd, Tony, 234, 238
tone
   metamodern slasher's, 17, 21, 24, 36, 56, 76–7, 78, 94, 119, 134, 143–4, 163, 216, 218, 232, 235, 254, 260; *see also* absurdity; inclusivity; optimism; sincerity
   postmodern slasher's, 18–19, 21, 26–7, 28, 29, 31, 32, 35, 36, 38, 44, 57, 58, 61–2, 76, 83, 84, 88, 97, 100, 101, 108, 109, 119, 129, 133–4, 155, 157, 159, 162, 174, 175, 194, 195, 223, 233, 240, 244; *see also* apathy; cynicism; duplicity; emotion: detachment; fatalism; insularity; irony
torture porn, 16, 169, 233, 240, 245–6
Toth, Josh, 20, 29, 57
Trackman (2007), 162, 225
Triangle (2009), 41–2, 50–5, 56–8, 76, 78, 98, 101, 127n, 152, 159, 182, 251, 253, 254, 255, 257
tropes *see* subgeneric conventions
Tucker and Dale vs Evil (2010), 16–17
Tudor, Andrew, 26, 29
Turner, Luke, 27, 41

upcycling, 249
Urban Legend (1998), 19, 25, 28n, 52, 64, 82, 119n, 223
Urban Legends: Final Cut (2000), 64–6, 70

Valentine (2001), 25, 38, 52, 223
Vanderbilt, James, 199, 200
Varndell, Daniel, 182
Verevis, Constantine, 183, 217
Vermeulen, Timotheus, 7, 21–2, 24, 33, 35, 37, 249, 252
VHS, 69, 139–40, 140–1, 154, 155–6, 157, 158; *see also* analogue aesthetics
Vietnam films, 171
viewers
  and assumed knowledge of the subgenre, 30, 88–9, 105, 111, 112–13, 135, 253, 258
  assumed sophistication of, 50, 66, 68, 72, 80, 84, 109, 135n, 156, 258
  as collaborators in meaning generation, 57–8, 72, 81, 104, 106, 107, 157, 208–9, 238, 253, 256, 257–8
  idiosyncratic perspectives, 15, 62, 140, 156–7, 158, 159, 208, 253, 257–8
  see also emotion: viewers' emotional responses to fiction; fans

Wacko (1982), 82
Walled In (2009), 169
Walton, Kendall L., 132

Warshow, Robert, 152
Waugh, Patricia, 56n, 63
Way of the Dragon (1972), 138
Wee, Valerie, 154
Welt, Bernard, 222
West, Alexandra, 1, 29n
West, Steven, 25, 27, 44
What's Opera, Doc? (1957), 214n
When a Stranger Calls (1979), 187
When a Stranger Calls (2005), 187, 232
Whitehead, Mark, 116
whodunit, 6, 44–5, 57, 73, 98, 115n, 256
The Wizard of Oz (1939), 214
Wrestlemaniac (2006), 225
Wrong Turn (2003), 49
Wyatt, Justin, 222

You Might Be the Killer (2018), 85, 86, 94–101, 103, 110, 124, 127n, 142, 157, 158, 255, 259

Zavarzadeh, Mas'ud, 21, 22n
zeitgeist, 2, 7, 8, 17, 18, 20, 22, 24, 26, 27, 32–3, 41, 153, 180, 186, 196, 210, 250, 259, 260; *see also* tone
Zeitlin, Michael, 218

EU representative:
Easy Access System Europe
Mustamäe tee 50, 10621 Tallinn, Estonia
Gpsr.requests@easproject.com

www.ingramcontent.com/pod-product-compliance
Lightning Source LLC
Chambersburg PA
CBHW052053230426
43671CB00011B/1895